The Southern Gardener

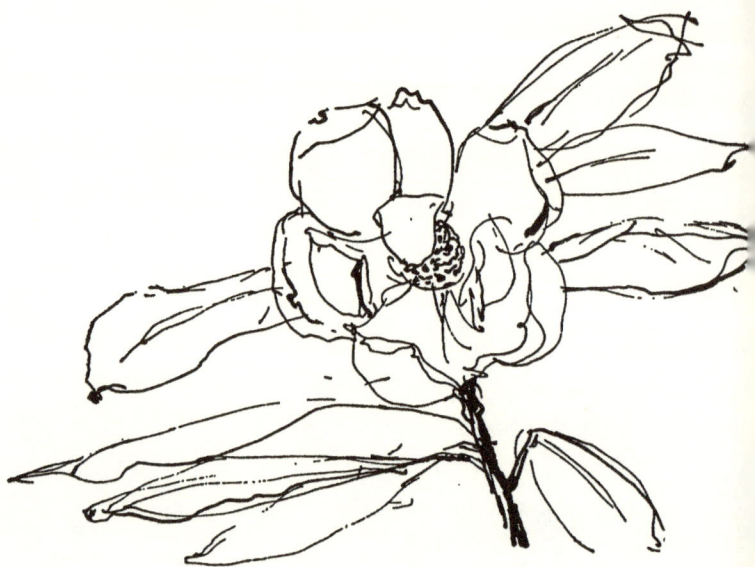

The
Southern Gardener

written and illustrated by

M A R Y   B.   S T E W A R T

Co-Author of *Gardening in New Orleans*

A FIREBIRD PRESS BOOK

PELICAN PUBLISHING COMPANY
Gretna 1998

Manufactured in the United States of America

Published by Pelican Publishing Company, Inc.
1000 Burmaster Street, Gretna, Louisiana 70053

To
My Husband and Daughters

Foreword

Gardens are not dormant things; they grow and mature and change. New plants are introduced and new methods are tried. In the last few years I have received many queries on particular aspects of home gardening; I have been asked about the culture and propagation of certain plants in the South, particularly in this peculiar climate of New Orleans. Hence my efforts have turned toward specialization, reports of new experiences and details of gardening experiments. No part presumes any particular skills, but rather is the result of my years of having fun outdoors. I look on gardening as a delightful therapy and a wonderful way to feel the closeness of our Creator. So, plan your grounds with care, have patience and understanding with the "green things" and they will reward you with much pleasure.

Everyone knows that climate decides what plants will grow where. That means that temperature, rainfall, drainage, exposure, nearness to coastline and topography all play important roles in a successful design.

The region of the South to which I refer in the following pages begins along a narrow margin of the coasts of North and South Carolina, stretches across the lower part of Georgia, the greater part of Alabama and almost all of Mississippi. It includes all of Louisiana, the coastal edge of Texas and reaches down into the upper half of Florida and the southern tip of Arkansas. I do not include any mountainous sections where elevations affect temperatures. Thus this region takes in parts of the Atlantic Coastal Plain and almost all of the Gulf Coastal areas. Needless to say, plants that do well along the Gulf Coast and in Florida, where the climate is tropical, will not thrive in regions farther north, more inland

and in arid sections of Texas. When I speak of the "deep South", I mean the lower coastal areas. When I refer to the "upper South", I mean the inland regions closer to the northern sections of the states mentioned. Planting for the whole area means landscaping in temperatures that range from an approximate low of fifteen to twenty degrees in the upper sections, to the humid coastal regions where the thermometer may register from ninety to one hundred degrees. Indicated flowering seasons are based on normal temperatures. Any unusually long periods of heat or cold may advance or delay the blooming time.

As of January 1, 1959, the new Horticultural Nomenclature Code, adopted by the Fifteenth International Horticultural Congress held in France, went into effect. Many points were clarified to insure international uniformity, but prominent among the changes was the substitution of the word "cultivar" for the term "variety." According to the International Code, a cultivar is "an assemblage of cultivated individuals which are distinguished by any characters significant for the purposes of agriculture, forestry or horticulture, and which, when reproduced, retain their distinguishing features." For instance, if Orange Cup were a new introduction of *Lilium umbellatum*, it would be presented as the Orange Cup cultivar of that particular lily. Heretofore the word variety was translated into the language of each country; henceforth, cultivar will be the term accepted the world over. This change has nothing whatever to do with the Latin titles, and names that have been in use prior to January 1, 1959, need not be altered.

I am sure that you will understand my reluctance to refer to the various fungicides and insecticides by their trade names, but there are instances where the chemical term is so formidable that its use would confuse not only the average reader but the average salesperson in the nursery as well. Need I point out that Phaltan is much simpler to ask for than N-trichloromethylthiophthalimide? Isn't Terraclor easier to say than pentachloronitrobenzene? My mention of one trade name does not necessarily mean that it is the only one by which the chemical is known.

I have used Latin names wherever feasible because each plant is accepted by that name the world over, while the common name varies from one section of the country to another. The first Latin name, always capitalized, is the generic or family name; the second shows the species and is not usually capitalized unless it is commemorative. When buying nursery stock I urge you to order by botanical or Latin names.

My special thanks to Rachel Daniel, Garden Editor of the *Times-Picayune*, for her interest and encouragement; to Mr. Edwin R. Lott, District Entomologist for the Louisiana State Department of Agriculture and to Dr. J. C. Schwegmann, plant pathologist, for their knowledge of pests, diseases and chemical controls; to Mrs. George W. Stem for her findings on Rose culture; to Mrs. William B. Wisdom for her pointers on Bromeliads; to Mrs. Joseph S. Ingraham, Mrs. Yorke P. Nicholson, Mrs. Frank G. Costley and Mrs. Frank L. Ramos for sharing their valuable gardening experiences.

MARY B. STEWART

Contents

The Southern Gardener

❈ 1 ❈

Soils and Additives

Would you go out and buy a houseful of highly expensive period furniture for a very ordinary, poorly-constructed house? Of course you wouldn't! You would be indignant that anyone should assume that you would do such a silly thing! But have you ever stopped to think that something just as silly as the furniture-buying spree is being done every day when people go out to purchase a plant without even considering the very poor soil in which it is to be planted? The earth in your garden beds is the mainspring of a successful garden and a good garden loam is about 40% Clay, 40% Humus and 20% Sand. Clay is what you start with—it is the "mud" that is in the ground that you break to make your garden bed. Humus is decayed organic matter, whether it be well-rotted manure, the residue of a good compost heap, peat moss or rich black loam, and should contain about 85% Carbon and about 10% Nitrogen; the other 5% being negligible components. Sand, as we all know, is finely ground particles of rock.

Animal manures must be thoroughly decomposed before being used. Peat moss is a combination of well-rotted sphagnum moss, sedge grass and other plant materials that have been left undisturbed for years in watery spots on the land. Incidentally, whenever possible, get the imported peat rather than the domestic type—it is so much older and richer. Rich black soil is the result of layer on layer of leaves falling from the trees and left standing for such a long time that it is teeming with animal and plant life. Good black soil is not always easy to get; some of the best looking black soils are quite alkaline and high in salt content, making them utterly undesirable. Not all of us are lucky enough to have compost heaps, so our best bet is peat moss. When you order black soil, always get it from a reputable dealer who would know where to get the quality that is salt-free.

If your soil is dry and caked, showing cracks, you may be sure that you need sand to help break up the thick sticky clay. If water runs off the bed too freely, then you need to add humus. In other words, besides the clay that you start with, you need sand for better drainage and humus for body and conditioning. Of the three constituents, humus is probably the key to good plant nutrition because it increases the breathing capacity of thick clay soils and helps sandy soils hold water. You must be ever-watchful; you must check your soil often, because in the South, more than anywhere else, it takes constant watching to keep a happy planting medium.

Basic soils in different parts of the deep South are variable, as you can readily see when you think of the abundance of sand on the Gulf Coast area and the prevalence of red clay in Alabama. In the former case, a great deal of humus is needed and in the latter, sand and humus are necessary. In Florida, rich black muck is easy to get in the swampy areas and luckily too, for there is need of it to condition the very sandy soils of the ridge section. In New Orleans, those of you who live in sections of the city where the original swamp humus still stands, will find that you must add clay and sand.

Then there is the business of topsoil and subsoil. Some areas of the deep South have no topsoil; it has been washed away by erosions. The lowlands, where the rivers and creeks are always overflowing, are perhaps the only places that have good topsoils. If you are in high dry areas away from the water, you must keep adding enough leafmold or peat moss to your garden to bring about the eventual decomposition that produces good top loam.

Subsoil is the name we give to the twelve inches or so of earth below the topsoil and because it is not often disturbed, it becomes stiff and caked. This is the reason I recommend digging a hole twice as deep as the ball of a large shrub or plant—the subsoil has to be broken up, aerated and combined with nutrients so that the roots will have a better place in which to live.

After adding the correct amount of humus and sand to your garden beds, stop to consider the three most important elements in plant growth: Nitrogen, Phosphorus and Potash. After them come Calcium, Magnesium and Sulphur. Minor plant foods, or "Trace Elements" are Boron, Manganese, Copper, Zinc and Iron.

Nitrogen, in its natural state, is an odorless gas that must be combined with other elements before it can be used as plant food. It produces rapid growth, improves the quality of leaves, flowers and berries of a plant and gives the dark green color that is so necessary for a good specimen. Lightening causes some nitrogen in the air to combine with oxygen to form products that rain will carry to plants. Nitrate of soda, ammonium sulphate (commonly found in mixed fertilizer) and ammonium nitrate are the chief commercial forms of nitrogen in use today. Cottonseed meal is said to be tops as a vegetable source of nitrogen and dried blood and fish scrap are valuable nitrogenous animal products and considered better than commercial and vegetable sources.

Phosphorus bursts into flame when exposed to air in its pure state, so it too must be combined with other elements when used as plant food. It gives a rapid and a vigorous start to plants, stimulates root and bloom formation and hastens maturity. It is obtained from bone and phosphate rock and as superphosphate in mixed fertilizers. Potassium or Potash is, like its sisters, also dangerous to handle in its pure state. When combined with other elements it imparts vigor and disease resistance to plants, produces stiff strong stems, increases size of fruit and seed and gives winter hardiness to the plant. Potash used to be obtained from wood ashes and in the nineteenth century, almost all of the potash used in the United States was imported from Germany and France. Since 1925 when first mining developments of potash began in New Mexico, it has been increasingly a domestic product. In Utah, muriate of potash which furnishes more potassium than other products, such as greensands, industrial wastes and seaweed, is actually a by-product of table salt production. Sulphate of potash is widely used but contains less potash and is more expensive than muriate of potash. Wood ashes are beneficial to the structure of heavy clay soils, but there is doubt as to how good it is to sandy soils because it not only lowers acidity of the soil but furnishes very little potash. When you buy a commercial fertilizer known as 8–8–8 or 5–10–5 or 4–12–4, the first figure stands for Nitrogen, the second for Phosphorus and the third, for Potash.

Calcium is found in limestones, oyster shells, phosphate rock, superphosphate and gypsum. It improves root formation and stiffness of stem, makes intake of other foods easier and neutralizes poisons produced in the plant. Magnesium is found in dolomitic limestone, magnesium sulphate and magnesium oxide. This element aids in maintaining the dark green color of leaves, regulates the intake of other plant foods and acts as a carrier of phosphoric acid through the plant. Magnesium sulphate is commonly known as Epsom Salts. The chief sources of sulphur are natural sulphur obtained from sulphur deposits, and from fertilizer materials such as gypsum, sulphate of potash, sulphate of ammonia and ordinary superphosphate. Sulphur increases root growth, helps with that dark green color and stimulates plant growth.

Boron is a newcomer to the fertilizer family and seems to be connected in some way to calcium—a deficiency in one shows a deficiency in the other. Usually cracked stems of plants and corking of the veins in citrus fruits are evidences that boron is necessary.

Borax, that we associate so closely to Death Valley and the Twenty Mule Teams (especially since the advent of television) is the chief source of boron. Use it sparingly.

You don't hear too much about manganese deficiency because barnyard manures usually contain enough of this material to suffice. However, it does seem to be the cure for the mottled leaves appearing on citrus fruits and other plants. Manganese sulphate is what we use to bring manganese to the plant and since the leaves of plants can absorb this nutrient, it is used widely as a spray. An application of 1% manganese sulphate in solution on Crape Myrtles, Guavas, Plumbagos, Ligustrums and Buddleias usually brings the discolored leaves back to normal.

Copper, obtained from copper sulphate, is widely used to check the yellowing and wilting of plant leaves—a condition that resembles Die-Back in Azaleas and citrus fruits. It seems to aid metabolism, to hasten oxidation of plant functions and to hasten the synthesis of chlorophyll. Don't use too much too often. Zinc, in the form of zinc sulphate, corrects the abnormal development of leaves of plants—the shortening, curling, malformation of foliage. It may be applied to the soil or used in the form of a spray on the leaves.

A definite yellowing of leaves of some plants is almost always caused by a deficiency of iron. When this symptom occurs in Azaleas, Hibiscus and Altheas, leaf and soil spraying with a solution of iron sulphate or Copperas is often the cure, especially in the summer months. Applications of iron chelates have also proved effective. Be careful with the iron chelates—you can burn a plant with an overdose. Follow the instructions on the label. I have been experimenting with liquid fertilizers that contain all of the trace elements, and so far their use has made it unnecessary to treat the deficiencies separately.

In the paragraph above, I spoke of "iron chelates", and remembering my own bewilderment when I first heard these words, I hasten to explain. First of all, the word chelate is from the Greek meaning "claw" and is pronounced "key-late." Chelation is the power of certain organic compounds to reach around like a claw and envelope metals to hold them together. At one time, regardless of how much effort was put to work on soil pH, plants died or remained sickly because the minerals were not absorbed. Then scientists discovered that minerals could be made "active" when surrounded by organic acids. They knew that rich soils often had enough humic acid formed by decomposition of organic materials to make the absorption of added minerals an easy matter. Citric acid had successfully been added to iron sulphate to make the iron effective when it was applied. So when you ask for iron chelates, you are getting the iron mixed with the organic acids necessary to make it do some good. New improved formulas supply not only iron but copper, zinc and manganese. These "medicines" may be applied to the soil, or plants and trees may be "Jet Fed" (on the order of our hypodermic needle) to obtain quicker results. There are several brand name preparations on the market, so ask your local nurseryman to let you have the literature on each product to make it easier for you to decide what you need. One chemical company offers a type of iron chelate for use on acid soils. It has also designed another type for alkaline soils. Another company lists its product as an iron chelate plus organics and soil conditioners. All are excellent, but just remember that none of the chelates replace fertilizers; the chelates are used in addition to the fertilizers.

What are the requirements of the particular specimen you are going to plant? Does it need alkaline conditions or is it an acid-loving plant? In some sections the soil is acid, but in others, like the New Orleans area, it is definitely alkaline. The sea coast is full of sandy soils and salt sprays. Right here I pause to explain the term "pH" that you see and hear so much about. The word pH is an expression of the amount of acid in the soil. Perhaps if I refer to it as a ruler measuring tenths of an inch, with the neutral point as the number 7, it will be easier to talk about.

You can buy a soil testing kit and if you follow directions you can discover just what the soil is in a particular bed. If the planting

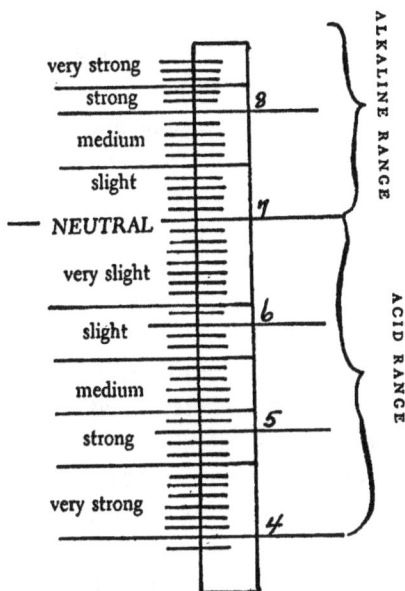

instructions call for a highly acid soil, you know that the pH should be between 4 and 5. If the specimen you are about to plant demands slightly acid conditions, bordering on the neutral, the pH should be 6 to 7. If requirements are alkaline, the reading should be 7 and up. When the soil condition registers a high pH or shows definite alkaline reaction you have trouble because high alkalinity makes the hitherto necessary minerals insoluble and unavailable to your plant. In short all soil machinery stops. Use either aluminum sulphate or sulphur to correct this condition, according to the directions in the ensuing paragraph.

In the following chapters you are going to read a lot about fertilizing and feeding and you will find that you can give a plant what it needs by using either chemical or organic fertilizers. Should your particular specimen call for acid soil add one tablespoonful of sulphur or about one-third cupful of aluminum sulphate to every square yard. Then keep the soil in good condition by using a well-balanced commercial fertilizer such as 4-6-4, testing occasionally to see if you need any of the acidifying agents. On the other hand if you wish to alkalinize or neutralize the soil use lime. Hydrated lime is faster-acting but is not kind to soils and fertilizers, therefore I recommend using ground or pulverized limestone. Using one to five pounds of pulverized limestone to every fifty square feet will raise the pH from 5 to 6. I ask you to be cautious in using chemical fertilizers because a little goes a long way. Be sure to read the directions carefully and follow them closely; you don't want to burn the plant that you start out to feed.

If you have access to organic fertilizers by all means use them in place of the commercial ones wherever feasible. Organic fertilizers come from plant and animal materials and I cite for example: bone meal, which is rich in phosphorus and can always be used around bulbs and tubers without fear of burning the plant as long as you do not apply it directly on or below the bulb; dried blood, which supplies nitrogen, and cottonseed meal which is so beneficial for acid-loving greens. And as I mentioned earlier, a good compost heap is a joy to have.

You can make your own leaf mold and compost if you have enough space in your garden. Layering oak leaves alternately with soil can be done in a small area but it takes from eight to twelve months to be ready to use. I would not suggest your starting a compost unless you have a corner of the garden to spare, a corner that is far enough away from patio and living quarters. Make an oblong bin of fairly close woven wire supported at the four corners with wooden posts. Make it at least five feet high. Put in a one-foot layer of dry materials such as grass, leaves, table waste, peat moss or fish scrap. If you can get hold of water hyacinths, add them because they are not only a wonderful supply of water but they supply potash and nitrogen. Then sprinkle with a layer of chemical fertilizer containing nitrogen, phosphate and potash. Wet thoroughly and pack down. Then spread a four-inch layer of manure over the wet materials and cover with a light blanket of superphosphate. Repeat the layering until the compost is about four feet high. The materials have to be kept wet, but wait at least a month before you turn them over for the first time, always keeping the heap lower in the center than on the edges so that water and rain won't run off. Turn at intervals and by the end of the second month it should be ready to use. In winter, it takes at least thirty to sixty days longer. The resulting compost is rich in nitrogen.

Animal manures, as I stated before, must be well decomposed before they are applied to plants and you must be sure that they are placed far enough away from bulb and stem to prevent burning. The chief objection to animal manures, as they come from the farm, is that they contain so many weeds. Cow manure is wet and heavy and horse manure is hot and dry. Both have to be used cautiously and both are good for making liquid manure when fresh. Sheep manure should be stored dry. It makes an excellent fertilizer, and is easier to use in the dry stick form that is now on the market. Poultry manure provides a good source of organic matter and is rich in the basic element, zinc. Peat moss is good for acid-loving plants provided it is well sifted. Wood ashes contain some potash, magnesium and lime; coal ashes have no nutritional value, but do loosen clay soils. Coal soot brings nitrogen, phosphorus and potash to the soil and seems to be of some value as an "enemy agent" to worms and certain fungi.

Make sure that your soil is healthy. There are several soil fumigants on the market, and one of the newest bears the handsome chemical title of: "3,5-dimethyltetrahydro-1,3,5, 2H thiadiazine-2-thione." Fortunately, it has the simple trade name of Mylone, and because of the heavier-than-air weight of its breakdown products, it has the punch to penetrate the silt in the soils of the South. It promises to be a good warrior against weeds, diseases and nematodes especially when used early in the season for sterilizing seed or the soil for new flower beds.

And there you have the soil and its problems. The old adage:

"An ounce of prevention is worth a pound of cure" applies very well to planting. Make certain that your soil contains the necessary elements for whatever you plan to put into it and you will find stronger plants with lovelier flowers of longer blooming periods.

❊ 2 ❊

Lawns

Once you have decided upon a tentative plan for your garden, sit down and tackle the lawn problem. The lawn is going to be the setting for your entire landscape and you will want to have it as green and luxuriant as possible.

There are four questions to consider:

1. Do you have a good foundation?
2. Is there sufficient drainage?
3. What kind of grass do you need?
4. Do you know how to plant the grass you may choose?

If your house has just been completed and your lawn is to be a brand new one, remember to rid the area of such debris as stones, bits of wood or brick used in the building process. Don't bury them. Haul them away. Rake the surface well and dig and turn the soil to at least a six inch depth. At this point stop and evaluate your drainage problem. If it is impossible to provide subsurface drainage through the medium of tile pipes, or if you think that what is already there is not sufficient, a good layer of shell or gravel beneath the top soil should serve the purpose as well.

The next step will be to grade the ground with a slight slope towards the street so that water can drain away from the house. Use a roller or a flat board to make sure that there are no low spots. It will be a waste of time and money to plant seed in an area where grass will stand in watery bogs too long. It just won't live.

Now consider your soil. If it is heavy and quite obviously clay you will want to add some decent garden soil and sand to make the ground more porous. Your grass will need oxygen, just as we do, to breathe. If the soil is too sandy you will want to incorporate some heavier garden loam to help the ground hold more water. Then work in a fair amount of a fertilizer that contains potash and phosphate to give the lawn a good start. You need not add nitrogen now because much of it will be lost before the seed or sprigs can get growing. Nitrogen can be added later. A little lime may be used at the same time as the potash and phosphate if you feel that there is an acidity problem to balance but do be careful if you plan to plant carpet grass, for it will not tolerate lime. To give you some idea of what quantities of materials to use in starting a new lawn, I offer a recipe that has been used successfully: for every five hundred square feet of area, use one to two cubic yards of well-rotted manure, one and one-half bales peat moss, and one to two cubic yards of humus. I like to see the prepared area stand for about two weeks to make sure that no low spots develop and to rid the ground of any further weeds that might show. Check the level again and you are ready to sow!

Select the grass that best suits the needs of your family and your vicinity. If you have plenty of time for garden care, there are grasses that have to be "nursed" to be beautiful. If you are a busy person, select a turf that will grow with a minimum of care. If you are in doubt about the type you want, study the problem and consult your State Agricultural Agent. *Don't* use the advice of all the neighbors. If you do you will get a jumbled idea of lawn care that will be costly in the long run.

There are several grasses that do well in the South. Some varieties do not produce seed and must be planted by sod, and by stolon or sprig, processes known as vegetative planting. Sodding means planting pieces of turf in small clumps or blocks or strips as close together as you can afford. The closer they are planted the quicker the coverage of area. The clumps or strips must be firmly packed into place. Sprigging means planting runners or stolons at intervals, or end to end. Perhaps the best method of presentation is to list the grasses and let you pick the one suited to your needs.

BERMUDA GRASS, *Cynodon dactylon* is probably one of the best known and most used grasses in our area. The common Bermuda, the one most planted in the South is the only variety of this grass planted from seed. Sow about two pounds to every five hundred square feet, using either a seed spreader or the hand method. This grass spreads by runners and its leaves are medium-coarse textured. It stands wear and tear and drought very well, but needs frequent mowing during the warm months. Because it turns brown with the first frost, it must be covered with winter rye if you would avoid an unsightly lawn. Bermuda need not be planted again in the spring. It comes back green and eager as soon as the warm weather sets in. There are several varieties of Bermuda on the market that may be planted by sod or stolon. The three best known are Ormond, Tiflawn, and Everglades, all deep green. Ormond is coarser and more upright than Tiflawn and Everglades. Of the three Everglades #1 demands the least care. Plant five square feet of sod or fifty pounds of stolons to every five hundred square feet of lawn area in early spring. No member of this family does well under shade trees.

CARPET GRASS, *Axonopus compressus* is widely used in the Coastal Plain down into Florida, where it is considered a perennial. It is coarser than Bermuda, has short stubby leaves up to one-half inch wide, and is inexpensive. Plant by seeds, two pounds per every five hundred square feet or by sodding, four to six square feet of sod to every five hundred square feet in spring or early summer. This grass needs frequent mowing but you will be glad to know that it is resistant to most diseases and insects aand retains its color fairly well in the cool months. It does not demand too much fertilization. Again I caution, if you intend to plant Carpet grass, never use lime in the soil.

CENTIPEDE GRASS *Eremochloa ephiuroides,* was introduced into our country from the Orient about thirty-four years ago and has been grown successfully throughout the South for the past twenty-five years. It is a short dark green turf that grows close to the ground by means of runners that put down roots at every joint. It actually resembles a centipede. Its texture is intermediate between St. Augustine and Bermuda and it does well in either sun or shade. More to its laurels are the facts that it can be planted anytime and lives through ordinary winters, surviving freezes, although it loses its green color. If it turns yellow in spots after a long wet season, it probably needs an application of ferrous sulphate to correct the deficiency of iron caused by the rains. Centipede is disease and pest resistant. It will withstand considerable drought if well established and needs to be mowed only once or twice a year! You can really enjoy this dense, springy green lawn. This grass is usually delivered and planted in square sections of sod. Plant it in about the same proportions as for Bermuda. Centipede may also be planted by seeding your lawn and in this medium is known under a trade name. I have tried the seed method and have not been too successful. In either method of planting, when you buy, beware of substitutes and imitations. There are several creeping grasses that are labeled "Centipede."

ITALIAN RYE GRASS *Lolium multiflorum,* is regarded as a supplemental green to those southern lawns that turn brown in winter. Prior to planting, fertilize the lawn with a well-balanced food, then rake smooth and water well before sowing. The seed should be sprinkled over the lawn in early fall and it needs plenty of water for germination. Never rake the tender grass too vigorously, especially when it is wet. Rye dies out as soon as warm weather starts in. I have never liked to see Italian Rye sown over St. Augustine grass, though the latter does lose some of its color in autumn. I have found that St. Augustine asserts itself faster in the spring when not crowded by a "visiting relative," so to speak.

ST. AUGUSTINE GRASS *Stenotaphrum secundatum,* a creeping perennial, is another popular southern lawn grass. It does its best when growing in slightly alkaline or neutral soil. Planted by sprig, runners or square plots of turf, it does very well in the shade and produces a thick luxuriant carpet if—and this is a big IF—it is not mowed too closely and a careful pest control is practiced. The mantle of the lawn mower must be raised as high as it can go when this grass is cut. Never mow too closely or the sun will burn it. You will want to allow the older varieties to remain a good two inches high at all times. Depending on the amount of rainfall, mowing is usually necessary at least semi-monthly during the warm months; in winter it is almost unnecessary.

"Bitter Blue" has long been considered the finest type of this grass. The variety Roselawn seems to produce more stems than leaves. The variegated St. Augustine is most unusual. The leaf is creamy down the center with margins of green, and a patch of this grass in a corner of the lawn or around the base of a tree is most effective.

Floratine is the newest member of the St. Augustine family to be introduced, in Florida in 1958. Blue-green in color, its short narrow leaves are close-growing in habit, thereby proving superior in resisting weeds. It hugs the ground and its rate of coverage is good. This variety is more disease resistant and can be clipped closer than most St. Augustine grasses. Its recommended cutting height is one and one-half inches.

Sad but true, St. Augustine is a perfect host for that sucking insect, the Chinch bug and I beg you to control it in its infancy, otherwise all is lost! It is also susceptible to army worm and several fungus diseases. Read more about these pests further in this chapter, under PESTS.

The ZOYSIA GRASSES *Zoysia* species and known in Florida as Manila Grass or Flawn, though beautiful, are all slow to establish and more expensive than other kinds of turf. You will need fifteen square feet of sod to every five hundred square feet when plugging, or three square feet of sod to every five hundred square feet when sprigging. These grasses are resistant to almost all diseases and insects, resistant to salt spray and remain green farther into the fall than the others. As far as I know, there are now four reliable Zoysia relatives on the market and all grow well in shade. They make such a thick green mat when established that they allow no room for the planting of winter grass; hence, when they brown during the cold months, you must grin and bear it.

MEYER ZOYSIA, or *Meyer Z-52 Zoysia* is better than *Zoysia japonica*, the Korean or Japanese grass, but both of these coarse blade lawns are topped by *Zoysia matrella*, the Manilagrass which has a narrower leaf. The latter needs more care and covers the area more slowly than the others, hence you must plant the sprigs closer together. EMERALD or VELVET ZOYSIA, *Zoysia tenuifolia* or Mascarenegrass, is a new and better hybrid of *Zoysia matrella*. All need plenty of water and lots of patience on your part. All should be planted in spring in rows parallel to the house and all should be allowed to become established before being mowed. Do not, however, allow any of these lawns to go too long without cutting. If you can afford it invest in the lawn-mower type lawn brush. It is so much more beneficial to this type of grass than the ordinary rake. From my own experience I have found the *Meyer Zoysia* the least susceptible to frost.

RENOVATING

So far I have discussed planting a new lawn; now for renovating your old one! If the grass you have had was planted in sprigs and there are worn spots here and there where traffic is heavy, your problem is solved by spot resprigging and resodding. Be sure to add soil if the area has worn low. Take runners of the established grass from the edge of the garden beds and plant them in the bare spots.

If your grass can be planted from seed, cut what is left of the old lawn as closely as you can, rid the area of all weeds and rake away all dry dead grass. Raking not only loosens the soil but aerates it as well. Then reseed, mixing your seed with sand or peat or other fertilizer to give even distribution. If you use fertilizer as a mixer, again I caution you to use one without nitrogen; give the seed a chance to begin to grow before you apply nitrogen because if nitrogen is too fast-acting it will burn rather than feed. Water well. Early spring is the ideal time to start any grass; early fall is the next best season.

FERTILIZING

Feed your grass! Like humans who have to eat to live, grass also needs its nourishment. But hit a happy medium; do not overfeed. As in humans it is not safe or healthy. No matter what type of grass you have established give it a meal of a good complete fertilizer, such as 8–8–8, early in the spring. Use from five to ten pounds per one thousand square feet. Then because all green things need just enough nitrogen for steady strong growth and because soils do not retain nitrogen for too long, feed during the late spring with an organic fertilizer, such as one of the sludge products or with a fertilizer such as 10–6–4. Or you may prefer to use one of the synthetic ureaform fertilizers which are excellent sources of slow-acting nitrogen. Organic forms seem to be better than the synthetic forms in the long run. The organics have to be acted upon by the bacteria in the soil before the nitrogen can be released, hence a slower-acting nutrient and subsequently a slower-growing plant. Nitrogen in the organic form will not burn the grass should you happen to use an overdose and under heavy rainfalls, it does not wash away as quickly as synthetic nitrogen. A good practice is to give the lawn a sprinkling of cottonseed meal in the fall; it will improve color and generally recondition the turf. Your grass should tell you when it needs nitrogen. If you see it looking anemic and being a host to clover and weeds you know it needs nitrogen. On the other hand try not to overfeed with nitrogen; too much of an overdose will make your lawn an easy prey for disease, especially Brown Patch. Whatever you apply and whenever you apply it be sure to water well immediately afterwards and regularly in the next few days. This is particularly important when the sun's rays are strong and hot.

PESTS

The pests most prevalent in grasses are Cutworms, Sod Webworms, Army Worms, Ants and the bugbear of all, the Chinch Bug.

If you notice your grass turning brown in trail formation you can be almost certain that you have CUTWORMS, *Agrotis* the smooth dull-brown, gray or black worms that chew their way in tunnels through the grass during the warm months. They feed at night on leaves, cut off the grass near the soil and damage seedlings of Bermuda and rye grasses. To make sure that you have these worms try soaking a spot of lawn with one gallon of water into which you have put one tablespoon of pyrethrum. This solution will bring the adults to the surface. Control with DDT, following the instructions on the package. Usually in spraying your lawn for the Chinch Bug you take care of the Cutworm at the same time but if you are treating solely for Cutworms, use one-half pound of 50% DDT wettable powder to twenty gallons of water over a one thousand square foot area.

The true ARMY-WORM is *Cirphis unipuncta,* a gray-black caterpillar with a narrow yellow stripe down the middle of its back and a wide chartreuse stripe along each side. It feeds at night, attacking the grass just below and at the surface of the soil. It is the

The Army Worm

larva of the dull brown moth and usually works in colonies or armies. Controls are the same as those for Cutworms.

The FALL ARMY-WORM, *Laphygma frugiperda* usually puts in its appearance after the true Army-worm and does most of its damage in the daytime. This one is about one and one-half inches long, greenish-brownish-gray with black stripes along each side and a line of black spots down the center back. Its feeding causes circular bare areas in the lawn. Controls are the same as those for Cutworms.

SOD WEBWORMS, *Pyralids* usually leave a tell-tale web through the grass. These are the larvae of the gray lawn moth that we have always called "millers," about three-fourths of an inch long and covered with thin hairs. This whole family is a night-shift group; the moths fly after dark, the females dropping eggs on the

Sod Webworm

lawn and as soon as the babies emerge they cover themselves with a silky web. These worms cut, eat and bury blades of grass, preferably on new lawns so get rid of them as fast as you can. You can check for them and use the same insecticides in the same way as you do for Cutworms.

Really gird yourself to battle the CHINCH BUG, *Blissus leucopterus insularis* and *Blissus hirtus*. This pest can destroy a complete lawn, especially St. Augustine grass unless controlled in its infancy. If you see irregular reddish-brown patches appearing

on your lawn and spreading quickly go to work at once and urge
your neighbors to get busy too, for I have seen this bug go from
lawn to lawn in a city block and destroy them all. The baby bugs
are red with a white band across the back; they are about as big as
a pinhead. The adults are small, about one-sixth of an inch long
with black bodies and white wings, closely resembling a beetle in
shape. They suck the sap from the stem of the grass blade at ground
level and cause the grass to die. To see them, flood the brown area
and watch these tiny pests try to keep their feet dry by climbing
onto the tip ends of the blades.

three stages of growth of
Chinch Bug

Use the insecticide recommended for Cutworms to fight the
CHINCH BUG and use it when you first see indications of its
presence. You may have to doctor the lawn more than once; in June
when the Chinch Bug is first noted and again in several weeks in
order to kill the next generation. It breeds rapidly in hot dry
weather. I have found one pound of 50% DDT wettable powder
to twenty gallons of water to be quite effective for every one thousand square feet of lawn. Or you may use one quart of 25% DDT
emulsifiable concentrate to twenty gallons of water for every one
thousand square feet of area. Soak the lawn with water before any
application of DDT. Because you have to be sure to get down to
the soil with the insecticide and because the heat of the sun causes
rapid deterioration of the power of DDT, if you haven't a spray

gun with sufficient force for the job, call in a nurseryman who has the necessary equipment. This may seem expensive but it is sure to be cheaper than having to replace your lawn. After spraying, the dead areas should be raked clean, sprinkled with peat or compost, turned over, raked smooth and then resodded.

Should there ever come a time when the Chinch Bug becomes resistant or immune to this insecticide try VC-13, an emulsifiable concentrate that is proving to be effective. VC-13 is an organic phosphate and is recommended at the rate of twelve ounces or twenty-four tablespoons to every one thousand square feet, with enough water to obtain sufficient coverage of the area.

Diazinon may also be used against the Chinch Bug. Available as a 25% emulsifiable concentrate, measure three ounces or six table-spoons of this one to every one thousand square feet, with sufficient water to cover the area. Inasmuch as VC-13 and Diazinon are very expensive, let us hope that the Chinch Bug can be destroyed with DDT for a long, long time.

FALSE CHINCH BUG, *Nysius ericae* is gray in color and is rarely a lawn pest.

ANTS, *Hymanoptera* build nests in the ground and hills around the doorway to their nests. These mounds smother grass around and under them and when ants nest near the roots of the grass, the roots die. These pests also destroy seeds in the ground and prevent a good carpet of grass from developing. Using 6% chlordane dust or one quart of 42% emulsion concentrate of chlordane to fifty gallons of water for every one thousand square feet of lawn seems a good method of getting rid of ants. I usually mix the liquid chlordane with the DDT when I spray for the Chinch Bug, thereby killing two birds with one stone.

Dieldrin, an organic insecticide, will also control the Argentine ant as well as fire ants, cutworms, white grubs, sod webworms, army-worms and red bugs or chiggers. In the granular form it is very easy to apply. Just follow directions on the package. You can even mix

Dieldrin with any dry fertilizer, thus accomplishing two jobs at once. A one-pound can of granules is usually sufficient for about three hundred square feet of soil.

GRUBS are grayish-whitish-tannish larvae of beetles and are usually found in a curled position in the ground. They feed on the grass roots. Fight them with DDT in the same proportions as for Cutworms, or use chlordane.

MOLE CRICKETS, *Gryllotalpidae* are about one and one-half inches long with a light brownish-green body and round beady eyes. Their forelegs are short and their feet are shaped like small

Mole Cricket

shovels, perfect for their business of burrowing and uprooting young grass plants. I control mine by dropping a handful of moth balls or paradichlorobenzene crystals into the burrows. Toxaphene is also being used to rout the mole cricket, but use it with care because it is very poisonous and not compatible with Bordeaux mixture or lime.

WIREWORMS, *Elateridae* are children of the click beetle, hard-shelled, brownish-black and about an inch long. They bore into the ground, feed on grass roots and eventually kill the lawn. Control is the same as that for Billbugs.

Wireworm

I mention the LOCUST-KILLER WASP, *Sphecius speciosus* because we do see it occasionally in the South, although it is more prevalent in the eastern part of the United States. This insect is about one and one-half inches long with a bright orange and black body. It digs round holes in the ground, disturbing the grass roots, then flies slowly out, kills the locusts and brings them back to the nest as food for the young. These wasps are seen in the summer and the important thing to remember, besides their damaging the lawn, is the fact that they will sting people if molested. Control is the same as that for Billbugs.

BILLBUGS, *Spenophorus* are reddish-brown beetles almost an inch long that chew on leaves and roots of Zoysia grass in the Gulf Coast region. One-half pound of 50% DDT wettable powder to twenty gallons of water to every one thousand square feet of surface will rid the lawn of this pest.

SCALE INSECTS, such as RHODESGRASS SCALE, *Antonina graminis* which attacks Bermuda and St. Augustine lawns; BERMUDAGRASS SCALE, *Odonaspis ruthae* which feeds on Bermuda and GROUND PEARLS, *Margarodes meridionalis* which cause damage to Bermuda and Centipede, all leave bare brown patches. They attack in long dry spells. I know that various insecticides will help control the spread but I suggest that you call your State Entomologist for the definite antidote for each. What is successful in one area may not be recommended in another.

DISEASES

There are many diseases in the turf world, even when one follows the rules of good drainage, proper fertilization and faithful methods of cutting. If you notice patches of your St. Augustine or other lawns turning brown in a more or less circular pattern, with the outer edge a smoky yellow color, in all probability the soil-inhabiting fungus, *Rhizoctonia solani* has begun to infest your lawn. To make doubly sure arm yourself with a hand rake, get down on your knees and scratch around the roots to see if you find any evidence of the pests I have already mentioned. If you find no trace of insects, this fungus *Rhizoctonia solani* has produced BROWN PATCH or *Pellicularia filamentosa* an infection that usually shows up in early spring and early fall, spreading rapidly in moderately cool temperatures and brought to a standstill with the advent of the extreme heat of summer and cold of winter. Starting with a small spot of dead, collapsed grass this fungus reaches out in all directions at approximately the same rate, eventually forming an area resembling a circle.

Although this fungus has been identified for some years, up to the present many fungicides have been recommended for its control, never for its elimination. Now, after many months of testing pentachloronitrobenzene has proved to be the fungicide to use. Sold under several trade names, including Terraclor, this chemical can be obtained in granular form or as a wettable powder. I recommend using one pound of the 75% pentachloronitrobenzene wettable powder to twenty-five gallons of water to each one thousand square feet of lawn, and this means the entire lawn, not just the infected area. Always use an agitator-type sprayer, since the powder is difficult to hold in suspension. One dose is usually effective for one season. Although more expensive, the granular form of this fungicide is easier to apply than the powder form; you can mix it with sand, spread it evenly on the lawn and wash it down into the ground with a hard spray of the hose. In using either form be sure to water down the lawn immediately after application in order to insure the chemical getting down to the ground around the roots of the grass. It is also necessary to wash it off the blades of the turf; delay will cause the grass to turn red for a short time. Should you inadvertently use a stronger percentage of this fungicide your lawn will in all probability, turn a bright crimson. This does not mean that you have killed the turf. The discoloration usually fades in several weeks' time.

Although the infestation of Chinch Bug is heavier in the hot months when Brown Patch is at a standstill you may have both conditions to fight at the same time. Since pentachloronitrobenzene is compatible with wettable DDT, you may mix the two remedies. One combined application should put an end to both troubles.

There are more fungus diseases that attack St. Augustine and other grasses, one of which is L E A F S P O T, caused by two fungi, *Piricularia grisea* and *Curcularia*. Other types, such as F U S A - R I U M , D O L L A R S P O T and G R E A S E S P O T are often troublesome but not nearly as destructive as Brown Patch. Their control is somewhat successful with use of turf fungicides sold under different trade names. S L I M E M O L D is unsightly but harmless. It appears after long wet periods, turning the affected areas into streaks of gray-black lawn. This infection is entirely superficial. It dries up and eventually disappears.

If you are unable to identify the particular type of infestation on your lawn, play safe and consult your local entomologist with the Department of Agriculture. He will be up to date on any new scale or disease and will be able to advise you accordingly.

And don't be afraid to continue feeding schedules when you are concerned about disease. Most fertilizers and fungicides are compatible.

G R E E N M O S S sometimes appears on bare spots of sod, and when it does you may be sure that the drainage is poor, that the soil is badly aerated.

WEEDS can be controlled best by taking good care of your lawn but since perfect "lawn-keeping" is almost impossible, the lowly weed will rear its head. Crabgrass, dandelions, chickweed and white clover can be eradicated with the many herbicides now on the market if you feel that it is too big a job to tackle by hand-picking. Just be sure to follow directions on the package and take care when you handle the poisonous ones. Some disinfect the soil so completely that nothing will grow in the area for months to come. In larger research laboratories tests are being made with a new formulation of calcium arsenate that if applied early enough in the spring promises to give nearly full control of the weed pests for twelve months duration. Keep in touch with your nurseryman for the latest introductions.

A word or two about encouraging your shade-tolerant grasses to grow under trees. Fertilize these areas more frequently than the rest of the lawn; feed the trees well so that their roots do not have to rob the grass of its nutrients; remove superfluous branches or thin out those that must stay on the tree; rake fallen leaves from shady spots and water more often and longer than in sunny locations. In short, be such a gracious host that the grass will want to remain longer as your guest!

✗ 3 ✗

Ground Covers

Your choice of ground cover depends upon whether you want a low creeper or whether you prefer something a foot or more in height. The place of use will largely determine the choice. Do you want something to enhance a bed, something to cut down the weedings? Try Ajuga or Saxifrage. Are you looking for a plant to cover the bare spots under a tree where "nothing ever grows?" Then Ivy and Ajuga are perfect. Or do you want to use a plant instead of bricks or corrugated edging to hold the soil and form the boundary of a bed? Think about Liriope. These and a few others are listed below for your selection, in the order of their approximate popularity.

ENGLISH IVY, *Hedera helix* and its sub-tropical relative that is tolerant to salt sprays, the ALGERIAN IVY, *Hedera canariensis* are both ground-hugging and lovely when eventually established. Although the English Ivy is really a plant of cool climates it is fairly hardy in the lower South. The Algerian Ivy also bears up well in the summer heat. Both are evergreen, will do well in sun and even better in shade, provided they get plenty of moisture. The variety from the Baltic provinces, *Hedera helix baltica* has very small leaves and is perhaps the hardiest of all Ivy. The silver variegated Baltic Ivy, known in the trade as Stardust is very beautiful. *H. canariensis variegata* has green leaves edged in creamy-white and it too is attractive. Use hairpins to keep the runners pinned to the ground until they take root. Make cuttings of all of these and root them in open ground in the fall. Keep watch for their chief enemies, the red spider and related minute organisms. Either hose them off with a forceful spray of water or use a miticide like Aramite.

Sometimes during periods of intense heat and heavy rains brown spots appear on English Ivy. These blemishes spread over the entire leaf and cause it to drop off; the entire plant may die. The culprit in this case is a fungus called *Phyllosticta concentrica*, a disease that may occur on Ivy everywhere but is more prevalent in the deep South. Control calls for collecting and burning the dead leaves and spraying with Bordeaux mixture or with one of the organic fungisides, such as Zineb or Captan. Incidentally be careful when you mix Captan with other products as it is not compatible with oil.

Another type of ground Ivy, *Nepeta hederaceae* is considered a creeping perennial. Its round leaves form a thick mat two to three inches high. In the lower South it remains green through the winter and grows fast, tolerating sun or shade. If frozen back it returns in the spring. This one has many nicknames but I think it is best known as "Creeping Charlie." Don't confuse it with another "Creeping Charlie," *Pilea Nummularifolia* or the Artillery Plant which is discussed in the chapter on Potted Plants.

There are several other ground covers that do well in either sun or shade and my favorite is A J U G A or the C A R P E T B U G L E P L A N T, *Ajuga reptans* an herbaceous perennial member of the Mint Family. Growing from one to three inches high, it likes a loamy soil and good drainage. When in condition it produces small spikes of blue flowers in the spring. The leaves are a deep green and grow in a rather prostrate manner. I use it as a ground cover in the rock garden, in the patio beds and between the stepping stones on the walks. *Ajuga metallica* variety *crispa* is a very low form. *Ajuga purpurea* is the copper-leaved form which is not at its best in the shade; it needs the sun to bring out its bronze tones.

The A J U G A, which dates back to Biblical days, has a new variety, Rainbow, which is just as colorful as its name implies. The variegated foliage has a metallic sheen and appears in rosettes of white, green, pink and bronze, the colors changing with the season and the amount of sun it receives. Growing to four inches, it is a hardy perennial that produces low spikes of purple flowers in May and June.

Although they are practically pest free you should watch for crown-rot on these plants in humid weather. Napthalene flakes worked lightly into the soil will rid the ground of spores. All varieties can be used in the middle and lower South and in the latter section it is practically evergreen. Plant from four to eight inches apart, depending on how fast a coverage you want. Ajuga increases by runners.

W A T E R M E L O N B E G O N I A, not really a begonia but actually *Peperomia Sandersii*, variety *argyreia* is a stemless creeping perennial member of the Pepper Family. The dark green leaves are fuzzy and round with lighter stripes between the veins. I use mine as an interesting ground cover under my Pyracantha bush where it has come through extreme cold with hardly a setback.

S A X I F R A G E, *Saxifraga* is a hardy perennial that looks most attractive in the bed and in the rock garden. I was amazed when I learned that the members of this family are native to the North and South temperate and arctic zones, excepting South America, Africa and Australia. There are a number of species, each with varieties of its own. *Saxifraga decipiens* is dwarf and mossy, producing white blossoms in summer and foliage turning a deep rose color in winter. *S. sarmentosa*, popularly known as the Strawberry Geranium, spreads by runners, grows to about six inches and may also be used in hanging baskets. These plants need no winter protection, thrive in moist earth and are particularly attractive when with the sedums.

STONECROP, *Sedum acre* forms a quick-growing creeping evergreen mat about two inches high in any type of soil in almost any southern area. The leaves are small and light green and the minute yellow spring flowers are very pretty. This is a good cover for rocks and crevices and stands either sun or shade.

MOSS PHLOX or *Phlox subulata,* sometimes called Ground Pink, forms a low thick mat if given full sun. Rarely exceeding three inches in height, its leaves are evergreen and its spring flowers are very colorful in white, pink and lavender. Since it tolerates any type of well-drained soil and most temperatures, Moss Phlox may be grown successfully anywhere in the southern area.

In the cooler regions of the South, JAPANESE SPURGE, *Pachrysandra terminalis* is a fine ground cover, making a thick carpet about six inches high. It does best in the shade, and is particularly attractive when mixed with its new variety, Silveredge, with lighter green leaves margined in silvery-white.

Besides being wonderfully adaptable to indoor culture, another low ground cover that tolerates any kind of soil is the perennial WANDERING JEW, *Tradescantia fluminensis* and *Zebrina pendula*. These botanical names are both of the Spiderwort Family but each is of a different genera. Both have one chief requisite: moisture. And after that, warmth. They will not stand being walked on. The green leaves of *Tradescantia* are white-tipped and striped and slightly tinted with lavender. The small white flowers appear in clusters at the tip of each trailing stem. *Zebrina's* foliage is almost metallic in appearance, purplish-green on the upper side and reddish beneath, and its tiny flower is a rosy-lavender. Cuttings of both will root rapidly in water, and both make ideal subjects for hanging baskets.

See *Liriope spicata* and *Liriope graminifolia* under Higher Growing Ground Covers.

The TRAILING LANTANA, *Lantana sellowiana,* tolerates poor soils so well that it is the solution to problem spots where nothing else will grow. It is perfect for covering old tree stumps and looks lovely when spilling from urns or boxes at the top of steps. It remains almost evergreen in the lower South and will do well in other areas if you have the patience to wait for it to come back after a freeze. The little clusters of lavender flowers show nearly the year around. A new, lower-growing hybrid with yellow blossoms has been introduced in California. Because it is reported to do well in heat and in dry soils, I see no reason why this Gold Rush Lantana, *L. Callowiana*, cannot be grown down here.

PERIWINKLE or Myrtle, *Vinca major*, the larger, and *Vinca minor*, the hardier, are both members of the Dogbane Family. The *minor* is known as the Running Myrtle. Both are shiny and evergreen, with lilac flowers that bloom in spring and summer; both spread rapidly in semi- or deep shade and like a fairly loamy soil, and both not only make superb covers for terraces and flat expanses of land, but are charming in lawn vases, urns and hanging baskets. *Vinca minor* even does well in the upper South where the summer season is not too long. Try the *minor*'s variety *alba* for contrast and the *major*'s *variegata* and *elegantissima* for leaves splotched and margined with yellowish-white.

The FIVELEAF AKEBIA, *Akebia quinata* known as a vine, grows laterally and serves well as a ground cover. It grows so fast in the mid and lower South that it has to be kept within bounds. Evergreen in the lower and deciduous in the upper regions. Pest free.

WINTERCREEPER, *Euonymous fortunei colorata* spreads rapidly and makes an excellent ground cover when kept within bounds. The leaves turn purplish-red in winter.

The VIRGINIA CREEPER or American Ivy, is *Parthenocissus quinquefolia*, a semi-evergreen climber that can be a pest if left to ramble over shrubs, but it can be put to use as a ground cover if carefully tended.

AARON'S BEARD or ST. JOHNSWORT was a favorite in old-fashioned gardens and should be used more near our patios today. Botanically it is *Hypericum calycinum*, a low grower, spread by suckers, that likes sun or semi-shade. The foliage is evergreen and the flowers are a golden yellow. It can be used all over the South.

Any HONEYSUCKLE makes as good a ground cover as a vine. *Lonicera japonica halliana*, the Japanese Honeysuckle, is a semi-evergreen perennial with white flowers tinted in cream. *L. semper-virens*, the Trumpet Honeysuckle, has orangy-red flowers. *L. Henryi* does well in shade and has a yellowish-red blossom. This one is hardy and keeps its leaves in winter. For details on CAPE HONEY-SUCKLE see VINES.

Have you ever thought of using the CONFEDERATE JAS-MINE vine as a ground cover? *Trachelospermum jasminoides* is most attractive used in this manner. Although a slow grower, it is just as shiny and full of tiny white stars on the ground as it is on the wall or on supports. Because it is so lovely, you would not want it planted where there is traffic. Keep it for the garden beds. Pinning it down here and there with long hairpins will help it take root faster.

Another aristocrat for the upper southern gardens is the evergreen BITTERSWEET, *Euonymous Kewensis*, a diminutive ground cover for small areas. Will grow in sun or shade.

The ICE PLANT, *Mesembryanthemum crystallinum* also known as *Cryophytum crystallinum* makes an attractive ground cover as well as a good filler for a hanging basket. Regarded as an annual herb, this member of the Carpetweed Family has low fleshy leaves that are covered with crystalline drops that sparkle in the sun. The single flowers are small, shade from white to deep rose, and usually remain open as long as there is sunlight. Other varieties produce blossoms of different colors. Propagated by seeds.

THE HIGHER ONES

Since ground covers need not always be very low creeping plants, there are a number of other specimens that grow higher and are not only considered covers but ornamentals as well.

The new dwarf CHRYSANTHEMUM, Golden Carpet, is perfect for bedding and edging. Each plant creeps across a two foot area and when in flower, never exceeds ten inches in height. It looks like a rug of deep yellow in the autumn.

LIRIOPE, *Liriope muscari* sometimes called *Liriope majestic* is the name usually given to this lily-like plant from China and Japan. Actually its parentage is doubtful. It has narrow dark, evergreen, strap-shaped leaves about twelve inches high. The lavender flowers that grow in spikes in the late summer are followed by blue-black berries. This one is an excellent edging plant that can be increased by division and seed, and does well in all sections. It is also disease and pest free. *Liriope variegata* is attractive with its leaves striped in creamy-white. *Liriope spicata*, growing to four or five inches and equally hardy, is generally known as the Dwarf Liriope, but it is also called Dwarf Lilyturf, Ophiopogon and Mondo. Its green leaves are broader and the flower spikes less prominent than *Liriope muscari*. It does best in shady well-drained beds.

Liriope graminifolia grows about twelve inches high and is a good substitute for grass in areas of dense shade. It may be mowed like grass and spreads quickly by underground stolons. *L. grandiflora* is the tallest of the family. Its leaves sometimes reach three feet but the flowers that come up on the outside of the clump grow only to about six inches high. All are pest and disease free.

The real OPHIOPOGON, *Mondo japonicum* is another species in this mixed-up category and is often confused with *Liriope spicata*, to which it is closely allied. It is also a good ground cover and is used in the same manner as the four-inch *spicata*. I have always had *Ophiopogon Jaburan* in my garden. This one grows two to three feet high, has green and variegated foliage and produces tiny white flowers on drooping scapes that are one and one-half to two feet long. These scapes will eventually root wherever the tip bends over and touches the ground. I use it as an ornamental filler in the beds and in hanging baskets.

A plant that closely resembles the *Ophiopogon Jaburan* is the *Anthericum Liliago* or the ST. BERNARD'S LILY. This herb of the Lily Family grows from rhizomes that look like tubers. The leaves are narrow and drooping; the blooms are racemes of small white flowers and the one to two-foot stolons that this plant sends out make it perfect as a ground cover because the tips root as they spread. The *Anthericum* is also ideal in lawn urns or window boxes, with the stolons hanging gracefully over the sides.

ASPIDISTRA, of the Lily Family *Aspidistra elatior* or *A. lurida* is almost taken for granted in New Orleans. Actually, if the old foliage is kept trimmed it serves its purpose as a ground cover or edging plant. The wide leaves are rather coarse, dark green, about fifteen inches high and will remain evergreen almost all over the South. If they happen to be frozen back in severe weather they lose no time coming up again. I like to vary the line by intermingling the *Aspidistra lurida variegata*, which has a leaf half green and half creamy-white. Both kinds spread by rhizomes.

HOLLY FERN, *Crytomium falcatum* has most attractive evergreen fronds and does beautifully in semi-shade and moist soil all over the southern area. Rarely exceeding fifteen inches, the foliage springs from the center of the plant and arches back to the ground, the lovely green color of the toothed leaves making a good contrast against a darker green hedge.

Another hardy and fast-growing plant is the BOSTON FERN, *Nephrolepis exaltata bostoniensis*. Although it will thrive anywhere in this region it does best in the shade. Spreading by under-surface root runners, this fern has to be kept within bounds or it becomes a nuisance. Keep clipped free of old fronds, otherwise it gives a scratchy appearance.

B R A C K E N, common name for *Pteridium* and commonly known as *Pteris*, is a beautiful addition to the shaded garden or patio. An herbaceous fern, the E N G L I S H B R A C K E N of the Polypody Family is graceful from the time the new leaf begins to unfurl until the feathery triangular frond droops its head. It grows from two to three feet high and dies back in winter if not in protected areas.

Juniper horizontalis is a creeping plant that makes an excellent ground cover. This class includes *Juniperus chinensis sargenti*, a pale green and *J. squamata*, a blue-green. While they will grow in warm climates, they are not too happy in the lower South. They need sun and time to spread; they will eventually cover a bare spot. Like all junipers, they are subject to red spider.

C O O N T I E or *Zamia integrifolia* although a native of the Florida swamps also serves as an excellent ground cover in the upper cooler regions. Growing to almost two feet, its heavy fern-like foliage gives a rather exotic appearance. It is sometimes attacked by red spider.

F U N K I A or *Hosta*, sometimes called the Plantain Lily, certainly deserves a place in this chapter. What would I do without it in my lily bed? It acts as a sunshade for the feet of the lilies, keeps them cool and looks pretty doing it. Funkia is a hardy herbaceous perennial of the Lily Family with either green or variegated leaves and slender spikes of small flowers in summer. The all-green variety, *Hosta caerulea lanceolata* has rather broad oval-shaped four to five-inch leaves and blue flowers in late summer. The *H. variegata's* leaves are lance-shaped and rippled, from six to eight inches long, creamy-white with light green margins. Its flowers are lilac-blue. The clumps enlarge and become more beautiful each year. Snow and freeze are beneficial to this plant, making it look lovelier and fresher than ever. I think that the flowers are really incidental. The leaves are the most striking part of the plant. Don't be alarmed if the Funkia dies down. It will be up again the following spring.

Experiment a little with your garden dwellers. There is a lot of joy in finding a new use for a plant. I have had wonderful success in using, of all things, the MERMAID ROSE CLIMBER as a ground cover. This climber is a rampant grower that sends its long lateral branches out in record time. Because of its thorns I do not recommend its use where bare feet must travel, but for show purposes in shady areas there is nothing as attractive or as quick-growing as the Mermaid.

✄ 4 ✄

Vines

Vines, whether clinging by tendrils or rootlets or trained by twining on supports, soften the harsh lines of any building or fence.
They generally enhance the landscape, be they flowering or non-
flowering. Nearly all of the vines listed in the following pages are
familiar to most of you, but for the gardener who likes to experiment I have included some that could be grown here with patience
and care.

ALLAMANDA, *Allamanda cathartica* is a vigorous tropical
climber. The variety A. *Hendersonii* with large trumpets of yellow-
gold, is the most popular in this area. Although it is not particular
as to soil this vine does need good drainage. Feed with well balanced commercial fertilizer during the growing season and then
keep the roots fairly dry until February when the vine may be
pruned and watered. The Allamanda may be propagated by cuttings of old or new wood taken in the spring. Should you wish to try
the lavender-flowered variety, A. *violacea*, be sure that it has been
grafted on A. *cathartica* variety *Hendersonii* stock, otherwise it
will not thrive.

BALSAM APPLE, *Momordica balsamina* is an herbaceous

annual climber that is interesting from the summer time when the yellowish-white flowers appear until fall when the spined fruit turns from green to yellow and then splits open to show the fiery-red seeds. Rampant grower in full sun.

BIGNONIA, like quite a few other plants, has been the subject of controversy as to its botanical name but the fast-growing, evergreen, yellow-flowered variety is popularly known as *B. capreolata*, the Trumpet-Flower or the Cross-Vine. It gets its last mentioned name because of the odd shaped cross markings that are visible when the stem is clipped. A fast grower, it has small leaves and clings to walls, trees and fences by means of tendrils. It blooms in spring and early summer and does well in either sun or shade through upper, middle and lower South. It is insect and disease free. Give it well-drained loamy soil and prune after flowering. Cuttings can be made from half-ripened wood.

I have had the Lavender Trumpet vine for years and have always called it *Bignonia violacea*, yet it is said to be in reality *Clytostoma callistegioides*, a member of the Bignonia Family. The leaves are evergreen and always shiny and the spring flowers are lovely lavender trumpets. This vine likes sun or dappled shade, is not particular as to soil, and does very well in the lower South. Mine has mingled with a Mermaid Rose Climber and the combination of the pale yellow roses and lavender trumpets is delightful. Never allow this vine to become so thick that air cannot circulate freely in the branches. I have found it disease free and I had always thought it pest free until I found it had visitors on the underside of the leaves, in the form of the Saddle Back Caterpillar, *Sibine stimulea*. This weirdly beautiful inch-long creature is dark tan in color and wears a saddle blanket of chartreuse trimmed with yellow fringe. The head, decorated with one white spot, closely resembles the tail which is marked by three white spots. Both head and tail are held high. Contact with the bristles that extend along the sides of this pest causes poisonous and painful injury. The Saddle Back has no feet but moves on a suction surface, so you can see how it presents double trouble. The bristles are poisonous to touch and if this beauty should fall on you it sticks to the surface of your skin by its suction cups. Arsenical sprays will rid the plant of the Saddle Back but if you should come in direct contact with it, by all means consult your physician.

BITTERSWEET or FALSE BITTERSWEET is *Celastrus scandens*. Although it has generally been accepted that this vine will not grow in the South, I see no reason why we shouldn't try, especially since it has been grown in climates similar to ours and particularly since its lovely orange berries that are borne in the fall are so much in demand for floral arrangements. The plant is woody and hardy, with semi-evergreen foliage and inconspicuous flowers; it will climb as high as fifteen feet. Be sure that you get a plant with both male and female flowers on it to insure seeding.

BOUGAINVILLEA is actually a climbing shrub, native to South America. At one time it was believed that this plant could only be grown in open ground in Texas but it has done beautifully in the lower South for some years, given full sun and a southern exposure. The leaves are soft green, oval and small; the flowers themselves are inconspicuous. The showy parts are actually the large bracts that surround the flowers. *B. glabra* will reach ten feet and is free-flowering, producing rose-red bracts; *B. Cypheri* shows deep rose blossoms and *B. spectabilis*, lavender bracts. I have seen the yellow and orange varieties, *B. hybrida*, but they are as tender as they are spectacular. They are strictly potted greenhouse subjects. Because my own Bougainvillea has been planted in a southern sheltered corner it has withstood all freezes, but I have seen those plants damaged by low temperatures. Snow and freezes cause the tops of Bougainvilleas to blacken. In these cases, the plant is topped and by the following summer it grows back considerably, the leaves as healthy and green as ever. I love to see the lavender Bougainvillea bloom next to the yellow Lady Banksia rose climber. They make a lovely sight. Keep Bougainvillea root-crowded for best bloom.

This vine may be propagated from cuttings made from the young growth in the spring. Place the cuttings in a cold frame in a mixture of sand, peat and good loam and keep at an even warm temperature until rooted.

CANARY-BIRD VINE, *Tropaeolum peregrinum* is so named because of its spur-bearing yellow flowers. They actually look like the birds in flight. Quick-growing, it will rapidly cover bare spots and is not particular as to soil. An annual, this vine will reach twelve to fifteen feet.

CAPE HONEYSUCKLE, *Tecomaria capensis,* although considered an evergreen shrub, climbs so well when properly supported by trellis or arbor that I am including it in this chapter. The orange trumpet flowers appear in clusters against dense green serrated leaves. Blooming is almost continuous through summer and fall. The flowers are followed by rather large seed pods. This member of the Bignonia Family is a native of South Africa and will do especially well along the Gulf Coast and into Florida if given fairly good soil and a southern exposure. Prune in early spring.

CAROLINA   JESSAMINE, *Gelsemium sempervirens,* the state flower of South Carolina, likes wooded areas and swampy river banks. The deep yellow spring flowers have a delicious scent and the evergreen foliage is small and fine. Insect and disease free.

Nothing is as lovely as the CLEMATIS, a fast growing perennial vine. *Clematis virginiana* or the Virgin's Bower, likes shade and produces masses of white flowers in midsummer. *Clematis paniculata,* which blooms in late summer and fall, produces clusters of white star-like fragrant flowers and seems to be the only variety that does fairly well in the lower South. Would that we could see more of the Clematis here! It does demand plenty of sun and likes to be pampered just a little bit. Give it a good support and by all means place low-growing plants around the base of this vine so that the roots will be shaded and cool. Mulch well too.

All Clematis vines like loamy well-drained soil and should be tied or pinned in place while young. They may be planted in spring or autumn and should be fed at least once in the growing period with a balanced fertilizer. The foliage of all is finely textured. Propogation is by seed, cuttings and layering. Prune in early spring when your vine blooms from young bottom shoots. Trim those that flower from old wood in late winter when they are dormant.

Here are some that are presently on the market: Montana Rubens, a hardy blush pink, producing its blossoms in late spring; Mrs. Robert Brydon, a late summer bloomer with pale blue flowers, and *Coccinea texensis*, a coral-red that flowers all summer. These are in the small flowered group. In the larger flowering category, Crimson Star, with its garnet blooms; the rosy-lilac Madame Baron Veillard; the double white Duchess of Edinburgh and the blue-lavender Mrs. Cholmondely are all outstanding.

The CLERODENDRON FAMILY includes small trees and shrubs but two twining members are *Clerodendron Thomsonae*, an evergreen with small red flowers surrounded by white calyxes and *Clerodendron speciosum*, with dull red blossoms circled by magenta calyxes. The leaves are large, dark green and heavily veined, usually opposite. The white *Thomsonae* is very often referred to as Bleeding Heart. The flower clusters last for weeks and the large dark green leaves are most attractive. This vine likes a well-drained spot and contrary to the fact that it likes to be sheltered from the north wind, I must tell you that I have had a white and a magenta clerodendron on the north side of our house for the past eight or nine years. Both vines are in a well-drained, raised bed and both came back up after recent big freezes. This past fall I separated a few of the roots of each of these vines, which incidentally bloomed profusely through the years, and planted one of each on the opposite side of the garden in a south-east exposure. All four vines are still doing nicely, thank you! Blooming too!

CLIMBING FIG, *Ficus pumila* is really a creeper that forms a thick mat over brick or wood surfaces. The leaves are evergreen and rather small and rounded. This one must be kept within bounds. The outstretching laterals with the small "figs" must be removed regularly in order to keep a neat appearance. It does well in either full sun or shade, is not bothered with insects or disease and will thrive in upper South if protected. It does best in lower South.

CLIMBING HYDRANGEA, *Hydrangea petiolaris* is slow to start but once it does, will cling by its tiny aerial rootlets to stone or wood. It likes a shady northern exposure and when in bloom in the spring, looks like a shower of medium-sized white flowering clusters. The deciduous leaves resemble those of the shrub Hydrangea but are smaller.

CLITORIA belongs to the Pea Family and *Clitoria ternatea*, often called the Butterfly Vine, is a tender one that will grow in the lower South. This perennial twiner has deep blue flowers accented at the throat with yellow. The variety *mariana*, with pale blue blossoms, is hardier and better for the upper South. Both are pest free and demand no special care.

COCCULUS is familiar to us as a drooping shrub, *Cocculus laurifolius*, but the vine is *C. trilobus*, one that does well in the upper and lower South. The evergreen foliage is shiny and three-lobed and the tiny creamy flowers are followed by small black berries in clusters. *C. Carolinus* has bright red berries. This vine is a graceful one to use over doorways or over an arbor separating patio from lawn. Give it good loamy soil and plenty of moisture. It always looks fresh and green.

CONFEDERATE JASMINE, *Trachelospermum jasminoides* is often called Star Jasmine and is an evergreen vine that does very well all over the South, particularly in the lower sections. A slow grower, it never seems to become heavy or thick. The snow-white flowers that look like tiny stars against the dark green glossy leaves are delightfully fragrant. It needs moist loamy soil and requires spraying whenever there is evidence of white fly or scale. Use an oil emulsion. This jasmine can be trained to a pointed or pillar-shaped support.

CONFUSUS VINE, *Senecio confusus* often called the Mexican Flame Vine, is one to plant only if you are prepared to keep it within bounds. A perennial, it will always reappear in spring if it dies down during a cold winter. Its yellowish-orange flowers, very similar to daisies, appear in terminal clusters in the first weeks of warm weather. *Senecio* is propagated by cuttings rooted in water or sand and by layering of its own accord.

The CYPRESS VINE is an old-fashioned favorite now known as *quamoclit pinnata*. An annual, its feathery foliage is even more delicate than that of the cypress tree. It is quick-growing, producing small orange-red trumpet-shaped flowers during the warm months.

Decumaria, very much like its cousin the Climbing Hydrangea clings by aerial roots to supports and produces clusters of white summer flowers against the nearly evergreen binate leaves. *D. barbara* is the hardiest of the species, will grow to twenty-five feet or more and thrives in swampy places from Louisiana and Florida up to Virginia.

Dioscerea is a twining vine that not only grows from tubers but bears the tubers as well, hence often known as the POTATO VINE. I have seen two varieties here. *Dioscerea alata* has heart-shaped leaves that look like those of the Anthurium in shape, heavily veined, with a "drip tip." This one has tubers on the axil and on the stem. *Dioscerea bulbifera* has a more rounded leaf and the "potatoes" are borne in the leaf axil. Both vines are grown principally for their foliage effect; both die down in winter.

Whenever I have blossoms on my DUTCHMAN'S PIPE VINE, *Aristolochia durior* I can always count on someone stopping to inquire the name of "those lovely little flowers that look like pipes." Besides making an excellent screen with its pretty round green leaves, this vine produces just such little pipes. The bloom is pale yellowish-green and tubular, veined in dark red-brown, curving down from the stem and up again to flare at the mouth. It will grow anywhere. Freezes will make it die back but you will find it again in the spring.

Fatshedera lizei is a fairly recent introduction of the result of the cross between the Japanese shrub Fatsia and the English Ivy,

Hedera helix. This is a most attractive evergreen with climbing tendencies for shady areas of the South. It lends itself beautifully to espaliering. Plant it in any fairly loamy soil in a spot where it will be protected from the wind.

FIRECRACKER VINE, sometimes called the CIGARETTE VINE is *Manettia glabra,* a tender thing that, though cut down by freezes is lovely to see. Not a rampant grower, it has tiny leaves and many tubular, bright red flowers about one and one-half inches long that look like little cigarettes.

FIVELEAF AKEBIA, *Akebia quinata* has as its name implies, delicate five-part leaves that are evergreen in the deep South in mild winters, and deciduous in upper regions. The fragrant spring blossoms are small and a dark purplish-brown. Both male and female flowers appear in the same cluster, the latter being larger and opening first. The extremely sticky pollen discourages the bees, so if you pollinate by hand you will have the pleasure of seeing the grayish-purple, oblong fruit, which is sweet and often eaten by the Japanese. There is a THREELEAF AKEBIA, *A. trifoliata.* Both vines could be considered ground covers because they spread laterally as well as upward and will grow in sun or shade.

GOLDEN TRUMPET, *Doxantha unguis-cati* clings to walls or trellis by tendrils that look like three little claws, causing this vine to sometimes be called the CAT'S CLAW VINE. Its large yellow trumpet-shaped flowers that bloom in the spring are its chief attraction. The foliage is yellowish-green and not especially noticeable. It does best in the lower South where it is perhaps known by its earlier botanical name, *Bignonia tweediana.*

The HONEYSUCKLE vines, of the genus *Lonicera* are all lovely and almost all evergreen, with grayish-green binate leaves that wrap around the stem. *Lonicera japonica* is good not only as a vine to fifteen feet, but also as a ground cover, producing white flowers fringed in lilac. The variety *halliana* has fragrant blossoms that change from white to a creamy yellow, while *L. sempervirens,* the Trumpet Honeysuckle, has red spring flowers. The hybrid variety, *L. Heckrotti* shows golden, purple-red flowers all summer.

Hoya carnosa is the best known species of the *Hoya* group, members of the Milkweed Family. Commonly known as the W A X P L A N T , it has trailing stems of dull green leaves and loose clusters of fragrant white flowers tinged with pink at the center. Evergreen, it attaches itself to support by means of tiny roots along the stem and will continue to bloom as long as you do not cut the flowers or prune the plant. It needs plenty of sun and a loamy soil well fortified with peat moss and bits of charcoal. Reaches eight feet.

I V Y , of the genus *Hedera*, has long been a favorite evergreen vine and ground cover, climbing by aerial rootlets. *Hedera baltica* has very small leaves and is probably the hardiest of all Ivy plants. I trained this type to cover a pair of three-foot cone-shaped supports that I had mounted on two large urns, and the results were charming. The Algerian Ivy, *Hedera canariensis* has larger leaves, grows faster than the English Ivy and does well throughout the South. The English Ivy, *Hedera helix* is also very attractive and probably has the edge over the Algerian Ivy by being a little more hardy. The varieties *H. variegata* and *H. striata* show delightful creamy markings, hence the name "variegated Ivy." Fall is the best season in which to start cuttings in the open ground. Keep well watered until established.

J A S M I N E , *Jasminum* includes both erect and climbing shrubs of the Olive Family and there are several varieties that may be treated as vines. *Jasminum multiflorum* or *J. pubescens* has simple hairy leaves and white flowers. It will stand frost. *Jasminum officinale*, better known as Jessamine, needs support. It has compound glabrous leaves and fragrant white flowers that bloom in clusters in the summer. It does well all over the South provided it is given some shade. *Jasminum primulinum*, called Primrose Jasmine, is an evergreen free-flowering shrub that can be trained as a vine. You will enjoy its fine foliage and big yellow spring flowers. It will stand frost. *Jasminum humile* reaches fifteen feet or more if given support and is lovely in summer and fall when its bright yellow flowers show in clusters against the thick leaves.

There is another Jasmine, called JASMINE NIGHTSHADE or the POTATO VINE, which is *Solanum jasminoides* a twining vine of the Nightshade Family. The foliage is small and evergreen and the tiny blue-white flowers that bloom in clusters in the late summer last a long time. This one does well in the lower South in sun or partial shade. *S. Wendlandii*, to fifty feet, is magnificent when its violet-blue flowers show in summer and fall. Nearly all Solanum will tolerate hot walls and steps.

KADSURA, *Kadsura japonica* a small compact vine, seems to have been forgotten and needs introduction again. The evergreen leaves are dark, oval and thick. The small summer-flowering yellow blossoms give way to red berries in autumn. It has proven itself along the lower and middle sections of the South.

I mention LEADWORT or *Plumbago capensis* in this chapter on vines because, although a shrub it will climb if trained on trellis or fence. See Plumbago in chapter on FLOWERING SHRUBS for details.

MONSTERA is a tropical climber belonging to the Arum Family. The one we know best is *Monstera deliciosa* with its very large perforated leaves and aerial roots. It attaches itself very strongly to walls and tree trunks. Sometimes called the "Swiss Cheese Plant," it thrives in semi-shade and does produce a fruit which the squirrels relish. A very dear friend who had a magnificent Monstera, habitually placed a cage made of hardware cloth over the cone-like fruit to preserve it until ripe enough to serve at table. The fruit has the flavor of pineapples and bananas.

New plants of the Monstera can easily be made by cutting the stem in sections and rooting the pieces in sharp sand or in a mixture of the sand and leaf mold. This vine does not stand freezes well. The leaves will burn and drop, but don't discard your plant too quickly, as it usually comes back in the spring.

The MOONFLOWER VINE, *Calonyction aculeatum* and a

member of the Morning Glory Family, is a *must* for our patios on summer evenings. This perennial twiner will grow to great heights and bears big heart-shaped leaves and fragrant white flowers that are trumpet-shaped. The beauty of this vine is that the blossoms open at night and close before noon the following day. So if you plan evenings in your patio and you want a conversation piece, plant the Moonflower. It demands little attention. I understand that there is a pink variety.

The MORNING GLORY, of the genus *Ipomaea* has more or less been considered a nuisance in the garden because of its rampant growth. It will grow anywhere under any condition. The flowers usually open early in the morning and close before the hottest part of the day, hence the name. True, for a quick screen, it is invaluable. *I. purpurea*, the purple variety, and *I. tricolor* the blue-flowered one, are the most popular. Heavenly Blue is an early flowering variety. Pearly Gates is all white. Darling is white-throated shading outwards to deep red.

The MUSCADINE GRAPE, V*itis rotundifolia* and the variety Scuppernong make nice ornamentation on walls and trellis. Even though they are deciduous these are ones to try if you are looking for something different. Besides, you will also enjoy the grapes! These vines will thrive in any fairly loamy, well-drained soil. Plant in January and February and fertilize in the spring with a feed high in potash and superphosphate to harden the trunk. Keep the nitrogen content low because nitrogen will produce too lush foliage and too little fruit. Always try to plant a young grape

make your supports of long-lasting materials

prune at these points in late winter

The Established Grape

vine. Those over two years of age are slow to renew growth after moving. Prune the side shoots to one joint allowing the strongest and center shoot to remain and serve as the trunk. This should be staked loosely until the vine is big enough to train on trellis or other supports. In the late winter of the following year prune back to three joints in order to allow the stems to become stronger. After that prune only weak shoots and overlong canes. Prune in late winter while the vine is dormant. All leaves and grapes are produced on shoots that begin to grow in the early spring.

A word here about supports or trellis. I discovered long ago when my Mermaid Rose Climber grew thick and heavy, that the wooden trellis does not last long in our humid climate. Since performing the mean task of having to replace worn timber I have used galvanized pipe to fashion a trellis. Anchor the main supports in concrete well below soil level and fasten to the cross pipes with elbows. The same idea may be applied to hold up any climber, even the Grape vine. The gray pipe is not unattractive nor too conspicuous and certainly affords the sturdiness that a good climber needs.

The big disease to worry about in the Grape vine is Black Rot, which spots leaves and grapes. Control this fungus by spraying with Bordeaux mixture in the early spring. This spray will also assist in routing mildew.

The PASSION FLOWER, *Passiflora* comprises a large group of trees, herbs and shrubs, but most of those in cultivation are equipped with tendrils for climbing. The most widely known Passion Flower is *Passiflora caerulea*, a rampant grower with delicate-looking leaves divided into five segments, two of the smallest of which are often again divided. The slightly fragrant flowers are a pale chartreuse in color, with the rays of the corona shading from blue to white to purple, and the styles, lavender. They usually measure two to three inches across. *Passiflora incarnata* is the Maypop with edible fruit, and its leaves are three-lobed. Both varieties do well from the deep South (where they are almost evergreen) to Virginia, where they freeze back in winter but do not die.

The pure white Passion Flower, *P. alba* is extremely beautiful and *Passiflora coccinea*, the red Bolivian Passion Flower, has recently been reintroduced to trade. There are many other varieties of different colors, ranging from white to deep crimson. My Passion Flower has a habit of harboring an orange and black caterpillar during the summer. This most uninviting specimen of pest is hard to discourage. Constant spraying with arsenate of lead is necessary.

This vine may be propagated by cuttings if they are made between January and March, and from seed. The mature plant thrives in a light loamy soil and does well in either sun or shade. Cut it back and mulch it well in winter. If you feel that you must, feed with liquid fertilizer in early spring. By all means thin this vine when necessary to keep its rampant growth within bounds.

Because the blossoms are so very beautiful, I think a note about the way in which they were named would be in order. Many years ago Italian and Spanish travelers gave the flower its name because they felt that it clearly depicted the Crucifixion, the ten sections of the floral case being the ten apostles present at the death of our Lord, the fringy corolla resembling the Crown of Thorns. The five stamens were said to be the five wounds; the three styles, the nails. The coiling tendrils reminded them of the ropes or scourges; the leaves, the hands of those responsible for Calvary. In 1610 Jacomo Bosio, author and artist, depicted the Passion Flower as representing the mysteries of the Passion and told of the Spaniards in Peru calling it the Flower of the Five Wounds.

I mention the P Y R A C A N T H A here because although considered a shrub the varieties *koidzumi* and *formosana* are excellent to be trained as a vine if properly supported. Cultural directions and care are the same as for the shrub Pyracantha.

R A N G O O N   C R E E P E R is the common name for *Quisqualis indica*, long considered a vine but actually a climbing shrub that is very hardy in the South. Besides being remarkably free of pests and diseases, the beauty of this specimen lies in the spikes of fragrant flowers that appear during the summer, hanging gracefully from the branches and shading from palest green to white as they open, to blush pink and deep rose as they mature. The name Quisqualis when translated means "what?", "where?" and is said to have been given the plant in earlier years because of its surprising growth habits. It reaches three to four feet as an upright shrub, then sends out long lateral branches that climb as a vine. Plant in loamy well-drained soil and mulch with peat. Prune immediately after flowering and propagate it by soft-wood cuttings.

ROSA DE MONTANA is also known as the CORAL VINE *Antigonon leptopus*, our familiar ROSA MONTANA that is such a joy to allergy-free gardeners and such a nuisance to hay-fever sufferers. It grows rampantly anywhere, blooms in summer and fall, stands dry conditions well and clings like mad to anything it touches by means of curling tendrils. Even in the lower South it dies down in winter, but it comes right back up again in the spring. It will reach thirty feet if unattended, showing masses of bright rosy-pink blossoms in long racemes.

SMILAX is a vine that has almost disappeared from lack of use. Perhaps because its summer and fall berries are insignificant and it has nothing but the evergreen leaves to offer, gardeners forget about its value in the Christmas season. Although there are many varieties *Smilax lanceolata* is the best for ornamental use, growing in almost any soil and spreading by underground tubers.

THUNBERGIA is a perennial climber which, like the Allamanda, dies back in extremely cold winters. The hardiest and best known of all the varieties is *Thunbergia grandiflora*, with dark green heart-shaped leaves and gloxinia-like blue tubular flowers that open in late summer and fall. *Thunbergia alata*, with its little yellow-orange blossoms with dark centers, is called the Black-Eyed Susan Vine. Of the white varieties *T. fragrans* is the one most popular with southern gardeners. All of these do well in ordinary soil and in full sun or partial shade. Prune after flowering. Cuttings may be made successfully from the new growth that appears in early spring.

The VIRGINIA CREEPER, *Parthenocissus quinquefolia* is a quick-growing vine that shows beautiful red foliage in the autumn before its leaves fall. Clinging fast to walls or trellis by means of tendrils that seem to have been touched with glue it covers an area in no time producing small greenish flowers and dark berries. There is another Creeper, the SILVERVEIN CREEPER *Parthenocissus Henryana* that shows its creamy-purplish leaves best in the shade. Both vines do well under any conditions in any soil all over the South although Silvervein is a bit more tender than the Virginia. *Parthenocissus tricuspidata* is commonly known as Boston or Japanese Ivy and is a favorite because of its hardiness to the dust and grime of cities. It presents a dense cover to any wall, ascends to great heights and its foliage turns orangy-red in fall.

WISTERIA is a beautiful sight to behold in the spring when the long clusters of lavender pea-shaped flowers hang gracefully from the pale, green-leaved branches. The variety we know best in the deep South is the Chinese Wisteria, *Wisteria sinensis* with bluish-lavender flower clusters from six to twelve inches long, opening all at once. Actually this one is not as hardy as *Wisteria floribunda*, the pale-green-leaved, lavender-flowered Japanese Wisteria, a woody deciduous twiner that does best in rich loamy soil and a good amount of sunshine. Its flower clusters are much longer and open from base to tip. The vine may be allowed to run rampant, may be trained to trellis or, if heavily pruned in may be kept to small tree size, in which case it is a lovely ornamental. The variety *alba* has white flowers. *Rosea* produces pinkish-lavender blooms. *W. frutescens* is the American species and thrives from Texas to Virginia, showing lilac blooms.

I have heard many complaints about Wisterias not blooming. The answer to this could be multiple. You may have overfed your vine in your eagerness to get it to show flowers. Wisterias that have good green foliage should not be fed often. Avoid any fertilizer containing nitrogen, because nitrogen makes for more foliage and less bloom in this case. Sometimes root pruning helps keep the

prune at these points
between July 15th and
August 15th

head in center trunk to
encourage growth as a small
tree

cut straight down with sharp
shovel to prune roots
18″ x 18″

Wisteria

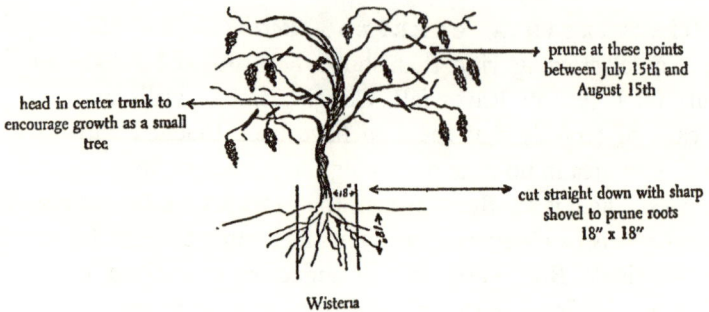

plant well-balanced and this is accomplished by pushing a sharp shovel straight down into the ground in a circle around the base of the plant about eighteen inches from the trunk. You will have to make the cut almost as deep because Wisteries have few roots and what they have go down very deep. You might mix some super-phosphate with the soil as you refill the cut to hasten blooming. Have you planted your Wisteria in the full sun that it needs? If it gets too much shade it certainly will not bloom. Then, if the winters have been too severe, you cannot expect many flowers. Some Wisterias are too young to bloom, so if you have a small plant don't be impatient.

Sex has nothing whatever to do with your vine flowering or not flowering. Did you know that every Wisteria bloom has both sexes present within that bloom? Seedlings very often fail to flower. It is always safer to buy a good specimen from your nurseryman.

The evergreen WISTERIA, *Wisteria megasperma* that comes from Australia, will stand low temperatures, has darker green and thicker leaves than the oriental species. The flowers bloom late in the spring or during the summer and their vivid wine-purple petals are pea-shaped, borne in twelve to fifteen inch-long panicles that are more erect than the other Wisterias. When the vine is allowed to grow rampant the blossoms are sometimes hard to find through the thick foliage. In the New Orleans area *megasperma* usually blooms through the months of June and July, but farther inland

and in Texas the flowers appear from July through September. This Wisteria grows well in a loamy soil that is fortified with peat and occasionally fed with a liquid fertilizer containing twice as much phosphorus as nitrogen and potash. It stands drought very well. It may be trained as a vine, in which case you must be faithful in giving it good support; or it may be allowed to grow as a "moundy" shrub. I have never seen *Wisteria megasperma* troubled with disease but the Io Moth caterpillar, *Automeris io,* that poisonous creature that dresses its red and white striped body in black-tipped green spines, does sometimes find this vine a delightful haven in the late summer. Rout this pest with a malathion spray.

The oval-shaped seed pods of this "summer-blooming" Wisteria begin to form in August and by December are brown and hard and flat. They do not open easily and therefore are not too often used in propagation. Layering seems the most successful way to reproduce this plant.

Wisteria megasperma is very often called *Millettia megasperma,* named in honor of Dr. J. A. Millett, a well-known botanist of the early eighteenth century. *Millettia,* of the *Leguminosae* tribe, includes over one hundred species of climbing shrubs and trees that differ from the American and Japanese Wisteria in the hard, flat, difficult-to-open seed pods.

W O O D   R O S E , *Ipomoea tuberosa* is a member of the Morning Glory Family and shows yellow blossoms amid its very long twining stems. It does well in frost-free sections, but outside of the tropics it seldom carries the flowers long enough for them to dry and form the lovely tan and brown wood roses that we use in dried arrangements. This tendency to shed its blooms could be caused by high humidity and high temperatures or the plant might need a certain insect to carry pollen, as is the case of the Smyrna Fig.

✣ 5 ✣

Evergreen, Deciduous and Flowering Trees

Your choice of trees and shrubs for your garden will depend largely on what effect you want to achieve. Here in the South we tend towards informality. Our needs are for the most part functional and our grounds are planted with the definite purpose of living outdoors most of the year.

It is well to plan carefully in selecting your landscape materials. If your budget will allow, consult a landscape designer or nursery-man and have him draw plans and furnish materials. If, on the other hand, you find that you cannot afford such luxury get busy and have the fun of doing it yourself. There is a great deal of satisfaction in watching your handiwork take form and grow.

Your success in landscaping will depend on how much you know about plants and on how you repeat them to give good balance to the over-all picture. Decide which spots need screening, which corner needs color and which area would make a restful patio. Remember to choose an evergreen tree if you are interested in having shade the year around and if you want a windbreak. It has been said that a perfect shade tree is worth at least "$5.00 per square inch of cross section at breast height". I understand that this means of evaluation has been upheld in the courts. Shade trees are very important to us. They provide cool spots in summer and help break cold blasts in the winter months besides enhancing the property and making it more livable.

Some of the deciduous trees make striking patterns with their bare winter branches and admit sunlight on cold days. Tapering trees like the Ginkgo will accent the width of a house while larger spreading specimen, such as the Oak, will make the height more pronounced. Trees like the Weeping Willow, Golden Rain, Jacaranda and Mimosa may be used to good advantage as ornamentals on the lawn.

True evergreens are all plants bearing cones and needle-like leaves, like the pines, firs, spruces and yews; foliage flattened against the branches, such as the cedars, cypress and junipers; and larger glossy leaves, like the Oak and the Magnolia *grandiflora*. All evergreens drop their old leaves gradually but they are constantly growing new ones, particularly in spring, so that the branches are never bare. Evergreens are slow growing, usually more expensive than the deciduous ones and should be moved with a ball of earth around the roots.

Read up on the growing habits of the specimen you have in mind. Unless you are impatient to have a mature garden it is definitely more fun and certainly more inexpensive to start with young plants and watch them grow. Consider the tree of your choice.

Is it suited to your locality?

Will it thrive in the exposure you have planned for it?

Will the roots spread so much that they will sap nutrients away from surrounding plants?

Will it present a constant job of leaf-raking?

Will it eventually grow too big for its original purpose?

It is often suggested that your best buy in an established tree is one less than ten feet tall and not any larger than three and a half to four inches in diameter at ground level. Plant small trees about twenty to twenty-five feet apart and large ones from twenty-five to fifty feet apart.

The winter months have proven the best planting time for most deciduous trees, that is, while they are dormant. I would hesitate to set out a deciduous tree after February. Broadleaved evergreens are usually moved in February and March and palms are successfully transplanted in June, July and August. So make your plans in the fall and remember that a lot of your success will depend on your choice of tall or dwarf specimen. Draw out the proposed plan on a large sheet of paper and use small circles to represent the proposed trees, lettering or numbering them to a corresponding check list. Bring this list to a reputable nurseryman and see which ones are available, which ones are more expensive and whether there are newer or hardier introductions. Don't rush your plans, "sleep on them."

PLANTING

If the tree that you buy comes balled in burlap prepare a hole at least one and a half feet deeper than the ball or if it is bare-rooted, at least six inches deeper than the length of the longest root. Fill the bottom of the hole with brickbats or gravel to insure drainage and then cover this with a layer of good garden soil. Pack this down well before lowering the tree to its natural level and fill in the remaining hole with loam to which several handfuls of superphosphate have been added and mixed thoroughly. Tamp the soil again until the tree is firmly in place and build a saucer-like basin around the base of the tree to keep water from running off too quickly. Water well for several days. Mulch well to preserve moisture.

STAKING

After your tree has been properly planted consider the staking problem. In cases of the Mimosa and Bauhinia trees where the trunk is supple and sways with the wind use strong wooden, or better yet, iron stakes and either a piece of plastic clothesline or a piece of wire encased in old rubber hose to attach the tree to the stake. Allow leeway for movement. Never tie a tree tightly to the stake. Using a covered wire for tying means preventing eventual decay that will almost always begin by constant rubbing of sharp material against the bark.

PRUNING

A tree should be pruned just as faithfully as you prune your shrubs. Do it after flowering or during the dormant period unless otherwise instructed. Top the tallest branches if the tree is of spreading growth habits and thin out the branches that rub together. If your tree is pyramidal in shape, light trimming of the outer straggly limbs should be all that is necessary. Sometimes just the thinning of crossed twigs and small branches to keep sun and air on all parts of the tree will suffice. Pruning, after the absolutely necessary amount is done, becomes a matter of personal choice. You will be the one to determine the height and shape of a tree or shrub and the manner in which it is to be utilized.

PESTS AND DISEASES

The minor but annoying enemies of trees and shrubs can usually be handled by the home gardener. For whitefly and scale, try an oil emulsion spray in mild weather or malathion in cold of winter and

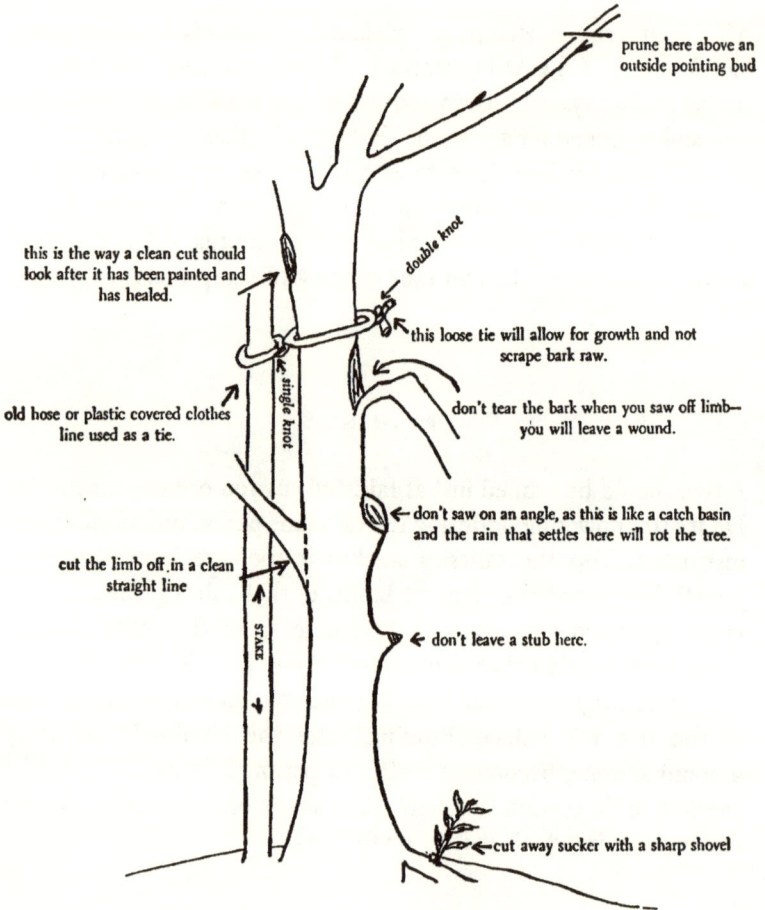

prune here above an
outside pointing bud

this is the way a clean cut should
look after it has been painted and
has healed.

double knot

this loose tie will allow for growth and not
scrape bark raw.

old hose or plastic covered clothes
line used as a tie.

single knot

don't tear the bark when you saw off limb—
you will leave a wound.

don't saw on an angle, as this is like a catch basin
and the rain that settles here will rot the tree.

cut the limb off in a clean
straight line

STAKE

don't leave a stub here.

cut away sucker with a sharp shovel

PRUNING AND STAKING TREES

heat of summer. Mildew is usually controlled with a dusting of sulphur or a spray of one of the wettable fungicides on the market. Aphids can be routed with a nicotine solution. Arsenate of lead is a cure for chewing insects. Consult your nurseryman about the trade names under which most of the insecticides and fungicides are sold, and follow instructions on the label. For further details on insecticides and fungicides, see pages 123–125.

Florida Red Scale does a lot of damage to small trees and shrubs, coating the underleaf until it causes gradual defoliation. Use a 2% oil emulsion spray in March and again in April, but be sure to allow a full thirty days interval between sprayings. Use six tablespoons of oil emulsion to one gallon of water. In warmer days, if you must repeat the sprays, use three tablespoons of oil emulsion to one gallon of water and add one tablespoon of malathion to this. The summer strength emulsion is not a cure, but it will arrest the scale.

In the case of bacterial blight on trees and shrubs the treatment calls for the use of such deadly poisons that it is safer and cheaper to call in your nurseryman to render first aid to the ailing plant. Bacterial blight closely resembles Die-Back on Camellias. The leaves suddenly take on a scorched appearance and the whole plant looks sick.

FEEDING

Avoid feeding a newly planted tree until it has become fully established. Wait until the following spring, when the leaf buds begin to swell, to fertilize. We all know that organic fertilizers are better than commercial preparations, but since most of our shade trees, and deciduous ones too, for that matter, are planted on established lawns and since using organic feed would mean digging a trench at spaced intervals, from the trunk to the outer spread of the branches, we almost always turn to commercial fertilizers which may be applied with a minimum disturbance to the lawn. Using a crowbar make holes in the ground about twelve inches deep, starting about fourteen inches from the trunk of the tree and extending outward, from two to three feet apart, to the drip-line of the outer branches. Fill the bottom of the holes with the well-balanced commercial fertilizer and the rest of the hole with soil. Water the ground thoroughly. There are many mixtures of commercial feed but I like the one containing 4% nitrogen, 6% phosphoric acid and 4% potash, known in the trade as 4–6–4. Use about a pound of fertilizer for each inch of the diameter of a tree, three feet above ground level.

Fertilizer just spread over the surface of the ground around the base of the tree will not satisfy the tree's appetite so I urge you to plug in the food. The latest methods of jet root-feeding and leaf-feeding have wonderful results but this entails the services of a tree man or nurseryman with the necessary power equipment.

Some trees will need additional fertilizing materials to build up the acidity of the soil in which they live. In the following lists of trees I indicate those needing just such special attention. Otherwise feed according to directions given above.

SOME DESIRABLE SHADE TREES

The OAK, of the genus *Quercus*. This is one of the stateliest and most beautiful trees to thrive anywhere in the South. It is a desirable evergreen although slow-growing to great heights, with varieties so numerous and distinctions so fine that I suggest only a few: our familiar LIVE OAK, *Quercus virginiana* which we see draped with Spanish moss has pretty new leaves of a light green that contrast nicely with the darker older foliage. The WATER OAK, *Q. nigra* and the JAPANESE OAK, *Q. acuta* make excellent screens. The HOLLY OAK, *Q. ilex* a European product of smaller statue should be grown here more than it is. It withstands salt sprays and a good amount of heat. A broad-leaved tree, the

Q. Prinus

Q. Phellos

Q. Alba

Q. Nigra

Q. Virgiana

Q. Rubra

OAK LEAVES

HOLLY OAK likes full sun and needs no special soil to grow successfully to sometimes thirty feet. The three-inch deep green leaves are shiny and spined, resembling those of the Holly. The roots grow deep and like dry conditions. Much has been written of the longevity of this tree. The word "holly" was spelled "holy" in days of yore and the HOLLY OAK is said to be the "holy" or "Holm" tree mentioned in the Bible. I have heard that there is one HOLLY OAK in the gardens of the Vatican that is older than the city of Rome.

The WHITE OAK, *Q. alba* with deeply lobed leaves presents brilliant fall foliage. The COW OAK, *Q. Prinus* with toothed leaves is not too ornamental. The leaves of the WILLOW OAK, *Q. phellos* are fine-textured and narrow and present a lovely gold color in autumn. The SOUTHERN RED OAK, or SPANISH OAK, *Q. falcata* or *Q. rubra*, does its best in the cool sections of the South. The OVERCUP OAK, *Q. lyrata* has foliage that turns yellow, orange and scarlet in the fall.

Did you know that the Tree-bark Aphids are responsible for the sticky substance that stains your automobile if it is parked beneath? These big Aphids reproduce at a fantastic rate and suck away on the underside of the leaves. If ants and bees are not busy enough to eat the honeydew secreted by the Aphids, when the leaves fall on the car they make a stain. The use of a nicotine spray while the trees are dormant and the Aphids are in the egg stage will usually prevent this infestation, but if they do appear later in the spring a second and third spraying at two weeks interval, is necessary. Actually all the trees in a neighborhood should be sprayed to prevent the trees that have been sprayed from becoming reinfested from untreated ones.

The GINKGO or MAIDENHAIR TREE, *Ginkgo biloba* is an exotic with small fan-shaped leaves that grows to fifty feet in height anywhere in the South. This tree is absolutely free of insects and disease and it is resistant to drought. I suggest that you buy a male tree which will not bear fruit because the ripened fruit

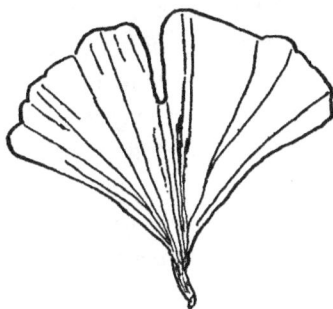

leaf of the Ginkgo Tree

of the female has an acrid odor. The G I N K G O does drop its leaves in winter but it makes a wonderful shade tree when grown. It has a peculiar way of branching, almost on a forty-five degree angle, giving it an oriental look. The leaves are fairly leathery to the touch. Some think that the leaf looks like a web foot; others see the resemblance to the Maidenhair Fern, hence the name M A I D E N - H A I R T R E E .

The M A G N O L I A , *Magnolia grandiflora* is one of the beauties of the South. It has large glossy leaves and great white fragrant blossoms; it grows to one hundred feet. It may be used as a street tree, lawn specimen, or it can be espaliered against a wall. Give it sun and lots of room to spread. Don't clip the lower branches if you can avoid doing so because the tree is so much prettier when its fullness comes close to ground level.

The S O U T H E R N S W E E T B A Y , *Magnolia virginiana* grows to sixty feet and needs an open moist location. It is evergreen in the South, deciduous farther North. Plant it in soil that is on the acid side and it will do equally well in sun or shade. The S W E E T - B A Y ' S oblong leaves are green on the upper and grayish-white on the under sides. White flowers are followed by red fruit. It does not take up as much space as *M. grandiflora*.

Of the C E D A R S , the S I L V E R or B L U E C E D A R , *Juniperus virginiana glauca* is a comparatively small tree, to twenty feet, with blue-green needles for foliage. A slow grower, it likes sun and a neutral soil. The CANAERT or RED CEDAR, *Juniperus virginiana Canaertii* has the same requirements. The DEODAR CEDAR, *Cedrus deodara* will slowly reach forty feet but its form and gray-green leaves are lovely. Give it full sun and a neutral soil.

A really beautiful tree for the upper South is the CANADIAN HEMLOCK, *Tsuga canadensis* which eventually reaches fifty feet. It usually does better in a sheltered southern exposure, in sun or partial shade and in neutral soil.

One of the specimens that I list in shrub materials also makes a satisfactory tree. *Photinia serrulata* or the CHINESE PHOTINIA will reach fifteen to twenty feet if trained to a single trunk. It will grow in any soil but I have found it will produce darker green foliage if the earth around it is slightly acid. The spring flowers are white and are followed by fruit that lasts well into the winter. It takes sun or semi-shade; the sun will bring out the bronzy-red color in the young leaves.

In the PINE family there is the SHORTLEAF PINE, *Pinus echinata* the SPRUCE PINE, *P. glabra* and the LOBLOLLY PINE, *P. tacda*. All thrive in the South where the soil is sandy and all slowly reach one hundred feet or more. The LOBLOLLY grows best in a neutral to slightly acid soil in sun or filtered shade. It is especially nice for background planting. The LONGLEAF PINE, *P. palustris* has larger leaves and cones than the SLASH PINE, *P. caribaea* although the cones have no stems. Both are hardy in the Southern Coastal Plain.

The ARAUCARIA is a graceful evergreen in this same family. The best known species are *A. excelsa* or the NORFOLK ISLAND PINE and *A. Bidwillii,* known as the BUNYA-BUNYA TREE. While these trees reach great heights in their native habitat, they are grown in this country in their juvenile state as potted plants or as ornamentals in large tubs. See chapters on Shrubs for the Landscape and Potted Plants.

PALMS, of the botanical family *Palmaceae* are familiar in our southern areas and give a tropical effect even without the use of other plant material. The P A L M E T T O, *Sabal palmetto* or the Cabbage Palm, is one of the few trees that withstands salt water and salt spray. It grows from twenty to forty feet in Florida and seems to be perfectly adjusted to any conditions in the rest of the South, as far up as North Carolina, although it does not reach as high. It is not bothered with pests or diseases. I was told many years ago that the soft-crown buds of this palm were considered a food, similar to the cabbage—hence the name.

For a smaller specimen try the S A W - P A L M E T T O, known as *Serenoa repens*. The S C R U B P A L M E T T O or *Sabal megacarpa* is a native of the coastal South. This one is used for certain difficult areas as barriers and as foliage contrast. Because it is a low grower with creeping, twisting stems that usually stay near ground level, it is sometimes included in the class of Ground Covers.

The majestic *Washingtonia robusta* grows to great heights (one hundred feet) in most southern locales but is slow in the process. The *Cocos Australis* and *Cocos plumosa* are beautiful and in comparison, more rapid in growth. The *Cocos Australis* has several other names (*Butia capitata* and Brazilian *Butiapalm*) but it is in the small category, eventually reaching fifteen feet, and has arching branches of a bluish-grayish-green tone. The trunk tends to thicken as it matures and is covered with the remnants of the leaf stalk. The orange fruit has an edible pulp. *Cocos plumosa* is known as the Q U E E N P A L M, and rightly so. Its smooth straight trunk of soft grayish-tan, sometimes showing rosy tones, rises to about forty feet. The long plume fronds are dark green and shiny and rise gracefully from the crown to arch and recurve. Its orange fruit is edible.

Several species of the D A T E P A L M, *Phoenix canariensis,* P. *sylvestris* and P. *dactylifera,* do especially well in the South. The first mentioned, commonly known as the C A N A R Y D A T E P A L M, reaches thirty to forty feet except in Florida, where it tops the scale at sixty feet. The drooping dark green branches are a nice contrast for its shower of bright orange fruit. The *Chamaerops*

excelsa, a low fan-leaved palm, is sometimes known as the W I N D -
M I L L   P A L M , *Trachycarpus Fortunei* so-called because the
blunt-bladed fans rise from a single slender trunk that is covered
with a thick black hairy fiber. Very slow growing, it eventually
reaches twenty-five feet in north and central Florida. Its fruit is a
shiny blue.

I like the graceful W A T E R F A L L   P A L M , Pindo Palm *Butia
spp.* really more shrub than tree, which gives the appearance of a
giant fountain on the landscape, with pendant fronds that rise from
the short trunk and arch downward. The Pindo needs plenty of
space and makes a fine ornamental for a corner of a long lawn.
Those in New Orleans reach twelve to fifteen feet but in Florida
their height is ultimately twenty-five feet.

Phoenix reclinata tends to be a leaning Date Palm and forms a
magnificent specimen when grown in moist rich soil in semi-shade.
If allowed to grow in clumps the trunks remain medium high;
otherwise, as solitary trees they eventually reach thirty-five to forty
feet. This one bears small red fruit.

A lovely related member of the Palm Family is *Rhapis flabelliformis,* also known as the R A T T A N   P A L M or Ground Rattan
and the L A R G E   L A D Y   P A L M . It sends up shoots from the
base of the plant. This one is a digitate-leaved palm, short (four or
five feet) and densely shrubby, a perfect specimen for the small
garden or patio. I have potted several small shoots with wonderful
results. I have even seen this palm used as a hedge, albeit slow-
growing.

The P I G M Y   D A T E   P A L M is *Phoenix Roebelenii,* a tree that
may be enjoyed as a potted plant in its miniature state or as a
twelve-foot tree. Its black fruit is half hidden by a thick crown of
dark green, feathery fronds.

The S A G O   P A L M , whence comes our traditional palms for
Palm Sunday, is really a member of the Pine Family and is termed
a "gymnosperm", meaning naked seed. You can see this seed in
the crown of the female of the species. The male tree bears the

fronds that are cut for church use. The Sago grows from six to eight feet but will bear even before reaching this height. You can propagate by merely planting some of the palms taken from the tree. It is long-lived.

Palms in general take little care and will thrive wherever they are not constantly frozen back. As a family they stand strong winds and salt sprays very well, even when transplanted. Set palms out in June, July and August, a little deeper than they grew before being moved. Dig the hole as deep as it is wide. Brickbats, bones and compost should be placed at the bottom, then a layer of a mixture of clay and manure. Fill in the rest of the hole with good top soil and well-rotted fertilizer. Nearly all palms need to be fed twice a year—in May when a good mulch will suffice and again in October, when the mulch is trenched in and topped with a generous application of a commercial food containing a high content of potash. The palm needs the potash to harden it against the cold. Water well, trim outer leaves and brace large specimen until established. Palm trees often develop shelf fungus on the trunk, indicating that the fungus has already invaded the inner tree. There is no cure that I know of.

Of the ELMS, the CHINESE ELM, *Ulmus parvifolia* and the AMERICAN ELM, *U. americana* from eighty to one hundred feet, are the best varieties for this area. If you wish a smaller tree for dry sections try the SIBERIAN ELM or *U. pumila*. The leaf of the Elm is small and rather pointed. Although these mentioned are almost entirely deciduous, there are some nurserymen who are experimenting with an evergreen variety for our section.

For wonderful fall coloring the SWEETGUM or REDGUM, *Liquidambar styraciflua* is fast growing and satisfying. The rich green summer leaves turn a beautiful reddish color in autumn and the round gum balls hang from the branches even after the foliage falls. Although the Gum will reach close to eighty feet in open swampy spaces, the ones I see planted along sidewalks are about twenty to twenty-five feet tall. The gum balls make attractive Christmas tree ornaments when painted and dipped in glitter.

Another tree that will lend grace to the landscape is the WEEPING WILLOW, *Salix babylonica*. The WHITE POPLAR, *Populus alba* has fine grayish foliage that is deciduous, leaving most attractive silvery-black bare branches. It grows rapidly to eighty feet all over our southern region.

TO HAVE OR HAVE NOT

I have saved the "Nuisance Group" of trees until last because although fast-growing, these become so much of an annoyance in one way or another that you finally pay dearly for having planted them in the first place.

The CAMPHOR, *Cinnamomum camphora* albeit evergreen and hardy through most of the South offers such a dining-room feast of camphor berries to the birds that you disregard the benefits of the shady leaves in your haste to get rid of it. Besides, nothing will grow long beneath it.

The SYCAMORE, *Platanus occidentalis* or American Planetree grows to sixty feet in the South but never stops shedding its leaves and bark. Your job of raking is never done. *Platanus orientalis* the Oriental Planetree, and its hybrid, the London Planetree, *Platanus acerifolia* also grow here but both have the same bad manners as the Sycamore.

Don't make the mistake of planting a HACKBERRY, of the genus *Celtis*! Cities of the South have large sidewalk plantings of the Sugar Hackberry *Celtis laevigata* but the nurserymen are replacing them rapidly because the roots simply take over the garden and the drainage system, the tiny Hackberry bugs cling to the house and screens, and the towering branches snap and crash when you least expect it. Although fast growing it is definitely more hazard than ornament.

The TUNG OIL TREE, *Aleurites Fordii* is beautiful in bloom but I do not recommend it for home gardens because the fruit and nuts are very poisonous.

You can take or leave the PECAN TREE, *Carya illinoensis* of the Hickory clan. Most of us have to take it because this tree was on the grounds when we bought our houses and it is no small financial problem to have it removed. It is certainly a shade tree and excellent in the orchard but aside from the pecan crop that the squirrels help eat, this tree must be sprayed against webworms and tent caterpillars and its roots sap a great deal of moisture from the ground below. It also litters the ground with falling blossoms in the spring and dried leaves in the fall.

the Hairy Webworm that spins
gray web in shade tree and feeds
on foliage.

I don't mean to be unfair. I have a Pecan tree so I know its problems but I also appreciate the fact that it shades my patio. I admit that the blossoms and leaves keep my children busy. So for those of you who may want to try it here are a few notes on its culture. The varieties best suited for areas above southern Florida are the Stuart, one of the oldest paper-shelled varieties, the Success, the Elliott and the Desirable. The Schley variety produces the best quality pecan but it is liable to scab disease and requires particular care.

Plant your tree in winter between November and February. Any type of soil will do provided the spot has depth and is well-drained. Feed in December or January with a fertilizer containing nitrogen, phosphorus and potash, making sure that the potash content is high. Plug in the fertilizer. If you must prune do it in January when the sap is down. The big pests of the Pecan tree are the caterpillars that weave their webs into tents around the succulent outer branches. Burn what you can reach with a torch on the end of a long pole, climb to reach the high ones or have the tree sprayed by the nurseryman. Most Pecan trees grow tall (some to sixty feet) so pest control becomes a problem.

It has been my experience that Pecan trees bear larger crops every other year. Technically the crop should be the same every season, but weather conditions vary. Heavy rains will knock off the pollen and the more the caterpillars the less the following year's crop.

FLOWERING TREES

To bring color and points of interest to spots in your garden I list below the Flowering Trees that do well in the South.

ALLIGATOR PEAR TREE or AVOCADO, *Persea americana* or *Persea gratissima* is a large evergreen tree up to sixty feet. Leaves are oblong to oval, green tinged with red at the base. Flowers hang in broad panicles shading from chartreuse to copper. While this tree is grown commercially in central and southern Florida and in California for its creamy buttery fruit, the loveliness of its foliage and blooms is what makes it attractive to us. The Trapp and the Pollack varieties are widely planted in the South for the market. Many of us in New Orleans find that our Avocado trees will show healthy foliage but rarely a bloom or fruit. Sometimes cutting the roots with a sharp shovel will force the flowering. Then the tree might bloom but fail to pollinate its own flowers, hence bear no fruit. Consult your nurseryman for suggestive remedies. Perhaps he will say that you need a companion tree to insure success. There are many trees here that are bearing fruit and the consensus of the owners is that it takes six or seven years for the tree to be old enough to bear, that a grafted tree will bear in five years, and that the Avocado needs frequent and heavy waterings and therefore demands good drainage. Other than that it calls for no further attention. The flowers usually show in late winter or very early spring followed by fruit which takes from six to twelve months to mature depending on variety, location and weather conditions.

BLACK LOCUST, *Robinia Pseudacacia* has white flowers in the spring followed by oblong brown pods in August and September. It is deciduous and grows to eighty feet. R. *Pseudacacia* variety *Rehderi* is a dwarf form. The Locust is said to be the only American tree which has become extensively naturalized in Europe.

BUCKEYE, or RED BUCKEYE *Aesculus pavia* is a small tree noted for its five-fingered leaves and reddish flower clusters that show in the spring. The fruits are poisonous and the leaves toxic.

CAJEPUT TREE, see PUNK TREE.

An import from the tropics is the lovely *Cassia alata*, popularly known as the CANDELABRA TREE. It does especially well in

Flower Heads of the Candelabra

southern Florida and has recently begun to be widely planted in
New Orleans not only as an ornamental shrub or small tree on
home lawns but on the neutral grounds of the city as well. Fast
growing from three to eight feet, this specimen produces lovely
golden yellow blossoms in candle-shaped racemes and is perfectly
beautiful in October and November. The leaves are large and
paripinnate, of a medium shade of green with orange rachis at the
base. The Candelabra likes light sandy loam and plenty of sun and
water. Unfortunately it is often killed by a freeze but new trees
may be started from seed in spring and these babies will mature
and bloom the following winter. It is well worth replanting every
year if necessary.

CASSIA, *Cassia fistula* is sometimes called the Golden Shower
Tree and is a sight to behold when its clusters of yellow flowers are
open in the late spring and early summer. A native of India, it
rarely exceeds ten feet and stands the cold very well. The pink
variety is *Cassia javanica* or Java Shower and another gem is the
Pink-and-White Shower or *C. nodosa*. All are dormant in winter,
not particular as to soil, but do best in full sun.

CATALPA, *Catalpa bignonioides* sometimes called Indian
Bean has white, pink or yellow blooms followed by cylindrical pods
and is deciduous. This is the tree that you sometimes notice in the
spring because the sidewalk beneath it is literally covered with
blossoms. You notice it again in the late summer when the very
long beans are hanging in clusters between the big heart-shaped
leaves. It grows to fifty feet. *Catalpa bignonioides* var. *nana* is the
dwarf form.

CHERRY-LAUREL, *Prunus Laurocerasus caroliniana* although more frequently considered a hedge material, if allowed
does grow rapidly to a tree of fifteen or twenty feet, almost anywhere in the South. The leaves are shiny evergreen and rather
small and the tiny white flowers are borne in racemes in the spring,
followed by dark berries. The Cherry-Laurel thrives in any type of
soil but will not live in swampy, badly-drained areas. It seems im-

mune to disease and pests and stands shearing well. The branches
and twigs are poisonous.

CHERRY TREE, *Prunus serotina* is medium-sized and bears
small white blossoms in racemes in March followed by dark purple
fruit. This is the cherry used to make Cherry Bounce.

CHINA-BERRY, *Melia Azedarach* also known as the Pride of
India and the China-Ball Tree, grows to forty feet and has become
naturalized throughout the South. A rapid grower, its lavender
flowers produced on many-branched leaf clusters are followed by
yellow ball-like berries. Since this tree is deciduous only during the
sharpest part of the winter and buds quickly in the spring it makes
a desirable shade tree and should be more utilized. The CHINESE
UMBRELLA TREE, *Melia Azedarach* variety *umbraculiformis*
also deciduous, grows to about twenty feet and produces a somewhat oriental effect with its stiff flat branches. *Melia sempervirens*
is evergreen. The leaves, berries, flowers and bark of these trees are
poisonous.

CHINESE TALLOW TREE, *Sapium sebiferum* has flowers
of two types on the same tree, yellowish staminate in erect clusters
and pistillate flowers below the staminate. The fruit is a green cap-
sule from which pop the waxy gray-white berries. These berries are
long-lasting in arrangements and are also used in candle-making by
the Chinese. Fast growing to twenty-five feet, it is deciduous.

CHINESE TREE-OF-HEAVEN, *Ailanthus altissima* is a
rapid grower to sixty feet even under the most unfavorable conditions. Avoid the male species with the staminate flowers which are
ill-smelling. Small greenish flowers give way to winged fruit. Though
deciduous, the large pinnate foliage makes this an excellent shade
tree with tropical effect. It may be kept dwarfed for use in the patio.

CONFEDERATE ROSE, *Hibiscus mutabilis* is a small deciduous tree to ten feet bearing flowers that open white in the morning
and change gradually to pink and deep red by nightfall. An interesting specimen.

The SOUTHERN CRABAPPLE, *Malus angustifolia* is probably the only one of the family that is successful all over the Southern Coastal Plain. Reaching to twenty feet, this deciduous tree has
horizontal branching habits with lovely flowers that appear in the
spring with the first leaf shoots, pink as a bud and white when
fully open. The blossoms are profuse and very fragrant and they
are followed by small green apples that are of no importance. This
one likes full sun and filtered shade. It needs staking when very
young.

CRAPE MYRTLE, *Lagerstroemia indica* grows from ten to
twenty-five feet throughout the South especially in inland sections.
In sandy coastal areas the Crape Myrtle is more likely to grow in
shrub form. It bears soft panicles of pink, lavender, rose and white
flowers during the summer. Its leaves are small, fine and bronze in
the fall and the trunk is a peculiarly lovely shade of tan. Those trees
planted in full sun are hardly ever attacked by the powdery mildew
that appears in damp weather. Control this fungus by dusting with
sulphur during the rainy season. Prune by heading back in the fall
after the leaves are shed and rub off suckers that usually come up
from the base of the tree.

Lagerstroemia speciosa comprises a large group of the Crape
Myrtles that do well in Florida and should be tried elsewhere in the
South. Of these, *L. flos-reginae* or the Queen's Crape Myrtle, which
must have full sun and bears pinkish-red flowers and *L. turbinata* a
late bloomer showing flowers shading from white to pink to violet
are the most attractive.

CRY-BABY TREE or CORAL TREE, *Erythrina Crista-galli*
has large deep orange flowers that appear sometimes twice a year
between May and September, provided it has had plenty of water
and sun. Deciduous, this tree can be kept as low as six to eight
feet or allowed to reach fifteen feet. The trunk becomes attractively
gnarled as it matures and the stems bear long spines. A new one to
try is the WHITE CORAL TREE or *Erythrina indica alba*. These
trees are called "Crybabies" because of the flow of nectar that

drips from the flower, resembling tear drops. The Coral Tree's blossoms are large, resembling sweet peas in shape, and shade from a rich orange on the wings to a deep orange-red towards the keel and the down-folding standard. The texture is suede-like. These flowers are borne in long racemes on the end of the branches. When cut they look lovely when massed with pale peach and copper-bronze glads. I have never seen bug or insect bother this tree. It is also comparatively free of disease. Since blooms appear on last year's wood prune immediately after flowering.

D O G W O O D , *Cornus florida* is a medium-sized tree that does well throughout this region growing ten to twelve feet and blooming in the spring. The small yellow-green flowers are surrounded by four white bracts, each with a darkened apex. The variety *rubra* has showy pink flowers. This tree needs aluminum sulphate or other feed suitable to keep the soil on the acid side. Test the soil often to make sure that you keep it so. It is a perfect companion to the Camellias and the Azaleas and truly a lovely thing. Since the Dogwood does not transplant easily I recommend starting off with a five-foot specimen from the nursery.

Sometimes the Dogwoods are attacked by borers that get into the trunk through an injury received in transplanting or through a split resulting from cold or excessive drought. Dig out the borer, clean and paint the spot with a good tree paint. If you keep a faithful watering program in dry weather you can avoid borers.

E U C A L Y P T U S , often called the Silver Dollar Eucalyptus, is the tree with the silvery gray-green foliage that is so much in demand by flower-arrangers. The bark is a gray-brown, the leaves are dull and round and grow in pairs along the graceful, slender stem. The flowers are small and creamy-white. Quite a few gardeners in New Orleans are trying this slow-growing tree, and so far it seems to be resistant to our prolonged summer heat and occasional freezing temperatures. This fact leads me to believe that this specimen is *Eucalyptus polyanthemos*, although the nurserymen in the area call it *E. cinerea*. Be sure to stake the young tree. *E. globulus compacta* is another member of this family worth trying. This dwarf blue gum forms a symmetrically rounded, compact tree.

I have recently experimented with some seeds of the CRIMSON-FLOWERING EUCALYPTUS, E. *ficifolia* that a friend brought me from California. I planted them in something new; little cubes that are made up of fibre fortified with plant food. I placed the seed in the hollow of the cube and covered it with perlite and then with a piece of gauze, so that in watering, the seed would not wash away. I kept the cubes damp by syringing with a hand bulb. In two weeks' time the tiny plants had appeared and in another two weeks, they had shown two sets of leaves, the bottom pair the traditional round shape that we associate with the Silver Dollar Eucalyptus, the upper leaves a little more oval. I cut the cubes apart from the block (they come in blocks of eight and twelve) with a sharp knife and I was delighted to find a beautiful root system showing at the bottom of the cube. I transferred the cube to a pot made of fibrous material into which I had placed the usual small pieces of brickbat at the bottom for drainage. The soil in the pot was good garden loam. In another three weeks I lowered the fibre pot into a four inch clay pot and brought my little trees outdoors. The point of the experiment was two-fold. I had succeeded in starting the Eucalyptus and I had grown them from seed to six inches in height without ever disturbing the plant itself. From seed to clay pot through the use of the cubes and the fibre pots, there was no shock to the plant. It is too soon to tell how long these Eucalyptus will grow but up to now they are doing very well. I have kept them in a cool place where they get lots of light but not too much moisture. When they have grown a little taller I shall set them out in the open ground.

These cubes and pots are sold under trade names and I heartily recommend them for starting any seeds of which you must take care. Together they eliminate the shock and set-back that the plant usually goes through in transplanting.

FINGER-LEAF TREE or CASSAVA, *Manihot cartha-*

ginensis is a small tree growing to about nine feet in height. Deciduous, it has small yellow-white flowers followed by round, perfectly smooth light-green berries the size of marbles. The leaves are five to nine-lobed closely resembling fingers of a hand. The roots of this tree when processed produce tapioca but in the raw state they are said to be poisonous. I have found that the area surrounding this tree will always be free of flies and mosquitoes, hence I use it in my patio. When the berries ripen, usually in summer, they split and the seeds burst out with a popping noise. Do not allow the children to put these seeds in their mouths. It has never been determined just how poisonous they are. Prune this tree way back in the late winter.

FRANGIPANI, of the genus Plumeria grows to fifteen feet and is known for its pinkish-white flowers that are particularly fragrant at night. The blossoms appear in summer. This tree, a native of Mexico and naturalized in the West Indies, does well in the Gulf region and in southern Florida. It is very common in Hawaii and as a matter of fact, the flowers are used to make the leis that are hung on the necks of visitors. *Plumeria rubra* has six inch broad leaves, about one foot long, with deep marginal veins and red, pink or purple blooms. *P. alba* has narrower leaves without veins and bears white flowers in terminal clusters. The Frangipani needs a sheltered spot in the garden.

FRINGE TREE, *Chionanthus virginica* is a slender tree to thirty feet, with bluish-white flowers composed of five strap-shaped petals one inch long blooming in feathery clusters in the spring. Deciduous, this tree does well in the mid and lower South, particularly in wet swampy sections.

GOLDEN-RAIN-TREE, *Koelreuteria paniculata* grows to thirty feet producing panicles of small yellow flowers in October followed by spectacular larger pods that range in color from deep pink to tan to brown. These are much in demand for dried arrangements. I once trimmed a summer hat with some of these beautifully colored pods. If dried correctly they keep their pink tones for a long time. This tree must be six or seven years old to bloom. The Golden-Rain thrives in hot dry sections and likes to be planted in full sun. A fast grower, it is reasonably free of pests and diseases but I know of several large specimen that developed root rot and had to be destroyed. Although the *paniculata* does well in most of the South the variety *formosana*, or Flame Golden-Rain is being widely used in the New Orleans area for sidewalk planting, replacing the enormous and annoying Hackberries. Another hardy variety is *K. bipinnata*. I prune mine back every year in December or January.

HOLLY, *Ilex* has several tree types in the American Holly *opaca* group that do very well in the South: L'Acadienne, Foster's

Ilex Opaca

Holly and East Palatka, usually to twenty-five feet, sometimes as high as forty feet. All have very green leaves and very red berries.

Ilex Opaca East Palatka

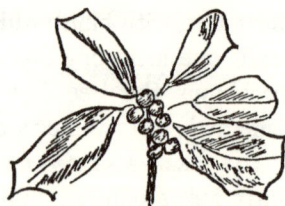

Ilex Opaca L'Acadienne

JACARANDA, *Jacaranda acutifolia* and *Jacaranda ovalifolia* are graceful trees to fifty feet with nearly evergreen fern-like foliage and great plumes of smokey-blue flowers in the spring. They are perfect foils for the pink and rose Mimosas, quickly recover from frost burn and stand pruning well. *J. ovalifolia* is sometimes called *J. mimosaefolia*. I have a dwarf *Jacaranda caerulea* in the garden that is very lovely. The panicles are blue-violet.

J A P A N E S E   P L U M   T R E E , *Eriobotrya japonica* sometimes called the Loquat Tree is densely evergreen, grows to twenty feet in the mid and lower South and through Florida. It bears small yellow-white flowers in compact upright panicles in autumn followed by yellow fruit in the spring. The leaves are heavy textured, serrated and fuzzy on the underside. This tree likes full sun and good drainage. Espalier it or dwarf it for patio use.

L O B L O L L Y - B A Y   T R E E , *Gordonia lasianthus* not often seen in Louisiana but grown from Virginia to Mississippi, is glossy and evergreen, showing white sweet-smelling blossoms in the warm months. Usually growing compactly to thirty feet or better, it likes lots of moisture.

M A G N O L I A , *Magnolia grandiflora* is listed again because of its lovely white blossoms in the spring and early summer. Evergreen and slow-growing, it eventually attains a height of seventy-five to one hundred feet in the deep South. A heavy feeder, the Magnolia needs rich soil, applications of a well-balanced fertilizer and space wherein to spread its enormous root system. The variety *gloriosa* grows only to forty feet, produces larger flowers and broader leaves that are brown on the under surface. Prune this tree during the growing season. It will not easily heal the cuts while dormant. Magnolias like a thick mulch. Transplant in late winter or early spring.

M A P L E , *Acer rubrum* sometimes called the Red or Swamp Maple grows to one hundred feet. It has scarlet flowers in the spring and deep orange-red foliage in the fall. Although deciduous, the tree is still lovely in winter showing grayish-silver branches. *Acer rubrum tridens* grows in the hilly regions of North Louisiana. The most beautiful red of all, *Acer rubrum drummondii* does best in the New Orleans and Mississippi river lowland areas. The S I L V E R M A P L E , *Acer saccharinum* grows from thirty to fifty feet and is so-called because its leaves are very silvery-white on the underside. The Maples need plenty of water in the arid sections and are more successful when planted in good, moist, loamy soil.

M A Y H A W , *Crataegus opaca* is a rounded deciduous medium-sized tree, with dark green leaves, whitish-pink flowers in the late winter and globular, bright red fragrant fruit in the spring. The fruit is made into jelly. *C. brachyacantha's* flowers fade to an orange color in May and the blue fruit ripens in August. *C. aestivalis* var. *Dormonae* is later to bloom and therefore fruits in late June.

M I M O S A , *Albizzia Julibrissin* is deciduous, grows to thirty-five feet and is the hardiest of the whole family, producing feathery gray-green foliage on spreading horizontal branches. The delicate pink blossoms resemble a powder puff. The variety *rosea*, sometimes called the Strawberry Mimosa, has deeper rose flowers. These trees do well in mid and lower South provided they get plenty of water and fairly good soil. Be sure to buy a tree that is resistant to Mimosa Wilt, a fungus that is new in the South. No effective spray has yet been found. I have grown all of mine from seed and so far I have been lucky to have avoided this disease.

O R C H I D T R E E , *Bauhinia variegata* is a tropical tree sometimes called Mountain Ebony. Originally a vine the young stalk must be staked until big enough to stand alone. Plant it in a sheltered southern corner of the garden. The flowers that appear in early spring range in color, with the different varieties, from purple *B. purpurea*, to lavender *B. variegata*, to white *B. alba* and *B. candida*, to yellow *B. tomentosa* and *B. picta*. The leaves are gray-green, heavily veined, shaped like a hoof and close like butterfly wings from dusk to sun-up. Semi-evergreen, depending on the severity of the winter, and growing to thirty feet, this tree may seem to die back in a freeze in its youth but don't be too hasty to remove it. It almost always comes back. Prune after flowering since the next season's blooms begin forming from the tips of the branches soon thereafter. A native of India, this tree is in no way related to the true orchids although the blossoms resemble the orchid on a smaller scale. If you examine the flowers carefully you will note that the fifth petal is larger and deeper in color than the other four. A long seed pod develops from the bloom, containing six to ten flat seeds that usually germinate. I have raised many from seed. My purple-flowering tree is seven years old, about twenty-eight feet high and was not injured at all through several freezes. I must admit that I very often wish that the leaves looked their best when the flowers open; they have a habit of being worn and scratchy-looking just at the time the blooms are so lovely. These tired leaves soon drop and the new foliage is most attractive.

Bauhinia Blakeana, an evergreen, was introduced in 1953 to the United States through Florida. Long beautifying the gardens of Hong Kong with its dark purple-crimson flowers, it does not set seed so it has to be propagated by air layering, by cuttings or by being grafted to other Bauhinias. So far it seems to be many-branched, many-flowered and shrubby. It sounds like a most attractive addition.

PARKINSONIA, *Parkinsonia aculeata* or Jerusalem Thorn, is a thorny tree with drooping feathery foliage and yellow summer flowers. Sprawly in habit, it grows to about twelve feet and the leaves remain through the year in the lower South. It is semi-deciduous in the rest of the southern areas. Other varieties reach forty feet but they all like full sun and sandy loam.

PEACH, *Prunus persica* bears fairly well in New Orleans though the peach grown for the table is nothing compared to the crops of named varieties like Dixie Gem, Sullivan's Early Elberta and Southland that thrive northwards. The varieties Red Ceylon, Waldo and Jewel seem to be well adapted for the southern area. Plant between December and February and feed the following year in early spring with a well-balanced fertilizer. If the leaves look yellow and sickly and begin to drop apply a light dose of nitrate of soda in June.

Here we are mainly concerned with the FLOWERING PEACH which should be pruned immediately after blooming each year. I don't think that there will be much difficulty in that respect because all of us cut the flowering branches to enjoy indoors. Cardinal is a double rosy pink and Iceberg a double white. There are Double Red and White Weeping Peaches with drooping branches that are most attractive. The dwarf Chinese Peach, a shrub to five feet, not only presents lovely blossoms but also bears small peaches. I have not tried this one as yet.

Peach trees sometimes show gum oozing from the trunk near the ground. This is a sign that borers are at work under the bark. Spray with DDT in late summer and mulch well to keep these pests from doing further damage.

PEAR, *Pyrus pyrifolia* or *P. culta* is the sand pear whose fruit must be cooked to be enjoyed. This deciduous tree is a vigorous grower through the South and is particularly valuable for the loveliness of its white blossoms on bare branches in early spring. It gets quite tall unless kept pruned back to within easy reach of its flowers. Plant between December and February and feed the following year with a mixture of 5-10-5 at the rate of one-half pound per year of age. Do this fertilizing in February or March. Unfortunately the Bartlett Pear is not for us. The Pineapple and Hood sand pears are best but still only fit for preserving. Do water copiously during the hot months so that in the following spring the blooms won't appear ahead of time and be nipped by frost.

Pear trees are often attacked by Fire Blight bacteria in early spring causing the flowering branches to turn black and die. Cut out the diseased parts, sterilizing your shears between cuts and don't give the tree too much nitrogen. Since there is no effective cure for this blight, my only advice is to try to buy resistant varieties.

PERSIMMON, *Diospyros virginiana* reaches twenty feet and produces fragrant cream-colored flowers early in May, the male and female flowers on separate trees. The fruit is very acrid (as we who have eaten a green persimmon know) until fully ripe at which time it is a brownish-red-orange color, and edible. Almost evergreen, its foliage is as attractive as its fruit. This tree needs rich moist soil and plenty of sun. It does best in the warmest sections of central and southern Florida but the Japanese Persimmon, *D. kaki* variety *Tane Nashi* of sprawly habits, has been grown above this area. The Persimmon is incredibly free of insects and disease and tolerates moving only when young so as not to disturb the tap root. Did you know that golf clubs are made from the wood of this tree?

PURPLE-LEAVED PLUM is *Prunus cerasifera pissardi* which reaches fifteen feet or more. Deciduous, its pale pink flowers in early spring are as lovely as its purplish-red foliage and bronzy fruit. It does well as a color accent in southern gardens and requires full sun. The variety *triloba* grows to eight feet.

PUNK TREE, *Melaleuca Leucadendra* sometimes known as the Cajeput Tree spreads to twenty feet, has a thick spongy bark that peels in layers and will withstand salt sprays, extreme heat, wind and frost. Almost evergreen, this tree has flowers of creamy-white that resemble in formation those of the Callistemon or Bottlebrush Family.

RED-BUD, *Cercis canadensis* is a deciduous tree from ten to twenty-five feet, with small rosy flowers blooming in spring before the large leaves appear. This variety is the most beautiful of the family. The variety called the JUDAS TREE is the European *Cercis siliquastrum. Cercis chinensis* is the Chinese species which does not grow as tall as the other two. These trees do well in almost any type of soil and under most adverse conditions in the South up to north and central Florida.

ROSE-ACACIA or LOCUST TREE, *Robinia hispida* grows to nine feet and bears rosy-purple blooms in the spring. It is deciduous and propagated easily from cuttings. The variety *hispida nana* is a dwarf form.

ROYAL PAULOWNIA, *Paulownia tomentosa* often called the Empress Tree has interesting plumose lavender blooms and brown pods that are valuable to the arranger of dried materials. Because it tolerates dry and adverse conditions, it should be planted more throughout our area. Deciduous.

SMOKE TREE, *Cotinus coggygria* formerly known as Rhus Cotinus, is a deciduous tree to fifteen feet, grown for its feathery purple panicles in summer and for its beautiful foliage that turns to bright autumnal hues.

STRAWBERRY TREE, *Arbutus unedo* is one that I have tried to grow, alas unsuccessfully to this date. It is a small evergreen, usually to twelve feet, with lovely white summer flowers that are followed by bright red fruit in the fall. Although it does not do well along the eastern coast of the South, by all the rules it should thrive farther inland and in our lower area. It really is too nice a specimen to ignore, so I am about to try again.

SWEET ACACIA, *Acacia Farnesiana* is an evergreen with handsome leaves and sweet-scented flowers in clusters which bloom several times a year. A slow grower, this tree will reach twelve feet. Give it good drainage.

TIBOUCHINA, *Tibouchina granulosa* is a Brazilian product sometimes called the Purple Glory Tree, and one that is being tried more frequently in the lower coastal sections. This evergreen does not need to be very large before the fall and winter violet flowers appear but it does eventually reach twenty feet. The foliage is as spectacular as the blossoms.

TREE HIBISCUS, *Hibiscus tiliaceus* and *H. elatus* are grown in Florida and are being experimentally used in our areas with good results to date. The first-mentioned variety grows to fifteen feet with yellowish-red blossoms. It needs plenty of water and sandy soil. The second variety is a smaller tree with orange colored flowers. Both are resistant to salt sprays and both are evergreen. *H. Waimeae* bears large white blooms and is somewhat shrubby in growth habits.

TULIP TREE, *Liriodendron Tulipifera* sometimes called the Yellow Poplar Tree, grows to one hundred and thirty feet in moist swampy places, with a trunk about ten feet in diameter. In more arid sections this tree will thrive but not to such heights. The flowers resemble tulips in shape. They are yellowish-green with deep orange markings at the throat. The deciduous blue-green leaves turn bright yellow in autumn and are most unusual in shape. I started two Tulip trees from ten inch seedlings and in two years time I had to move them to a wider open space than the confines of my garden because I knew that they would not transplant easily when over five feet tall. Given plenty of air and sun in their present locale, they are on the way to being towering specimens today.

TUNG OIL TREE, *Aleurites Fordii* is a tropical grown for its oil-producing seeds but also known for its showy reddish-pink to white flowers in the spring. Grows ten to twenty-five feet high and is deciduous. The seeds or nuts are extremely poisonous.

VARNISH TREE, *Firmiana platanifolia* also known as the Chinese Parasoltree, reaches twenty-five to thirty feet in height. Deciduous, its flowers have no petals. The fruit, at first closed, hangs in panicles and then opens to five petal-like pieces, each having one or two seeds attached to the edges. Shading from tan to gold, they are most attractive in dried arrangements. The oil from the fruit is used in making lacquer. The fruit is poisonous.

VIBURNUM, *Viburnum odoratissimum* grows into tree size, sometimes to fifteen feet and makes good background planting. It bears white flowers in the spring and has long been known in Louisiana. V. *rufidulum* and V. *dentatum* both grow taller and also bear white flowers, the former in the spring, the latter in June and July. Most Viburnum are evergreen in the deep South and deciduous northwards.

WAX LIGUSTRUM, *Ligustrum lucidum* has spreading branches that reach twenty feet. A most desirable evergreen, it is used also as a hedge because it stands shearing well. Small white flowers appear in racemes in the spring. This specimen harbors the white fly so keep your oil emulsion handy. L. *vulgare* is also widely used as an ornamental, though smaller.

YAUPON, *Ilex vomitoria* has glossy evergreen foliage and is more tall shrub (to fifteen feet or more) than tree. White flowers give way to scarlet berries. It is well adapted to most soils in the South.

I purposely omitted the ROYAL POINCIANA in the list above because it is so very tender to any freeze. But it is so beautiful that my conscience hurt me, so here it is.

ROYAL POINCIANA, *Delonix regia* formerly known as *Poinciana regia* is one of the most brilliant of the tropical flowering trees, with orange-red flowers and feathery leaves. It dies with the first freeze in sections above Florida but it is quite worthwhile having in the garden even for a short time. Who can tell in our climate? We may have several winters in a row without very low temperatures and this tree can give us so much pleasure in that time. Deciduous, it will reach twenty feet although I have never had the opportunity to see one grow that tall.

✯ 6 ✯

Trees with Edible Fruits

THE FIG TREE

I discuss the Fig because it not only serves as a fruit tree but is now becoming popular as a potted ornamental in patios and is being espaliered with much success against garden walls.

The F I G , *Ficus Carica* grows in almost any soil in the southern coastal region and into northern Florida provided that soil is well-drained, is fed regularly and contains plenty of moisture. An historic tree mentioned in the earliest religious writings and songs its black branches grow rather stiffly, bearing large dark green, heavy-textured leaves. The fig itself evolves from small flowers that are enclosed in a tough shell. Our Celeste and the other varieties that do well here do not require "Caprification", the method used to pollinate the Smyrna Fig. In California and Europe the flowers of the Smyrna Fig have to be visited by the specially imported fig wasps that live in the wild fig or Caprifig trees. The Smyrna type does not thrive here because our summers are too hot and humid and the temperatures change too suddenly in winter. So our trees mature their figs regularly, or may I say more easily, without the aid of the Caprifigs and their pollen. Our blossoms swell as they absorb starch and sap and change to juice and sugar, eventually softening into edible fruit. They are considered mule flowers that become pomologically mature but rarely botanically mature. A fig that ripens on the tree more than doubles its size in the last two or three days before picking, its cheeks puffing out and showing pinkish tints.

VARIETIES

There are quite a few varieties that do well here, some bearing earlier than others but the one we know best is the Celeste, a hardy tree with medium-sized fruit that shades from a bluish-tan to brown and contains a sweet rose-colored pulp. The Florentine variety which is as hardy and bears at the same time as the Celeste, has larger fruit that is a bright yellow. A less vigorous type fig is the Hunt which produces its brown fruit later and a little longer than the Celeste. The Mission Fig is well known on the west coast and has been grown down South for some time. While it is not as hardy nor is its crop as large as the Celeste, it bears late in summer producing a large black-skinned fruit with a very short stem. The figs

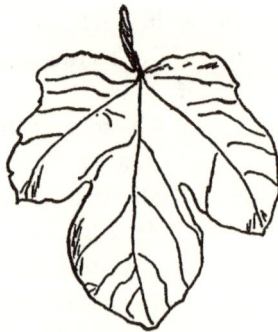

Brown Turkey Fig Leaf

of the four above-mentioned trees are edible fresh or preserved, the Mission fig being the only kind that must be peeled before cooking.

Two more varieties, the Brown Turkey and the Magnolia are also grown here, but more for preserving than enjoying fresh from the tree. The Brown Turkey is sometimes known under the names of Harrison or Texas Everbearing. It produces a small crop of medium-sized figs several weeks earlier than the Celeste and then a heavier crop some weeks after the Celeste. Another name for Magnolia is Brunswick, a very hardy type tree that bears big, hollow, brown-ribbed fruit that hangs from the branch with almost no stem. The eye of this fruit remains open giving it a tendency to sour quickly. It must be picked immediately as it ripens if it is to be fit for preserving. If you have space in your garden, purchasing several varieties of fig trees will give you fruit over a long period of time.

TREE OR BUSH?

Before purchasing decide whether you want the tree or the bush type of fig. The advantage of buying the latter lies in the fact that you will never have to climb the tree to pick the fruit. If you already have a tree type pruning can convert it into the bush type if you head back the inside branches to make the top open up and thin where necessary. Do your trimming in February and March after danger of freeze is over and before growth starts because the figs are produced on the current year's growth.

PLANTING

When you plant your fig tree in February or March plant the tree type two inches deeper and the bush type four inches deeper than they grew in the nursery. Prune the top branches of the tree type, leaving them about three feet above the ground. Trim the bush type to within two feet above soil level. Fig trees have a shallow root system so after setting them out, mulch them well with leaves or any other mulching material and do not allow grass to grow around the base of the tree.

PROPAGATION

If you cannot find the variety that you wish to plant through your nurseryman and a friend has the type you want try making cuttings, a fairly easy and usually successful procedure. The best time to do this is from December to February or March, depending on the weather you have that particular winter. In any case cuttings must be made in cold temperatures while the tree is still dormant. Since roots will appear only at points where the leaf stems arise make your cuttings about ten inches long, just below one of these points or nodes. Plant about eight inches deep in furrows in the open ground in semi-shade and keep well watered. Set the cutting deep enough so that only one bud remains above or level with the soil surface and pack the earth firmly around it. By the next winter they will be rooted sufficiently for you to transfer to the spot where they will remain indefinitely. Fig suckers may also be removed and planted in the dormant season when there are no leaves and transpiration is at a minimum but while the sucker still maintains root growth. Keep well watered. Never let them dry out.

PRUNING

A mature fig tree needs very little pruning other than to cut out diseased and dead limbs. However in the second and third year after planting a new tree you will have to head back the lower limbs slightly and trim the inside branches to force the top to open up. Whatever pruning you do perform the operation with a clean sharp shears and paint the cut surfaces with a good tree paint. Always cut a branch even with the surface of the limb or trunk from which it grows. Leaving a stub not only makes for an unsightly tree but offers a wonderful breeding nook for insects and disease. Pruning done in late winter is always the most successful because the more dormant the tree, the quicker the cuts heal.

Quite often a severe freeze will kill back the fig tree. In this case allow the new shoots to grow out close to ground level, cut out all dead wood and burn it. From this point with careful pruning, you have a perfect opportunity to develop the bush type fig.

PESTS

Keep your eyes open for the insects that plague the fig tree, the fig mealybug and the three-lined Fig Tree Borer. Mealybug is a cottony mass that nestles on trunk, limb, leaves and fruit and can be controlled by spraying the trunk and limbs with a 3% oil emulsion to which is added one teaspoon nicotine sulphate and one ounce of soap to each gallon of spray solution. If the weather is too hot or too cold to use the oil emulsion, spray with malathion, two pints of 50% liquid to one hundred gallons of water. Use these solutions *only* while the tree is dormant, before the leaves appear. To avoid the shock of seeing the mealybug attack the tree after the leaves appear and the sick feeling of realization that you cannot spray at that time, take this precaution: as the new leaves bud, tie a two-inch band of tree Tanglefoot or burlap soaked in insecticide (nicotine-soap or pyrethrum-soap) around the trunk of the tree about three or four inches above ground level and scratch the surface of the band frequently to avoid crusting. The band will prevent the mealybugs from crawling onto the tree or from being carried there by ants.

And herein hangs another tale: ants and mealybugs work beauti-

fully together, unfortunately towards the destruction of the tree!
Ants offer free taxi service to the mealybug, transporting it to different parts of the tree. Their fee for such service is the sweet sticky
substance exuded by the mealybugs. So in order to be happy with
a healthy fig tree use the suggestions in the previous paragraph or
other preventive measures. Since ants help bring the other pest
begin by clearing the whole area of dried leaves, trash, etc., and
then just as the new growth appears spray everything in the garden
including lawn and trees, with chlordane, using about five gallons
of solution (50% wettable chlordane powder to fifty gallons of
water) to every one thousand square feet. This should rid the
grounds of ants for at least a month. The dose may be repeated
after that time but never apply it to the fig tree after the fruit
begins to ripen.

If you keep your tree well-pruned of broken and diseased limbs
and paint all cuts with a good tree paint, you will probably avoid
the three-lined FIG TREE BORER, *Ptychodes trivittatus* which
feeds on the bark before it bores into the wood of the tree. If you
see sawdust next to a hole in a limb or on the ground below the tree
as if someone had been using a drill or saw, arm yourself with a
sharp knife and dig out the borer and paint the scraped surface
with your tree paint. If the borer has infiltrated beyond your control call in your nurseryman. He may suggest spraying with ethylene
dichloride emulsion or he may have other methods of control
available.

The full grown borer is a gray-brown beetle measuring about an
inch wide and bearing long horns. Three white wavy stripes show
on its back, one on each side and one down the center. It lays its
eggs in March in loose bark and injured areas of the tree trunk and
branches. When the eggs hatch the young white beetles feed on
the bark for two or three weeks and it is in this stage that you can
dig them out with a sharp knife. After this period they begin to
bore deeper into the tree and then you will have to call for help.

DISEASES

One of the diseases to look for is RUST, *Uredo fici* a condition that causes leaves to fall from the tree. Small brown spots on the under surface of the leaves multiply until the leaf turns brown and falls. Whereas this blight does not badly damage the fig crop it makes the tree unsightly. Spraying with Bordeaux mixture usually takes care of this condition but keeping your tree clean of dead leaves and twigs seems to be the best preventive medicine that I can recommend. This cleanliness can be augmented by a spray program using Bordeaux mixture beginning during the dormant period and again in the spring when the leaves have first developed. Then your tree should be sprayed a third time in early August.

A much more serious leaf disease very often occurs in May or June and is called Thread Blight. Caused by a parasitic fungus that lives on dead wood or dead leaves, it is first apparent at the base of the green leaf and spreads like a wave to the outer tip, causing the entire leaf to wither and turn brown. The dead leaf is then held to the branch by brown threads. This disease will ruin the entire crop for that year if not immediately checked. Applications of a 4-4-50 Bordeaux mixture as soon as it is noticed will do some good but the blight can be controlled for the following year by the application of a more effective spray during the dormant period. This spray, recommended by the Agricultural Experiment Station of Louisiana State University, is made up of:

21 oz. copper sulphate (blue stone)
14 oz. lime
14 oz. zinc arsenite
3½ oz. monocalcium arsenite
14 oz. fish oil
10 gal. water

Never use this spray unless you know that your tree is infested.

When the branches of the fig tree look like they are dying and a pink coating appears, your fig is attacked by the Fig Blight, a fungus. The pink coating is produced by the fungus as it forms spores to spread the disease. Cut off the infected limbs and burn.

FEEDING

As to feeding I recommend using one pound of a fertilizer to the analysis of 5–10–5 or 6–8–8 for each year of the tree's age. Apply between February and March. Inasmuch as the fig has a shallow root system, instead of plugging in the feed remove the mulch, carefully cultivate the topsoil and mix the fertilizer with it. Replace the mulch and water well for several days.

THE FRUIT

Sometimes a fig tree will drop its fruit before it ripens. In most cases this is caused from lack of water or quick changes of tempera-

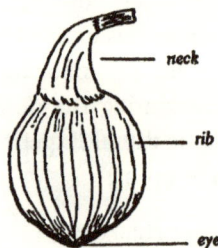

— neck

— rib

— eye

Celeste Fig

ture. Figs also sour rapidly, especially in a rainy period. The fruit must be picked just before the juice seeps through the skin and while still firm enough to handle. Should the skin burst naturally or should the birds get greedy enough to puncture the fruit and help themselves, bacteria quickly sets up fermentation. In some varieties the eye of the fig opens from lack of sugar and spoilage begins at this point. This condition is rarely seen in the Celeste.

Now that you have heard all that can happen to the fig tree don't let the account of its pests and diseases discourage you from planting it. Actually, if you take care of your tree and keep it clean, half of these troubles will not appear. It responds rapidly to good treatment. I am afraid that I must use the old adage here: "An ounce of prevention is worth a pound of cure."

THE FIG AS A POTTED PLANT

The fig makes an unusual addition to the small garden or patio when grown in tubs or large pots. Nurseries offer varieties suited for such use, or you may start a cutting of any of the varieties mentioned and grow it in a pot. Take the same care of it as you would the larger tree. You will have to be particularly careful of the pruning in order to keep it to the desired size, and the size is a matter of personal choice.

THE ESPALIER

In some instances the walls of a small patio offer a perfect opportunity to espalier the fig tree. Long ago the French people learned to train their fruit trees, not only against farm house walls but out in the fields as well. To espalier is to train a tree to two arms or into the shape of a U. When branches are trained into four or six arms, that is, two or three on each side of the center, the term used is Palmette Verrier espalier. The English gardeners introduced the Fan espalier with a number of branches allowed to grow in the shape of a fan. They also use the Gridiron espalier, a lower and much wider form of the Palmette, slightly resembling a pitch-

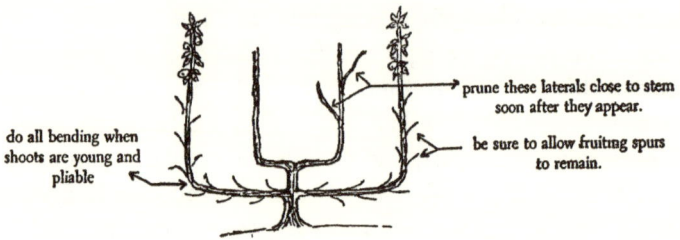

do all bending when
shoots are young and
pliable

prune these laterals close to stem
soon after they appear.

be sure to allow fruiting spurs
to remain.

Palmette Verrier Espalier

fork in shape. Any of these methods can be used against a wall or trellis.

To train the tree in the field is to stretch the branches on wire or cord, hence the term "cordon". This method may be single, with one branch stretched horizontally from each side of the main trunk, or triple cordon, with three tiered branches stretched horizontally on each side of the center trunk. While we have no fields in which to try this method, planting a row of pear trees along a driveway and training them cordon fashion would be most effective. I suggested the pear in this last instance because I think the fig needs a solid background on which to be espaliered.

Here we tend to go at the espalier a little more informally. The planting, feeding and spraying are the same as for the regular fig tree but you must prune so that you keep the branches to a definite number to suit the space. Usually, from the center trunk one to three branches on each side are trained for some little distance horizontally, then bent gently and turned vertically, allowing the arms to grow as high as the garden wall or to whatever point you desire. The branching must be started low and this is encouraged by heading back the main shoot and pruning all unwanted branches as they begin to grow. When you cut unnecessary shoots by all means cut them all the way back to the branch from which they sprout. Never leave a stub. Do all bending of the branches when they are young and pliable. The older they get the more brittle they are.

Sink ring bolts into the wall and attach the branches with raffia taking care not to tie too tightly. Espaliering is successful only if you are determined to pay close attention to the specimen so grown.

THE PAPAYA TREE

The PAPAYA TREE, *Carica papaya* belongs to the Pawpaw Family and is in reality a tough-stemmed herb that grows erect to fifteen and twenty feet in the lower South and into Florida.

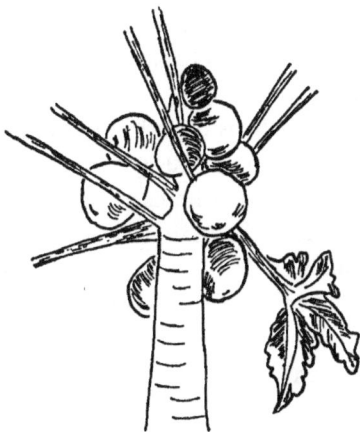

Papaya Fruit

The Papaya's leaves are dull green, seven-lobed and quite broad. The melon-like fruit hangs from the axils of the leaves. This tree can almost be considered an annual because it grows, blossoms and bears fruit within the year of planting. I started my seeds in December in fibre pots and placed them where they were protected from frost until I set them out in the spring. I planted them on the south side of the garden because these trees are susceptible to cold. Papayas will grow in ordinary soil but thrive best in rich loam that is well-drained. They are hungry feeders so fertilize with a liquid food since the shallow roots allow for little or no soil cultivation. Use a well-balanced fertilizer.

In July and August, the flowers appear. The female flowers are pale yellow and funnel-shaped, about one inch long and are close to the stem. The male flowers are borne on long slender pedicels, are more fragile than the female and resemble stephanotis blooms. The male and female flowers may or may not be on the same tree but only the female tree bears fruit. After pollinization the fruits begin to grow like melons, first green, then light yellow and finally bright yellow-orange. Pick only when fully ripe. When open the inside resembles a melon with black seeds. It can be eaten as breakfast fruit or as a dessert or salad with a little lime or lemon juice added to bring out the taste. Papaya trees are a sight to behold when they are heavy with fruit.

If you are as unfortunate as I was to lose your male tree to severe weather and the bees are not as busy as they should be, do as I did. Hunt up a neighbor or friend who has a male tree in bloom, borrow some of the pollen from the male flowers and apply to the open flowers of the female tree. In no time you will see the fruit forming and soon you will have passersby leaning over your garden fence, asking whether you have a cocoanut tree or "What *is* that tree growing in your garden?"

THE CITRUS TREES

All Citrus trees do better in the humid coastal South rather than in the more arid inland regions. They need light porous soil, good drainage and a fertilizer containing nitrogen, phosphoric acid and potash in ratios of 5–10–5 under ordinary circumstances, or 8–10–3 for trees that seem to have difficulty in bearing. They also need magnesium, calcium, boron, zinc, iron and manganese—nearly all of the trace elements, to a pH of about 6. So check the planting area regularly to keep them happy. Apply the feed under the trees just outside the spread of the branches so that the feeder roots that lie near the surface can assimilate the fertilizer. Feed in early spring and then in June, applying one-quarter pound of nitrate of soda on one-year-old trees, one-half pound on older trees.

Planting time is winter, from December fifteenth to February fifteenth. Place the trees from twelve to fifteen feet apart and plant the balled roots so that the tree sits at least two inches higher than it was in the nursery to allow for settling. Then hill up the soil around the trunk saucer-fashion to keep the water from running off too quickly.

Pruning to the extent of thinning out the inner branches should be done only after the tree has become well established. After the initial pruning only trimming of dead or withered branches is necessary. By no means trim immediately after a freeze; wait until new growth appears and then you can see just what has to be eliminated.

I suggest the Duncan variety of the GRAPEFRUIT, *Citrus grandis* or the *paradisi* variety, either of which takes four to six years to produce. The *paradisi* has a spreading growth habit; its leaves are broad and its white flowers large. The fruit is usually pale yellow and heavy, bending the branches. Grapefruit sometimes grow to maturity with bumps on the fruit. Control this scab fungus by spraying before and after blooming season with a copper spray. Very often you will notice a yellowing of the leaves meaning that the tree is suffering from a deficiency of magnesium. Apply one or two pounds of low-grade Epsom Salt to correct this condition.

In the LEMON Family, *Citrus Limonis* the Meyer or *Limonia Meyerii* has small leaves, spreading branches (albeit a semi-dwarf) and takes three to five years to produce good table fruit. The Everbearing and the Ponderosa varieties are also good. *Limonia ponderosa* grows from eight to ten feet, shows more spines and bears larger fruit than the Meyer.

The ORANGE is *Citrus sinensis*, a tree that reaches twenty-five to thirty feet. Its spines are rather soft and the regular branches bear dark green leathery leaves. The flowers are white and fragrant

Meyer Lemons

and the fruit is sweet. The Louisiana Sweet, the Washington Navel, the Hamlin and the Omaii Satsuma are good. The Satsuma is the hardiest of all. The variety Deliciosa in the MANDARIN or TANGERINE group *Citrus nobilis* do well. These last two groups bear in four to six years.

LIMES, *Citrus aurantifolia* must be grown where frosts are unknown, hence I do not recommend them; instead try the LIMEQUAT, a hardier hybrid and the ROUND KUMQUAT, *Fortunella margarita* and *F. japonica*. The Kumquat makes an attractive small tree reaching six to eight feet. Tiny white sweet-smelling flowers are evident in summer, replaced in winter by miniature edible fruit which is used also for marmalade.

All Citrus trees should be kept mulched the year round. Pine needles are good for this purpose.

Keeping the trees clean will not eliminate pests and diseases. The Citrus group is subject to white fly and its resulting black mold, which you can rout with an oil emulsion if the temperature is moderate, or with malathion at other times. Rust is treated with applications of sulphur; mealybug with nicotine sulphate; caterpillars with arsenate of lead. Just be careful not to injure the plants around the fruit trees when you spray.

Dwarf forms of the Orange and Lemon trees make interesting

specimen for the patio. I have had several Meyer Lemons in pots for years and I did not have to treat them for anything until this spring when I found a few white flies.

Mangos, *Mangifera indica* and the pineapple *Ananas sativus* while not Citrus fruits, bear in the warmest parts of central Florida and in southern Florida proper. See chapter on Potted Plants.

✂ 7 ✂

Shrubs for the Landscape

The type of house in which you live will influence your choice of plant material for the garden. A formal dwelling on stately lines will almost demand the tall stiff hedge and dignified tree, while today's low ranch-type home asks for the informal, gracefully branching shrubs and trees. When in doubt consult your architect or landscape designer. He is in the position to suggest the texture and types of greens as well as the construction of the walls and walks that do much for a successful garden.

After suggestions are made study the list to decide which shrubs will do best in your soil conditions and exposures. You will also have to make a decision about the colors. After all you are the one who will have to live with the things you plant.

I hope that the following lists of shrubs will assist you in planning your garden. I have noted next to each one whether it is evergreen or deciduous and the (s) next to some means that those particular ones will do well in semi-shady spots. You may find some of these same shrubs mentioned again under Flowering Shrubs, but in these lists I am concerned with background planting. Following the listed shrubs I have made a few recommendations for planting and care.

**TALL SHRUBS TO BE USED
AGAINST HOUSE OR GARDEN WALL**

A B E L I A , *Abelia triflora* evergreen, to ten feet.

A R B O R - V I T A E , *Thuja occidentalis* to thirty feet or more, *T. compacta* to fifteen feet, *T. pyramidalis* to twelve feet, *T. aurea conspicua* or the Golden Spire, upright to ten feet. Evergreen.

A Z A L E A S , of the *Rhododendron* Family. I suggest varieties of the *Indicum* species for height. Evergreen. (s)

B A M B O O , *Bambusa vulgaris* or Feathery Bamboo from twenty to fifty feet, *Bambusa Arundinaria japonica* to ten feet, semi-evergreen.

B A R B E R R Y , *Berberis polyantha* semi-evergreen, to twelve feet; *Berberis vulgaris*, the common Barberry, and *B. aristata* evergreen, to eight feet. (s)

B O X W O O D , *Buxus sempervirens* the common Box, slow-growing and evergreen, to ten feet or more. Bark and leaves contain toxic poison. Boxwood turning yellow to brown to red in winter could be signs of the infection of the roots by nematodes. Consult your nurseryman for a suitable fungicide. Before you do this however, feed the plants with a liquid fertilizer containing trace elements. This may be all that it needs. Keep Boxwood happy with a semi-annual (March and October) application of well-rotted manure. (s)

B U T T E R F L Y B U S H , *Buddleia Davidii* to eight feet, *B. madagascariensis* to fifteen feet. Semi-evergreen.

C A M E L L I A , *Camellia japonica* and *Sasanqua* evergreen, to fifteen feet. (s) See Flowering Shrubs for details on varieties.

C A S T O R B E A N , *Ricinus communis* a tropical annual grown in lower South and Florida. Stems and leaves are green (*R. africanus*) or red (*macrocarpus*), large and shaped almost like those of the Rice Paper Plant although thinner in texture and smaller in size. Insignificant flowers are followed by spiny round fruit borne in clusters and these may be green or red depending on the variety. They make a valuable item to the flower arranger, the red variety being more in demand. Seeds may be broadcast in the open ground in March, April or May. When a hard freeze forced me to cut back my Viburnum hedge I used the fast-growing Castor Bean as a substitute until the hedge had reasserted itself. The Castor Bean usually comes up the following year from seeds dropped by parent plants. Remember the seeds are poisonous.

CHERRY-LAUREL, *Prunus Laurocerasus caroliniana* although sometimes used as a tree is best as a hedge. A fast grower, it can be clipped to any size. Evergreen. (s)

COCCULUS, *Cocculus laurifolius* or the Laurel Leaf Snailseed, to fifteen feet in lower South. Its drooping branches of evergreen leaves that always look as though they have been polished, makes it ideal for screening purposes.

COMMON PRIVET, *Ligustrum vulgare* to fifteen feet, *L. lucidum* or *japonicum* to twenty feet. Evergreen. The new introduction, *Ligustrum* Suwanee River is particularly hardy. All are subject to white fly for which you must spray with an oil emulsion or an all-purpose malathion solution. (s)

ESCALLONIA, of the Saxifrage Family, evergreen. I suggest *E. floribunda*, to twelve feet. Likes neutral or slightly alkaline soil. Not too hardy where frosts are heavy for long periods.

FIRETHORN, *Pyracantha coccinea* var. *Lalandii* grows as a bush to twenty feet or more and has bright red berries, *P. leucocarva* has yellow berries; evergreen.

HOLLY, *Ilex opaca* or the American Holly, sometimes to forty feet; evergreen. *Ilex cornuta Burfordii*, Chinese Holly with large leaves, to fifteen feet. *Ilex cassine* or Dahoon, as it is frequently called, will grow to tree proportions of twenty feet anywhere in the South if you trim off the lower branches. Its bright red berries are attractive during the winter and it is completely adjusted to the different conditions prevailing through the South. (s)

H O N E Y S U C K L E , *Lonicera tatarica* to ten feet; nearly evergreen. (s)

I T A L I A N   C Y P R E S S , *Cupressus sempervirens stricta* is still seen occasionally in the landscape. Its liking for dry, alkaline soils makes it good for the inland arid sections of the South. Tall, narrow and slow-growing to a pointed tip, it is a most attractive background plant for the long vista.

J A P A N E S E   M A G N O L I A , *Magnolia Soulangeana* to twelve and fourteen feet; deciduous.

J U N I P E R S , *Juniperus chinensis* var. *sylvestris* light green pyramidal, to fifteen feet; *J. excelsa stricta* or Greek Juniper, bluish-green with spiny leaves, to forty feet; *J. virginiana Canaertii* Red Cedar, and *J. virginiana glauca* the Blue Cedar, to twenty feet; both are pyramidal and both can be sheared. The Pfitzer Juniper, *J. pfitzeriana* develops horizontally and eventually reaches eight to ten feet. The Irish Juniper, *J. hibernica* is the slim gray-green upright bush that you see so often in doorway plantings. All are evergreen and most of them reach greater heights farther north.

K E R R I A , *Kerria japonica grandiflora* to eight feet, deciduous.(s)

L I G U S T R U M , see Common Privet.

M O C K O R A N G E , *Philadelphus pubescens* eight to ten feet, deciduous.

M Y R T L E , *Myrtus communis* to ten or more feet, evergreen. (s)

N A N D I N A , *Nandina domestica* to eight feet, evergreen. (s)

O R E G O N   G R A P E   H O L L Y , *Mahonia bealei* to ten feet, with yellow flowers in spring followed by bluish-black berries. Needs acid soil. Evergreen but not as hardy as the variety *aquifolium* which is discussed under Flowering Shrubs.

P H O T I N I A , *Photinia serrulata* to twenty feet, is evergreen with bronzy-red foliage when young. Fast grower in sun.

P I T T O S P O R U M , *Pittosporum Tobira* to ten or more feet, evergreen.

PODOCARPUS, *Podocarpus macrophylla Maki* is most popular through the South for clipped hedges and screens. So many of us have been under the impression that Yew and Podocarpus were one and the same plant. Actually, Podocarpus belongs to the Yew Family, in the group with needle-type foliage. Growing from ten to thirty feet, its leaves are two to three inches long and medium-textured. Its flowers are incidental but its great merit lies in the fact that it can be sheared so beautifully. *P. nagi*, the Japanese Podocarpus, is erect, formal and good for corners though more tender than the *macrophylla*. *P. elongata* is finely textured and sprawly in growth habits. It grows very slowly. All are evergreen.

POMEGRANATE, *Punica Granatum* to fifteen feet, semi-evergreen.

SWEET OLIVE, *Osmanthus fragrans* to thirty feet, evergreen. (s)

VIBURNUM, *Viburnum suspensum* to fifteen feet, V. *odoratissimum* to twenty-five feet, evergreen. (s)

YAUPON, *Ilex vomitoria* to twenty-five feet, evergreen. Will tolerate winds and salt sprays.

YEW, of the genus *Taxaceae*, offers *Taxus baccata* of spreading habits, to forty feet. Evergreen.

SMALLER SHRUBS TO USE IN
FRONT OF BACKGROUND PLANTING

ARBOR-VITAE, *Thuja occidentalis Bonita* with rounded growth habits, to six feet. *T.* Golden Berkman, also to six feet, popular in lower South. Evergreen.

BAMBOO, *Bambusa disticha* or B. *multiplex* to six feet, does best in lower sections of South. This semi-deciduous fernleaf variety will grow higher but stands shearing well and makes a luxuriant gray-green screen. To avoid having roots take over the garden, once a year dig a trench between the Bamboo and the lawn or flower beds. Dig deep enough so that all roots are cut. In planting in the spring break roots into clumps and set divisions about six feet apart. Cut canes back to nearly ground level.

B A R B E R R Y , *Berberis Thunbergii* and B. *Darwinii* to five feet, the former semi-evergreen, and brilliantly colored in fall; the latter evergreen but tender to frost. B. *buxifolia* from six to ten feet, hardy and evergreen. B. *julianae,* often called Wintergreen Barberry makes excellent hedge, growing to six feet. Flowers are yellow in the spring, foliage is almost dense enough to hide autumn blueblack berries; evergreen. All do best in moist loam and light shade. (s)

B O X W O O D , *Buxus japonica* or Japanese Box to six feet, stands shearing well and will thrive as far south as mid Florida. B. *harlandi Hance* reaches four feet, with leaves larger than other Box. Feed twice a year, in October and March, with well-rotted manure. Keep well watered and well trimmed. Does well in sun or shade.

B R I D A L   W R E A T H , *Spiraea reevesiana* to six feet, S. *Thunbergii* to four feet, deciduous. S. *reevesiana* blooms later than S. *Thunbergii* and is almost evergreen in the lower South. They are both more prolific in cooler sections of the southern region. See Flowering Shrubs for other varieties.

C O M M O N   P R I V E T , *Ligustrum sinense* and *amurense,* var. *Stauntonii,* with spreading habits, to five or six feet; evergreen. (s)

E S C A L L O N I A , *Escallonia Berteriana* to six feet, evergreen.

F I R E T H O R N , *Pyracantha angustifolia* and P. *crenulata* var. *yunnanensis* to five feet. Evergreen.

F L O W E R I N G   A L M O N D , *Prunus triloba* to five feet, P. *glandulosa* to four feet. Deciduous.

F L O W E R I N G   Q U I N C E , *Chaenomeles lagenaria* from six to ten feet, deciduous.

H O L L Y , *Ilex crenata convexa* and I. *crenata rotundifolia* to six feet. Evergreen. (s)

H O N E Y S U C K L E , *Lonicera fragrantissima* to five feet. Almost evergreen.

H Y D R A N G E A , *Hydrangea macrophylla* to four feet, deciduous.

JASMINE, *Jasminum floridum* is graceful drooping shrub with yellow flowers; *J. humile* upright, *J. primulinum* more trailing, both yellow and all three of these to five feet. *J. sambac* or Grand Duke, white-flowered and to six feet. All evergreen in the South except in severe winters.

JUNIPER, *Juniper communis* var. *hibernica* the Irish columnar, to six feet; variety *depressa*, the prostrate juniper, to four feet; evergreen.

LILAC, *Syringa persica laciniata* or the Persian Lilac, is not recommended for the lower South. This plant likes full sun and rich loamy soil. Its fine leaves and beautiful blossoms have tempted me on several occasions, with no success. Lilacs like cooler climates and longer winters. To six feet. Deciduous.

·OREGON GRAPE HOLLY, *Mahonia aquifolium* three to six feet, evergreen. (s)

PHOTINIA, *Photinia glabra* from six to eight feet, evergreen. This one does well in almost all sections of the South and is desirable for cutting when the new foliage shows its vivid red coloring. Plant in sunny spot to enhance scarlet tones.

PITTOSPORUM, *Pittosporum Tobira variegata* or Japanese Pittosporum, three to six feet; evergreen. (s)

ROSE, *Rosa odorata* varieties lend color to the landscape. Although I recognize the fact that most roses need a special bed of their own in order to do their best, there are a few small bushes that will do well treated as a shrub. The old favorite Louis Phillippe, *Rosa chinensis* with its dark red blossoms, has been used for years as a low-growing hedge that not only stands pruning well but is faithful in producing its blooms, even though they are not of the prize-winning group.

SAGO CYCAS, SAGO PALM, *Cycas revoluta* mentioned in the chapter on Trees, has for years been mistakenly called a palm. It is actually related to the Pine and Yew Families and to my friend the Ginkgo tree. Very slow-growing to six feet, this one makes an interesting and unusual note in the whole southern landscape, especially when the orange fruit appears in the tan fuzzy crown of the female plant. It does well in sun or shade and is resistant to heat and drought. It is free of pests and diseases except in Florida where it is sometimes attacked by blight for which there is no cure as yet.

S N O W B E R R Y , *Symphoricarpus albus* to six feet, deciduous.(s)

S W E E T   B U S H , *Clethra alnifolia* three to six feet, semi-evergreen.

S W E E T   S H R U B , *Calycanthus floridus* six to eight feet, deciduous. (s)

V I B U R N U M , *Viburnum suspensum* to six feet in colder sections of the South and to fifteen feet in warmer areas. Evergreen if not killed back in prolonged freeze. This shrub makes a very beautiful hedge that more than tolerates clipping. Small white flowers incidental to its lush foliage. V. *acerifolium* is compact and low-growing to four or five feet. Both will thrive in sun or shade and although they are considered pest free, in the deep South they are sometimes attacked by white fly which leads to the sooty mold on the leaves. Spray with an oil emulsion.

W E I G E L A , *Diervilla florida* of the Honeysuckle Family, to six feet. Deciduous.

W I L D   C A M E L L I A , *Stewartia* or *Stuartia malachodendron* from six to twelve feet. S. *pentagyna* var. *grandiflora* also desirable. Deciduous.

Y E W , *Taxus baccata*, var. *fastigiata* from six to twelve feet, is columnar with thick upright branches, spirally arranged leaves and is remarkably beautiful and fine for formal setting. *Taxus Hatfieldi* is one of the finest pyramidal English Yews. *Cephalotaxus Harringtonia*, another member of the Yew Family, is graceful in habit. All evergreen. (s)

DWARF SHRUBS THAT MAKE GOOD HEDGES AND FILLERS

Dwarf plant material is always being sought to break the long high lines of the taller shrubs and to frame ranch-type houses.

ALTERNANTHERA, to three or four inches, green and cream or green and red leaves. Semi-evergreen.

ARBOR-VITAE, *Thuja occidentalis globosa* variety Tom Thumb and *T. aurea nana,* to two feet. Evergreen.

ARDISIA, *Ardisia japonica* grows to eighteen inches. A good dwarf form that seems to be doing well all over the South. It is miniature replica of the larger Ardisia described under Flowering Shrubs. (s)

ARTEMISIA, though perennial herbs of the Composite Family, they do make fine small shrubs in the garden and are in demand for the gray-white aromatic foliage. A. *abrotanum* grows in any soil to two and a half to three feet tall, is finely textured, stands heat and is disease and pest free. *Artemisia albula* the Silver King, likes lots of moisture, grows to about three feet, and gives a misty-white appearance. There is a new variety called Silver Mount which has a compact habit of growth to about six inches in height and ten inches in diameter. This one prefers dry conditions. A. *absinthium* has silvery-white leaves and is one of the sources of the liqueur, absinthe. All of these are often called Sage-brush. They should be pruned back each year to keep their compactness. They show their tiny flowers, usually white, in late summer so prune in early spring.

AZALEAS KURUME, *Rhododendron obtusum japonicum* make fine dwarf shrubs throughout the southern region. Compact and horizontal-branching in growth habits, they rarely reach three feet in height. Leaves are small and evergreen and the plants may be had in a variety of colors. See Azaleas in Flowering Shrubs for name varieties and culture.

BAMBOO, *Bambusa pygmaea* is a semi-evergreen that grows to two feet. Roots of this one have to be controlled just like those of the larger relatives. Variety *Sasa* is a fairly new intermediate type growing to two and a half feet. It is very lovely. Bamboos are best set out before June in sun or semi-shade. Feed occasionally with a fertilizer high in nitrogen. Should you see any scale, spray with an oil emulsion early in the spring. Bamboos range in cane size from pencil thickness to a width of four inches.

BARBERRY, *Berberis verruculosa* reaches three feet and has dark reddish foliage that is lined with silvery-red. It produces the tiny flowers that are characteristic of the whole family and is at its best in cooler sections of the South. The variety B. *Thunbergii atropurpurea* or the Red-leaved Barberry, grows well all over our section, reaching two feet and liking full sun. The miniature of this one is the Dwarf Barberry Crimson Pygmy, slow-growing to one foot but very full. It must have sun to keep its bright red foliage. Mild winters are kind to the foliage (you seldom notice leaves falling) but I will have to call them semi-evergreen because normally cold winters cause most of them to lose their leaves. And remember, with the exception of a few, Barberries are thorny.

BOXWOOD, *Buxus sempervirens* var. *suffruticosa* and *Buxus koreana* var. *microphylla* are both fine dwarf forms. The former is commonly known as English Boxwood and in English gardens of old these plants and their taller varieties were sheared to represent animals, birds and minarets. Such topiary is still done today in Colonial Williamsburg. The Korean Box is said to be hardy enough to try where other Boxwood ordinarily will not grow. While all Boxwood will grow in any type of soil it heartily dislikes chemical fertilizers so as I have recommended before give it the organic food that it loves, either well-rotted manure or cottonseed meal. Make sure that it gets enough moisture, good drainage, adequate light or full sun. Cuttings may be taken anytime from October until spring, and they must be given shade to succeed. Plant the young Boxwood from six to eight inches apart. Evergreen. Leaves poisonous. (s)

Transplant Boxwood from September to November and from February to April, making a point to move it with a good ball of earth around the roots. Replant about two inches above original level so that the specimen, when settled, will eventually be at the primary soil level. Box that begins to look old and scratchy should be doctored with a dose of organic fertilizer such as dried blood or cottonseed meal in the fall. Spread it over the soil and wash it in with a gentle spray of the hose. Then in March chicken manure mixed with a little bonemeal or superphosphate may be administered around the plants. Mulch well over the summer. This particular care should bring the plant back to its original vigorous health and is given the plant in lieu of the usual feedings.

D E U T Z I A , *Deutzia gracilis* to three feet; *D. Sieboldiana* to two feet; deciduous.

D W A R F   F L O W E R I N G   Q U I N C E , *Chaenomeles japonica* to three feet; deciduous.

G A R D E N I A   R A D I C A N S , *Gardenia jasminoides radicans* grows to two feet with waxy variegated leaves; branches reach out horizontally. *G. stricta nana* grows more upright. Both have tiny flowers exactly like the large Gardenia and both have the same lovely scent. Like the larger bushes these dwarfs are also subject to white fly which leads inevitably to the black sooty mold on the leaves that prevents them from breathing. So if you must have Gardenias make up your mind to take care of them. Use an oil emulsion if the attack is bad; ordinary soap and water will sometimes do the trick in milder cases and an all-purpose spray containing malathion is effective. See Flowering Shrubs for culture.

H O L L Y , *Ilex crenata Bullata* and *I. convexa* are dwarf forms with dense growth. *Ilex crenata helleri* known commercially as Heller Holly is a compact grower to two feet and can be used all over the South if sufficiently watered. Others to try are the dwarf Yaupon, *Ilex vomitoria nana; Ilex cornuta rotunda* or the dwarf Chinese Holly, which is grown more for foliage than for berries; *I. crenata rotundifolia* makes a good substitute for Boxwood. Evergreen.

K E R R I A , *Kerria japonica* var. *vittato-ramosa* and var. *argenteo-variegata* from two to three feet, deciduous. (s)

L I G U S T R U M , *Ligustrum vicari* is a new dwarf that is golden yellow and green. Grows from eighteen inches to two feet. Needs full sun. Evergreen.

MALPIGHIA, *Malpighia coccigera* though a relative, is not the same as the Barbados Cherry referred to in the list of Flowering Shrubs. *Coccigera* has holly-shaped evergreen leaves and small pink spring flowers followed by red fruits. Likes partial shade and moist loam and does best in the lower sections of our South.

MOCKORANGE, *Philadelphus microphyllus* to three feet, deciduous. (s)

MYRTLE, *Myrtus communis* var. *microphylla* dwarf form with small dark green leaves perfect for border planting. Evergreen. *Myrtus communis compacta* rarely reaches three feet and does best in the hot dry areas. Evergreen leaves have a delightful aromatic scent. Var. *italica* also attractive. These true myrtles like full sun and slightly alkaline soil.

OREGON GRAPE HOLLY., *Mahonia repens* rarely grows over one foot high. Good as underplanting to trees and leggy shrubs. Evergreen. (s)

PFITZER JUNIPER, *Juniperus chinensis procumbens* is dense and low and good for foundation planting throughout South. Horizontal in growth habits, its foliage is a gray-blue-green. It likes sun, wind and dry conditions. Given room, it will spread from eight to ten feet horizontally. Evergreen.

POMEGRANATE, *Punicus Granatum nana* from two to three feet, with narrow leaves, small orange-red flowers in summer followed by burnt-orange colored fruit in fall. Almost evergreen in the lower South, it is deciduous in colder sections. Pest and disease-free, it tolerates any soil and exposure. Lovely for patios and for small gardens.

SERISSA, *Serissa foetida* to two feet in warmer areas; evergreen. This one has small, dark green glossy leaves and tiny white winter flowers. Needs protection from north winds. *S. foetida variegata* has yellow-margined leaves, also evergreen. Prune annually for compactness. Makes dainty hedge.

ST. JOHN'S WORT, *Hypericum Chinense* and *Moserianum* the latter called the Goldflower, to two feet, semi-deciduous. *H. patulum Henryii* to three feet; quite hardy.

SWEET SHRUB, *Calycanthus fertilis nana* to three feet. Deciduous.

VIBURNUM, *Viburnum Opulus nanum* shrubby evergreen to two feet. (s)

YEW, *Taxus canadensis stricta* to one foot. Evergreen. (s)

ORNAMENTALS TO DRAW ATTENTION TO GARDEN CORNERS OR PARTICULAR SPOTS IN THE LANDSCAPE

ALOE, *Hesperaloe parviflora* grows well in dry Texas. Its twelve-inch foliage resembles that of the Spanish Bayonet and its chartreuse-green or rose-colored four-foot flower stalks show up in summer. A slow-growing, perennial, succulent member of the Lily Family.

CAMELLIA JAPONICA, choice of variety up to individual gardener. See Flowering Shrubs.

CENTURY PLANT, *Agave americana* forms low mound. Pale green leaves, very large and recurved, tipped with thorns that should be cut as soon as the leaf unfurls. Flower spikes sometimes twelve to twenty feet or more, look like candelabra and are sent aloft after ten to twenty years of favorable growing. Resistant to salt spray and strong winds and poor soil. It takes a lot of cold to freeze back this plant. *Agave americana marginata*'s leaves have wide yellow margins. There are numerous other varieties.

NORFOLK ISLAND PINE, *Araucaria excelsa* sometimes misnamed the Monkey Puzzle Tree, is such a slow grower that it can be enjoyed in its juvenile state for many years before it becomes a tree. As a tree it is still an ornamental. *Araucaria glauca* with white tipped branches is new and beautiful; it is known as the "Silver Star." Both varieties make excellent pot plants too. For those of you who are curious, the Monkey Puzzle Tree is *Araucaria imbricata* or *A. auracana.*

PAMPAS GRASS, *Cortaderia argentea* to ten feet, with long graceful plumes. Perennial.

PONY TAIL, *Nolina Beaucarnea*, is a member of the Lily Family that has the ability of storing water in its bulbous base for several months. It is an exotic that is as attractive in a garden urn as it is in the open ground. Its narrow, bright green leaves resemble those of the Yucca, except that those of the Pony Tail are not equipped with spines. The leaves grow straight up from the center of the plant and then droop over gracefully. It thrives best in sandy soil and full sun and slowly reaches a height of about twenty feet. Feed in early spring and again in May, preferably with an organic sludge that will furnish nitrogen at an even, slow rate through the summer. Never dormant in the lower South, it may be planted anytime except during spells of very cold weather.

RIBBON GRASS, *Phalaris arundinacea picta* to six feet. Perennial.

YUCCA, *Yucca aloifolia* and *Y. gloriosa* sometimes known as the Spanish Bayonet and Spanish Dagger, grow to three or four feet while creamy-white flower spikes reach six feet or more. Both are lovely throughout the South but dangerous to children and pets because of the needle-sharp tips of the dark green leaves. Adam's Needle is *Yucca filamentosa*, native of Florida. All are evergreen and do well under adverse conditions of wind and weather provided they are given sun. Pest and disease free.

Caution! Please don't choose your shrubs for their sizes at the time of purchase. Always remember that shrubs sometimes outgrow their location and the results will be over-crowded corners. Instead of constantly trimming a plant to keep it small enough for good landscaping, acquaint yourselves with the dwarf species and buy a small variety in the first place.

PLANTING AND MOVING

Take care of your shrubs. All of the evergreens, be they coniferous or broadleaved, will grow in a well-drained soil that is kept moist. Since the evergreens have no true dormant season, they may be moved if properly balled in burlap, anytime of the year except during the extreme heat of the summer. The best time for moving deciduous materials is in the fall and winter when the flow of sap has practically stopped. Both may be planted in late winter and very early spring.

Get your hedge materials off to a flying start by preparing the beds or spots before planting. Either spade in a good layer of fertilizer and turn the earth well before digging the hole into which you plan to sink the balled specimen, or dig a trench the length of the line to be planted. Dig it deep and wide enough to spread the roots if it is bare-rooted, or for roots to spread if it is balled. Incidentally, soak bare-rooted plants for several hours before planting. Always make the hole into which your plant is to go about one foot wider and deeper than the ball around the plant. Give the bottom of the hole a good coverage of brickbats, well-rotted manure and leafmold and fill in the next several inches with good garden soil. It is always a good idea to plant deciduous shrubs to the same depth in which they stood in the nursery, placing evergreens about one inch lower than they were previously planted. Lower the plant and pack the ground around the ball with a heavy weight, loosening the sacking at the top of the ball. Cover with loamy soil and edge with a miniature levee about three inches high to compel the water to go to the roots. Water well until established.

SPACING

A good rule of thumb is to find out as near as possible the height of the plant at maturity, then space your young specimens about two-thirds of this measure apart. This gives room for growth. Or set dwarf shrubs from one to two feet apart; medium ones, two to three feet apart; and large plants, three to four feet apart. The results may seem empty at first but you plant for the future not for the present. Actually the space allowed between bushes depends on the particular plant, its ultimate size and growth habits.

FEEDING

All shrubs will do well after being planted in a good well-balanced loamy soil but after about a year of akaline rainfall and absorption of soil nutrients by the plant, feeding should be carried on at regular intervals. I like to feed my hedge materials, both broadleaf and coniferous, twice a year—in March and again in May with a complete fertilizer such as 5–10–5. It can either be spread over the ground near the base of the shrub or more effectively, plugged into several holes in the earth near the base of the trunk. In either case, mulch and then water well. *Do not* plug the feed to those shrubs that have shallow root systems, such as Camellias and Azaleas. That method is reserved for those trees and shrubs whose roots run deep. Do not feed any nitrogenous material to your shrubs after June because it promotes new fall growth that is liable to be killed in cold weather. When the plant requires acid soil supplement cottonseed meal with one of the acidifying agents mentioned in Soils and Additives. Some shrubs like the Boxwood, should be fed with a top dressing of well-rotted cow manure twice a year, in March and in October. Do not allow the fertilizer to touch the branches and trunk of the plant.

There are many named plant foods on the market and when using these be sure to follow the directions on the package. Besides plant foods *per se* there are several supplemental agents recommended for the plants that need "toning up".

MULCHING

Mulches are so necessary to successful gardening! They serve as an insulation against heat and cold, they keep moisture around the plant and they help keep out weeds and eventually add to the soil content of the bed.

There are several types of mulches. Pine needles are excellent and form a light covering. Peat moss and oak leaves are slightly acid in reaction and bagasse is good if it doesn't bring ants. I was once told that bagasse contains nineteen pounds of plant food per ton, same as cow manure.

MULCHING AND CARE BEFORE AND AFTER FREEZING WEATHER

The best way to protect your outdoor plants and shrubs from freezing is to wet the earth surrounding the plant thoroughly before the drop in temperature and then pile a thick mulch up around the trunk. If you haven't any of the mulches mentioned above available, use burlap or old newspapers. Then when the thaw starts remove the mulch and water copiously. Any ice that forms on a plant in a freeze acts as an insulation. It is the fast drying-out of the roots after a freeze that causes so much loss of plants. The ice protects but also dehydrates ground and plant, and to water well also after a freeze is to replace the moisture. Wrapping the top of a shrub with paper or old sheets and leaving the roots exposed offers little protection from the cold. It really does no good at all. The whole plant, such as Hibiscus, Poinsettias and tender annuals can be covered with sacking or paper or boxes weighted down around the base with bricks or stones. Sweet peas may also be protected in this manner but everything should be watered before covering. For a prized plant, one that should not have the wrapping touch the foliage, drive four stakes around the plant to support the covering. Should Hibiscus or Poinsettias show blackening from the freeze despite care, prune the branches just below the blackened area immediately after the freeze, otherwise the frozen sap will continue to drop back and blacken more of the stem. For all other plants be very slow about pruning until time has told just how much damage was done, even though it means tolerating a forlorn-looking garden for a few weeks.

Snowfall actually can serve as a protective blanket. It is a sustained freeze that does damage to plants. Plants that receive direct sun immediately as the thaw begins fare badly while those plants and shrubs that have a chance to warm up before the sun hits them thaw slowly and show very little damage. One thing I beg of you. Remove the wrappings as soon as danger of freeze is over. I have seen plants remain covered for a week at a time, and have also observed their sad state afterwards.

PRUNING

Evergreens require very little pruning especially if they are of the conifer group. Those of the broadleaved family that are used as hedges will naturally need shearing and trimming, but coniferous trees, because they grow outward and upward only at the tips of the branches cannot be pruned in the same manner as deciduous trees and broadleaves. If the tips are pruned heavily conifers will never sprout out again lower down on that same branch, so to keep their conical shape just pinch off regularly a small bit of the new light green terminal growth, and do this in the spring. If this is not done the branches separate and the whole shrub takes on a

PRUNING HEDGES

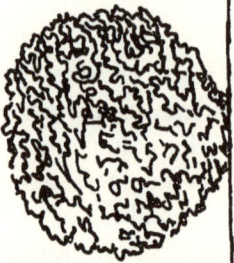

FIGURE 4

FIGURE 3

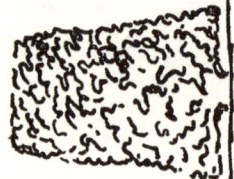

FIGURE 2

FIGURE 1

FIGURES   Prune this way—so that you leave the bottom of the shrub thick and with enough
1 AND 2   leaves on it to absorb sunlight and moisture.

FIGURE 3   This is bad! Sunlight will never reach lower leaves.

FIGURE 4   Boxwood is often clipped thus—fairly successfully

bedraggled appearance. The junipers are fastigiate. You hardly have to worry about them at all.

Unless absolutely necessary, try not to prune your broadleaves during the winter because the cut surfaces furnish added means of evaporation of moisture from the shrub. If there is a freeze and you think that some of the branches have died, wait until the first spring growth appears to be sure that you do not cut off a living part of the plant. For a good clean look for evergreen hedges try to keep them trimmed to a certain height and width by systematic clipping at intervals through the year. Always trim the sides of your hedge so that the bottom is slightly wider than the top. This allows the sun to reach the lower branches and helps keep them thick. To get the top level fasten a string at the level you wish to cut, from one stake to another, pulling it tight. This gives you a guide line for even pruning.

In pruning deciduous shrubs the main idea is to remove dead wood and crowding inner branches so that light and air may readily penetrate the bush. Then clip the outer branches to the shape you desire, cutting above an outside bud. Do this pruning immediately after flowering if the shrub is a spring-blooming variety because this type sets its buds in the fall. If the shrub blooms in summer or fall prune while dormant or very early in the spring. Don't ever prune recklessly. Regard each shrub as a "special patient"; otherwise you lose much of its charm. And please use a sharp clean shears!

PESTS AND INSECTICIDES

Besides the other pests mentioned in the beginning of the chapter on Evergreen, Deciduous and Flowering Trees, in which chapter I also discuss diseases, I want to add the insects most prevalent on the Cedars, Arborvitae, Junipers and other evergreens: the Bagworm and the Red Spider. In the fall the female Bagworm moth lays the eggs in a cocoon-like bag cleverly concocted of bits of leaves

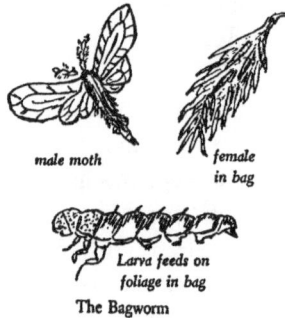

male moth   female
                             in bag

Larva feeds on
foliage in bag
The Bagworm

and web. This bag hangs from the limbs until spring, when the young caterpillars hatch. Pick off the bags and burn them as soon as you see them; or if you are too late in doing this spray in the spring with lead arsenate, three to four tablespoons per gallon of water. You may add one teaspoonful of nicotine sulphate to this mixture if the infestation is bad.

You will notice the Red Spider on Azaleas, and on other shrubs as well, by the sudden reddening and scorching of the foliage and by the appearance of fine webs stretching from leaf to leaf. This mite is so small that you have difficulty seeing it with the naked

Spider Mite   Aphid

eye but you can tell it is there by the look of the foliage. First try routing the spider with a hard spray of the hose and if it persists, spray with nicotine sulphate or Aramite. Nicotine sulphate may also be used against aphids but remember it must be mixed with a soap spreader. Use two teaspoons nicotine sulphate and one tablespoon soap flakes to one gallon of water. Aramite may be purchased as a wettable powder and used according to instructions on the label.

Read up on any new insecticide before purchasing to make sure that it will be compatible with whatever you have been using. Remember never to use anything with sulphur in it in warm weather because sulphur burns the foliage. And never use sulphur on Viburnums since they are "allergic" to it. Sulphur comes in wettable powder and dusting powder forms. Use two tablespoons of the wettable powder to one gallon of water *only* in cool weather. Go to the nurseryman for this powdered sulphur and you will get the fungicide sulphur that you need for your plants. Don't shop at your drug store for flowers of sulphur. It is not the same thing. Ferbam is a good substitute for sulphur in hot weather. It mixes readily with insecticides, thereby allowing you to fight fungi such as mildew and rust and a chewing insect like the aphid at the same time.

Oil emulsions should not be used when temperatures are very high or very low and they should never be used with sulphur. Although there are several trade names on the market the most familiar to us is Volck which is now available combined with lindane. This mixture of oil emulsion and insecticide is said to control aphids, thrips, lacebugs, red spider, mites, scale insects, white flies and mealybugs. Follow the directions on the label.

There are many other insecticides and fungicides on the market, available as wettable powders, emulsions and dusts. By all means read the contents of, and instructions on the package.

✄ 8 ✄

Flowering Shrubs

Flowering shrubs serve as "breaks" or color notes against your background greens. They add to the good composition of your landscape and if you choose wisely, you can insure not only an attractive spring flower display but lovely autumn foliage tones as well. Study the growth habits of the various shrubs. Get to know which ones grow faster than others, which prefer sun to shade, which must be placed in sheltered south corners and which do well in the wide open spaces. Sprawly bushes need lots of room in which to spread. Compact ones can be used to better advantage in smaller areas. Following these suggestions will save you a lot of heartache as well as many backaches. It is always a disappointment to realize that your shrub is sickly and must be moved simply because its requirements were not considered prior to planting.

ABELIA, of the *Caprifoliaceae* or Honeysuckle Family is a many-branching shrub with small green glossy leaves and pinkish-white flowers. *Abelia grandiflora* is one of the hardiest and blooms from June to November through the South down into northern Florida. Its ultimate height, eight feet; evergreen. Grows in any soil provided it is well-drained. Prune regularly to head in succulent canes that appear in the spring.

A B U T I L O N , of the *Malvaceae* or Mallow Family is sometimes known as the Flowering Maple or Chinese Bellflower. A semi-tropical, it will bloom and remain evergreen almost all year if the temperature does not go too far below freezing. I have had the

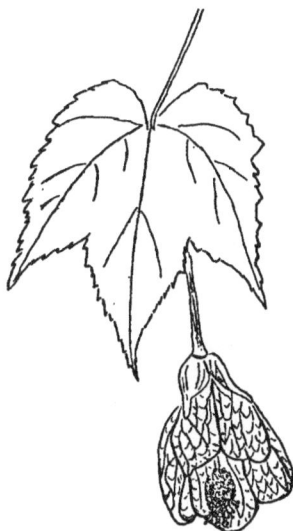

Abutilon

variety *pictum* in my garden for years. The leaves are three-lobed and the flowers, which measure from one to three inches long and look like hanging bells, are orange-yellow with crimson veins. The stamens are exserted as in fuchsias. Abutilon is very easy to root from cuttings and will grow to twenty-five feet. Because I like the plant compact and full, I keep mine down to eight or ten feet and I root cuttings whenever I prune. Boule de Neige is pure white, Erecta is pink, Golden Bell rich yellow, and Sanatan deep red. *Savitzii*, a dwarf, makes a good bedding plant. All will grow in any type of soil.

ACACIA, *Acacia Farnesiana* and A. *longifolia* of the *Legumi-nosae* or Pea Family, sometimes called the Golden Wattle, are hardy evergreen willowy shrubs with yellow flowers in late winter and early spring. Grow to eight or ten feet. The blooms of *Farnesiana* are used in making perfume. The Acacia does well, especially in the lower South. It likes sun and loamy soil. Keep trimmed of dead canes.

ACALYPHA, *Acalypha Wilkesiana* sometimes called the Copper Leaf, is a member of the Spurge Family. This is a tender foliage plant or shrub, much used in summer gardens in the lower South. This particular variety reaches ten feet, has erect alternating bronzy leaves and inconspicuous flower spikes that tend to droop. A. *hispida*, or Red-Hot Cat-Tail is better known as the Chenille Plant. It is grown especially for its droopy red flower spikes that grow much longer than its leaves. The most beautiful Chenille I ever saw grew to the roof of a greenhouse in New Orleans. Because it is tender it weathers the winter better if treated as a pot plant or greenhouse ornament. The variety A. *Macafeana* has green leaves marked with dark red and bronze and is perhaps the most common. A. *musaica* has green leaves with red and orange splotches. A. *triumphans* has very large leaves of green, red and brown. The last three tend to be lovely and thick, making ideal low shrubs for the spring and summer garden.

All of the Acalypha need a soil mixture of three parts loam, one part well-rotted manure and some sharp sand. They are all subject to mealybug, scale and red spider. The best cuttings are made from well-ripened wood. All varieties must be protected from low temperatures. They are tender and do best indoors in the winter months.

ACANTHUS, often considered an herbaceous perennial, is a small shrub that grows three to six feet tall and is noted for its lovely shaped leaves and spiky flowers that shade from white to lavender. I must confess that the thing that first made me curious about the Acanthus was my hearing someone say that it had "pinnatifid" leaves. The word bothered me until I found that it meant leaves deeply cleft, with such clefts reaching almost halfway to the midrib. And that is an exact description of the Acanthus leaf, the leaf that was undoubtedly the inspiration for the acanthus decorations on the capital of the Corinthian columns and on pieces of furniture.

Since the Acanthus is native to temperate zones it should be mulched against freeze. Mine froze back this year but is budding again from the base. It does best in well-drained loamy soil and demands lots of sunshine. There are about twenty species in the family but the best grown in the South are A. *mollis*, to two feet, which is most frequently used as a pot plant, A. *mollis latifolius*, to three feet, and A. *spinosus*, which has very heavily indented leaves. The *latifolius* can be used to advantage in the open ground.

A L L A M A N D A , *Allamanda neriifolia* an evergreen relative of the Allamanda vine and a member of the Dogbane Family, does not climb but remains a shrub to about three feet in height. It bears small yellow flowers and pointed leaves, is not attacked by bugs or disease and does well in warmer sections of the South, down through southern Florida.

A L T H E A , or Rose of Sharon *Hibiscus syriacus* is a slender deciduous shrub with flowers ranging in color from white to mauve depending on variety. Reaching fifteen feet, the foliage is incidental to the flowers which bloom over a long period of summer and fall. The double-bloom varieties are prettier. Mine is a double which appears magenta color in bud and opens to a luscious shade of pink. The Althea demands no care at all, is fast growing and stands clipping very well. Not recommended for colder sections of the South.

A N G E L ' S T R U M P E T , *Datura arborea* or *D. suaveolens* remains evergreen unless hard freezes occur. Growing to fifteen feet, the white trumpet-shaped flowers of double and triple varieties are beautiful and bloom several times a year. This member of the Nightshade Family is considered an annual in the North; a peren-

nial in the South. Those in New Orleans remain green and keep
blooming through the year if the winters are mild. Prune after
flowering in the spring. Leaves and seeds are poisonous.

ARDISIA, of the *Myrsinaceae* or Myrsine Family is a small
columnar bush with white flowers followed by red berries in the
fall, and these in turn last through the winter into spring. *Ardisia
crenulata*, the best known variety, will grow to two and one-half
feet in shade provided it gets good, loamy soil. The berries of this
evergreen are much in demand at Christmas time. If you feel that
you are robbing the bush by cutting the berries, why not pot a few
specimens so that they can be brought indoors? This plant does
well from the lower South to South Carolina. It is subject to brown
scale, which can be controlled with an oil emulsion. Propagated
by seeds and cuttings.

AZALEA, or Rhododendron, of the Heath Family, is an evergreen flowering shrub in the South. If planted in the correct manner and in the right soil, it is a lovely addition to any garden. There
are some varieties farther north that are semi-evergreen.

The soil for Azaleas is the same as that for Camellias. The correct pH for Azaleas should be between 4.5 and 5.5. If your soil test
shows a pH of 6.0 or over put in from five to six pounds of aluminum sulphate per every one hundred square feet and add a fair
amount of peat to the soil. Check your soil frequently so that you
will not overdose. There is always the danger of the ground becoming toxic when too much aluminum sulphate is used. If you prefer
to use sulphur, only about one pound per one hundred square feet
is sufficient but it is slower acting than the aluminum sulphate.
This plant needs plenty of water and must be kept mulched
against the heat of the summer and the cold winds of winter.

As to varieties, we have the *Indicas* or Indian Azaleas that are
hybrids in origin and are large spreading bushes, six to eight feet in
height and growing taller as they grow older. These do well in the
warmer sections of the South. The dark green leaves of the *Indicas*
are larger than those of the other varieties. I recommend:

Red and Deep Pink	Prince of Wales; Pride of Dorking, late bloomer.
Light Salmon	Duc de Rohan, early bloomer; Duke of Wellington.
Clear Light Pink	Elegans, early bloomer.
Melon-pink	Pride of Mobile, very free-flowering, mid-season.
Pure White	Fielder's White, early bloomer.
Lilac-lavender	Formosa, very large, easily grown, mid-season. The George Lindley Taber, a blush-pink to white slightly marked with lavender, blends well with the Formosa.
Orange	Macrantha; Prince of Orange, mid-season.

The *Kurumes*, or dwarf Azaleas, are low-growing thick plants with rather small leaves, getting their name from the town of Kurume, Japan where they were discovered. They also thrive in the deep South. In this class I suggest:

Bright Carmine Red	Christmas Cheer, mid-season bloomer.
Orange-red	Firebird.
Salmon	Salmon Prince; Salmon Beauty.
Melon-pink	Peaceblow; Coral Bells, a hardy plant with semi-double flowers; early bloomer.
Shell-pink	Pink Pearl, early and prolific bloomer.
Pure White	Snow, mid-season; Snowflake, semi-double flowers.

The Belgian type Azaleas are lovely but slow growers and demand extra care. The Mollis and Pontica types include a multitude of colors, bloom later, are deciduous and do better in the North and East. *Rhododendron prunifolium* blooms in July and shows yellow-orange blossoms. Two of the prettiest are Chevalier de Reali, a sunny yellow, and Queen Emma, an apricot with buff tones. *R. serrulatum* flowers in August and has white fragrant blooms. *R. canescens* shows color in pink, white and rose. *R. obtusum kaempferi*, or the Torch Azaleas, do well in the colder sections of the South, albeit deciduous.

Pruning the Azalea means pinching the new shoots before the terminal bud reaches the height of the upper branches and this is done in the spring immediately after blooming. Use clippers to shape your bush if you like, but do so right after the flowers are finished, otherwise you will lose next year's blooms.

Nearly all Azaleas of the South are the victims of Azalea Petal Blight, a fungus, *Ovulinia azalea,* athough I contend that if you check the pH of your soil often enough to keep just the right amount of acidity, you can very often save your plants from this unsightly scourge. If your plants are affected by this fungus you will first notice white spots on the petals of the open flowers and then the blossoms wilt and hang, dejected and wet-looking, from the bush. There is an accepted commercial spray containing zinc sulphate and Dithane to use on Azaleas to combat Petal Blight, but once you begin, prepare to continue the spraying every third day throughout the blooming season.

If your Azaleas begin to look droopy and the leaves appear dull, dried and yellow, particularly during the summer months try spraying the foliage and roots with a solution of iron sulphate or Copperas, one tablespoonful to a quart of water. The leaves absorb the solution through their pores and will in about ten days, change to a healthy dark green color. And who knows? You might have avoided serious infestation of Die-Back by so doing. Just bear in mind that Copperas, like the leaves of the *Indica Azalea,* is poisonous.

Chief pests are red spider and thrips that stick to the underside of the leaf and turn it red-brown. If you keep your Azaleas well watered during the dry hot months these insects should not present a problem. You may spray with Aramite for the red spider and with lindane for thrips; malathion will check both. Spray with nicotine for the Azalea Lace Bug.

Feed the Azaleas with the same materials and at the same time as you do the Camellias.

BARBADOS CHERRY, *Malpighia glabra* is a semi-evergreen

shrub with rosy flowers followed by red berries. It grows to six feet as far as southern Texas.

BARBERRY, *Berberis Thunbergii* the Japanese Barberry is known for its low horizontal growth habits (rarely to five feet) its red flowers and scarlet autumn leaves. The branches are spiny and will not lose their leaves except in a hard prolonged freeze. The Common Barberry, *B. vulgaris* grows to eight feet and a new spineless form is on the market. *B. Thunbergii atropurpurea* has deep bronze-red foliage in summer; in autumn it changes to orange-red. This one will grow from two to four feet and needs full sun. It has a dwarf form, *B. Thunbergii atropurpurea* var. Crimson Pygmy.

BAYBERRY, *Myrica cerifera* sometimes called the Southern Wax Myrtle, grows all over the South. It is an evergreen shrub to fifteen feet or more. The female plant is noted for its aromatic leaves and small clusters of gray-white berries from which Bayberry candles are made. Other than demanding sun it thrives with no particular care and may be clipped and pruned at will. Oddly enough the Northern Bayberry, *Myrica caroliniensis* is found in swampy spots of Louisiana, Mississippi and Florida. This one does not grow much over eight feet, is deciduous and is beautiful in winter when its bare branches are covered with grayish-white berries that remain intact until spring. Try arranging it with sweet peas and early spring flowers. Both types of Bayberry seem well-suited to sandy soils and salt sprays. Plant male and female specimens for good berry yield.

BEAUTY BUSH, *Kolkwitzia amabilis* is a small deciduous bush with slender arching branches and pinkish-yellow flowers that bloom the second year after planting. Grows to seven feet.

BIRD OF PARADISE, *Caesalpinia Gilliesii* is a tropical evergreen, growing to eight feet and bearing blossoms closely resembling those of the Royal Poinciana, *Poinciana regia*. As a matter of fact it is often called that name in error. The foliage looks very much like that of the mimosa. This shrub does well in sandy soil and tolerates dry conditions, sunny locations. *C. pulcherrima* is a dwarf form, perfect for patios.

BOTTLEBRUSH, *Callistemon coccinea* a shrub belonging to the Myrtle Family, has narrow pointed leaves and bright red flowers with so many stamens in a cylindrical shape that they resemble just what the name implies, a bottlebrush. This ornamental is very difficult to transplant and slow to start from seed. You must open the small round balls on the stem (the seed cases) and plant the minute dust-like seeds. Prune in the fall to increase bloom. Grows to about twelve feet in the mid and lower South, never entirely loses its leaves and prefers moist sandy soil.

The BUCKEYE BOTTLEBRUSH, *Aesculus parviflora* has long startling blossoms of white in the summer and does better in the southeast sections, although it is not too well known. The RED BUCKEYE, *Aesculus pavia* likes wet swamplands from Louisiana and Florida as far north as Virginia.

BRIDAL WREATH, *Spiraea* is an ornamental, informal and deciduous, noted for its profusion of flowers in the spring. Best of this family are *S. prunifolia plena* and *S. Vanhouttei* which grow to six feet or more, with double white blossoms on thin drooping branches. *Spiraeas* like moisture and are subject to root rot, for which there is no remedy so keep them happy with the average soaking. Do not flood them. There is also a pink Bridal Wreath, *S. Billiardii* to six feet, a deep pink, *S. Bumalda* and a bright crimson, *S.* Anthony Waterer. The last two are dwarf forms that rarely exceed two feet. *S. tribolata* or Swan Lake is a new introduction from North China and Siberia. This one never grows over four feet —perfect for the small garden.

Prune immediately after flowering. This shrub thrives well all over the South and through northern and central Florida, but blossoms are more beautiful in colder sections because the flower buds have more of a chance to mature in longer, colder winters.

BRUNFELSIA belongs to the Nightshade Family, *Solanaceae* and blooms in the South in late winter and spring. Semi-evergreen (a severe freeze will cause the leaves to drop), this shrub is charming in that the flowers, larger than periwinkles, may be three different colors depending on the length of time they are open. The foliage is dark green; the bark, gray. Variety *undulata* though slow growing, will reach ten feet here and fifteen feet in the tropics. Flowers change from white to cream. *B. americana*, to six feet, with blossoms white to yellow, is fragrant at night, hence is called Lady of the Night. *B. latifolia*, or Yesterday-Today-and-Tomorrow, carries flowers ranging in color from violet to pink to white and reaches four to five feet. They all grow in fairly ordinary soil but do demand moisture, good drainage and plenty of sun. They like to be crowded in pots or beds.

BUTTERFLY-BUSH, *Buddleia* is a semi-evergreen shrub that needs lots of sun, good drainage and rich loamy soil. Flowers are borne in racemes that droop at the top, in colors ranging from white *B. asiatica*, to lavender *B. japonica* and *B. Davidii* and these usually reach six feet. *B. officinalis maxim*, a pale lilac with orange eye, grows to eight feet.

Vitex

Buddleia

Don't confuse the *Buddleia* with *Vitex*, the Chaste Tree. *Buddleia* has simple leaves, *Vitex* has leaves that look like a hand with outstretched fingers. *Buddleia's* racemes are longer and more lavender than blue and droop at the tip.

Perhaps the reason for our not seeing the Butterfly-bush in the garden as often as we would like to is because it does play host, in some instances, to the red spider and other troublesome sucking pests but your hose and spray gun should take care of these annoyances. Prune the *Buddleias* in the spring after flowering by cutting out old canes at ground level.

C A M E L L I A , of the *Ternstroemiaceae* or Tea Family, was named in 1735 by Carolus Linnaeus, world famous botanist and originator of the binomial system of plant classification, for George Joseph Kamel, a Jesuit priest who traveled in Asia in the seventeenth century. Camellias are woody plants native to Asia, with glossy evergreen leaves and flowers that bloom from September to April depending on variety. One variety might have as many as four different trade names and entirely different flowers. Their interesting shapes and textures make them good landscape shrubs in the ground and in large tubs throughout the South to Arcadia, Florida. It was satisfying to hear that on Thursday, August 27, 1959, the Camellia became the official state flower of the state of Alabama.

Camellias are slow-growing, reaching heights from five to fifteen (and sometimes to twenty-five) feet, according to growth habits. They produce single, double, semi-double, peony and pompon-formed blooms, in almost any shade from white to magenta. There are three outstanding types of Camellia: *C. japonica, C. Sasanqua* and *C. reticulata. Camellia japonica,* although branching, has an allover, rounded, or sometimes columnar appearance, blooms in the late fall, winter and spring and produces many varieties. With rare exceptions the *japonica* has no fragrance. The flowers vary from those of several petals with a mass of stamens in the center to those of many petals and no visible stamens. All have five green sepals that remain until the round or oval seed pod develops. This pod, containing from one to five seeds remains dark brown and hard. When it begins to split, gather the seeds and have some fun growing your own seedlings. The results are often amazing and most satisfying. The *Camellia japonica* usually ranges from four to ten feet in height, depending on variety.

Here are some of the old favorites: *Alba Plena* is a regular complete-double white with imbricated petals; it is an early bloomer and makes a fine corsage. Debutante, a peony-type, and Pink Perfection, a formal full-double, are pink and early to mid-season flowering. Purple Dawn, a regular full-double, is a deep rose-pink with purple tinge to the edge of the petals; blooms mid-season to late. Victor Emmanuel, an incomplete-double, is red and a late bloomer. Herme and its sports are all lovely, from the reds to the red-and-whites, to the whites streaked with pink; all are semi-double. One of the most unusual of the variegated is *Collettii Maculata*, a dark, red and white peony form that looks like peppermint candy and enjoys a long flowering season. The plant is bushy, with round deep green heavy-textured leaves, and a profuse bloomer. It is one of my favorites. Gigantea, sometimes known as the Emperor Wilhelm, is a red splotched with white—a loose anemone type. A good example of the incomplete-double is the lovely Chandleri Elegans, a soft, deep pink touched with white, showing its center stamens very clearly. I have seen magnificent blooms of the Ville de Nantes, a semi-double, deep red, with scattered markings of white on its fimbriated petals. C. M. Hovey, sometimes called Colonel Fiery, is a formal-double that bespeaks its name. Sunset Glory is a reddish-coral, anemone type; Carolyn Tuttle is a rosy-pink with crinkly foliage. There are so many varieties in so many wonderful colors that you would do well to visit a Camellia fancier or nurseryman when these plants are in bloom to see which ones strike your fancy. If you can't get out consult a book on Camellias wherein the color plates will be helpful for selection.

Camellia Sasanqua, native of Japan, is an early fall and winter-flowering plant, sometimes reaching twenty-five feet. It is more columnar in growth habits than the *japonica*, the blossoms stand more cold and the foliage is a darker green and heavier-textured. Cleopatra is a semi-double to peony form and a delightful rose-pink; Maiden's Blush is flesh-pink and Dawn is a semi-double ivory tinged with pink. C. *Sasanqua,* whose blooms have a slight fragrance, makes fine hedging material and can be espaliered as well. Try espaliering Snow-on-the-Mountain, sometimes known as White Doves; or Mine-No-Yuki, an early pure white, semi-double bloomer with willowy growth habits. Hino de Gumo, with large single white flowers edged in pink is also spreading and informal. Briar Rose, a soft single, clear pink; Hugh Evans, a single pink and profuse bloomer; Velvety, an early crimson single, and Rosea all make beautifully full, clipped hedges because of their vigorous, upright growth habits. Dawn or Akebono-Shibori, an early, pinkish-white semi-double, and Texas Star are two to be used as narrow clipped hedges where there is little space. For patios try two *Sasanquas* that are noted for their low, spreading growth: Tanya, a rosy-pink and Lavender Queen, a violet-pink.

We in the lower South are very proud of Mr. René Casadaban **of Abita Springs, Louisiana,** for his production of the Sasanqua Sparkling Burgundy, the All-America Camellia Selection for 1960. A glowing ruby-rose color, as rich as the vintage for which it is named, it is the result of a cross between Hino de Gumo and Showa-No-Sakae. It was tested for three years in all sections of the United States and was found to be a variety well-suited to the usual Camellia sections and to the colder sections of the South. As a matter of fact it withstood the exceptionally hard freezes of Norfolk, Virginia, disastrous to many Sasanquas and most japonicas. Sparkling Burgundy begins to flower about the first of October and will continue until the end of November, an unusually long blooming period for a Sasanqua. The crisp blossoms are fully-double and measure three and one-half to four inches across, very often showing an overlay of a lavender sheen.

Camellia reticulata is a large shrub, sometimes growing to fifty feet in its native China, with rather dull green leaves prominently veined and saw-toothed, and loosely arranged flowers. It never grows near such heights in this country. The *reticulata* blooms last of all in the spring, usually showing purplish-rose in color. More and more interest has been shown in this type since the introduction of the variety from the Yunnan Province of China, sometimes called the Kunming *reticulata*. The blooms are large and fluffy. Captain Rawes is a semi-double, clear pink to purple; the Lion's Head, vigorous as its name implies, is an incomplete-double, turkey-red with white markings; Shot Silk, a free bloomer, is a large semi-double, rose-pink dotted with deep rose, and Willow Wand has whorled petals on its formal-double, orchid-pink blossoms, with stamens divided in groups.

There are about one hundred other species under cultivation in Asia and in the future we will probably be able to enjoy some of these. A few Camellia fanciers in this country are experimenting with the *Oleifera, cuspidata, Pitardii* and *saluenensis* species. In 1956, *Camellia Hiemalis* began to be regarded as a new classification; it is said by its originator to be from China and closely related to the Sasanqua species. Because the *Hiemalis* tends to be dwarf and bushy in growth habits, it is ideal for low borders. Blooming somewhat later than the *Sasanqua*, the flowers are fuller and do not shatter as easily as those of the majority of the *Sasanquas*. The variety Shishigashira usually shows its bright red blooms at Christmas time. Showa Supreme is a new cultivar of this group.

Although the *Granthamiana* species was found near Kowloon, China in 1955, and although it has not yet been placed on the market it seems to be one worth awaiting. Named for the Governor of the Hong Kong colony, Sir Alexander Grantham this type has oblong leaves of rough texture and flowers usually sporting eight petals clustered around a center of yellow stamens.

All of these Camellias should have partial shade, some protection from extreme cold, plenty of water and air drainage and an acid soil. Placing the plant in a spot that does not get the morning sun too quickly is a safeguard against the rapid thawing after a freeze that is so injurious to the Camellia.

I do not presume to be an authority on Camellias. There are so many books by so many well-known authors on the subject of this flower and its culture that I offer only a few pointers on Camellia care. These are the results of the notes that I took as I experimented with and care for the scant dozen that I have in my garden.

PLANTING

Camellias may be planted or moved any time during the year except in the very hot months provided the roots are well-balled and bagged in burlap. The ideal time is when the plant is semi-dormant. Decide where you want to place your Camellia and dig the hole for it several weeks before planting. Make the hole about twice as wide and twice as deep as the ball of soil around the plant roots and lay brickbats, broken pieces of pottery or gravel at the bottom to insure drainage. Add about six inches of organic matter mixed with a little superphosphate and settle this with water. The ideal range for a good Camellia soil is a pH of 5.0 to 5.5 and with this in mind mix good black humus, peat moss and sharp sand, about one third each, and test the resulting mixture with your soil test kit. If the soil does not prove acid enough add an acidifying agent until you get the right pH. Camellias have grown in different types of soils, from the red clays of inland Georgia and the sand of coastal Georgia to the arid soil of Texas and the muck of the coastal lower South. But no matter what the planting medium they must have enough acid-reacting organic matter to thrive. It is not acid *per se* that the plants need but the minerals that are made available to the Camellia by the acid-reacting agents that you use.

Fill the hole further with from twelve to eighteen inches of this soil mixture, the amount depending on the size of the hole, water well and allow to stand until you are ready to plant the Camellia. Sufficient time having elapsed, set about the business of placing your specimen, remembering never to plant it any lower than it grew in the nursery. Just loosen the burlap around the top of the ball (it is not necessary to remove it) and after lowering the plant, keeping the top of the ball about two inches above ground level, fill in the spaces around the ball with the soil mixture and water well, tamping until the Camellia is firmly in place. Planting a Camellia too deeply is defeat before you start because if the plant is too low the rate of growth is nil, leaves are dull and begin to fall and twigs and branches gradually die.

Repeat the filling and watering process until the hole is filled and the top is shaped to a saucer-like depression to make further watering easy. Mulch with peat moss or leaf mold before the final watering to keep the soil surface loose and to aid aeration and water penetration. Keep the layer of mulch about one-half inch thick near the trunk of the plant. The mulch on the outside edges can be as thick as three inches. Thereafter it is wise to check the acidity of the soil around your Camellia at least twice a year. If the results show a reaction of a pH above 7.0 applications of some acidifying agent such as sulphur or aluminum sulphate are required.

Sulphur is almost three times as strong as aluminum sulphate and should not be used too often. It has been said by many experts that the wettable grade of sulphur is the best kind and even that should not be used more than one to two pounds to every one hundred square feet of area. Water the soil, mix the sulphur thoroughly with the soil and then water again. Aluminum sulphate is probably the acidifying agent most used by home gardeners. It changes the reactions quicker than sulphur but its effects do not last as long and it does tend to tie up soil nutrients. Hence it may be used more often than sulphur, but with restraint.

FEEDING

Camellias should be fed right after the blooming period in the spring and again in June. I always spread the feed over the existing mulch. The mulch acts as a buffer between the tender top roots and the heat of the chemicals in the fertilizer. I start from about one inch from the base of the plant and work to the spot directly under the outer tips of the branches. I use 5–3–2, or five parts of cottonseed meal, three parts phosphate and two parts sulphate of potash. If the root circle is three feet, I use one-half pound on each plant or one pound to every twenty square feet. Then mulch with peat. With correct feeding there may be no need for an acidifying agent. And again I caution, do not over-acidify. Check your soil frequently. To get too much acid in the soil is as injurious as to have too little. If the soil gets too acid the leaves turn brown at their tips and fall, the rate of growth will be retarded and the plant will eventually die. If these signs exist drench the Camellia with water to dilute the fertilizer. If, on the other hand there is too much alkalinity growth will be practically nil, leaves will turn yellow and the whole plant gives a sickly appearance. Now don't confuse this yellowing of the leaves with a yellow mottling that I have noticed on the leaves of one of my Camellias. I have been told that it is of virus origin. It is nothing to fear. Mottling seems to be all that this virus does. It is not spread by touch and does no other damage.

WATERING

Some summers are kind to us and bring a hard shower every other day or so, in which case we have no watering problems. But in the long dry spells we must soak our Camellias (not just sprinkle) every third day to keep them going. Water them when they are in shade or the leaves will show sun-scald, and water them with force because it helps to rout pests. As our water tends to be alkaline, we must be constantly on the watch for signs that the soil is losing its acidity: drooping sickly-looking, curling leaves. Those danger signals mean to start checking the soil at once to see if it needs acidifying. I know that I am repeating myself, but acidity is so important to good Camellias!

If you have quite a few Camellias you will find that having them power-sprayed once a year after flowering by a reputable nursery-man will usually keep them free of pests and diseases. Here are some of the things to look for.

White Tea Scale, *Fiorinia theae Green* is a hard scale that infests the under side of the leaves, causing the upper surface to turn a sickly yellow. Eventually the foliage falls and the growth of the plant is retarded. Spray with a summer strength oil emulsion, one part oil to fifty parts of water, or with any of the new preparations, like malathion, that may be recommended by a good authority. I don't use parathion because it is a very poisonous substance and should be handled with rubber gloves and a face mask. And please don't use the oil emulsion when the temperature is above seventy-five degrees or below forty degrees. Oil emulsion will burn the foliage if the weather is too hot and it will coat the leaves and prevent thawing if there should be a freeze. Should you be forced to spray with the emulsion in the late fall when the flower buds are almost fully developed, pick a day when the temperatures are between seventy-five and forty to do the job. I would rather lose some of the flowers than to take a chance of the Tea Scale spreading to other Camellias. Then if a sudden drop in the temperature is predicted hose the plant with force enough to wash off most of the emulsion.

Peony Scale, *Pseudaonidia paeoniae Ckll* and the Camphor Scale, *Pseudaonidia duplex Ckll* so unwelcome, are comprised of minute female insects that attach themselves to branch, twig and leaves and just feed and multiply. The wind and the touch carry them from plant to plant. The Peony Scale is hard to detect. It is the color of the bark and does damage to the woody parts of the Camellia, causing death of twigs and branches. Camphor Scale is yellowish-brown and wreaks as much havoc as its companion. Rout both with a spray of oil emulsion or an all-purpose spray in the summer when these insects are at the crawling stage.

Florida Red Scale, *Chrysomphalus aonidum Linn.* appears as dark reddish-black spots on both sides of the leaves and young branches of Camellias. This one is a soft waxy scale also known as Camellia Scale. It can be controlled by using a 2% oil emulsion spray in March, using six tablespoons of oil emulsion to one gallon of water. If you must repeat the dose be sure that at least thirty days have elapsed between doses and this time use three tablespoons of oil emulsion to one gallon of water and add one tablespoon of malathion to this. Be sure to cover the leaves and branches when you spray. The emulsion acts as a coating that prevents the insect from breathing, and so destroys it.

Red Spider sucks out the juices of the leaves and causes the foliage to take on a dry, reddish-brown appearance. Spray with nicotine sulphate or Aramite.

Spraying with a nicotine solution will rout aphids, and arsenate of lead will get rid of caterpillars but a spray of lindane and chlordane will not only kill these two but take care of ants as well. I am waiting to see what tests have proved about DDT being injurious to Camellias.

Sometimes Die-Back, a fungus, attacks the bark of the Camellia and the only cure is to cut off the affected limb well below the damaged area. The attack is first noticed when leaves of a branch suddenly turn scorched-looking. If you cut one of the twigs and see a circular brown area in the center of the cut surface, then you should be a little suspicious. Cut further down the branch and if the brown area persists you may be positive that Die-Back is present. Waste no time cutting off the branch until you reach a spot where the inner bark is normal. Iron sulphate or Copperas, one-fourth of a pound per foot of the height of your bush, applied annually does a lot to prevent Die-Back which is generally caused by some kind of an organism that is encouraged by lack of acidity and moisture. It is also aided and abetted by too much sun on delicate, young or newly-transplanted shrubs. One summer, I used Copperas in solution on several of my sick bushes and after the application I set up a moss-draped lathe frame over each plant to keep it cool and preserve moisture. Some Camellias, like Eleanor of Fairoaks tend to have Die-Back. It was the only one that I lost to this disease. Don't be alarmed if you see brown spots on otherwise healthy leaves. They may be nothing more than sunburn.

Camellia Petal Blight, *Sclerotinia camelliae* is becoming more and more serious. This fungus goes from soil to flower and back again, forming a vicious circle. Allowing flowers that fall to remain on the ground around the base of the Camellia encourages the growth of definite organisms under the top soil. These organisms eject spores that reach the open flower, causing it to turn a soggy-looking brown. The flower falls to the earth, more organisms form, and the cycle starts all over again. The blight does not seem to affect the growth of the plant as yet but it certainly makes an unsightly bush. Representatives of the Department of Agriculture have been going from house to house spraying every Camellia in the neighborhood because this blight spreads rapidly. The ground in which the Camellia is planted is sprayed, not the leaves or flowers. So to help combat this disease, do your part by picking up the fallen flowers and burning them if you know that you have the blight in your garden. If you have a suspicion that it is present there are two remedies that you might try. One is ferbam, usually sold under its trade name. Used at the rate of one pound in 25 gallons of water, applications of this organic fungicide to the ground around the plant every two weeks from early January until the end of March will prevent the spore cycle from recurring. The other fungicide to try is pentachloronitrobenzene, sold under several trade names including Terraclor. Use this one at the rate of a little over two pounds to every one thousand square feet, and to be effective apply in the latter part of December, say between Christmas and New Year's day. One application soaked into the ground around the plant is usually sufficient for the season. Try using the wettable form of pentachloronitrobenzene in a watering can, making sure that you keep the mixture well agitated.

Should the blight still persist after use of these measures call your local entomologist and he will advise. Even if you know that your Camellias have not yet become infested be a good housekeeper anyway and pick up the fallen blooms, put them in a bag and then into the trash container that is well covered.

Leaf Gall or deformity of leaves and swelling of twigs, usually in early spring, is caused by a fungus. Sometimes Bordeaux spray will help; otherwise, remove the affected part and burn. Crown Gall attacks the roots and underground portion of the Camellia. Other than slowing growth it does no other damage and I know of no control.

Camellia Scab comprises a variety of spots that do nothing more serious than discolor the Camellia leaves. There are Black Spots, White Spots and a Gray Spot that attacks only the Sasanqua. They are all caused by a fungus and there is no control. Sometimes poor drainage causes raised brown spots on the under surface of the leaves, so it would be wise to consider whether your plant is getting the proper attention in this direction. Then there is a gray spot called Alga Spot, that sometimes attacks the japonica species. This is usually controlled by a copper sulphate spray.

So many of us are concerned about Bud Drop and Bull-heading. Camellias will drop their buds if too much fertilizer is applied, if poor drainage exists, or after a sudden extreme change of temperature or humidity. And we in the lower South are only too well aware of these changes! Since we cannot control the weather the only thing we can do to at least remedy this situation is to choose the ideal protected planting site for the plant and give it care. Sometimes the plant inherits a tendency to drop buds, as is the case with Molly Moore Davis and Admiral Nimitz. You can usually tell when a bud has been injured by cold. Its center blackens and the petals fall away at a touch.

Bull-heads are buds that begin to show color and then drop before they open. This usually happens to buds that develop during late stages of growth when a very warm spell of weather follows a cold snap. Sometimes this condition is an inherited trait in certain varieties of Camellias. On the other hand the plant can be just plain "ornery". I have a lovely bush that I have nicknamed "Amazing"; although in apparent good health it will bull-head year after year and then suddenly in the next season amaze me with a display of perfect blooms.

WINTER PROTECTION

I covered almost all points on care before and after a freeze at the end of the previous chapter but I must repeat that winter protection calls for a thorough watering and a good mulch before a freeze. The greatest danger comes to a plant through the rapidity of its thawing-out after a freeze. The quicker the thaw, the more damage is caused. That is why Camellias that are planted in semi-shade fare better than those in the open where full sunlight will hit them and cause too rapid a thaw. Water the ground well after a freeze to keep the roots of the plant moist through the process of thawing. When you cover a plant with a sheet or paper you are actually protecting it against frost not against the cold. The waterings and the mulch are still necessary.

Now I must again run up the red flag of warning and urge you never to spray your plants with oil emulsion when the temperatures are too low or too high. And never use an oil emulsion and sulphur within thirty days of each other. They fight! Do not spray your Camellias with any insecticide in the dead of winter unless it is an emergency.

The Camellia is propagated by cuttings, by grafting and from seed. It makes a perfect companion for the Azalea since both require the same soil and culture. Read up on the Camellia, look at color plates, attend Camellia shows, join your local and national

Camellia societies, and then visit your nurseryman to make your choice. One nice thing about this plant is that you can buy it and plant it while in full bloom. You can find the pillar-type Camellias, such as the Abbe Wilder and Professor Sargent, for formal doorway planting and for low, rounded forms the Magnoliaflora, with pale pink blossoms, cannot be outdone. Informal sprawly ones are Rainy Sun, Lady Clare and Gigantea, while the Herme and Mathotiana will provide thick heavy growth for empty corners.

CAPE JASMINE, *Gardenia jasminoides* grows from four to six feet high, has evergreen foliage and lovely white fragrant flowers that closely resemble the Camellia. It blooms from spring to September and is hardy as far north as Virginia. It should be planted in March or April in full sun in a bed where a bottom layer of manure will furnish bottom heat and a top layer of good sandy loam will insure success. Never set the plants down directly on the bottom layer. Let several inches of loam cover the manure and then lower the plants. Because the Cape Jasmine needs acid soil (to a 5.0 to 5.5 pH) to flower properly mix a little aluminum sulphate in the bed. Then test frequently to see if the soil is sufficiently acid. Keep moderately moist and mulch well. Hard sprayings of the hose will help rout pests from this plant. Chlordane will kill ants and oil emulsion will eradicate black mold, a fungus disease, on the leaves. Caution: never use oil emulsion in very hot weather. A good washing of mild soap flakes and water will do the job when temperatures are high.

Sometimes the leaves of the plant will yellow and look sickly. This is probably due to chlorosis or lack of iron, caused by not keeping your soil acid enough. A foliar spray of one teaspoon ferrous sulphate and one-half teaspoon soap suds to one gallon of water will usually correct this condition quickly. But you must acidify the soil within a week or so or the leaves will yellow again. The ferrous sulphate is just a temporary cure.

Gardenia Veitchii, a newer introduction, is winter-flowering and stands a great amount of heat. This one should be planted in June.

The culture is about the same as that of the *jasminoides* except that in the fall just before blooming the *Veitchii* needs a light mulch of well-rotted manure to aid in flower development. *Gardenia radicans* is low and lovely for borders.

Mulch your Gardenias well to avoid infestation of root nematodes which will cause the leaves to drop and for which there is no cure. The bushes grafted on the strong *Gardenia Thunbergiana* stock seem fairly resistant to nematodes.

CASHMERE BOUQUET, *Clerodendron fragrans* has clusters of rosy blooms in bouquets as its name implies. Grows to five feet and the leaves usually fall if there is a hard freeze. This shrub will take over the garden completely if not carefully watched. It spreads by underground runners. And I must warn you, as beautiful as it appears, the blossoms harbor millions of ants! So if you must have it, spray!

CARYOPTERIS, of the *Verbenaceae* or Vervain Family is a low shrub, upright in growth habits, reaching two to two and a half feet. The variety Heavenly Blue has deep blue flower spikes in autumn and is particularly beautiful when planted in front of pink Duchesse de Brabant roses. Deciduous, it likes full sun. The variety *candida* has white flowers.

CASSIA or Senna, *Cassia corymbosa* likes the sun and blooms in late summer and fall, showing clusters of yellow flowers on upright stems. Semi-deciduous, it is hardier in the lower South than farther north and grows from five to ten feet. *Cassia bicapsularis* has a weedy habit of growth and will reach a height of ten or more feet, lovely against a wall from early fall to the first frost. This evergreen should be cut back after flowering to insure compactness. And of course there is the dazzling *Cassia alata'* small tree or shrub, discussed in the chapter on Evergreen, Deciduous and Flowering Trees.

CHINESE RED BUD, *Cercis occidentalis* a member of the Pea Family grows to ten feet and has deeper rose flowers than the tree form.

COTONEASTER, *Cotoneaster horizontalis* is a half-evergreen shrub with low horizontal branches, pink flowers in June and bright red fruit in August and September. Likes sun and dry conditions and does better in the colder sections of the South. Variety *pannosa* is the Silverleaf Cotoneaster and is more upright in habit, reaching six feet. The variety *Franchetii*, to ten feet, is thickly branched and does well in most of the South.

CRAPE JASMINE, formerly known as *Tabernaemontana coronaria* and now known as *Ervatamia coronaria*, is also called Nero's Crown and Fleur d'Amour. This is a tender shrub that must be planted in rainy spells of spring in sandy soil and full sun. Most evergreens are set out in fall and winter but this one must become established before cold weather. It has shiny green crimped leaves and white fragrant flowers in clusters, throughout the summer. Grows to eight feet from Florida to the Carolinas. The double-flowered form is *E. flore-pleno*.

DAPHNE, *Daphne odora marginata* is a lovely little evergreen shrub with fragrant pink clustered flowers in winter and spring. The leaves are variegated. Grows to four feet in partial shade.

DEUTZIA, *Deutzia gracilis* of the Saxifrage Family is an upright bushy shrub to four or five feet, known for its blush-white flowers in spring and summer. Deciduous, it is easy to cultivate, especially in the upper sections. Two of the hardiest species are *D. grandiflora* and *D. parviflora*, both of which grow to six feet. Var. *compacta* is dwarf form.

DURANTA, see Golden Dew Drop.

ELAEAGNUS, of the Oleaster Family, is grown chiefly for its lovely gray-green foliage. The evergreen varieties such as *E. macrophylla* and *E. glabra* are hardy in the upper South. They grow to ten feet and produce red fruit with silvery-brown scales after the autumn flowers. *E. pungens*, taller and with leaves edged with yellow and white, and *E. angustifolia* the Russian Olive, to ten feet, are both familiar to us in the deep South. They all like sun and are more attractive when kept well-trimmed.

ERANTHEMUM, of the Acanthus family, is a tropical shrub that dies back with a freeze but makes a quick return. Does well in shade and if the winter is mild blooms almost constantly through the cold months. Variety *laxiflorum* which grows from two to four feet tall, has violet-blue flowers and leaves that vary in size from small near the blooms to large oval at the base of the plant. The variety *nervosum* sometimes known as *Daedalacanthus nervosus*, averages from two to five feet in height and has deep blue flowers. Both make a picture when planted among the azaleas that bloom at the same time. Give them plenty of sun and water. Both root readily when cuttings are made of the new wood.

ESCALLONIA, of the Saxifrage Family, is an evergreen that is easy to grow in neutral or slightly acid soil and where frosts are not too heavy. It bears very thick foliage and flowers in clusters in spring: pink, *E. organensis*; white, *E. floribunda* or red, *E. rubra*. These reach nine to twelve feet. *E. Berteriana*, a white, grows to ten feet. This shrub is easily clipped to mound shape. One characteristic of this species is the amount of glands that may appear anywhere on the plant and the oily spots that appear on the leaves.

EUONYMOUS, or Evonymous, of the *Celastraceae* or the Staff-tree Family, is often called the Spindle-Tree and is grown especially for its evergreen foliage and very attractive autumn berries. *E. japonica* is upright to eight feet, *E. radicans* has trailing habits and may be espaliered successfully and *E. vegeta* grows to five feet. There are some deciduous varieties. *E. americanas*, often called the Strawberry Shrub, reaches six to eight feet.

EUPHORBIA, classical name of the Spurge Family, includes the Poinsettia. *E. pulcherrima* is a shrub to ten feet, the Crown of Thorns, *E. splendens* is a pot plant and Snow-on-the-Mountain, *E. marginata* is an annual. The Castor Bean, known for its ornamental foliage and grown for screens is *Ricinus communis* and is also a member of the Euphorbia Family. Its seeds are poisonous.

The Poinsettia, the shrub of this group with which we are concerned, is easy to grow from cuttings of soft and hard wood. There are white, pink and red varieties, single and double, that bloom in November and December and I urge you to keep them in sheltered spots so that a pre-Christmas freeze will not affect them. Let July be the last month in which you prune them back. If frozen back the Poinsettia always puts out new growth in the spring. The flower is actually the cluster of small yellow flowers in the center. The large red "petals" are really bracts that surround the flower.

Poinsettias do well in almost any type of soil, as a matter of fact they demand very little care but do try to brace them and shelter them enough so that the winter winds cannot play havoc with the blossoms before time to cut them. The day before you plan to bring the flower into the house pull off the leaves under the flower so that the "bleeding" or milky juice can coagulate. Cut the bloom and immediately burn the stem to prevent further "bleeding". I have tried plunging them into hot water but unless you have a means of preventing the steam from hitting the flowers this method is not always successful.

Softwood cuttings made in July and August will bloom for Christmas. Hardwood cuttings should be made in the spring after blooming and continued until new growth begins. Make the cuttings from twelve to fifteen inches long and plunge half of the piece into pot, ground or coldframe.

Prune one half of the current season's growth in July and as I mentioned before, do not prune any later in the summer or you will lose some of the blooms.

F A T S I A , *Fatsia japonica* is a small evergreen shrub reaching to about five feet. It belongs to the Aralia Family and does well in the upper and lower South. The leaves are not too unlike Ivy leaves in shape but they are larger and glossier and more deeply lobed. The flowers show in white panicles. Plant in fairly good well-drained soil in a spot where it will be protected from strong winds and where it will get the morning sun. It likes afternoon shade.

Another Fatsia, *Fatshedera lizei* is the result of a cross between *Fatsia japonica* and the English Ivy, *Hedera helix*. Its leaves are evergreen and smaller than those of the japonica and it is more low shrub than vine although it is included in the list of vines because it lends itself beautifully to espaliering. Hardy all through the South, it will grow in any well-drained soil and does prefer shade.

FLOWERING ALMOND, *Prunus triloba* to eight feet, has tiny pink flowers on bare or semi-bare branches in early spring. Dwarf Flowering Almond, *Prunus glandulosa* to four feet. Varieties *Prunus gladulosa sinensis* has double pink flowers, *albo-plena* double-white. All deciduous, no particular soil but some sun needed.

FLOWERING PEACH, *Prunus Persica vulgaris flore albo-plena* (I don't blame you, it is so much easier to say Flowering Peach) a lovely deciduous southern shrub, bears double white blossoms on bare branches in the spring. The variety *Roseo-plena* has rose colored flowers. Reaching ten feet, they are lovely with spring flowering bulbs.

FLOWERING PEAR, of the genus *Pyrus*, is another southern beauty that bears white blossoms on bare branches in the spring. Varieties of *Pyrus communis* when propagated on Quince roots produce dwarf forms that are very ornamental in the garden. To keep them to ten or twelve feet the pears should be thinned out and pruned each year preferably in March. They like loamy well-drained soil.

FLOWERING PLUM, *Prunus triflora* is the Japanese Plum and is not to be confused with the Japanese Plum or Loquat Tree, *Eriobotrya japonica*. The *triflora* has reddish-brown branches, showy white flowers and sometimes pale red fruits. We are not too concerned with the fruit, hence we keep the shrub clipped to about six feet and treat it as an ornamental which it definitely is when the blossoms appear on the dark twigs.

FLOWERING QUINCE, *Chaenomoles lagenaria* formerly included in the *Cydonia* tribe, is a delicate-looking branchy deciduous shrub that is most attractive in early spring when the bare branches are covered with small rosy-red blossoms. Grows to five feet in lower South and to eight feet in upper sections. Needs no pruning and likes to be planted in heavy soil in filtered shade. In nursery catalogues, Flowering Quince is often listed as *Cydonia japonica*. Both *Chaenomoles* and *Cydonia* belong to the *Rosaceae* Family, sub-family *Pomeae*.

FORSYTHIA, sometimes called Golden Bell, is a member of the Olive Family. It is lovely in the upper South 'but is not recommended for the lower regions and the New Orleans area. Growing to eight or nine feet it keeps its green leaves well into the winter, is practically pest and disease free, likes sun and will thrive in almost any soil. *F. suspensa* is pendulous and gracefully drooping, *F. viridissima* is more upright and *F. intermedia spectabilis* is the lower form. Prune immediately after flowering by cutting out old canes at ground level. Never shear this shrub uniformly. It is irregular in growth habits.

GARDENIA, see Cape Jasmine.

GOLD DUST TREE, *Aucuba japonica variegata* is an evergreen shrub known for its shiny green foliage that is spotted in yellow, its small purple flowers in terminal panicles and its bright red Christmas berries. It does well all over the South but because it prefers heavy soil, it does have to struggle a bit in the sandy loam along the Gulf Coast. Since the plants are dioecious there must be female plants with the male. These shrubs may be kept as low as four feet or allowed to reach twelve feet. *Aucuba japonica nana* has thick compact foliage and small lavender flowers followed by red berries in late summer and fall. This form, like the larger *variegata*, is also dioecious and must be planted in a good moist, heavy, well-drained soil, in a shady position.

GOLDEN DEW DROP, *Duranta repens* can easily be pruned to a round bush, a drooping shrub or a small tree. Lavender flowers in racemes appear in winter and early spring, followed by graceful hanging yellow berries in summer. Branches are armed with spines. Nearly evergreen in the deep South, this shrub needs plenty of sun and space in which to grow. It is not particular as to soil and may be trimmed any time of the year, although late summer is a good time to remove the old berries and January a good time to get rid of all dead wood.

HIBISCUS, of the Mallow Family is *Hibiscus Rosa-sinensis* closely related to the Abutilon and Althea. It is said that *H. Manihot* from China and Japan is the Queen of the summer hibiscus and this is the one that has been naturalized in the South. This perennial shrub has many varieties that produce single and double flowers in a wide range of colors. It will do well in almost any soil as long as there is plenty of moisture and grows to a height of from three to nine feet. To avoid losing your plant when the temperature drops to freezing I suggest that you water the ground around it well, mulch it high or wrap the main trunk to about six to ten inches above the ground with burlap, holding the burlap to the grounds with weights. Concentrate on covering the base not the top. If the top of the plant freezes and turns black cut it back well past the discolored section before the frozen sap can drop back and kill the healthy part. Do not be in a hurry to dispose of an apparently dead bush as new shoots can appear as late as May.

Mealybugs and aphids often cause bud drop on Hibiscus if they cluster around the flower bud. A spray of summer oil emulsion and nicotine sulphate will rout them if the weather is cool. If the temperatures are high malathion will do the trick. Poor drainage will also cause bud drop. See that the bed is well-raised so that the plant is never surrounded by puddles of water. Besides good drainage the Hibiscus needs sun and at least one feeding of a well-balanced fertilizer per season. I work in a handful of 8-8-8 around the plant in the spring. Then if the leaves show a yellowing I give occasional sprayings of a liquid fertilizer containing the trace elements. Use chlordane to control ants.

As to varieties, Hibiscus Ruth Wilcox is a large single white that remains open until midnight, a desirable quality in a family of flowers that usually open in the morning and fold at eventide. Delicata is a blush-pink with lavender overtones, and single. Crown of Bohemia is a magnificent crested yellow with copper shadings and a red throat, one of the best yellows. Luna is large creamy-buff and single with a pink eye. Flamingo Plume is a large loose double red, Kona double rose, Burgundy a double dubonnet to maroon. Thes Double Apricots and Double Salmons are very striking. There are many others from which to choose. The fringed species is *Hibiscus schizopetalus* with small flowers. Psyche is a good red and Dainty White is stunning. The Hybrid Mallows are most interesting, with huge white, red or rose-pink blossoms that are actually plate size.

H O L L Y or *Ilex* is an evergreen and a deciduous shrub grown for its deep green leaves and bright red berries. *Ilex opaca*, the American Holly is the tallest (to forty feet if allowed to become a tree) of the evergreen species and is much in demand at Christmas time. It grows far to the northeast and down into Florida. *Ilex verticillata*, sometimes called Winterberry is a deciduous, acid-loving, spreading shrub that is startlingly lovely with its scarlet berries on bare branches. They all grow best in well-drained spots and in rather sheltered positions.

Chinese Holly is *Ilex cornuta*, to twelve feet, with very large berries and beautiful foliage in autumn. Variety *Burfordii* is a good one of this species. It is said that this is one of the female Hollies that will bear fruit without a male plant in the neighborhood. The English Holly, *Ilex aquifolium* is slow-growing but may be clipped into almost any shape. There are some variegated species in this group. The Japanese Holly, *Ilex crenata rotundifolia* and *I. crenata microphylla* will reach six and four feet respectively. The foliage of the latter is small and pointed while that of the *rotundifolia* is rounder and larger. Both like light shade, are fairly free of pests and diseases and take kindly to a semi-annual clipping in fall and spring. The Boxleaf Holly, *Ilex crenata* var. *convexa* grows like boxwood as a hedge and is inclined to be disease resistant. *Ilex crenata* var. *helleri* grows from twelve inches to two feet and is ideal for low borders albeit a slow grower.

Hollies are dioecious so choose mostly pistillate plants and several staminate ones in order to let the former stand out. Early fall is the best time to move hollies particularly the evergreen species and in the case of *Ilex opaca* and *Ilex aquifolium* nearly all of the leaves should be stripped from the plant in transplanting. This is a *must* if the transplant is to be a success. I know, I hated to do it too!

Hollies are sometimes attacked by scale, in which case spray with an oil emulsion in early spring.

HONEYSUCKLE, *Lonicera tatarica* or the Tatarian Honeysuckle is a semi-deciduous shrub noted for its fragrant white and pastel flowers. The Winter Honeysuckle, *L. fragrantissima* grows to eight feet in nearly all sections of the South, is half evergreen and has sweet-smelling white flowers. *L. thibetica* reaches five feet and has pale lavender blossoms. *L. spinosa* var. *Alberti* is low-growing. They are all easy to grow, need little pruning and last many years. I have a lovely Honeysuckle bush that remains about three feet high and bears deep orange flowers. It was given to me by a friend who did not know its botanical name. I have never found out definitely what it is but as nearly as I can trace it, this variety is *Lonicera involucrata*. It is a perfect companion for the dwarf pomegranate.

HYDRANGEAS, of the Saxifrage Family, are deciduous shrubs that do well in loamy soil and require plenty of water. *H. arborescens grandiflora* or the Snowball Bush, likes shade, grows from three to five feet and produces blossoms in June, July and August. *Hydrangea paniculata grandiflora* is a taller shrub that likes sun and has the largest flowers of all but it is not too well known in the lower South. The blossoms form in loose umbels. *H. Domotoi*, a low-growing type with large leaves is a stout plant about two or three feet high and just about as round. *H. macrophylla Hortensia*, the French Hydrangea is the old-fashioned favorite that has been grown for years in southern gardens. Although deciduous in winter, if given proper care the summer foliage and blossoms are rewarding. One of the hardiest, if this one freezes back it still produces flowers the following summer.

In alkaline soil, the Hydrangea blossoms are pink; when you add an acidifying agent, such as sulphur or aluminum sulphate to the soil the flowers turn blue. The addition of rusty nails to the earth around the Hydrangea is simply a slower means of attaining your blue blossoms, and in the process you will notice that the flowers will first be a lavender-pink, then a lavender and finally blue. To produce my blues, I use one level tablespoonful of Copperas combined with two level tablespoonfuls aluminum sulphate in three gallons of water. I often have to repeat the dose to get the shade I want. I do this in January, February and March and I feed them with a well-balanced fertilizer in February. When Hydrangea leaves turn brown and there is no sign of pests it might be that the plants need a dose or two of potash, about three-fourths of an ounce to a gallon of water.

Prune immediately after flowering or not any later than August and September, otherwise you cut off next year's flowering branches. All weak and dead twigs may be pruned again in early spring before leaves appear. The Hydrangea may be propagated by cuttings made from the woody section of the stem, in August, September and October. Keep well-watered and shaded until rooted. Aramite will control red spider which sometimes burns the foliage in summer.

Hydrangea Quercifolia or the Oak-leaf Hydrangea, is a graceful bush that grows to six or eight feet and is sometimes used as an informal hedge. The leaves are big and resemble those of the oak tree although they become somewhat scratchy-looking in winter. The white summer flowers are borne in loose panicles in a drooping manner. This one does well in shade in almost all sections of the South. Prune after it has flowered.

Hydrangea *petiolaris* is a climber that clings to tree trunks and walls, producing white flowers through the warm months. See Vines.

Here is a .tip about cutting Hydrangeas for use in the house. Make the cut down in the old wood and in the late evening when it is cool. Cut in this manner the flowers rarely wilt.

I N G A is a delicate-looking shrub with leaves like the Mimosa and showy, feathery red flowers. Grows to fifteen feet and is hardly ever deciduous. After studying the confusion of botanical names associated with this lovely thing, I have concluded that this shrub is *Inga Guildingii* of the Pea Family. It is also known as *Calliandra Guildingii* and is said to come from Trinidad, where there is also a white variety. "Calliandra" comes from the Greek, meaning beautiful stamens, and the flowers of this *Inga* are actually green with red stamens that are so prominent that the whole blossom appears to be red. Whatever its botanical name, it is a striking thing. You have to be patient and wait to see it grow big enough to produce these red puffs but it is definitely worth it. The seed pods are small and flat and split completely, each half recurving. I have been successful in raising a good many plants from seed. Incidentally, with no intent to confuse you further, I do want to mention that I have seen this shrub listed in catalogues as *Calliandra haematocephala*.

I N K B E R R Y , *Ilex glabra* is perfect for either wet or dry places where drainage is a problem. Used in the entire region, it makes a good hedge, three to eight feet high. Its evergreen foliage blends well with other plants. The berry is black.

I X O R A , member of the Madder Family, is an evergreen shrub with attractive dark green foliage and small flowers borne in clusters in the summer. It has a compact habit of growth and is best left unclipped. Reaches five feet. The Ixoras do well in a loamy acid soil fortified with charcoal, peat and sharp sand. Because they are tender I like to keep mine on the south side so that they are more or less protected. But all of them whether in sun or shade demand acid and very well-drained soil. Feed monthly in summer and every other month in winter. They can be grown in pots in the upper South and in the ground where the winters are warm.

Although I have always associated Ixora with brilliant colors I love the latest introduction called Biscuit, an entrancing buff color. This does not mean that I am forsaking the old favorite *Ixora chinensis*, a native of China and Malaya. Its dense round heads of scarlet flowers and stemless leaves will not tolerate sun so be sure that you set this one in filtered shade. *I. coccinea* has to have care. It is the only one that is susceptible to frost and yet it will not behave indoors so it must be placed in a semi-shaded, protected spot. This one has a pretty cousin, *I. rosea* with flowers shading from blush to deep pink. *Ixora incarnata* needs a dose of cold weather to bring out its pink blossoms. *I. fraseri II* a new hybrid of *chinensis* is a good pinkish-coral in shade. Propagate by cuttings in spring and fall.

Two more reds, both beautiful but both sensitive to cold are *I.* Superking and *I.* Trinidad Giant Red. *Ixora aureo-rosea*, yellow-orange; *I. lutea*, yellow and *I. parviflora*, a white, are all lovely. The last one grows to six feet. I think the best of all the whites is *Ixora finlaysoniana*.

Ixoras very often need trace elements to take care of nutritional deficiencies. You can tell the minute you see the leaves turn yellow that the plants need something more than the monthly feeding, so apply chelated iron, ferrous sulphate, or the liquid fertilizer containing the trace elements that I have already mentioned.

Mealybugs and red spider, the only pests that I have ever seen on the Ixoras can usually be routed with a hard spray from the hose, or use a spray containing malathion. The Ixoras are favorites of mine, as you may have guessed. Perhaps you will be interested to know that the Chinese offer these flowers to their native idol Ixora. In India, where the Ixora is widely grown, the *Coccinea*'s seeds are a delicacy for the peacocks.

Keep all varieties on the dry side for about a month after flowering, then feed with the well-balanced fertilizer and with whatever acidifying agent you need.

JACOBINIA, of the Acanthus Family is easily grown to five

feet. Leaves are large and heavily veined; summer and autumn flowers are clusters of tubular, rosy-hued blossoms rising to an arch and then recurving. Semi-deciduous. *Jacobinia carnea* is probably the best known and is often confused with *Justicia*, a close relative which is distinguished by its spurs at the base of the anther lobe. Most of our garden plants known as *Justicia* are really *Jacobinia*. Prune to shape in the fall. Cuttings will root in water.

J A S M I N E , of the *Oleaceae* or Olive Family, also called *Jasminum* and Jessamine, is a member of a group of evergreen erect, sprawling and climbing shrubs that do well all over the South. *J. officinale* is a white-flowered climber that needs support. *J. grandiflorum*, also called Spanish Jasmine is an erect shrub with white, very fragrant blossoms in summer and fall. The variety called Grand Duke, *J. Sambac* is exceedingly sweet-scented with double creamy-white flowers. Showy Jasmine, *Jasminum floridum* has beautiful green foliage and panicles of small yellow flowers. This one is hardy and worthy of a trial. It seems to have been forgotten in the southern garden. *J. humile revolutum* has spreading habits, dark green leaves on angled branches and fragrant lemon-yellow flowers in terminal clusters. Blooms from June to September and is hardy all over the South.

J A V A   S H R U B , *Clerodendron speciosissimum* or *C. fallax* is a good stout medium shrub with large green heart-shaped leaves and erect panicles of deep red flowers that show through summer and fall. It grows in ordinary soil, is not bothered by pests or disease, likes filtered shade and is easily transplanted. Though it dies back in a freeze, it comes right back up in the spring.

J U S T I C I A , another member of the Acanthus Family, has spurred anthers that distinguish it from the Jacobinia that so closely resembles it. This shrub is also semi-deciduous, has lavender-pink flowers and needs close attention to keep it from getting scraggly. Grows to four feet in the lower South, to eight feet in Florida and wherever the climate is more tropical.

K A L M I A , *Kalmia latifolia*, of the Heath Family, *Ericaceae* is the American or Mountain Laurel and is sometimes called the Calico Bush. This evergreen shrub, which might be tried more in the lower South is medium to low, with whitish-pink and purple flowers in early summer. It does beautifully in South Carolina where it can be kept as low as four feet or allowed to reach eight to ten feet. It likes a sandy, loamy, slightly acid soil, plenty of moisture and will grow in sun or shade.

KERRIA, Japanese shrub belonging to the Rose Family, does best in partial shade. *K. japonica* grows to eight feet and is as broad, showing yellow-orange blossoms in June and July. The branches are an attractive greenish-yellow after the leaves drop in the fall. Be watchful for twig blight on this shrub. A treatment of sulphur or Bordeaux will take care of this reddish-brown cankerous disfigurement.

LANTANA, of the genus *Verbenaceae* or Vervain Family will keep its leaves and will bloom all year if not burned back by freezes. It is considered a sub-shrub because of its sprawling habits. *L. Camara* grows from two to four feet with hairy leaves and verbena-like flowers that shade from yellow to pink to orange. It is our well-known Ham and Eggs but I do not recommend it as a cut flower because it has a disagreeable odor. *L. Sellowiana* is the weeping or trailing variety with lavender flowers. This one drapes nicely over steps and garden boxes. All of the Lantanas like sun.

LIGUSTRUM, *Ligustrum japonicum* or the Japanese Privet is well-known all over the South especially for its adaptability to hedging. The leaves are evergreen and the white clustered spring flowers are followed by bluish-black berries. The only trouble that I have had with my ten foot hedge is occasional attacks of white fly which can easily be controlled with an oil emulsion.

MAGNOLIA FUSCATA, *Michelia fuscata* is grown in the middle and lower South for its magnolia-like evergreen leaves and reddish-yellow blossoms that are tinged with brown. It is also known as the Brown-flowered Shrub and Banana Shrub, the flowers having a strong banana fragrance. Reaching ten feet, it is very hardy. It likes sun but will tolerate shade and needs a slightly acid soil to bring forth its spring and summer blooms. Pest and disease free. As a child I remember members of my family saving the tan petals of the *Magnolia fuscata* to place in the chest of drawers to scent the table linens.

MAGNOLIA SOULANGEANA, the Saucer Magnolia of the Magnolia Family is one of the beauties of our very early spring gardens. It is said to be a hybrid of *Magnolia liliflora* and *Magnolia denudata*. Large green leaves drop in the fall and the magnificent cup-shaped white and pink flowers are borne on bare branches, usually in January and February. Ultimate height, twenty feet. The variety *nigra* has dark purple flowers and blooms later in the spring. *M. Lennei's* flowers are crimson and *M. speciosa's* reddish blooms are very large. These shrubs are symmetrical in growth habits and rarely need pruning. They like full sun and moisture and do well all over the South, looking particularly beautiful when used with spring flowering bulbs.

During the last several years, friends were troubled because their *Magnolia Soulangeana* was covered with a black scale. Leaves curled, blackened and dropped and even the bark looked scorched. We tried an oil emulsion spray, since the attacks appeared before the weather turned too warm, but this was not effective and it finally became necessary to resort to parathion, a potent poison, to get rid of the scale. So watch your precious plant carefully and if you happen to see the beginning of the scale, act quickly with the oil emulsion or with one of the new combinations of insecticide and oil emulsion; you may be successful in the very beginning and not have to fall back to stronger measures. Parathion, although effective against mealybugs, scale, aphids and spider mites, is very dangerous to handle. It should never be used unless all precautionary measures recommended by the manufacturer are followed.

The Star Magnolia, *Magnolia stellata* is another hybrid that produces white flowers. Its variety Pink Star has pink blossoms.

MOCKORANGE, *Philadelphus coronarius* belongs to the Saxifrage Family. It is deciduous and reaches eight to ten feet. This plant is noted for its supremely fragrant flowers that are white tinged with pink, opening in June. If you must prune do it immediately after flowering because the flowers appear on wood formed the previous year. *P. Zeyheri* is a good medium-sized variety and *P. microphyllum* is the dwarf form that reaches three feet.

MYRTLE, *Myrtle communis* or *Myrtus communis* is a lovely scented evergreen, reaching nine or more feet. The aromatic leaves are small, dark and shiny and the white flowers are followed by blue-black berries. A slow grower, it needs a sheltered spot and lots of water. It also grows healthier when planted in slightly alkaline soil. It is perfect to cut and bring into the house for arrangements. This is the myrtle worn by the gladiators of ancient times. Some varieties have white-margined leaves.

NANDINA, *Nandina domestica* is often called Heavenly Bamboo, the Japanese name for this evergreen member of the Barberry Family. It is an erect shrub with delicate-looking foliage that becomes tinged with red in the fall. The clusters of small white flowers in summer are followed by pyramids of bright red berries that linger on the bush for quite a few months. This shrub does well in sun or semi-shade and grows to eight or nine feet. Give this most desirable plant plenty of water and leaf mold to aid its growth. If you must prune remove the stalks at ground level if there is no show of foliage except at the top. Leaves will not bud on the stem once the top has been clipped. However, if there is growth appearing half way down the stem, cut just above this growth.

OLEANDER, *Nerium oleander* is an evergreen that is widely cultivated in the South, especially near the coast. It attains eight to fourteen feet in height and blooms in the spring and early summer. Its leaves are long and narrow; the double and single flowers range from white to pink to rose to salmon to dark red, with shades of these colors in between, depending on variety. Prune this shrub after blooming, from June through July and sometimes into August. Thin out by removing the old canes at ground level, and generally shape your bush. A hard spraying of the hose will rout scale and mealybug which attack this shrub. Otherwise it is completely hardy even under adverse conditions.

One word of caution! Do not let your children, or any adult for that matter, chew on the stems, leaves or flowers. They are poisonous. Even the smoke of burning oleander twigs will make some people violently ill.

ORANGE WILD COFFEE, *Daubentonia* or *Sesbania* of the Pea Family, is also known as *Daubentonia Tripetii* and is a deciduous shrub or small tree with feathery leaves and pale yellow-orange clustered flowers from June to August. Grows from five to ten feet.

OREGON HOLLY GRAPE, *Mahonia aquifolium* is an evergreen shrub with spiny dark green holly-shaped leaves and small

Mahonia Aquifolium

yellow spring flowers followed by blue-gray-green berries. Red tints dapple the leaves in the autumn. The *aquifolium* and M. *Wagneri,* another hardy variety grow to six feet very slowly. M. *nervosa* is the dwarf form, M. *repens* rarely grows over one foot in height and is the most resistant to sunburn. M. *bealii,* or M. *japonica* is also called the Leatherleaf Mahonia because of the texture of its bluish-green leaves. This is hardy in the South and does not exceed ten feet.

PENTAS, of the Madder Family, is an old-fashioned shrub to three feet, that seems to have been lost in the shuffle of recent times. It does well in the South all year long if the winters are mild. If frozen back it comes right back up again in the spring. Pentas likes a soil mixture of loam, sand and peat, needs good drainage and takes plenty of water in warm weather. Insects and disease seem to overlook this plant which comes from an African herb and sub-shrub tribe. In short it is a gem that blooms and blooms. The flesh-pink variety is *Pentas lanceolata* and the *alba* is a pure white. *P. kermesina* is carmine-red and the flowers of all grow in small bouquets of tiny star-like blossoms. My dark pink is *P. lanceolata Quartiniana* and looks especially pretty flanked by a double-pink Althea and a large blue Plumbago. Pinch the new shoots to produce compactness and propagate by cuttings, usually made from March to June when you use half-ripened wood. Since the Pentas makes an excellent cut flower, you automatically prune the bush as you clip.

In the last freezing weather my Pentas was blackened by ice and frost but fortunately I had mulched the base of the plant prior to the cold so whereas the top branches had to be removed, the roots had not been harmed and my plant has begun to sprout again. Fast-growing, it will be back to its original size by summer. I was also happy that I had made a few cuttings late last spring. These, rooted in my coldframes were not injured by low temperatures.

PERSIAN SHIELD, *Strobilanthes* of the Acanthus Family, is another so-called sub-shrub that rarely exceeds three feet. It has dark bronzy-green leaves that are long and pointed, each with a distinct metallic overlay. *S. isophyllus* has blue and white flowers growing in clusters. A smaller variety, *S. dyerianus* with lavender blooms, is best treated as a potted plant. Both grow well in shade in sheltered spots and need plenty of moisture. It would be wise to make cuttings of this shrub so that if it is killed by freeze you will have a replacement.

PHOTINIA, of the Rose Family has evergreen varieties *P. ser-*

rulata, P. arbutifolia and *P. glabra*. The deciduous ones are *P. villosa* and *P. subumbellata*. All will grow to fifteen and twenty feet if allowed and all are particularly noted for the scarlet coloring of the leaves in the fall and the bright red berries that linger through the winter. We are in luck with this one. The birds do not eat these berries. These shrubs are not particular as to soil but the deciduous ones do require more sun than those that are evergreen.

PINEAPPLE GUAVA, *Feijoa Sellowiana* of the Myrtle Family is not a guava at all but so-called because the foliage and fruit are so much like those of the guava. An evergreen that grows to fifteen feet, it has leaves that are glossy green above and silverygray beneath. Pinkish-white flowers with red tufty stamens, most attractive in the spring, give way to oval dull green fruit in the fall. The fruit makes good jams and jellies tasting strongly of pineapple. Although this shrub is fairly free of disease it does need good drainage and does well in partial shade. It has always been a favorite in our gardens in the deep South and its popularity is spreading to the mid regions.

PITTOSPORUM, *Pittosporaceae* is a very woody evergreen shrub used extensively all through the South for hedging. The Japanese variety, *P. Tobira* is quick-growing, blooms in late winter and spring and reaches ten feet. It will withstand salt sprays. Its leaves are thick, green and rather round, its flowers are creamywhite and fragrant. *P. Tobira variegatum* has thinner leaves touched with white. Pittosporum can be pruned to various shapes and like the Ligustrum needs occasional spraying with oil emulsion to keep it free of the white fly.

PLUMBAGO, of the Leadwort Family is a graceful southern perennial. Its rather sprawling growth habits can be corrected by training it with supports. *Plumbago capensis* has light green leaves and sky-blue phlox-like flowers in spring and summer. The variety *alba* has white blooms. This shrub lends itself to sparsely foliated bases of other plants and likes fertile soil and full sun. I have a lovely blue Plumbago growing in front of a Mermaid Rose Climber and next to a dull red Clerodendron vine. The Plumbago and the Clerodendron have used the lower thorny stems of the rose on which to climb and the combination of colors is lovely. If the winter is mild Plumbago will remain green but if a freeze occurs it will die back until the following spring.

POMEGRANATE, *Punica Granatum* used to be called the Apple of Carthage. This is a large shrub, from ten to fifteen feet, with small grayish-green glabrous leaves and orange-red flowers in late spring and early summer. The blossoms ripen into large seeded balls. Hardy, it does well all over the South. There is a double white-flowered pomegranate, *P. alba*. The dwarf form, *P. Granatum nana* is interesting for small gardens and patios. Plant them all in deep rich loam, in full sun and if the winters are not too severe they will not lose their leaves. Propagation is by hardwood cuttings made in February or by softwood cuttings made in summer. Prune while dormant in the fall. In the home garden the Pomegranate is more valued for its flowers than for its fruit. In some locales it is grown commercially.

PYRACANTHA, *Coccinea Lalandii* or Firethorn has tiny evergreen leaves and is literally covered with small star-like white flowers in the spring followed by fiery red berries in autumn. A vigorous grower all over the South, it not only reaches twenty or more feet as a bush but can be espaliered to walls and fences and trained to pillar shape. *P. pauciflora* is of low dense habits and is suitable for hedges. *P. crenulata flava* is one of the varieties producing yellow fruit. *P. yunnanensis* has coral-red berries, is hardy and grows to five feet. *P. angustifolia,* the very narrow-leaf variety shows orange-red berries. A new dwarf form, *P. koidzumi nana* has just been introduced and should be the answer to landscaping where low evergreens are in demand.

This shrub is subject to Fire Blight, a bacterial disease that causes Die-Back, so prune well below the scorched areas. Paint the cut surface with Bordeaux paint and disinfect your shears. Pyracantha is also attacked by the lace bug which sucks the sap from the undersides of the leaves and causes them to take on a rusty appearance. Control with a contact insecticide, preferably early in the spring when the young bugs begin to hatch. Your Pyracantha can also become anemic and develop chlorosis or yellowing of the foliage. This is due to the alkalinity of the soil and a dose of iron is indicated, either iron sulphate or one of the chelates.

As for regular pruning, after the berries turn dark and shriveled cut the branch back to the cane from which it grows. But don't take off any of the new non-fruited growth that has appeared because this will bear next year's berries. The only safe time to transplant the Pyracantha is in the month of January and in the first two weeks of February unless the plant is container-grown. Plant in slightly alkaline soil. Pruning in the spring to the extent of bringing flowering branches into the house for arrangement is not injurious to the shrub but it does rob you of future berries.

RICE-PAPER PLANT, *Tetrapanax papyriferus* also called the Chinese Paper Plant, is a tropical that has foot-broad felty leaves and huge wooly panicles in winter. No insect spray or particular culture is needed. As a matter of fact you have a hard time controlling the roots from spreading all over the garden. Used for paper in Asia, the leaves give a superb tropical effect for patios and the fuzzy blossoms are much in demand by flower arrangers. It is grown through the lower coastal plain and Florida but is killed back by the first frost. Next spring it is up again.

SHRIMP PLANT, *Beloperone guttata* grows three or four feet tall and sometimes reaches five feet. An evergreen in warmer sections of the South, it is considered a perennial elsewhere. This shrub has slender drooping three-inch racemes of white flowers tinged in dark red. These flowers are small and enclosed in heart-shaped copper-colored bracts that overlap in such a fashion as to show a tip of the bloom. The leaves are medium in size and a soft green in tone, much more tender than those of the Acanthus plant to which it is related. There is a fairly new hybrid, *B. angustiflora* with darker, more slender and heavier leaves and bracts that are a deeper shade of orange and not so uniformly overlapped, and more tubular than heart-shaped. These racemes are half the length of those of the *guttata*. They look almost stubby but they make a nice contrast when grown in front of the taller *guttata*. These tropicals are easily propagated by cuttings and like a moist, well-drained soil and plenty of sun. They withstand our deep South winters and to my knowledge have never been molested by pest or disease. They also make excellent cut flowers; so with all of these points in their favor it is hard to understand why they are not more widely grown. In the upper South where winters are more severe, the Shrimp Plant makes a wonderful potted plant that can be brought indoors when frosts and freezes are predicted.

SNOWBERRY, *Symphoricarpus albus* is a deciduous shrub with branching habits that reaches a height of four to six feet. *S. albus laevigatus* is the pink-flowered variety most widely cultivated and in summer its arching branches are heavy with snow-white berries that last well into fall. *S. orbiculatus* is the Coralberry, with purplish-red berries. The variety called White Hedge is a low compact form suited to small gardens.

ST. JOHN'S WORT, *Hypericum aureum* is an ornamental plant known for its attractive yellow summer flowers and interesting semi-deciduous foliage. It grows to three feet and will bloom longer in a partly shaded spot. *H. patulum Henryi* also to three feet has large flowers, *H. kalmianum* is lower and hardy, *H. calycinum* is such a low grower that it can be used as a ground cover. This last one is evergreen, perhaps because it is always so protected by higher-growing plants.

STEWARTIA, also spelled STUARTIA and often called the Wild Camellia is of the Tea Family, *Ternstroemiaceae*. This is a deciduous shrub noted for its large single summer flowers and bright green foliage that becomes tinged with red in autumn. Although it is not too well known nor widely planted most of the species of Stewartia are native from Virginia, North Carolina and

Georgia to all points south. S. *pentagyna* one of the hardiest, reaches fifteen feet, showing white filaments and yellow anthers in the large white flowers. S. *Malacodendron* the Virginia Stewartia although not as hardy as *pentagyna,* grows to twelve feet and bears very large flowers that show purple stamens. S. *Pseudo-Camellia* though reaching fifty feet in Japan will grow here to twelve feet and its flowers show orange-colored anthers. All varieties do best in rich peaty loam and in sunny locations.

STRAWBERRY GUAVA, *Psidium Cattleianum,* a member of the Myrtle Family is the Cattley Guava and bears fruit that is much in demand for jellies. This shrub which sometimes grows to fifteen feet has become naturalized in some parts of the lower South and in south and central Florida. Elsewhere it is quite hardy and will stand temperatures as low as twenty-five degrees. An evergreen, it has thick rather leathery elliptical leaves. The white-petaled flowers bearing rosy stamens are followed in summer by greenish-lavender fruit. The smooth brownish-green bark adds the final touch to make this a most desirable compact bush. It is not too fussy either. It does not mind dry conditions, requires no particular soil and is relatively free of disease and pests. It does need good drainage. The Guava of the tropics is *Psidium guajava.* Did you know that the guava fruit is a source of Vitamin C?

SUMACS or RHUS, are woody plants of the Cashew Family grown for their colorful autumn foliage and attractive panicles of berry-like fruit that remain intact during the winter. Almost evergreen (and I say this because a hard freeze will defoliate but not kill them) *Rhus typhina, R. glabra* and *R. copallina* are good ornamentals of this family. *R. typhina,* the Staghorn Sumac has striking brilliant foliage and panicles of green flowers that turn to red fruit in the fall. Grows to twenty feet and better in the upper South. *R. glabra,* even more beautiful than *typhina* is the Smooth Sumac and reaches twelve to fifteen feet. You can tell the *glabra* from Poison Ivy by noticing the undersurface of the leaf, white in *glabra,* green in Poison Ivy. *R. copallina* the Shining Sumac, is widely distrubuted in Louisiana and into the middle South. It has glossy green foliage and red panicled fruit. *R. aromatica* is the Fragrant Sumac. A low shrub, it has tri-foliate leaves, inconspicuous flowers and attractive red berries.

I do not recommend *Rhus radicans* Poison Ivy, a shrub when it is low and a vine when it reaches something on which to climb. Poison Oak is *R. quercifolia, Rhus verniciflua* is the Varnish Tree, *R. succedanea* is the Wax Tree and *R. vernix* is Poison Sumac. They are all dangerous. Be careful of this whole last group. They are rank growers and could take over the garden if allowed. Poison Ivy's three-inch stemmed leaves are tri-foliate and may be smooth-edged or toothed. Fruit and berries are green. Killed by frost. Poison Oak is a low shrub never more than two feet high. Its leaves are evergreen and also tri-foliate, lobed like the oak leaf, and leathery. Fruit and berries are greenish-yellow. Poison Sumac has gray stems and narrow elliptical leaves. Berries are white and hang in clusters. The poisonous varieties cause the skin to blister, and if home remedies fail call your physician at once.

SWEET PEPPERBUSH, *Clethra alnifolia* grows to nine feet from New England to Florida but can be pruned as low as six feet. Semi-deciduous and known for its fragrant panicled white flowers from June to September, it is also called Summersweet. This shrub likes moist swampy conditions with plenty of peat mixed in the soil.

SWEET OLIVE, *Osmanthus fragrans* is listed as a shrub as well as a tree because it is a slow grower and because its height, sometimes to twenty feet, can be controlled by careful pruning. This evergreen has handsome leaves and very fragrant clustered white flowers that bloom during the winter. This is an old southern favorite and in recent years has been taken somewhat for granted. Although it is true that the Sweet Olive demands no particular soil it does need good drainage and does appreciate occasional feeding with a well-balanced fertilizer. If you knew how hard it is to find these shrubs I am certain that you would realize that your

Sweet Olive is not just "that old bush that has been in the garden for years".

Another familiar variety O. *fortunei* has spiny leaves and doesn't grow as tall as its cousin *fragrans*. This one blooms in the spring and is also fragrant. O. *Aquifolium* or Holly Osmanthus has, as its name implies, leaves resembling those of the Holly. Its sweet-smelling flowers are creamy-yellow and the plant though slow-growing, will reach sixteen or seventeen feet in height, making it ideal for background planting. A. *aureo-marginatus* has yellow variegated leaves and A. *argenteo-marginatus* is white-variegated. O. *americanus*, to twenty feet, is still another variety that should be planted more in the lower South. It grows more rapidly and needs more shade and moisture than the others mentioned.

SWEET SHRUB, *Calycanthus floridus* sometimes called the Strawberry Bush, is deciduous, grows to six feet and is aromatically fragrant as its name implies. The leaves are green above and grayish-brown beneath and the dark red-brown flowers that bloom in summer are followed by oblong fruit. This shrub does well in either sun or shade.

TAMARIX or TAMARISK is a deciduous ornamental known for its graceful cedar-like foliage and racemes of pinkish-white flowers. Because it tolerates salt spray it is frequently called Salt Water Cedar. T. *hispida* blooms towards autumn while T. *parviflora* and T. *chinensis* are spring and summer-flowering. Attain twelve feet. This shrub should be cut back drastically when transplanted in order to insure successful results. This whole family is well adapted to warm dry areas and thrives best in alkaline soil.

THRYALLIS, *Thryallis glauca* is a tropical summer-flowering, semi-evergreen shrub that grows to five or more feet. Plant in late winter while dormant, in ordinary garden soil, in an open sunny location. Feed with a balanced fertilizer as growth begins. The blossoms are yellow and prolific, almost hiding the medium-small soft green leaves and making a brilliant summer bed. Prune to shape in January or February because the flowers appear on the current season's growth. Insect free. Cuttings of softwood may be made in late spring, of hardwood after the plant defoliates in late November.

TIBOUCHINA, *Tibouchina semidecandra* is a tender tropical shrub to six or eight feet, that should be planted in the spring in a protected spot. Placing it next to a wall would be ideal because this plant lends itself superbly to espaliering. It needs sun and filtered shade to bring out the lovely deep pink buds that change to a dark satiny lavender when the petals are open. The stamens are yellow and shaped like a sickle. The leaves are green, covered with a velvety down and deeply veined. Feed with 5–10–5 in spring and again in June. Insect free. The Tibouchina may freeze down in a very cold winter but if planted near a wall or other shelter, it almost always revives in the spring.

TREE WISTERIA, of the Pea Family, is actually the Wisteria vine that has been cut back to six or eight feet when young and pruned in for several years so that the trunk thickens until it needs no support and the top spreads like an umbrella. Prune yearly between July fifteenth and August fifteenth and cut back new growth to the fourth bud. Give the plant a dose of well-rotted manure when transplanting and then in late winter feed with a well-balanced fertilizer. Never feed in the spring because spring feeding brings on more growth than flowers. The Japanese Wisteria, *W. floribunda* is the hardiest of all, with violet-blue flowers. The variety *alba* has white flowers, variety *rosea* has pink and rose blooms tipped with purple. Variety *violaceo-plena* is double-flowered but fades rapidly in rainy seasons. For further details see Wisteria in Chapter on Vines.

TURKSCAP, *Malvaviscus arboreus* is a fine old shrub noted for its resistance to insects and low temperatures. It grows in the mid and lower South to about six feet, is branching in habit, with deep scarlet flowers that resemble those of the Abutilon but which never fully open. This plant has a long blooming season and is easily propagated by cuttings. A later-flowering smaller variety has a tiny red flower that looks exactly like a wrapped turban and is sometimes known as The Sultan's Turban.

VIBURNUM of the Honeysuckle Family, is considered an evergreen that is excellent for hedging throughout the South. Some are more tender than others and some are deciduous.

I have always enjoyed my hedge of *Viburnum suspensum*, which is listed as an evergreeen and certainly behaves like one except on rare occasions. It has frozen back to the ground in a prolonged freeze but it comes back beautifully. Naturally it takes some time to reach six feet again but I plant the quick-growing Castor Bean in between each *suspensum* bush and at least I have the privacy we need during the following summer. By the next spring the Viburnum hedge graces the garden again. But here in New Orleans such freezes are unusual. In subsequent freezes only the tips of the hedge were blackened. I don't think I clipped any more than six inches from the top. Perhaps the older the *suspensum* gets the more resistant it becomes to cold. Or perhaps this winter's cold was wetter and the earlier freezes were drier. The leaves are always a pretty green. The flowers are incidental, but an attractive white, appearing in panicles.

Viburnum tomentosum, to eight feet, is the Japanese Snowball and is hardy. This one is known for its beautiful display of white clustered flowers that are so rounded that they look like snowballs. This variety is sometimes referred to as *V. japonicum*, which is not hardy in the upper regions of the United States. The *tomentosum*'s leaves are most beautiful and the flowers give way to bright red fruit before they change to black.

The Sweet Viburnum, *Viburnum odoratissimum* to ten feet, is the old plant that may still be found in the plantations of Louisiana. It is more easily damaged by cold. *Viburnum Tinus rigidum*, the upright variety will reach ten feet. It is bushy in growth habits. *V. Sieboldii*, with handsome green foliage and *V. Burkwoodi*, whose leaves turn scarlet in the fall are both deciduous and do best in the upper South. They are ornamentals so not used much as hedge material. You would want the evergreen Viburnum if you were planting for privacy.

V. *rhytidophyllum* to ten feet, with wrinkled dark green leaves is evergreen and does well all over the South. So does V. *acerifolium* whose leaves turn dark purple in the fall. Then there is *Viburnum grandiflorum* that is superb in New Orleans in July, after a cold winter. It is covered with clusters of red berries. It doesn't flower too often down here. These berries may be planted, when mature, for more plants.

Viburnum is subject not only to white fly for which you use an oil emulsion spray, but also to fireblight, lace bug and red spider. Control all three in the cooler months by using a spray containing 1% malathion and 2½% oil emulsion. In the summer use 1% malathion and 1½% oil emulsion, on a cloudy day or late in the evening.

VITEX, of the Vervain Family *Verbenaceae* is a deciduous shrub that needs cutting back each winter to keep it compact. *Vitex Agnus-castus* sometimes called the Chaste Tree and the Hemp Tree, has grayish aromatic foliage and dark green leaves resembling the fingers of a hand. The flowers appear in long spikes of bluish-lavender and usually are at their height in May and June. Don't confuse the Vitex with Buddleia, whose racemes of blossoms are predominantly lavender-purple and have a tendency to droop over at the top. A rapid grower, Vitex will reach ten feet if planted in a moderately rich loam in a sunny spot. Feed at least once during the growing season with a balanced fertilizer. It may be pruned to any shape and is practicaly free of pest and disease. Propagate by softwood cuttings in the spring and hardwood cuttings in autumn. The variety *macrophylla* is another good one, a broader-leaved form. Don't be alarmed if your Vitex does not come into bud in early spring, it does not bring out its leaves until warm weather.

WEIGELA or DIERVILLA, of the Honeysuckle Family *Caprifoliceae* is a deciduous ornamental shrub of spreading growth habits. Showy flowers that begin in spring and last until autumn range in color from white to red. W. *florida* has white flowers changing to pale pink, W. Bristol Ruby is a rounded bush and like the others, takes plenty of sun and lots of moisture. The dwarf variety is W. Eva Rathke.

Y A U P O N , *Ilex vomitoria* although a plant native to swampy regions along the coast will also do well in upper, drier climates. Dark evergreen leaves look lovely in contrast to the gray bark and the scarlet berries that appear in profusion in the winter. It stands clipping well. Same culture as Holly.

By this time you must have a fairly good conception of planting, feeding, pruning, etc., from the chapters on Shrubs and Trees but the following is a reminder.

PLANTING

Though your shrub comes to you with a ball of earth around the roots you must always dig the hole into which the plant will go at least one foot wider and deeper unless the plant is container-grown. You do this in order to loosen up the soil surrounding the ball to give the roots comfortable space in which to spread.

If your shrub is bare-rooted by all means dig deeper and wider than the length of the roots. Never twist and double over the roots to avoid making a larger hole. Don't forget to soak bare-rooted plants in water before planting and if you have a drainage problem, by all means use brickbats in the bottom of the hole. Refer to the first chapter on Soils and Additives for remedying clay and sandy soils and to the chapter on Shrubs for the Landscape for further planting and spacing directions.

CONTAINER-GROWN PLANTS

Horticultural experimental stations have found that container-grown stock retains nearly all of the plant's root system. This is good news to the gardener because now he does not have to wait until the dormant season to buy his plants. He can see them in leaf and flower, can have the nurseryman slit the cans before he takes the plants home, can keep them at home in the container until the right planting time and he can be sure that they will escape shock in transplanting.

Quite a few flowering shrubs, tropicals, shade trees and even roses are now being sold in containers, and the procedure for transplanting container-grown stock is a little different than the steps taken in transplanting balled and bare-rooted stock. The depth of the hole has to match the depth of the plant in the container so that the soil level of the plant is even with the ground level. The hole may be twice as wide, enabling you to fill in the sides with loam that is well-mixed with fertilizer and peat. A container-grown plant may be fed at the time it is planted. Use one pound of a well-balanced commercial fertilizer to every two hundred square feet of ground. Then continue feeding at the routine intervals during the year. Balled plants should never be fed until they have been in the ground about a year. Mulch and water your container-grown plant but keep in mind the fact that over-watering can be as dangerous as none at all.

FEEDING

Unless otherwise specified in the foregoing pages, I recommend feeding your flowering shrubs with a good balanced fertilizer immediately after they have bloomed. Scratch it into the soil with a trowel and water well or in the case of larger plants make about three holes, about eight inches deep midway between the outer circumference of the branches and the trunk and fill half-way with fertilizer. Fill the remainder of the hole with soil and water well. Never allow the feed to touch the base of the trunk and never plug in the feed on plants that have a shallow root system, such as the Azalea and Camellia. If you plan to feed your shrubs in the fall use a fertilizer that is slow-acting, otherwise you will bring on new growth just in time for frost to kill. By slow-acting I mean one that takes several months to go to work on the plant and one that is low in nitrogen. Blood meal, horn and hoof meal and the synthetic ureaformaldehydes are all sources of slow-acting nitrogen. Don't forget to use the acidifying agents on those shrubs that demand acid soil.

Be careful of the commercial fertilizers that carry no breakdown or analysis of content on the label. And go slowly on the new "wonder feeds" because most of them are still in the experimental stages. I always check them by using them on one of a pair of potted plants, and I allow enough time for them to prove themselves. Liquid fertilizers are easier to use than the dry chemicals but they are more expensive.

Experiments have been and are being made with foliar feeding as a substitute for ground feeding. To date the consensus of opinion is that the foliar sprays are not full substitutes for the standard soil fertilization. So far it has been decided that the best way to use a feed is to put it in the ground. However foliar feeding does have its place. Plants often show need of additional nutrients besides nitrogen, phosphoric acid and potash, and then the trace elements may be fed to the plants through the leaves. Azaleas and other shrubs may show that they are in need of iron by the yellowing of the leaves, particularly in summer. Chelated iron, sold under trade names, or a solution of iron sulphate or Copperas may be sprayed on the leaves to correct this condition.

To get back to soil feeding, do not confuse the plant hormones or soil conditioners with fertilizers. Hormones do help in making rooted cuttings, and the conditioners tend to improve the texture of the soil but they are not substitutes for food. The gibberellins are on the market under several brand names. They are new growth stimulants to plants and are still in the experimental stage. I have tried some of them with very good results on some plants, and absolutely none on others. It is still too early to tell.

Testing is still going on with ground glass, called "Frits" as a nutrient. The window glass of commerce is actually a blend of sand and certain amounts of lime, sodium, boron, iron and potassium. When ground up this glass becomes frits that are being tested as a possible source of nutrition as trace elements to the soil.

PRUNING

Flowering shrubs are usually pruned after the blooming season but not too long afterwards because most of them set the next year's buds rather quickly.

Pruning does not mean merely whacking off a piece of this branch or that one to insure bushier growth. Pruning should be regarded almost as a clinical operation, a rejuvenation process, to be done with tools that have been well-sharpened and disinfected from past usage on diseased limbs. Study your plant before using your clipping tools. If it is a leggy spindly one you will want to top it heavily so that it will produce more branches and leaves. Remove all dead or broken branches and wherever you see one branch rubbing against another, remove one of them. If you should find a matted area of stems you will want to thin some of them out so that air and sunlight may reach the lower parts of the plant and encourage new growth. This is especially common in hedges of boxwood and pyracantha.

Do not prune immediately after a freeze. If you don't mind bearing with a rather sad looking garden it is wise to wait until spring growth appears before you cut back. The exceptions are Hibiscus and Poinsettia which must be pruned back before the frozen sap sinks further down into the stems to spread the damage.

If there are suckers or wild growth showing at the base of the shrub (nearly all grafted stock will show this) prune them off.

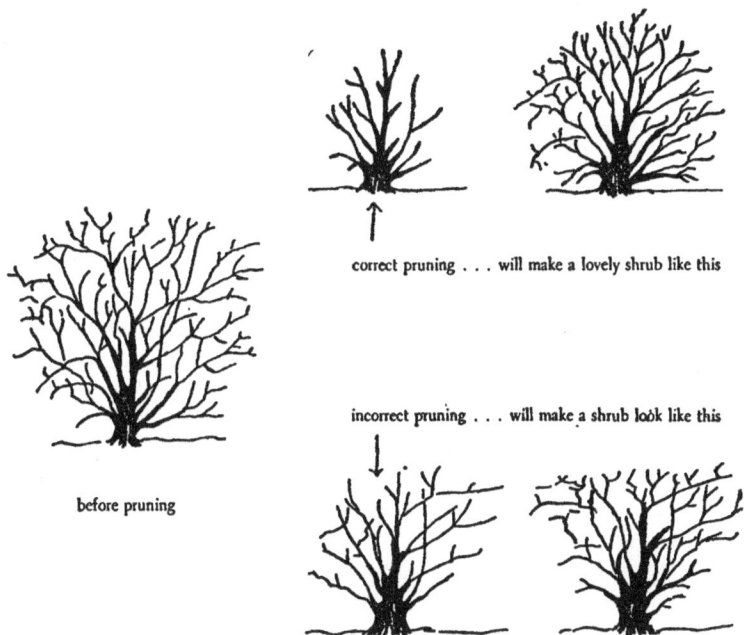

correct pruning . . . will make a lovely shrub like this

incorrect pruning . . . will make a shrub look like this

before pruning

SHRUB PRUNING

Watch for this condition especially in Tree Roses, Camellias, Dog-woods, Flowing Almonds and Plums. Make the cut with a sharp shovel, with the curve of the blade turned away from the trunk of the shrub. If you wish to keep a plant to dwarf dimensions you will have to prune top branches and roots, thin out the whole plant and keep pinching out the new top green shoots as they appear.

Many of you are trying the fairly new multiflora hedge, *Rosa multiflora*, the hardy Japanese rose. When the first growth appears it will seem long and leggy and most unwieldy, and you will wonder if you have received a climbing rose instead of the multiflora hedge that you ordered. Just keep it clipped back to about a three-foot height until the bottom has thickened and allow it to gradually grow to the height desired. The results will be a thick, luxuriant hedge.

All summer-blooming and fall-blooming shrubs should be pruned during their dormant period in January and February because their blooms will usually be on new wood produced during the current growing season. There are some exceptions to this rule. The Gardenia need never be pruned as long as you cut the blossoms regularly or unless it is damaged by a cold spell of weather, in which case you cut it back severely. Those shrubs that flower but are used as hedges must be kept trimmed. But I urge you not to prune immediately before a predicted cold snap or freeze.

A word about pruning the Nandina. Since it does not actually branch it increases its size by sending up new shoots from the ground. Never just trim a Nandina; if you do, the rest of the stem will wither and die. Be sure to cut the whole cane off at ground level unless there is growth midway down the stem. In this instance you can top the cane just above this growth of leaves.

PROPAGATION — CUTTINGS

There is no definite rule as to the best time to make cuttings but generally soft-wood cuttings (the current season's growth with matured leaves) of deciduous plants are made in late spring and early summer. Soft-wood cuttings of the broad-leaved evergreens and conifers are begun in the late summer and may be continued through the fall and into the winter. Hardwood cuttings of woody plants are also made of the current season's growth but usually from the canes that grow from the base of the shrub. Soft-wood cuttings are usually made from three to six inches in length; hardwood, from six to eight inches long. You want to keep in mind the fact that the shorter the cutting, the less foliage and therefore the less evaporation of moisture and eventually the less

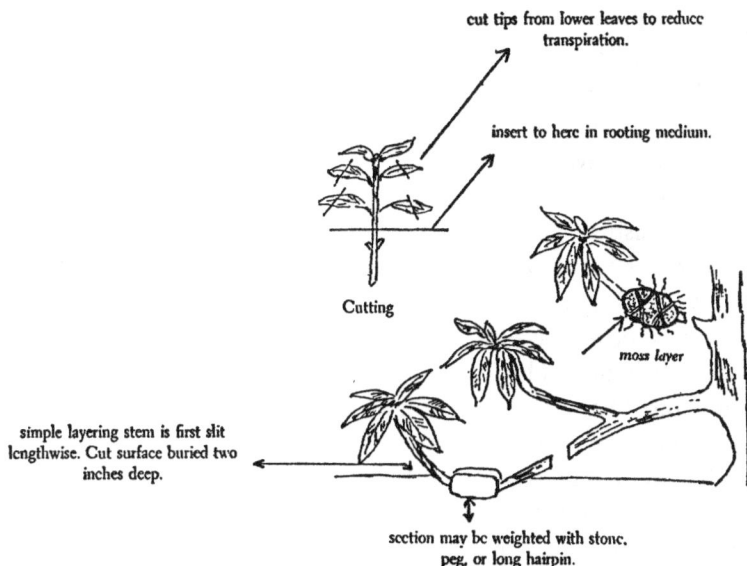

cut tips from lower leaves to reduce transpiration.

insert to here in rooting medium.

Cutting

moss layer

simple layering stem is first slit lengthwise. Cut surface buried two inches deep.

section may be weighted with stone, peg, or long hairpin.

PROPAGATION

wilting. A sharp knife can be used to cut the softwood, thereby avoiding any squeezing of the plant tissues that might be done by a pruning shears. On the other hand, hardwood cuttings almost always necessitate the use of the shears. Just make sure that they are sharp and clean.

Whichever type of cutting you make, cut on a slant or forty-five degree angle and try to make it just below a leaf node. Remove the leaves from the lower third of the cutting. Some gardeners like to pull the leaf completely away from the stem but I have found my cuttings root with more success if I leave a little "heel" or stump of the leaf on the stem. Dip the basal end of the cutting in a hormone rooting powder, shake off the excess and insert into the planting medium on a slant, from one-third to one-half the length of the cutting.

There are several rooting mediums; clean, sharp, builder's sand,

vermiculite, or a mixture of sand and peat moss. I prefer using
⅓ sharp sand, ⅓ peat and ⅓ good garden loam which I have previously sterilized. I place the rooting mixture in my coldframes,
which I describe in the chapter on Annuals and Perennials. These
coldframes have covers made from window sashes which can be partially lowered when the cuttings are first placed within, to con-
serve moisture. The cuttings must be kept moist but never soggy
and for the first week or so they must have light shade. Plastic
bags can be put to use as covers for the containers that hold your
cuttings, or plastic bread and refrigerator boxes may serve as flats
with their own lids. When the cuttings have produced roots at
least one to two inches in length, remove them carefully to either
pot or open ground.

The next time you feel in the mood to make a quantity of cuttings why not try the comparatively new "Mist" method? Mist
Propagation entails the use of a sunny, well-drained site and good
planting medium surrounded by a windbreak of plastic or other
transparent material. A very fine mist of water is allowed to play
over the inserted cuttings from sunrise to sunset. The principle
behind this method of propagation is that there is almost no water
loss from the cuttings while they benefit from the full heat of the
sun. This comparatively new garden practice has three advantages:
the home gardener can root larger cuttings, the rooting time is cut
almost in half, and cuttings otherwise difficult to root are almost
always a success.

A greenhouse is a perfect setting for Mist Propagation but the
average home gardener can either avail himself of one of the wire
and plastic, ready-made domes or if he is ingenious, he will rig one
up for himself. One mist nozzle to every four square feet will
usually do the trick, and make sure that the ones you buy have the
smallest possible opening. Misting may be used steadily or intermittently through the daylight hours and it is successful only
through the summer season.

The rooting medium may be a mixture of peat moss and vermiculite, with a heavy layer of gravel or brickbats beneath to insure good drainage. Cuttings of plants that have hairy leaves, Azaleas included,`cannot be rooted in this manner because the water does not drip fast enough from the surface. In all other instances, cuttings are prepared as usual, removing only the leaves from that part of the stem that will be inserted in the rooting medium. You do not have to use a rooting hormone unless you feel you must. Place the cuttings far enough apart so that there will be no overlapping of leaves, and turn on the mist. This method reduces fungus that usually besets cuttings, to a minimum. Instead of the familiar struggle to root a cutting—careful shading, frequent waterings, etc., the Mist Method is really easier, and productive of rooted cuttings in ten to twenty-one days.

PESTS

There are numerous pests and diseases on flowering shrubs that you will have to fight from time to time, and these include bacterial blight, aphids, scale, mildew and other chewing insects. Fire Blight makes the leaves and branches of Pyracantha, Quince and Plum trees look wilted and scorched as if they have been burned. It is most dreadful because there is no cure. You must simply cut off all affected twigs and branches and remove them from the garden to the trash burner. Cut the diseased parts well past the sickly area, disinfecting your cutting tool each time you clip. There are several formulas that I could give you to use as a disinfectant for your cutting implements but the substances are so poisonous to handle that it will be safer in the long run for you to obtain a prepared mixture from your nurseryman and follow the directions closely.

Use sprays containing nicotine, lindane or malathion for the aphids, preparations containing oil emulsion or malathion for scale and white fly, arsenate of lead to rout the chewing insects and applications of wettable sulphur in cool weather and ferbam in warm weather to get rid of mildew. Here again I caution not to use sulphur or full strength oil emulsion if temperatures are too high and don't use sulphur and oil emulsion on the same plant without allowing at least thirty days to lapse between the two. Aramite is a good insecticide for red spider, chlordane for ants, lindane for thrips, and if you have a combination of thrip and red spider to fight, use malathion. For further details on insecticides and fungicides, see pages 123–125.

A note about POISONS: Besides the previous commentary notes made about plants and insecticides being poisonous, there are several more trees and shrubs that might give trouble to you allergic readers. Poinsettia "milk" produces an irritation on sensitive skin, leaves of the Tree of Heaven, flowers of the Catalpa and fruit of the Ginkgo produce rashes. In the insecticides, parathion, an organic phosphate, is extremely poisonous to man and beast. DDT, malathion and lindane can do damage if absorbed through the skin. Chlordane is not so toxic. Pyrethrum, lead arsenate and rotenone present little hazard through absorption.

9

Bulbs

True bulbs are either tunicated or formed in rings or layers like the hyacinths and onions, or scaly like those of the Liliums and Amaryllis. But for the commercial purposes and to be popularly understood, the term "bulb" applies to a large class of plants that includes besides the true *bulb,* the solid *corms* such as crocus and glads, the *tubers* which are succulent and have buds or eyes near the surface, like the dahlia and the potato, the *rhizomes* or fleshy roots that creep underground like certain iris and ginger, the *pips* or the flowering crowns of the Lily-of-the-Valley, and other fleshy roots or herbaceous tubers like the ranunculus.

The bulb is a storehouse for the plant, wherein is formed after flowering the new stem, leaf and flower. In fact the bulb as you buy it, contains a new plant that is protected and sustained within the bulb by the reserve food and energy collected therein during one season's growth. After the flowering period the plant above the bulb and the roots beneath it ripen off and die away and the bulb enters its dormant state. If you must lift a bulb don't do it until the foliage is brown and dried-looking or the new plant contained in the bulb will not fully develop.

A true bulb lives indefinitely as a single unit and reproduces by seed or by splitting. The corm dies after producing flowers for one season and is replaced by a new corm that forms either above, below or alongside it. The rhizomes and tubers multiply through the roots and tubers.

I have found through the process of trial and error that bulbs have certain locales in which they do their best. So don't order all of the beautiful blooms that you see in the catalogues. First find out which ones do best in your area and then choose accordingly. What the upper South might enjoy year after year may be short-lived in the lower sections. We in the New Orleans area with our famous short winters, long hot summers and great humidity have to battle the three-letter word that is the bulb's worst enemy, R O T .

PLANTING

Prepare the bulb bed by filling the bottom with a layer of white shells or brickbats. This will insure the good drainage that is so necessary to successful bulb growth. If the bed is a raised one you have additional insurance against the bulb wasting away. Be sure that the soil you add is of a sandy, loamy texture. It is always a good idea when you dig to plant, to set your bulb or tuber on a handful of sharp builder's sand to increase good drainage still further. I have also noticed that some bulbs do well in a neutral soil condition in one exposure and that these same bulbs will thrive in slightly acid soil in another exposure. My amaryllis, habranthus and tigridias do very well in a south bed in neutral to slightly alkaline conditions and they flower equally well in a north bed where I plant my hybrid lilies in soil that tends to be acid. I do not add any chemical fertilizer to make the earth acid. I simply use the same soil mixture as I do for my camellias and azaleas, one-third black humus, one-third sharp sand and one-third peat moss. Occasional light mulching with peat moss seems to keep the soil just acid

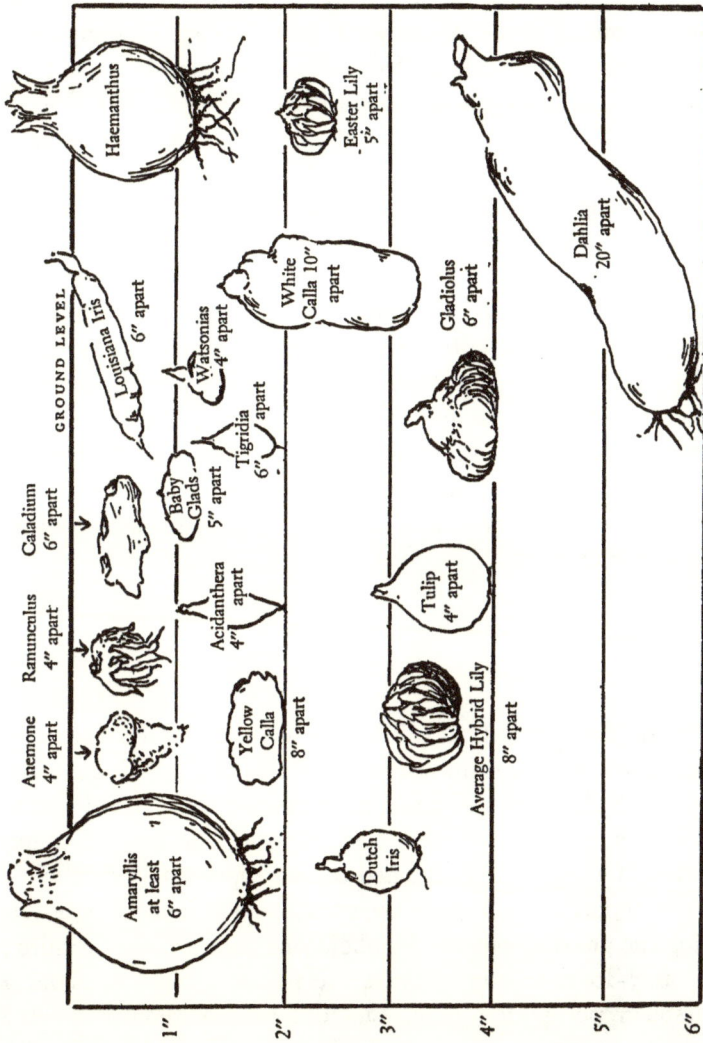

AVERAGE PLANTING DEPTHS FOR BULBS, TUBERS AND RHIZOMES'

Amaryllis
at least
6" apart

Anemone
4" apart

Ramunculus
4" apart

Caladium
6" apart

GROUND LEVEL

Louisiana Iris
6" apart

Haemanthus

Yellow
Calla

Acidanthera
4" apart

Baby
Glads
5" apart

Tigridia
6"
apart

Watsonias
4" apart

White
Calla 10"
apart

Easter Lily
5" apart

Dutch
Iris

8" apart

Average Hybrid Lily

Tulip
4" apart

Gladiolus
6" apart

Dahlia
20" apart

8" apart

1"
2"
3"
4"
5"
6"

enough. Be sure to sift the peat moss before using as a mixer or as a mulch. Sifting through hardware cloth gets rid of lumps and prevents consequent caking. With ideal soil conditions and exposures you will find that bulbs will need only an occasional feeding with a well-balanced liquid fertilizer that also contains trace elements.

Most catalogue instructions on planting are geared to cooler climates. We in the lower South cannot plant our bulbs as deeply as directed. A good rule of thumb in this area is to set them out from one and a half to twice the depth of the bulb. If you must err with bulbs it is better to plant too shallow rather than too deep. Bulbs can find their own depth by means of their roots but they cannot pull themselves up. There are exceptions to the rule of course, such as the anemone and ranunculus that must be planted just below the ground surface; the amaryllis, whose neck must stand above the soil level and the dahlias, which should be planted four to six inches deep.

FEEDING

For those that need it an initial dose of bone meal at planting time is good because it furnishes phosphorus to the bulb but some of it is not absorbed and bulbs need the additional nourishment of nitrogen, potash and other trace elements. So feed all bulbs, whether in a slightly alkaline bed or in a slightly acid one, when the new shoots break through the ground and at monthly intervals during the growing period. Use about one pound of dry fertilizer, such as 5–10–5, to every fifty square feet of ground or about a tablespoon per potted bulb. Liquid fertilizers should be used according to the directions on the package. Withhold food, with the exception of an occasional dose of bone meal, during the bulb's dormant period, at which time watering should be done sparingly. And a word of caution! Never let any powdered fertilizer come in direct contact with the bulb or you will burn the bulb. Further, remember that bulbs will split if over-fed. It will take at least three years for the split to mature enough to heal. There has been recent interest in a newly introduced bulb food embodying a high potash formula, similar to that used by some of the commercial growers in Holland. This new fertilizer also has a soil insect control mixed with it to provide protection against pests.

DIGGING AND STORING

Most of us have felt at one time in our gardening experience that we should dig and store bulbs after each blooming period. Because we humans are potentially lazy we more or less strive to steer clear of work and therefore we tend to avoid planting bulbs. But actually the situation is not as big a bugbear as we think it is. Tulip bulbs can be dug once their foliage has died, brushed of excess earth, dusted with an insecticide and stored in a cool dry place. I usually place mine in old nylon stockings and hang them from a rafter in the garage. Chill them in the refrigerator for two months before planting again. They will return blooms a second year and sometimes even for a third year but the stems will not always be as tall as the original ones. Whether certain bulbs do well in succeeding years depends on the weather. I have noticed that snow and prolonged freeze allowed my tulips to come up for the third year and bloom on stems nearly as tall as those of the two previous years. You can take the same chances with the hyacinths.

Amaryllis and amarcrinum need not be disturbed unless you feel that they must be thinned out and then you do the dividing in the dormant period of September and October. Callas do better if not disturbed or divided for four or five years. Easter Lilies need not be dug every year. Once every three or four years is usually sufficient. The bulbs of the anemone and the ranunculus disintegrate into roots as the foliage fades. As many times as I have dug gently around the plant in the hopes of finding a tuber to store I have only found a stringy mass of roots, so pull them up and plan to reorder a batch for the next year.

There is one thing that I beg you not to do. Don't cut the bulb foliage until it browns. Because it is unsightly when it turns yellow we are all tempted to remove the leaves at once but I suggest that you try plaiting the foliage and rolling it down near the base of the plant. Most bulbs need the leaves to store up food in the bulb for next season's blooms so bear with the sad-looking foliage until time to cut it off.

PESTS

APHIDS are small sucking insects that attack lilies, dahlias, tulips, glads, anemone and ranunculus, iris, oxalis and many others. Control: nicotine sulphate or malathion.

BORER is a small brown caterpillar that attacks lilies, dahlias and glads, iris and cannas. Control: DDT or arsenate of lead and burn old foliage to insure total destruction of the borer.

CUTWORMS, green and brown, attack dahlias and glads at soil level. Control by handpicking or by wrapping the base of the plant with a strip of tar-paper, or with a 5% DDT spray.

MEALYBUGS, the wooly-white oval sucking insects attack amaryllis, callas and others. Control by removing with stick covered with cotton and dipped in alcohol, if there are only a few. If the infestation is large spray with nicotine sulphate or malathion.

MITES, those minute organisms burrow in bulbs, causing bulb rot in amaryllis, callas, glads, tulips and lilies. Control by spraying with Aramite or by destroying rotted bulbs.

RED SPIDER, very small but very much of a nuisance, attacks under-foliage of dahlias, amaryllis, lilies. Control: Aramite.

SCALE, sometimes on amaryllis leaves, can be controlled by spraying with malathion.

s l u g s , snail-like chewing characters, feed on lush foliage and blooms of dahlias, lilies and anything else that looks tempting. Control with trade-name baits, but beware! The baits are poisonous.

t h r i p s , minute winged insects, usually brown, cause deformed flowers and brown leaves on glads, amaryllis, iris and daffodils. Spray with 5% DDT or chlordane.

DISEASES OF BULBOUS PLANTS

g r a y m o l d appears on amaryllis, anemones and ranunculi, dahlias, glads and some lilies. Control with Bordeaux mixture or in extreme cases burn infected plant.

r e d b l i g h t appears as reddish-brown spots or streaks on stem and leaves of crinum, amaryllis, Eucharis Lily, narcissi. Prevent by soaking bulk in disinfectant before planting and by not watering too heavily after planting. Control by spraying with Bordeaux mixture fortified with soap suds or by destroying the most seriously affected plants.

m o s a i c is a virus disease that shows its presence by dwarfing growth and mottling the foliage. These "mottles" or spots turn brown and then dry out, giving the leaf the appearance of having been skeletonized. Control is not easy. It is a wise gardener who removes infected plants and burns them rather than run the risk of the disease spreading.

Most spring and summer-flowering bulbs should be planted in the fall and winter while they are dormant. Below is as complete a list as I can give.

a g a p a n t h u s , *Agapanthus umbellatus* is better known to us as the Lily of the Nile. This plant has rhizomatous roots that like to be pot-bound before it sends up its magnificent late spring and summer blooms so your best bet is to pot it in the fall and sink the pot into the ground. The light green strap-like leaves usually remain on the plant the year around. As a matter of fact, the leaves of my plant were covered with snow for two days and showed no damage whatsoever. The Agapanthus likes a sunny location, loamy alkaline soil and good drainage. If you don't give it too much attention it rewards you handsomely. Its flower is a spherical cluster of small blooms on long stems. It is sometimes called the perfect umbel. *Agapanthus orientalis umbellatus* is the Blue Lily of the Nile that we see so often in our New Orleans and southern beds. A. *orientalis alba* often called Albatross, is pure white. A. *Mooreanus* is a dark blue and very hardy. Storm Cloud is lovely and different, with a grayish-lavender umbel.

Allium Neapolitanum is the FLOWERING ONION, a bulb that produces slender graceful heads of pure white flowers that are wonderful for cutting in the spring. There are several other varieties. A. *azureum* is blue, A. *Cernuum* is pale lilac and A. *Drummondi* is pinkish-purple. All grow easily anywhere in the sun and in any type of soil. A. *Zenobiae* does well in Texas. A. *Schoenoprasum* is the Chives of the herb shelf, A. *sativum* is the Garlic Chive of the kitchen and A. *Cepa* is the common Onion. The shallot is A. *ascalonicum*. No need to dig and store these.

Alpinia or SHELL GINGER can be set out anytime although planting in the fall gives it a better start for spring bloom. Its robust rhizomatous roots must be checked every now and then to prevent their spreading out of bounds. The Shell Ginger we know so well is *Alpinia nutans speciosa*, tall-growing to eight feet, evergreen except in severe winters when the foliage burns, demanding light shade, slightly acid soil and plenty of water. The long leaf blades are coarse-textured and dark green and the flowers that appear in spring and summer and sometimes intermittently during the year, hang downward like strings of shells. They are white tipped with pink and veined in orange-red and they have a sheen that reminds you of porcelain. A. *nutans alba* is pure white. Two rare varieties, A. *calcarata* and A. *mutica* are white with crimson veining and bloom in late summer and fall. All are propagated by root division in spring or fall.

Alstroemeria, sometimes called the Peruvian Lily, is not grown much any more, sad to say. This tuberous-rooted member of the Amaryllis Family can be planted outdoors in the lower sections of the South and treated as potted plants where winters are colder. Free-flowering, they bloom in May and June on tall stems, the blossoms ranging in color from yellow A. *aurantiaca,* to violet-pink A. *Pelegrina,* known also as the Inca Lily, to orange and green, A. *pulchella,* the Parrot Flower. A. *chilensis,* the Chilean Lily, has larger umbels of flowers shading from white to pink to red. I have had A. *pulchella* for years. The stems of this Parrot Flower are taller than the other varieties and the dark orange and green funnel-shaped flowers make a perfect background companion to the paler orange of the Shrimp Plant. The small round satiny tan seed pods of the Parrot are the reason for this plant sometimes being called the Popcorn Plant. Set out the tubers horizontally in the fall in partial shade and place them about three inches deep in any kind of soil. They need plenty of water during their growing season. In very cold weather the foliage, which turns yellow as soon as the blooms fade, disappears entirely but the plants are back again next spring.

Amarcrinum Howardii is said to be the bigeneric hybrid of *Brunsvigia rosea* and *Crinum Moorei.* This large bulb planted with its neck well above ground level produces blooms that are a perfectly beautiful shade of muted pink. The fragrant trumpet-shaped flowers show during the summer on two-foot high scapes and the foliage is an attractive addition to the Amaryllis bed. Hardy throughout the South. I quote from my garden diary:

"June 10th—Amarcrinum appeared in bud, deeper pink than five previous years. 20 buds in open sheath.

June 12th—Three buds open . . . beautiful color . . . deeper pink streaks down mid-rib of petals, which are slightly recurved . . . heavenly scent.

June 14th—Five flowers open and first ones not yet fading. Straps are dull green with a deep indentation down middle. They are slightly longer and thinner in texture than those of Amaryllis.

June 16th—First flowers fading in color . . . other buds opening·

June 20th—Five fresh flowers showing.

June 24th—Last of open blossoms wilting."

Culture is the same as that of the Crinums.

A M A R Y L L I S are bulbs originally from South Africa. They have become popular with gardeners all over the South because their large trumpet-shaped blossoms of many colors do much to grace the garden in the spring.

The Amaryllis should always be set out in the fall when they are dormant, with their necks well above soil level. Make sure that the earth is loamy and that it is supplied at intervals with a well-balanced fertilizer. The mixture 6–10–4 is good if applied to the soil near the bulbs (not directly on them). Liquid fertilizers are easier to use but follow the directions on the bottle. As I indicated in the beginning of the chapter, if your bed contains slightly alkaline soil and it is in a southern exposure it is still a good spot for your Amaryllis. Dig the hole, place a scant handful of bone meal down in the hole, then add a layer of sharp builder's sand and then set your bulb directly on the sand. Fill the remainder of the hole with soil up to the required level. I must remind you too, that I have had excellent results with Amaryllis planted in azalea soil in the north bed and I know that quite a few of the bulb fanciers prefer the latter planting medium. Whichever soil you choose do not plant too close to tree roots which steal all moisture near them. Give the bulbs filtered shade or nearly full sun and never use sulphur or aluminum sulphate on or near the bulbs. Instead if you wish to maintain the slight acidity with which you began use peat moss, good compost or a small amount of well decomposed cow manure.

Amaryllis may also be potted, and I like a mixture of one-third sand, one-third peat and one-third leaf mold to which I add a little bone meal and a very small amount of blood meal. Use pots at least two inches in diameter larger than the bulb. I feed my potted Amaryllis about once a month with liquid fertilizer. Amaryllis may also be grown in the new cedar and redwood fibres provided drainage is almost perfect and provided you feed them regularly and give them added winter protection. Amaryllis may even be potted in medium-sized charcoal chips if you make sure to place a layer of sphagnum moss in the bottom of the pot to give the roots something to hold onto. Add a spoonful of dried cow manure twice a month and feed weekly with liquid fertilizer.

Amaryllis include the Dutch and the American Strains. In the Dutch family the showiest is the Warmenhoven Strain with many name varieties. Red Master, considered the best of all of the dark reds, usually measures ten inches across, Moreno is a medium red. Joan of Arc, the white and Sweet Seventeen, a large deep pink, are lovely but my favorite is Prince of Orange, a warm rich orange. Two late introductions are Beacon, a frosty salmon and Cherokee, a reddish-orange with metallic overlay. In the Dutch Ludwig Strain, you will find flowers of high quality, great size and delicate shades. This strain is also noted for its pure whites. Since Dutch Amaryllis arrive in the nursery in late fall the planting time for these bulbs is usually November, December and January.

The best American Strains are the Smith and the Howard and these are pollinated by hand and grown from selected seed. One of the loveliest of the Howards is the Maiden's Blush, a delicate pink. Dwarf Amaryllis, with blooms of one-third to one-half the size of the large type, are available in the American and Dutch Strains.

Leave your Amaryllis bulbs undisturbed as long as possible. There is no need to dig and store them annually. If a freeze is predicted mulch the top of the bulb with leaves or peat and remove when the temperature returns to normal. So treated, these Amaryllis survive our southern winters very well.

It is fun to cross your Amaryllis blooms, be they imported or domestic. Plant the resulting seeds and watch your new seedlings mature and flower. Remove the pollen from one flower and dust it on the pistil of another. Cover with a paper sandwich bag, or if you apply the pollen heavily enough you can forget about the bag because there is little or no chance for cross pollinization from insects if you apply sufficient pollen. Allow the flower to go to seed and as the seed sacs begin to split gather the black wafer-like seeds and plant in shallow trenches in flats or coldframes. The soil in the flats should be the same as the first-mentioned potting medium. Allow the seedlings to remain in the frames until the fall of the next year when they may be transplanted into open ground. They should bloom in two or three years if regularly fed.

I would suggest that you bring your pure white Amaryllis indoors if you self-pollinate it. Don't give the bees that outside chance of ruining your work. Return the pot outdoors after the seed pod has formed. I know that there are those of you who claim that allowing the Amaryllis to go to seed makes for an untidy garden and keeps some nourishment from the bulb. This is true but you don't have to make a yearly practice of it and it is part of the fun of gardening.

I cannot leave the subject without mentioning the Helen Hull, a double Amaryllis of the American Strain. The petals are very large and ruffled on the edges and the color is a deep orange tinged with streaks of white. This is one of the double hybrid Amaryllis originated by the late Captain J. J. McCann in his Florida nursery.

A lovely late summer-blooming bulb is the *Amaryllis Belladonna*, known also as the Belladonna Lily and said to be the only true type of Amaryllis. It has been often confused with *Brunsvigia rosea*, another member of the Amaryllis Family. The *Belladonna* is a large bulb that needs to be planted deeper than the ordinary Amaryllis, likes sandy loam in a well-raised bed and if left undisturbed year after year produces tubular flaring flowers from a deep pink, like the *Belladonna rosea perfecta*, to a white variety, *blanda*, and a purplish-rose, *purpurea*. My *rosea perfecta* blooms are at their best in July and August. The variety *Parkeri*, the result of a cross between *Amaryllis Belladonna* and *Brunsvigia Josephinae*, is very beautiful. Mine rewarded me by blooming this August in the north lily bed. The amethyst-colored scape rises to about three feet and the flowers are produced in a circular umbel, sixteen crisp, trumpet-shaped blossoms about four inches long, at right-angles to the stem. The edges of the trumpets are margined in a wide band of shocking pink that fades to white, which in turn shades to a bright orange at the base. The throat of the lily is the same orange color. The scape needs no support against the wind and the flowers do not seem at all perturbed by sun or rain.

The *Belladonna* has been the object of a botanical nomenclature controversy for many years. The plant Carolus Linnaeus first described is called *Bella Donna*, a red lily from the West Indies. The pink forms were apparently brought in from Bolivia. Other botanists have attempted to use the name for the belladonna lilies of the South African Capes, which is really *Brunsvigia rosea*. Bear with me! It is confusing! *Amaryllis Belladonna* of Linnaeus has a hollow scape, while *Brunsvigia rosea* has a solid scape. In my experience both bloom before the leaves appear. *Belladonna's* scape has a dull lavender tone. I have noticed that it rises from the bulb when the bulb has moved from its original upright position to a more prostrate position in the bed, as if lying on its side, which may have some bearing on the contention that the *Belladonna's* bulb is stoloniferous.

Be on the lookout for *Amaryllis Evansiae*, recent introduction from Bolivia named for the noted horticulturist, Mrs. U. B. Evans of Ferriday, Louisiana. I understand that it has been grouped with the *Amaryllis Belladonna*. I have seen pictures of it and it looks striking, varying in shades of blush to yellow to pink.

The ANEMONE and the RANUNCULUS, both of the *Ranunculaceae* or Buttercup Family, are always paired off together because besides being cousins they make perfect team mates and wonderful cut flowers in most of the South. The "De Caen" type Anemone is a single poppy-like flower often measuring four inches in diameter. The St. Brigid strain encompasses the doubles and semi-doubles in exciting colors. The Persian Ranunculus R. *asiaticus*, a double camellia-type flower is the one best known to us, with blooms of every color except blue. The tubers of the Anemone are hard, dark and rock-like in feel and appearance. The Ranunculus tuber looks like a little claw. Both should be planted in October and both should be soaked for two or three hours before planting, after which time they swell and the tops of last year's crown are easily distinguished. They can then be set out about six inches apart just below the surface of the soil, cushioning each tuber on a little mound of sand. Ranunculi should always be planted with the claws going *down* and don't ever make the mistake of planting otherwise. Several years ago a shipment of Ranunculi failed to bloom in the New Orleans area. Immediately word went out that they should have been planted with claws facing up. This was a mistake. The tubers were just not good, the method of planting was not faulty. So remember, Ranunculus claws go *down*.

Snow or freeze does not stop these tubers from showing their parsley-like leaves and colorful flowers in the spring and the blooming season usually lasts over a month. As to their keeping over for the next year, there is not much luck in this direction. Although every now and then a gardener will claim that the tubers can be dug and stored after blooming I have never had such good fortune. I have tried to dig carefully when the plant dies back but I have never found any sign of a rock-like tuber or a claw, only a mass of fine roots that dry and wither after a day out of the ground.

Each Anemone plant will produce about one and a half dozen blooms and each Ranunculus, more than two dozen flowers. Set out in a row in a long bed, they make a beautiful display in the spring garden.

Did you know that the BANANA or *Musa* was named after Antonio Musa, the physician to Octavius Augustus, the first Emperor of Rome, 63–14 B.C.? This plant of the long green leaves, lavender flowers and yellow fruit has a perennial rootstock and enjoys filtered sunlight, sandy soil and lots of water. Widely grown in the tropics for its edible fruit, the Banana is in demand in the lower South as an ornamental.

Musa paradisiaca sapientum is the Banana grown for commerce. It reaches great heights. *Musa maurellii* has leaves of deep maroon fading to green towards the center, greatly resembling the foliage of the bronze-leaved Canna. It does not grow quite as large as *Musa Enseta*, the Abyssinian Banana which reaches almost thirty feet and is probably the most popular of the decorative Bananas. *Musa Cavendishii*, a dwarf that grows from four to six feet, and *M. rosea nana*, the rose-flowered plant that rarely exceeds eight feet, are nice for patio use. I have had *rosea nana* in my garden for many years. It has attractive bluish-green leaves with a magenta midrib. Planted in the fall, the leaves will flourish through a mild winter. If a freeze occurs cut back the blackened stalks and foliage. In the spring new shoots always appear. The blossoms arrive in the summer. Bananas are always more presentable when kept trimmed of torn and tattered leaves.

The spectacular BIRD OF PARADISE, *Strelitzia reginae* named for the Princess of Mecklenburg-Strelitz, wife of King George III of England, is another member of the Banana Family. Not fragile by any means, the exotic blooms that resemble bright blue and orange birds rise on stout green two to three-foot stems amid thick-textured green foliage. Even the unopened buds are tinted in blue, purple, pink, orange and green. Some still think of the Strelitzia as a hot-house plant but it actually does very well outdoors especially if two or three plants are grouped together. Plant in full sun in coastal areas, in light shade further inland. The soil should be rich and loamy, slightly on the acid side, and fortified occasionally with doses of iron sulphate and a top dressing of well-rotted manure. Water well. Set out in early fall so that the rhizomatous roots can become well established before winter. Most

Strelitzias should bloom the second winter after transplanting. They show practically no damage from snow or frost.

The variety *Nicolai* has very large banana-like leaves, eventually reaching fifteen to twenty feet. Its flowers, shaped like those of the *reginae*, are large, very heavy and blue and white. It takes several years to bring this plant to blooming size. It is grown chiefly for its tropical foliage effect.

The BLOOD LILY, *Haemanthus*, native of South Africa bears a bloom on a single scape that grows up from the side of the bulb in the early summer. The spherical blossom is made up of about one hundred tiny star-shaped flowers that stand out from the base of the bloom. Sometimes the mass of color measures ten inches across. Luxuriant green leaves slightly rippled on the edges grow from a ten inch stem that is usually stained with red splotches. This plant does better in pots, likes loamy, sandy, slightly acid soil and stands reasonably cold weather. If very low temperatures are predicted, bring the Haemanthus into a shelter until the freeze is over. In one freeze I was forced to leave a pot outdoors because it was too heavy for me to move. I covered it with a hamper and though the foliage died back, new leaves turned out immediately afterwards and the bulbs showed no damage.

Haemanthus Katherinae is such a handsome red it has been frequently called the most beautiful of the flowering bulbs. It blooms in July and August. *H. coccineus* is a blood red. *H. albiflos* bears white flowers in the fall. *H. multiflorus* has a stem spotted with brown and its flowers are not as red as those of *H. Katherinae*. This last one is a more tender variety. Plant your *H. albiflos* with the greater portion of the neck of the bulb above the surface of the soil. *H. Katherinae* and the others may be a little more covered.

Four years ago I purchased one *H. Katherinae* and this past year I separated the "family" of bulbs that had multiplied. I now have thirteen in the patio, all in semi-shade. I treasure my *Haemanthus albiflos* and my *Haemanthus albiflos*, variety *brachyphyllum* that

I was lucky enough to find several years ago. Both were scarce then and I believe the *brachyphyllum* is even harder to get at present. These have umbels a little smaller than the *Katherinae* but they are a lovely white and they last so long on the plant. All are members of the Amaryllis Family.

Brunsvigia rosea is sometimes called the N A K E D L A D Y because the rose-colored, very fragrant flowers appear in July, August and sometimes September before the leaves show. This member of the Amaryllis Family is often confused with Amaryllis Belladonna. The Brunsvigia does well in the upper South, particularly where summer rains are scarce but in our New Orleans and the lower coastal areas it very often stubbornly refuses to bloom. Dormant all winter, it makes you wait in suspense. Sometimes it flowers, sometimes it just shows lush strap-like foliage, in which case you wait for another year and hope for better luck. The blooms are well worth awaiting. Having tried them in pots unsuccessfully I moved them to open ground in the southeast bed where soil is slightly alkaline and sandy and where there is filtered shade in summer, plenty of sun in winter. They must have been grateful. They bloomed.

The variety *Josephinae*, named after Napoleon's Empress after she added the bulb to her gardens at Malmaison, bears smaller clusters of darker reddish flowers.

C A L L A S , generally accepted botanically as *Zantedeschia*, are bulbous tuberous-rooted East African plants that should be set in the ground about three inches deep and left undisturbed. Since the Calla produces better blooms when enjoying "bottom heat" prepare the bed by first putting down a layer of well-rotted manure, then add a thick layer of sharp builder's sand on which to place the Calla tuber. Never let the tuber touch the manure or it will burn before it grows. Plant from September to January.

I have the white Calla that we all know so well, *Zantedeschia aethiopica* which grows to three feet and produces a long yellow spadix surrounded by a pure white spathe. The leaves are large and oblong, dark green and beautifully rippled. I have had many lovely blooms from these plants in the last few years and I find that there are very few months in which they do not produce flowers. I have them planted well-raised on the north side of the house in a spot where they are protected from the north wind. They grow in full sun and in semi-shade. They demand plenty of water, good loamy soil slightly on the acid side and frequent applications of liquid fertilizer. Mulch with peat.

Z. *Elliottiana's* spathe is a rich yellow. Its leaves are oval and green spotted with white. It also grows to three feet. The pink Calla, Z. *Rehmannii* is a dwarf perennial but most attractive. Both of these may be planted from November to February. The black Calla, Z. *melanoleuca* is not really black but actually has a cream-colored spathe darkened at the throat with a deep purple-maroon. It should be set out from October to December. Culture for the last three mentioned is the same as that of the *aethiopica*.

An unusual plant that some call a Black Calla is not really a Calla at all but a member of the Arum Family, a type of wild ginger. This so-called Black Calla is *Arum palaestinum*, with leaves that resemble those of the Caladium and with a long pointed spathe shading from green on the outside to blackish-purple on the inner surface. The spadix is dark and much shorter than the yellow spadix of the white Calla. Some Arum are hardy but this one is tender, must be potted and kept in the shade. Protect from cold.

CLIVIA, known as the Kafir-lily, is one of the most attractive of the potted bulbs. A fleshy-rooted member of the Amaryllis Family, Clivia does not like to be disturbed once it is potted and prefers loamy soil rather on the neutral side. So keep the pH 7 in mind when you feed about every three months with a well-balanced fertilizer. The straps or leaves are dark and evergreen and droop gracefully. The flowers of shades of deep orange, salmon and orange-red are trumpet-shaped like lilies on a small scale and are borne in umbels of from twelve to twenty-five, on tall stems in the spring usually in March or April.

Plant the small Clivia in eight-inch pots and as they grow in size, never divide but transfer carefully to larger size, or twelve-inch pots. Do not repot too quickly, the Clivia likes to be pot-bound. Place brickbats in the bottom of the pot to insure drainage and water and feed well during the summer and autumn. Keep moist over the winter as it never appreciates being completely dry. Place the pot where the plant will get plenty of light and air but just spots of sun. I keep mine under a big Pyracantha bush.

I have never seen this plant so beautiful after a snow and freeze. Of course I bring the pot into the garage for shelter from the snow but the cold seems to make the flowers bigger and a more luscious color. Often called the Aristocrat of the shade gardens, Clivia is a boon to patio use. It may be planted anytime although the fall is ideal because it has a chance to become established before spring. My plant is *Clivia miniata,* the original species from South Africa and the one most commonly known. It has leaves narrower than the hybrids and the flowers are a salmony-orange with yellow centers. Most of the *miniata* hybrids and the Belgian hybrids have wider straps, blossoms of a deeper orange-red and are more expensive.

As to bugs, I have never seen Clivia attacked by anything but an occasional mealybug, in which case a forceful spray with the hose or Qtip soaked in alcohol quickly eradicated that problem.

Most of the CRINUM are very large tropical or semi-tropical bulbs of the Amaryllis Family that should be planted with their necks well above ground level. They are ideal under trees and among shrubs all over the South. The whole group which comprises many varieties is divided into the long-necked bulbs which are more or less evergreen and the round members that are usually deciduous. If planted in moist, rich, sandy soil that is fortified with some peat moss they do as well in garden beds as in ridges and pinelands. In the upper regions they may be planted a little deeper than in the lower South and they should be mulched in winter. Although Crinums are best planted in the spring in the North they can be set out anytime in the South. I like to plant them in the fall so that they can be well established by summer. Most of them thrive in full sun and semi-shade.

Here are some of the many that do well in the South.

Crinum americanum, known as the Florida Swamp Lily blooms in spring and summer along mud banks and rivers and in beds where the soil is always moist. The leaves are about two feet long and dark green and the flowers open on three-foot scapes, spidery and white with purple filaments. The foliage dies down in the winter.

Crinum asiaticum is a great big bulb about twelve inches high and should be planted well above the ground. The three-foot leaves are wide at the base, narrow towards the tip and evergreen. About twenty funnel-shaped fragrant flowers, pure white with deep wine filaments, appear on tall stems. This one is hardy along the Gulf Coast and blooms off and on during the year, even in a warm winter.

Crinum augustum, often called the Great Mogul of Barbados is the largest of all Crinums, the whole plant often measuring four feet high and six feet round. It too needs rich moist soil and good feedings. The four-foot long evergreen leaves just about drape over the bed and the wine-colored flower scape, four feet high, is so heavy with the twenty-odd fragrant purplish-pink blossoms that it needs staking. It is slow to multiply. *C. augustum* looks very much like and is often confused with *C. amabile.* They are very similar but *augustum* is smaller and has more blunt, rounded leaves.

Crinum Moorei is a very large bulb, almost six inches round, with a long neck. It likes heavy clay soil to produce its long slender rippled foliage and pink, fragrant, bell-shaped flowers, usually eight to the sheath. Blooms in March and April in Florida. Another Crinum popular in Florida is the Milk and Wine Lily.

Crinum Sanderianum, small in comparison to the others. The flower stalk is about three feet high, bearing five or six white blossoms keeled with red.

I enjoy my *Crinum variabile*, called the showiest of all the family. The very large bulb sends up tall scapes high above the foliage, which is long and glossy. The fifteen to twenty trumpet-shaped flowers are white, striped with pale pink. They open at dusk and are crisp and fresh until dawn when they begin to droop. Two or three flower stalks rise at the same time and make a beautiful sight in the patio on a moonlight night. This plant is hardy up to Missouri and Kentucky. One of the best hybrids is *Crinum* Cecil Houdyshel, a deep rose-pink flowering variety on tall stems. It blooms all through the summer and will remain hardy up to Missouri. C. Ellan Bosanquet is almost wine color and very fragrant and C. Louis Bosanquet is deep pink on tall scapes and has a long blooming season.

Another Crinum that I consider an addition to my patio is *Crinum giganteum*, sometimes called the Friar Lily. The bulb is about five inches round with a short neck. The leaves grow to about two and a half feet and are three inches wide. The filaments are white and so are the tulip-shaped flowers that usually appear six to the sheath. The pollen changes in color as the flower remains open, from a pale gray to a black. This crinum does well in the shade of the pecan tree and freezes do not seem to hurt it. Due to hybridization there are hundreds of varieties of Crinum and nearly all of them are beauties.

All JONQUILS, NARCISSI and DAFFODILS belong to the species *Narcissus* of the Amaryllis Family, but those Narcissi with the trumpet-shaped center are called DAFFODILS or *Narcissus Pseudo-narcissus*. The smaller Narcissi that may be grown in water and that bloom in fragrant clusters are known as NARCISSUS or the Polyanthus Narcissus, *Narcissus Tazetta*. JONQUILS, *Narcissus jonquilla* or *Narcissus poeticus* the Poet's Narcissus is the plant with hollow reedy leaves and many flowers supported by one stem. The hybridizers have been so busy with this tribe that they have given blooms of many shapes and colors to the gardening world.

As often as I have tried I have never been successful in having my Daffodils bloom more than two years. Our usual winters are just not quite cold enough for them and our summers are too hot and too long. So I am forced to admit that for lasting qualities the upper South and North will have the pleasure of the lovely new Pink Trumpet Daffodils, the fragrant Louise De Coligny with her apricot-pink cup and white perianth, Pink Glory and Lady Bird. Of the yellow and white Daffodils, King Alfred is the largest and perhaps the best known. It will grow in the lower South but not as successfully as Aerolite, Lord Nelson, whose cup is a deeper contrast to the perianth, and Mount Hood, which changes from pale yellow to pure white as it opens. Other good ones are Gloria, Carlton, Solario and Semper Avanti. To thumb through a garden catalogue is to discover just how many new hybrids there are. Green Emerald gives the effect of chartreuse coloring, Confuoco has a reddish-orange ruffled trumpet against wide yellow petals, and the Duke of Windsor is yellow and white. There is a new apricot collection available, all short-trumpeted. Planted correctly they will all bloom the first year in the lower South. After that you take your chances.

There are a number of "Little Daffodils" that do well in rock gardens and in spots where a bloom of six to eight inches high is needed. Several of these like the *Narcissus Bulbocodium citrinus* and the *Narcissus Bulbocodium Conspicuus* are the yellow "Hoop-Petticoats" of the family.

The Narcissus, with its flowers in clusters is better adjusted to our climate and of the doubles, Mary Copeland is my favorite. The petals are white streaked with yellow and the shorter center petals, more ruffled than the outer ones, are yellow and orange. It gives the appearance of a full six-pointed star. Poet's Narcissi are available in quite a few color combinations. The orange Prince and Innocence are good and Cheerfulness is a fragrant double, fine for cutting. The variety known as *orientalis*, cream and yellow, is known as The Chinese Sacred Lily.

Paper-white *Grandiflora* and Soleil d'Or are two Narcissi that grow well in water. They sometimes produce twenty-five to thirty individual blooms. Start them off in November in a bowl three-quarters full of water into which you have placed several handfuls of pebbles and a few pieces of charcoal. The charcoal keeps the water sweet. Place the bowl in a cool dark place for several weeks and then bring into the light. Use several bowls and stagger your planting for a continuation of bloom.

The Jonquils are also more successful here, withstanding more heat than their cousins, blooming a little later and lasting a long time when cut and brought into the house. A small one called Queen Anne's Daffodil is a pretty golden single, Campernelle is a good double.

Plant your Daffodils in October or at the latest early in November, in sandy loam, in full sun or filtered shade. Use a raised bed or a high spot of ground because they need good drainage. Dig the hole about four inches deep and fill in the bottom with sharp builder's sand. Set the bulb directly on the sand and cover with soil. Keep moderately moist all through the growing season. You cannot plant Daffodils too shallow because their foliage needs anchorage against winter winds.

These bulbs should bloom well the first year and if left undisturbed should give you a second season of color provided you do not cut the foliage before it dies down. The bulb needs the foliage to manufacture food and strength for the next year. You do not have to dig and store your Narcissi or your Jonquils. These will bloom for years after the Daffodils are through. Any member of this family is an asset to the spring garden, especially when planted with the blue and purple Dutch Iris.

Before I leave the subject I might caution those of you who are allergic (as I am) to certain plants that you can develop an irritation on hands and arms from the juice of the Daffodil foliage. It itches like mad and the only thing that stopped my discomfort was plenty of hot water and soap and then a coating of carbolated vaseline.

DAYLILIES or *Hemerocallis,* a genus of perennial herbs of the Lily Family, need no introduction anywhere in the South. Now available in a myriad of colors they will bloom anywhere where there is a fair amount of sun. They thrive in any kind of soil and demand little more than a thinning every fourth or fifth year. They are practically disease and pest free. The only bugs I have seen, at sparse intervals, were thrip and red spider, in which case I spray in early spring and late fall with a mixture of malathion, lindane and DDT.

I am convinced that every gardener has a conscience, and, since these lovely lilies do so much better with good drainage and with some well-balanced fertilizer dug into the earth in the spring and fall, do give them this minimum of care. Well-rotted compost or cow manure is good. And the Daylilies can take it! They show practically no damage from snow and freeze. True, their spring growth is slowed but the plants survive.

Actually the Daylily may be planted anytime but the ideal time to divide and reset is autumn. Dig the entire clump and pull the individual plants apart with your hands. Work at it gently. Then clip off the straggly overlong roots and trim the fan, or leaves, back to about eight inches. Dig a hole big enough so that the roots will not be cramped and set them about two feet apart, one to two inches deep. Water well after planting and at blooming time. Mulch against heat and cold.

Another method of propagation is by seed. My husband and I have had a great deal of pleasure with cross-hybridizing. We go out into the garden before eight o'clock in the morning (and I say that time because the pollen vessels will have emptied after that time) and take a pollen-laden stamen from one flower and either tap it against the stigma of either the same flower if you wish to self-pollinate that one, or another flower of different hue if you want to cross-pollinate. We find that using the stamen of a light-colored Daylily on the stigma of a dark mahogany one brings some surprising results. Four years ago using several named varieties of the

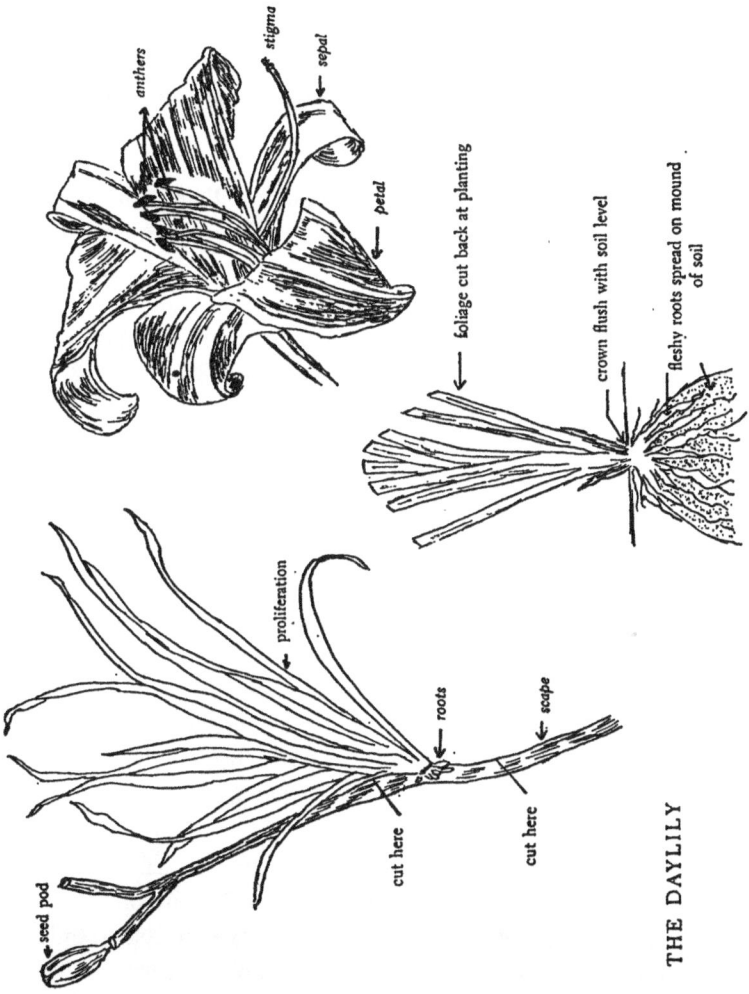

anthers
stigma
sepal
petal

foliage cut back at planting
crown flush with soil level
fleshy roots spread on mound of soil

seed pod
proliferation
roots
cut here
cut here
scape

THE DAYLILY

darker colors we crossed our lemon yellows with them, bagged the flowers with sandwich bags and waited for the seed pods to form, mature, dry and begin to split. As soon as we noticed the split we gathered the shiny black seeds and planted them at once in our cold frames. The following spring we edged all of our garden beds with our new hybrids and last year it was a thrill to go out each morning to see what new Daylily was blooming. The color range was wide, from dark reddish-brown to pale beige and pink, some with beautifully marked eye zones and others with delightfully rippled petals. We even have a night bloomer and that one is a bi-color. If you want to have fun in your garden and really feel that you are accomplishing something, try getting your own hybrids.

Daylilies may also multiply by proliferation, or small plants that grow along the flower scape. Cut below the proliferation and set the new plant in water until roots begin to show, then plant in the flower bed. Flowers from a proliferation will always be true to the parent plant.

Hybridizers have been so busy with this plant that you can now have Daylilies blooming in your garden from early spring to fall, from tall ones to dwarf. True, the flower lasts but one day but the scape usually carries several buds, so that you can enjoy the blossom for at least a week. Some varieties bloom twice in a season. Nearly all of the new ones are descendants of the species: *flava* or Lemon Lily, and Hyperion is a large one; of *fulva,* the tawny orange, and of *middendorfi,* a dwarf.

Some of the prettiest of the new ones are Golden Heart, a big soft yellow early bloomer whose sepals and petals are brown-tipped, Bambi, a light rosy-red with an iridescent overlay that stands sun well and blooms at midseason and Apollo, an apricot-yellow of deep beauty, flowering midseason to late. I like Nigrette, very dark mahogany with a golden throat, only about twenty inches high and flowering in June and July. I have used the pollen of Nigrette on pale yellow seedlings to secure some fascinating results. Some other beauties are Pink Bowknot, a salmon-pink with ivory midrid,

Cradle Song, a medium yellow, Night Hawk, an ivory that opens late in the evening and remains open through the following day and Ebony Prince, a deep maroon with black velvet overlay, mid-season to late.

My garden includes the fragrant yellow Primrose Mascotte, the Chinese-coral Tasmania, the rosy-orchid Show Girl that likes partial shade. Just pick up a garden catalogue and see the hundreds of Daylilies from which to choose. If I have succeeded in interesting you just a little bit, inquire into your local and national Hemerocallis societies. They can give you many more details on the subject.

The E A S T E R L I L Y that we of the South know best is *Lilium longiflorum* and it is offered in the *alexandrae, eximium Harrisii* and *formosum* varieties. These are the white, heavy-textured trumpet-shaped flowers that are so beautiful in the spring garden. Plant in September and October in rich loamy soil in a well-raised bed. The lily must have good drainage. Set the bulb on the regular cushion of sand from two to three inches deep. My Easter Lilies in the north bed have lived through exceptionally cold winters. Only the blooming time is delayed several weeks after Easter. To insure flowers for Easter try counting one hundred days from planting to blooming. Pot firmly in a mixture of three parts soil, two parts humus and one part sand. Add a five-inch pot of bonemeal to a bushel of the mixture and plant with the nose of the bulb showing above the level of the soil. Place the pot under a bench in semi-darkness until there are several inches of growth. Water sparingly until brought into full sunlight.

I don't disturb my Easter Lilies every year, but dig them only when they seem to be crowded. Then I examine for bulb rot to which they are subject. If there is an indication of this condition I cut the affected area out and soak the remaining part in a solution of one teaspoonful commercial formaldehyde to three parts of water for one hour. Then I replant right away.

Quite often bulblets appear at the base of the stem at soil level.

I remove these carefully, plant in my cold frame and then the following year move them to the garden bed. Another year, and I have a blooming plant.

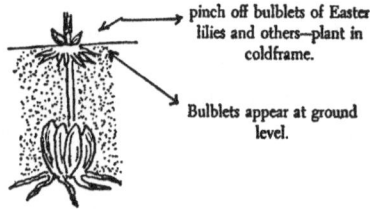

pinch off bulblets of Easter lilies and others—plant in coldframe.

Bulblets appear at ground level.

The E U C H A R I S   L I L Y , *Eucharis grandiflora* often called the Amazon Lily, is one of the finest bulbs of the Amaryllis Family. Resembling a daffodil in shape, the four large pure-white spring flowers with a touch of green inside the crown appear on one and a half to two-foot scapes and the dark green leaves are stemmed, basal and broad. This lovely thing needs high night temperatures and likes to be crowded in a pot in coarse loamy soil to which charcoal and sand have been added. Make sure the inevitable brickbats are at the bottom of the pot for drainage and plant the two-inch bulb with neck above the soil. Since its native habitat is the Colombian Andes it may be grown outdoors in the lower South in filtered shade. In the upper sections it becomes a greenhouse dweller. Stimulate late spring and summer flowering by watering copiously, treating it to occasional doses of sunshine and then withholding water for a few weeks. When offsets appear in early spring and you feel that the pot is overcrowded, gently separate and repot. From one bulb you should soon have several. Feed occasionally during the growing period with manure water or a well-balanced liquid fertilizer. Keep an eye open for red spider. The *grandiflora* is often sold under the name *amazonica*. The Eucharis is also frequently mistakenly named Star of Bethlehem, which is *Ornithogalum*.

You may be interested to know that the *Eucharis grandiflora* was crossed with *Urceolina pendula*, a scarce yellow urn-shaped member of the Amaryllis Family, and the resulting hybrid, called *Urceocharis* proved to be a lovely thing. Winter-blooming, the flowers are white, more bell-shaped than the Eucharis, and about two inches across. There are about ten or twelve blossoms to the umbel. *Urceocharis* is sometimes called *Eucharis Clibranii*. If you are fortunate enough to get one, culture is the same as that of *Eucharis grandiflora*.

FAIRY LILIES are *Zephyranthes*, sometimes called Zephyr Lilies, a group of small bulbs of the Amaryllis Family that flower all over the South. They are also known as Rain Lilies because the blooms spring up as soon as the spring and summer rains begin. They should be planted in loamy soil, in a rather shallow hole. Mulch with peat. The leaves are narrow straps, dark green in color and the flowers are funnel-shaped, held straight up by thin hollow stems, one bloom to a stem. A border of these lilies is always an addition to the lily bed, especially when combined with the pale pink Habranthus. They need not be dug in the lower South, but where winters are colder lifting and storing should be practiced. I have enjoyed the rosy summer-blooming ones, Z. *grandiflora*, Z. *carinata* and Z. *rosea*. The white, Z. *candida* a late bloomer and the yellow, Z. *sulphurea* are lovely. Z. *texana* native to Texas, is a yellowish-copper with lavender markings.

A fragrant, night-blooming relative of the Zephyranthes is the COOPERIA, another small bulb that is often known as the Prairie Lily. It too is sometimes called Rain Lily. *Cooperia pedunculata* is white and probably the largest of the varieties; C. *Drummondii* or Evening Star is a smaller white. C. *Smallii* is a rare yellow from the southern part of Texas.

If the fall and winter prove to be good and cold in the lower South, then FREESIAS may be tried here as well as in the upper sections. Trouble is, we have no way of foretelling. At any rate, because this cormous member of the Iris Family needs a cool temperature day and night (between fifty and sixty degrees) to thrive, you can see why the blooms would be disappointing if the winter turned out to be warm and sticky. I took a chance one year and planted a batch of Freesias in late October in the loamy soil of my north bed in full sun. I put down *F. refracta alba* the white, and a collection of *hybrida*, the blue, pink, yellow and rose-colored ones. I set them all about two inches deep. The leaves are very much like those of the Glad in shape and color, only growing to about two feet. The fragrant tubular flowers come out on the end of slender spikes, taller than the leaves and usually five to the cluster. They take plenty of water. The weather was with me. The occasional warm, humid spells did not last long and I had blooms in January. I let the foliage die down and I allowed the bulbs to remain in the ground through the summer. They returned next fall but because the autumn and winter were more warm than cool, the flowers were nothing to brag about. If you don't mind reordering these corms I think you would enjoy them.

True G I N G E R is *Zingiber* and *Zingiber officinale* is the rhizome that is grown commercially in the East and West Indies for preserving, spices and relishes. The dried roots are used for medicinal purposes; the young tender rhizomes make the candied ginger and the green part of the plant is utilized for flavoring. *Officinale* thrives in Florida in good loamy soil and partial shade. I planted mine in October in a southeast bed and it has been doing beautifully, although I have not yet seen it bloom. It only grows about two and one-half feet high and unlike Shell Ginger, its leaves are slender and wavy. The infrequent flowers are a dark purple, almost black and the bracts are a dull green margined in yellow. I am also growing *Zingiber Zerumbet* or the "Red Pine Cone Ginger." Its height ranges between two to three feet and its cone of red bracts is most attractive in the fall. Its flowers are small and white. *Zingiber Darceyi* is a lovely rare Ginger with rippled creamy-margined leaves, and deep red blossoms. When the winters are mild these perennials remain evergreen. Propagation is usually by division of the roots.

If you wish to try another member of the Ginger Family, plant

KAEMPFERIA, a tuberous-rooted gem that likes rich moist soil fortified with leaf mold. It is best to pot this one and sink the pot in the ground during the warm months. Use it as an attractive house plant in the winter. The foliage rises directly from the base of the plant with practically no stem; the round leaves are either green or bronze and the small low flowers are differently colored, depending on variety. *K. rotunda* also known as the "ground Orchid" and the "Resurrection Lily", has fragrant white flowers with purple tints and upright lanceolate leaves that taper into the petiole. The foliage is variegated green above and greenish-purple beneath. This one is dormant in winter and blooms in spring before the leaves. *K. grandiflora* has stemmed oblong leaves with blue flowers that also appear before the foliage. See chapter on Potted Plants.

Still another Ginger relative, from the East Indies, is COSTUS or CREPE GINGER. It is sometimes called the Spiral Flag because its handsome leaves, shorter and more rounded than other Gingers are arranged spirally on the stem. Easily propagated by division of the stalk, *Costus speciosus* grows from three to ten feet tall showing bell-shaped ruffled white flowers that arise behind dark red bracts. This perennial does well in the lower South and in Florida in sandy soil and in partial shade. Propagation is by division of the stalk or stem. I think the most attractive parts of this plant are the bracts that form elegant heads after the flowers have bloomed, remaining on the stems for some time.

GLORY-OF-THE-SNOW is *Chionodoxa*, another member of the Lily Family, so named becaunse it blooms so early in the spring. It is more successful where winters are cold for long periods. Plant two inches deep and close together because it makes a better show when set out in groups. These bulbs grow in any soil provided they have light and good drainage. They need plenty of moisture at growing season. I had reasonable success with *C. Luciliae* whose strap leaves were a little shorter than the three-foot scapes that bore about a dozen little blue, funnel-shaped, droopy flowers. The throat is white. These need not be dug. *Chionodoxa* grows well with the early flowering Blue Bell or *Scilla*, bulb of the Lily Family whose culture is the same.

A few years ago a dear friend gave me a dozen seeds of H A - B R A N T H U S , *Habranthus robustus* the South American member of the *Hippeastrum* tribe of the Amaryllis Family. Today, having self-pollinated the flowers and planted a yearly crop of seeds I have four beds bordered with these lovely little flowers that look like Amaryllis in miniature. The small bulbs planted in the fall produce narrow, dark green, strap-like leaves about a foot long and single flowers on a slender twelve-inch scape. They bloom from mid-May into July, pale pink and white. *Habranthus Andersonii* variety *Texanus* is an unusual copper-bronze lily from Texas. The Habranthus form seed pods just as the Amaryllis do, each small black wafer a miniature of the Amaryllis seed. Plant in flats or cold frames as soon as harvested and transfer to open ground in the autumn after they are one year old. Be watchful of the baby plants. The leaves are like thin grass reeds until they mature.

Mine are planted in the slightly acid soil of the north bed and in the slightly alkaline ground of the southeast beds, and both conditions are good. The pale pink Habranthus, with its flower at an angle to the stem, is a fine companion to the rose Fairy Lily or Zephyranthes whose blossoms are a deeper pink and upright on the scape.

H Y A C I N T H S are hardy, early spring-flowering members of the Lily Family. Most of them come from South Africa and others, like the kind with which we are familiar, from the Mediterranean area. Those grown in Holland have become known, like the Iris and Tulips, as Dutch Hyacinths. These have short strap-like leaves and one large cluster of flowers from each bulb. The Roman Hyacinths which really come from the south of France have narrower, taller leaves and produce three or four smaller flower spikes. Both are tunicated bulbs.

Growth of the Hyacinth flower depends entirely on the growth of the roots, so plant as early as you can in the fall and stagger your planting in sets of six or more so that you can have blooms all through the winter and spring. Hyacinths will grow in any soil provided drainage is good. But get the best results you can. Prepare the bed in the beginning of October by turning the earth at least a foot deep and incorporating some well-rotted cow manure and if the soil is heavy, add sharp sand. The ground must be loose and porous enough for the roots to wander. Set the bulbs six inches apart about four inches deep in the deep South and about six inches deep farther north, and mulch for winter protection. When the shoots first appear scrape some of the mulch away, leaving enough to afford cover in case of late winter frosts.

Dutch Hyacinths may be grown in water in special glasses sold just for that purpose. Fill the bottom with water and add a few pieces of charcoal to keep it sweet. Set the bulb in the top of the glass so that the base of the bulb just touches the water. Keep the glass in a dark closet until the top shoot is about four inches tall and the roots have put out growth. This procedure should take about eight weeks. Bring to light gradually until it can be moved to a north window. Add water when necessary.

Hyacinths may also be forced in pots. Plant in September in four or five-inch pots into which you have placed plenty of brickbats to insure drainage and which you have filled with rich loamy soil. Bury the pot in the ground so that the top is covered with at least two inches of soil. When the top shows about two inches high above the bulb (you will have to watch it) remove to a cool spot until the new growth is good and green, then keep the plant at seventy-degree temperature. Feed occasionally with liquid manure. By Christmas you should have beautiful blooms.

Hyacinths, like Tulips, do not always return flowers a second year in the lower South but you can dig, clean and store in a cool place over the summer and take a chance on their blooming again. When planted in the fall a great deal depends on what kind of winter we have. Just be sure to allow the foliage to die down completely before digging them up. In cooler climates they can be left undisturbed in the ground from season to season.

There are many colors to choose from. Queen of the Whites, Queen of the Pinks, Delft Blue and Marie, a deep purple, are very good. Pink Pearl is a deep rose, Cyclops is scarlet and Grand Maitre, a porcelain blue. City of Haarlem is a lovely yellow.

The GRAPE HYACINTH is *Muscari*, a small bulb also of the Lily Family. The blue or white flowers are tiny and bell-shaped and appear in compact heads in very early spring. Growing in any kind of soil under almost any conditions they make attractive border plants since they reach only five or six inches. They do equally well in sun or shade. *Hyacinthus azureum* is a bright blue and the Plume Hyacinth, *Plumosum*, which flowers in May is exceptionally pretty with its feathery plumes of violet blooms. These bulbs do best undisturbed from year to year.

The IRIS Family, *Iridaceae* is a large one ranging from the bulbous type to the rhizomes, from the stately Dutch to the luscious Louisiana species. We cannot enjoy them all but now and then we can experiment with a few new ones and perhaps find one to add to our collection.

This might be a good place to stop and review the parts of the Iris flower. It is the fleur-de-lis that you see so often in heraldic designs, with the three upright petals called "standards", three wider lower petals termed "falls" and the in-between strap-like petals that are known as the "style branches". The foliage of some is evergreen and wider than that of others.

To start with the bulbous beardless type, we are all familiar with the DUTCH IRIS, the early birds of the spring garden. They are said to be the result of a cross between some varieties of Spanish Iris and *Iris tingitana* from Africa. These are small bulbs that must be set out in the fall in full sun, in raised beds and planted at least two to three inches deep so that the tall slender stems are well anchored and balanced against wind and rain. The soil should be light and loamy and definitely *not* on the alkaline side. I have found mine do best in a soil mixture that has been rendered slightly acid by the addition of peat moss or oak leaf mold. They like moisture while growing but prefer dry conditions after they have bloomed. And here again, I cushion each bulb on a handful of sand when planting.

As to varieties, there are the deep purple, Imperator, Blue Pearl and a new hybrid, National Velvet; the lavender-blue, Wedgewood, Delft Blue; the lavender, King Mauve, The Orchid; the white, Excelsior, Joan of Arc and White Perfection; the yellow, Golden Harvest, Belle Jaune, Pride of Holland; the bronze, Le Mogul, Orange King and Ankara. These bloom in the spring, usually in March in the lower South and later than that farther north. I say "usually" because the extremity of the winter governs the exact time of bloom.

I cut the reed-like foliage after it has turned brown and dry and I do not dig the bulbs every year, only about every third or fourth year so that they don't choke themselves out. I have had mine down for four years and I'm still enjoying their glorious colors each spring. This far down South the third and fourth year's blooms and any after that will never equal the first and second year's flowers in size. I have never noticed a lessening quality in color. It is not a bad idea to reorder a batch each year to keep up the crop. And remember when you cut the bloom to wear, leave as much of the foliage on the stem as you can. This foliage is necessary to the health of the bulb. Never cut the stem off until it has died back.

The ENGLISH IRIS, *Iris xiphioides* and the SPANISH group, *Iris Xiphium* also need to be planted deep enough for the foliage to remain erect. Their culture is the same as that of the Dutch Iris and they bloom about the same time. The English and Spanish tribes give us very beautiful blooms ranging in color from bronze, brown and gold to pale yellows. Although they are lovely and may be purchased in collections their success in the South is overshadowed by the Dutch Iris.

The only other two in this group are the JUNO and the RETICULATA IRIS. Both bloom in early spring and while the Juno's culture is the same as that of the Dutch, Reticulata seems to need a limed soil. The foliage of the Juno does not look like Iris foliage at all but more like that of the Hybrid and Easter Lilies. The flowers are produced in the axils of the upper leaves. A clump of these is most unusual and *Juno Bucharica* is a good white and yellow variety. *Reticulata Hercules* is a commanding bronzy-purple with an orange crest. Its falls are very round.

The RHIZOMATOUS GROUP is a large one and is so called because the plant grows from a thick root that creeps horizontally just below the surface and sends roots downward to anchor it. The stiff leaves that come from the rhizome resemble and are called, the "Fan". In the Bearded or *Pogoniris* class I still have my Mother's "white flags" blooming in my garden. They are years old and as children we always referred to them as the German Iris. Actually they are *Iris florentina*, from whose dried roots and those of the *Iris germanica* is extracted the orris root used in cosmetics. The foliage of *florentina* is stiff and short, the flower scape reaching to about eighteen inches. There is a definite beard or hairy growth in the center of the falls. These Iris like dry, rather neutral soil conditions and plenty of sun. Every two or three years I dig them up after blooming and scrub the rhizomes with a solution of half Lysol, half water. Then I separate and replant immediately. I have also enjoyed beautiful results from the *Iris germanica*, of the dark purple tones. Gentius, Red Orchid and Espada, ranging respectively in hues of blue-purple, red-purple and an almost purplish-black, are most attractive. These do well and look pretty in the same bed as the "flags" and bloom in April and May.

BEARDED IRIS, those of the large standards and wide falls do very well in the North and East. They do not tolerate our dampness and long hot summers too well. But if you can afford to try some, even the few resulting blooms are worth seeing. I ordered six several years ago, Grand Canyon, a coppery plum color; Great Lakes, a medium blue; Prairie Sunset, a deep apricot; Lady Mohr, white, lavender and chartreuse; Black Forest, a bluish-black and Sable, a dark blue-violet. The falls of all of these bear beards in a gold or bronze color. I received them in October and planted them at once in the same bed in which my flags and *Iris germanica* were growing. These, the flags and the germanicas should all be planted in a shallow trench with just enough soil on top to anchor the tops until they take root. I enjoyed all six for three years. They all grew to about thirty-six inches, bloomed through May and early June and the foliage remained evergreen through our mild winters. Each June when flowering was over I dug the rhizomes, scrubbed them with Lysol and water and re-planted immediately. The Prairie Sunset was the most beautiful of all. I was very proud to wear it. Now, seven years later, I have three still living and blooming. The only change that I have noticed in the flower is the slight fading of the blue in Great Lakes and of the lavender and copper in Lady Mohr and Grand Canyon. I lost the other three to bacterial rhizome rot, try as I did to save them. Feed the above mentioned Iris in the growing season by scratching the ground surface and sprinkling a handful of well-balanced commercial fertilizer on the soil around the plant.

The introduction of the DWARF BEARDED IRIS has brought new color combinations to add to the garden: Tantalizer, a bronzy-buff and April Shower, shading from blue to purple are very lovely. The INTERMEDIATES are the results of crossing the tall with the dwarf and bloom after the dwarfs and before the tall group.

As I have already pointed out the Bearded Iris like light dry conditions and full sun. Now I must stress the fact that the following group of rhizamatous, but BEARDLESS or *Apogon* Iris thrive best in moist rich, heavier soil, in sun or semi-shade. The SIBERIAN IRIS does not stand the heat of the lower South very well. It is too bad because they are fine for cutting. Eric the Red and Snowcrest are attractive. Nobody knows why the

SPURIA or Butterfly Iris is so called but this tall species, very much like the Louisiana Iris will do well over most of the South if left undisturbed from year to year. Lark Song, a frilled white and yellow and Dutch Defiance, a shaded blue and gold are good ones, reaching nearly four feet.

Some of the most beautiful Iris are the JAPANESE IRIS, *Iris Kaempferi* that need plenty of moisture especially during the growing season and acid soil in which to grow. Blooming in June and July they really do their best in the region of the Great Lakes but like the Bearded Iris they are lovely enough to try a few here. They can be had in a myriad of colors and are usually grouped in early, midseason and late bloomers. Should the leaves turn yellow it is a warning that the soil is not acid enough so get out the peat or oak leaves and act accordingly.

VESPER IRIS, or *Iris dichtoma* belongs to the Japanese Family and blooms in July and August. Easily grown from seed, this one has clusters of delicate lavender flowers that open about three or four o'clock in the afternoon and close by the next day. The lavender in the blooms is sometimes streaked with copper, lemon or orange-brown markings and the stems sometimes reach four feet in height. Vesper Iris likes rich soil, will stand heat and cold, full sun or shade and produces fibrous roots instead of rhizomes. It is lovely when planted close to your Daylilies, which also enjoy blooms-for-a-day, and should really be used more than it is.

The LOUISIANA IRIS, each of which bears blooms at the top and at several spots along the scape, has been found to be hardy in nearly all sections of the South. Natives of the Mississippi Delta, these rhizomatous roots should be planted in August and September just below the soil surface. They will grow in sun or partial shade and must have water in the growing season. Prepare the bed by digging and turning the soil about nine inches deep. Mix whatever organic matter you have on hand or use about six pounds of a well-balanced commercial fertilizer like 8-8-8, to every one hundred square feet. Planting should be shallow so place the rhizomes horizontally with their tops level with the surface of the ground ànd mulch with peat about two inches thick on the day of planting. Water copiously until fall growth begins, then you can scrape away a little of the mulch. Divide rhizomes and rework beds in August when the plants are semi-dormant. Although the foliage usually grows to three feet, after a snow and freeze the leaves can reach a colossal four and a half feet. A cold winter also makes the flowers bigger and the colors deeper.

Besides the russet, lavender and purple Louisiana Iris so long familiar to us there are some lovely hybrids well worth having. I have added Bayou Sunset, so close to the vivid tones of the Bearded Iris, Prairie Sunset, the Abbeville Yellows, a handsome beige hybrid of the Abbeville Yellows, and some of the rose and pink shades. Bayou Vermilion is one of the best large-flowering reds in the Abbeville group. Violet Ray is a very large pansy purple with creamy markings, one of the most beautiful of the Louisiana Iris. Barbara Elaine Taylor is a pure white and Black Widow is the darkest purple I've ever seen, the bloom measuring about seven inches across. Native Louisiana Iris may be moved anytime of the year but the best time to divide and reset is in August. If they are not crowded do not disturb.

There are many other varieties of Iris too numerous to list but I would like to mention a few pretty ones. There is a tall yellow Iris, *Iris Pseudacorus* that produces stately fresh foliage almost four feet high each year and yellow spring blossoms only after a cold winter. It likes good loamy soil and plenty of sun and makes a perfect filler for a difficult corner. In the deep South we are forced to enjoy its foliage more often than its blooms. The so-called WALKING IRIS is *Marica gracilis*, a tropical member of the *Iridaceae*. The root is a short rhizome which should be planted in full sun and in fairly good loam. Mulch well with peat through the winter. In spring and summer the leaves grow sword-fashion to about two inches and the taller flower scape becomes so heavy with the three-inch blossoms that are streaked with blue, yellow and brown, that it bends down and touches the ground. Wherever it rests on the soil it takes root and up shoots another plant. Do not disturb this one unless you wish to transplant to another spot, in which case do it while it is dormant in the fall. *Marica Northiana* is white tipped with violet, a good plant for a hanging basket.

There are many other species of Iris that are not too well known and might be interesting to try. *Iris susiana*, or the dark Mourning Iris, is a native of Israel and belongs to the bearded O N C O C Y C - L U S group. This spring bloomer is difficult to grow even if lifted and stored regularly. It requires a limed soil and needs perfect drainage. Does best where rainfall is heavy between October and March. Water sparingly after blooming.

The R E G E L I A are bearded Iris related to the *Oncocyclus* but are taller and bear two elongated flowers on each stem. Beautifully veined, they do well in the same bed as the tall Bearded group. Its *Iris Hoogiana* blooms in May and is lavender-blue; the variety Bronze Beauty is a dark violet, fading at the tips to a cinnamon brown. *Iris foetidissima*, the Christmas Iris is an evergreen with small lavender flowers. Planted in fall, this one likes shade. The seed pods stay on the plants during the winter, popping open to show bright red seeds that last for weeks.

Others of the Bearded group are the E V A N S I A or Crested Iris, with spring flowers that resemble orchids. They like shade, acid conditions and a mulch of leaf mold. All are tender except the variety *cristata*, a dwarf amethyst-blue touched with gold and delightfully fringed and crested. This dwarf is pretty as a border plant. Variety *tectorum alba* is the rare white-flowered Roof Iris of Japan. It grows easily in full sun.

The only real pest is the Iris Borer. The moth lays its eggs at the base of the leaves in the autumn and these eggs hatch in spring. DDT or lindane will get rid of these if you spray in the fall. The so-called Bulb Rot is actually started by the inroads of the borer. The only hope to save an Iris from rot is to soak the rhizome in a weak solution of bichloride of mercury, which is a *deadly poison*.

I X I A S , bulbous corms of the Iris Family, are popularly known as Corn Lilies and here again are spring-blooming plants that do better in the upper South. The grass-like leaves and cup-shaped flowers are attractive and coming early in the year they make nice companions to the S P A R A X I S , another bulbous corm of the same family, smaller than Ixias. Both come in a variety of bright colors. Both like sandy loam, full sun and plenty of water. Planted in October, they grow and bloom and return best in an even forty to fifty degree temperature.

When I speak of L I L I E S , *Lilium,* I speak of the true species and their Hybrids, those stately beauties of the garden that most of us in the lower South thought were not for our hot and steamy climate. But I did try *Lilium* Enchantment some years ago and the results gave me the courage to try others.

Most Lilies are herbaceous perennials with bulbs made up of overlapping scales, and if given proper care will last several years. True species of Lilies are the results of types selected and intercrossed with other members of the same species until a healthy strain is established. There are trumpet-shaped, cup-shaped, cap-shaped and bowl-shaped Lilies. Hybrids are the results of crossing different species and groups, thereby producing flowers of various types. Lilies are propagated by seed, by scales and by bulbil and bulblet. Those plants produced by seed do not always come true to the parent plant. Reproduction by scale, bulbil and bulblet, called the vegetative method, is referred to as a clon, and each Lily raised within the clon is true to its parent.

I decided to try the Hybrids in the same well-drained, raised bed on the north side of the house where my Callas and my *Lilium* Enchantment, one of the Mid-Century Hybrids, had been doing so well. The soil in the bed is rich and loamy; there is plenty of peat moss in its content and I knew that in the length of the bed some parts got full sunlight, others only partial shade. I ordered my bulbs from a reputable bulb house and when they arrived the

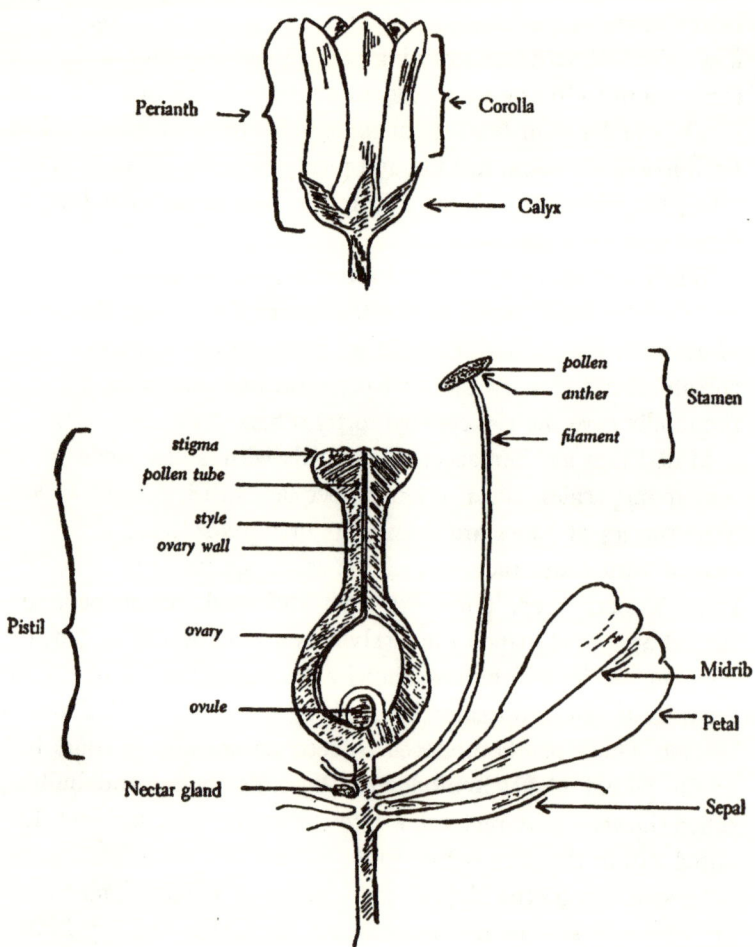

ANATOMY OF THE FLOWER

colors and shapes of the bulbs were so lovely that I really hated to put them down in the dark black earth!

I do not plant any of these Lilies as deep as the instructions directed. I subtract from two to three inches from each stated depth. Farther north of course, the planting should be a little deeper than in the lower area of the South. I set out the bulbs as soon as they arrive from the bulb house, usually in October, and I do not dig the bulbs in the winter after the foliage has died down but leave them undisturbed. I throw a light mulch of well-sifted peat over the bed about November fifteenth and I feed them as the new shoots break through the ground with a liquid fertilizer containing all of the trace elements.

Here is my list. I name these Lilies in order, from their places in the northeast end of the bed, which gets morning sun and is in semi-shade the rest of the day, to the northwest end of the garden bed, which besides getting the morning sun is still in full sun by three o'clock in the afternoon.

1. *Lilium speciosum rubrum* and its American counterpart *L. speciosum* Red Champion. Anthers heavily laden with deep orange pollen and white recurved petals deeply spotted with wine-red. Planted two inches deep and bloomed prolifically through July and August. The flowers face downward. Actually, I planted one dozen of these rubrum lilies in the bed between other hybrids so some got full sun, some partial shade and others full shade in the afternoon. All of them were full of blooms. When foliage died down in autumn I cut off the stems and allow the bulbs to remain in the ground through the winter. In spring the stems and leaves are beautiful and the lilies just as lovely as the first year's crop. Height of stem: from three and a half to four feet. I have also tried *L. speciosum album*, snow-white with yellow and green coloring down the center of each petal. Pollen is dark burnt-orange on long filaments. This one is as hardy as the *rubrum* but to me not as exotic. Remarkably free of disease and pests, these bulbs should be fed occasionally with a well-balanced liquid fertilizer.

2. BELLINGHAM HYBRID, *Lilium Shuksan* has three-foot stems

to carry lovely little cap-shaped lilies that bloom in June in blended shades of yellow, maroon and brown. Planted three inches deep. I lost this one after three years of bloom from bulb rot.

3. *Lilium Auratum* the gold-banded lily of Japan, died after two year's bloom. It is a great big flower, ivory-white petals specked with reddish-brown dots and each carrying a band of golden yellow down the midrib from throat to tip. The slender foliage appears on dark green sturdy stems about two and a half feet tall. Very fragrant. Planted three inches deep. Blooms in June in lower South where I find that two or three years is average time for *Auratum* to last. In upper sections it lasts longer and blooms later.

4. *Lilium* Green Mountain Hybrid is as beautiful in the bud as it is when wide open. The outside of the petals is a shaded brown, the inside white with a green throat. Texture is heavy and velvety. Long anthers with brown pollen. June blooms held sturdily on three and one-half foot stems. These are planted three inches deep in light shade.

5. *Lilium Rubellum* is almost a dwarf, growing to about one foot in height. Rose-lavender recurved blooms in May or June. Light shade.

6. *Lilium* Sunset, a prolific bloomer of late May and June in tones of yellow, amber and brown. Stem measures three feet. Planted three inches deep. I had this one for four years.

7. *Lilium Formosanum*, or the Formosa Lily, planted about three inches deep, does well in either full sun or partial shade. The trumpets are pure white, with greenish throats, borne on stem from three to four feet tall. Usually six to ten in number, the flowers are about the size of Easter Lilies or a little larger, are deliciously fragrant, and long-lasting. The leaves are not as wide as those of the Easter Lily. Besides being excellent cut flowers, if allowed to go to seed the golden beige pods are much in demand for dried arrangements.

The Formosa Lily usually blooms in July and August, showing no signs of damage from the heat. When the pods begin to split open in October plant the seeds immediately in cold frames or flats, or in the open ground and in two years you should have a blooming plant. If you do use the cold frame transplant the seedlings to open ground when they are about four to six inches tall and space them about one and one-half feet apart. The bulb needs no digging or storing; although it stands cold very well it does have the habit of splitting into two or three pieces, making it necessary for each piece to grow to maturity before blooming. Sometimes the bulb will just deteriorate but the abundance of seeds that each bloom presents and the rapidity of growth to maturity and bloom make up for the short life of the bulb.

Years ago *Lilium Formosanum* became confused with a tender lily that strongly resembles it, the *Lilium Philippinense*, native of the Philippine Islands and sometimes called the Philippine Lily. Some catalogues erroneously list it as *Lilium Philippinense formosanum*.

8. Jan de Graaff is one of the pioneers in the Lily field. He does his hybridizing in Oregon and he has given us many new strains of magnificent Hybrid lilies. His Mid-Century Hybrids are the results of crossing *Lilium tigrinum* and *Lilium umbellatum*. *Lilium* E N C H A N T - M E N T, introduced in 1949, is one of the most beautiful. It has been in my garden for eight years and this past year was more striking than ever. The three to four-foot stems bear ten to twelve large flowers of intense brilliant nasturtium-orange, spotted in dark blackish-brown. The bulbs were planted three inches deep and usually bloom in late April and May. This is another Lily that I have gradually added to all spots in the bed so that some are in full sun and others are in filtered shade. All are vigorous and the flowers last as well on the plant as they do as cut flowers in the house.

I stated that the Enchantment usually blooms in April and May and this is the normal flowering period in the South. But as is often the case in our very temperamental climate I have had them bloom in late January and early February, even during a freeze. When the low temperatures were predicted and I saw the buds showing color, I covered half of the ready-to-bloom plants with plastic bags and left the other half uncovered. Both sets of plants, protected and unprotected, did equally well with twelve to fifteen blossoms on each stem. That same year another batch bloomed in April and early May, another in June and four more plants flowered in late July and early August. That year I really had Enchantments for a long period. All were normal size on standard stems.

A rare characteristic of this lily and a very few others is to reproduce by means of bulbils that are found along the stem. These bulbils are tiny growths which appear all along the stem in the axil

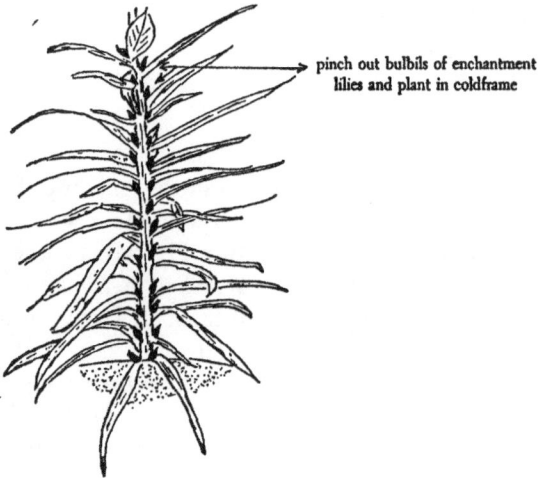

pinch out bulbils of enchantment lilies and plant in coldframe

of the leaf after the plant has finished blooming. They look like pixie caps that turn from green to brown as they mature. I have had a lot of fun propagating the Enchantment by picking these bulbils with my fingers, planting them point up in my cold frame that contains a mixture of one-third sharp sand, one-third peat moss and one-third humus. The frame is in sheltered, filtered shade. I water the bulbils with a fine spray just enough to keep them moist and I feed them once a month with a well-balanced liquid fertilizer. After one year, in the month of October I transplant the young lilies to another frame where the sun is a little stronger. I leave them here until the following October when I place them out in the open ground. When the babies are three years old I have normal size blooms.

Not only is propagation by bulbil economical but the bulbils run true to the parent plant, which is not always the case in propagation by seed. Moreover the plants that mature from bulbils are practically disease free and much more resistant to the different types of virus that usually attack lilies.

9. *Lilium* Flamingo. The bulbs were so beautiful, the color of a flamingo, that I hated to plant them. The blooms were equally lovely but alas, the foliage soon withered and the bulb rotted. They had been planted two inches deep. I'm going to try again.

10. *Lilium Testaceum,* the Nankeen Lily likes full sun and is one of the bulbs that you must plant as shallow as you dare, the other being L. *Candidum.* Although all catalogues point out this lily as the one that should do best in any climate, I saw plenty of foliage but no blooms. I am still coaxing.

11. *Lilium Martagon Album* has dainty waxy-white flowers and likes sun. It too likes shallow planting and blooms in May on three to four foot stems.

12. *Lilium Amabile* is an interesting red lily spotted in black. Planted three inches deep it is the first to bloom in early May and the foliage dies down soon after bloom. The stems measure two and a half feet in height.

13. *Lilium Amabile luteum* is another May bloomer. The flowers are yellowish-red and are borne on two-foot stems. It should be planted very shallow.

14. *Lilium* Campfire whose bulb is as fiery red as its blooms, is most gratifying. I planted it at the head of the bed in full sun and it also flowered in May on two-foot stems. Depth of planting is three inches.

15. *Lilium Henryi* is sometimes called the Yellow Speciosum because it resembles that species in flower but not in growth habits. It blooms in May and June, a lovely shade of mellow orange, not as bright as Enchantment. Filaments are chartreuse with orange pollen. Stems are dark green mottled in brown up to three feet and the leaves are ordinary normal size up to that point. Above three feet the stem becomes

smooth green and leaves grow smaller until they are about one-fourth as large as the lower ones. When the stem reaches five feet it divides into three branches, two having two blooms each and the third dividing again, each branchlet setting two buds. Stake this lily before it blooms. Plant it three inches deep.

16. *Lilium* Orange Perfection was introduced as being even better than *Lilium* Enchanment but I do not find it so. Although a lovely orange, it does not have the intensity of color or proliferous habits of the Enchantment.

17. *Lilium Candidum* or the Madonna Lily is pure white and delightfully fragrant. Don't plant these singly, but in groups of three or four. Usually bloom in June and July on three to four-foot stems. Said to be the oldest lily in cultivation the Candidum has a habit of increasing rapidly. It likes shallow planting, about one and a half inches deep so bear this in mind when you set them out in September and October.

18. *Lilium regale*, the Regal Lilies are white shaded with lilac and brown on the outside and yellow on the inside of the petals. The texture is heavy. Mine grow to five feet and the flowers bloom in clusters in May and June. Planted four inches deep.

19. Early in June, *Lilium* Royal Gold, or the Golden Regale Lily begins to show its wide buttery-yellow petals. The slender three-foot stem, with its narrow green leaves, has to be staked to hold the flowers that open on an angle to the stem. The texture is so like suede that I am always tempted to feel it. The filaments are chartreuse, bearing coral-colored pollen. Planted three inches deep. This one is a beauty!

20. I think that the biggest moment of Lily-growing came when I saw my first *Lilium* Theodore A. Havemeyer open in mid June. This is a Hybrid of the cross between *Lilium Henryi* and *Lilium myriophyllum*, and has proven to be a very rare and choice Lily, winner of a special gold medal in the New York World's Fair. The flowers are borne on three-foot stems and the foliage is very dark green and slender. The three inner petals of the blossom are very large and heavily ridged and the three outer sepals are indented at the center and gently ruffled at the edges. The whole flower is the color of old ivory, sprinkled at the flare of the perianth with amber-orange and deepening at the throat to dark green. The filaments are chartreuse bearing anthers heavily laden with

burnt-orange pollen. The pistil is a deep green. The Lily opens wide and almost flat, measuring nine inches across and it has the most delicious fragrance I have ever found. This is one of the times when I wished I could have captured the beauty and the scent and held onto them longer. The cut flower lasts three or four days in the house. Planted three inches deep.

21. When I planted my PINK PERFECTION Lilies I chose a section of the long lily bed where dappled shade begins at noon. These are the new Pink Selections of the Olympic Hybrids, a new race of the Centifolium group. They grow strong and straight to six feet and bear beautifully shaped trumpets of pale pink and velvety texture. They bloom in May. The color is not as deep in the South as it is in other parts of the country. I am afraid that we have our intense heat and high night temperatures to blame for that. Planted three inches deep.

All of these Hybrids bloomed earlier than the time set forth in the catalogues. There are many others to choose from and I suppose that the only way to discover which ones do well is to go through the process of trial and error. Given ideal conditions the *Liliums* certainly are not demanding. They need no lifting, pruning, pinching or careful watching. I have never found many pests on my Hybrids. I hand-pick the snails because I cannot use poisoned pellets due to my children and their pets. I use a hard spray of the hose if I see any spider webs. If aphids make their appearance I act immediately to get rid of them by spraying with a solution containing DDT, malathion and lindane, because aphids carry the Mosaic disease that sometimes affects lilies. This disease, evidenced by a mottling of the leaves is a virus that attacks not only the foliage but stem and bulb as well. Since there is no cure your best bet is to discard the lily quickly. Just be sure to order bulbs from a reputable bulb house and examine them carefully for any signs of spotting or decay.

If the leaves of your lily turn yellow and the plant seems to stop growth before blooming your bulb may be affected by a brown rot fungus called Fusarium Rot. Look over the bulbs you are about to plant and if the scales are loose and fall easily and if the bulb as a whole feels spongy, do not plant it. The fungus will stay in the soil once it is there and it will take a good many applications of fungicide to get rid of it. If you dig a suspected bulb and you find only part of it affected cut the sick area away well past the decay and treat it with a fungicide. Fumigate the soil too before re-planting. The Nankeen Lily, *Lilium testaceum* is prone to this disease.

Botrytis Blight, another fungus, creates brown spots on leaves, flowers and stem but rarely kills a plant. Furthermore in damp humid weather if the infected leaves fall to the ground and stay there another crop of spores have a chance to form and the disease spreads. Spraying with Bordeaux mixture will eventually control Botrytis but good housekeeping in the garden will do a lot to keep it out entirely.

These three diseases may sound dreadful but actually they do not occur too frequently. I think that losing two or three lilies out of twenty-one is a good average. One thing I have learned: keep the lily bed free of fallen leaves and weeds to avoid disease. And dusting the bulbs with a fungicide before planting is a good precaution. It discourages spores that cause disease.

Pips of the LILY-OF-THE-VALLEY *Convalleria majalis,* a low perennial member of the Lily Family are lovely to see. Though they can be planted outdoors in December in the upper South down here in our lower section we must be content to force a few in pots in the dark and then enjoy the blooms indoors. The outdoor bed must be fortified with a heavy layer of well-rotted manure or rich compost and must be kept moist. Use the same mixture in pots. The pips do best in shady spots. For use indoors place a set of pips in a bowl and steady them by packing sphagnum or peat moss and a few pieces of charcoal around them. Fill the container with tap water and place in a window. Add water as it evaporates. You should have blooms in four weeks.

L Y C O R I S , bulbous members of the Amaryllis Family are often called the Spider Lilies of the autumn. Originally from China and Japan they are also known as Naked Ladies because the flowers bloom in clusters on long stems before the leaves appear. The petals are narrow and fluted and the stamens quite prominent. Although you can plant them in the spring you may not always have them bloom that same fall; it is wiser to get them established in the late autumn and early winter. As soon as the foliage dies back you can transplant them. They are hardy, don't seem to mind low temperatures, and I have never seen them attacked by disease or pest. Do not disturb them often; every five or six years is often enough to thin them out. They bloom better in colonies that are left completely alone as long as possible. *Lycoris* will bloom in any kind of soil fortified with bone meal. Originally planted with the tip of the bulb showing, they soon disappear entirely below the soil level as they remain in the ground until about the fifth year when they seem to warn you that they need attention by showing their necks even after blooming and losing their foliage. So when they are first planted, it is not a bad idea to put name markers on the spot so that the bulbs are not injured when you cultivate the soil. As a matter of fact I label all of my lilies by sticking long-handled white plastic markers down in the ground several inches in front of the plant. It is a nice way to keep track of what you have and it certainly makes a garden more interesting to visitors.

Lycoris radiata is the one best known to us, perhaps under the incorrect names of Guernsey Lily or Nerine. This one is a lovely shade of melon-red with an overlay of dusty gold. *L. aurea* is larger and a very beautiful golden-yellow, more expensive and scarce. *L. incarnata* not too well known, is a pale flesh color. I have enjoyed this one and the *L. alba*, a rare white not easily found. *Lycoris Sprengeri* is lavender-rose. All of these bloom in the fall before foliage appears.

Lycoris squamigera, known as *Amaryllis Hallii* is often nicknamed the Hurricane Lily. It shows its foliage in March and the lavender blossoms do not appear until August after the leaves die down.

MERTENSIA, of the Borage Family is an herbaceous perennial of many species, the most popular of which is *Mertensia virginica* known as Virginia Cowslip or just as Blue Bells. Planted in ordinary soil they do best in shade and grow to about fifteen inches high, producing little blue funnel-shaped, drooping flowers that change to pink as they mature. They do not like to be disturbed so place them with other flowers that will hide the foliage as it yellows and dies. The Blue Bells will not always return the second year in the lower South as they do further north.

The MONTBRETIA, bulbous corm of the Iris Family is known botanically as *Tritonia*, but since this plant is almost always listed in catalogues as Montbretia I'll stick to it. This summer and fall bloomer requires the same culture as does the Glad, needing no digging and storing anywhere in the South. It looks especially well when planted in clumps. The leaves are narrow and pointed, flat like those of the Glad and the flowers are small funnel-shaped and borne on tall spikes. Most nurseries sell Montbretias in a mixture of colors including the varieties *crocata* reddish-orange, *Pottsii* yellow, *rosea* tall and red and yellow. The hybrid *crocosmaeflora* is the largest of the reddish-orange group. Plant from November through February.

Quite a few gardeners consider the OXALIS as a weed but I have always enjoyed seeing my little yellow ones bloom in their border in the spring. These members of the Oxalis Family are known for their leaves that not only close at night but look like clover leaves, leading to the popular name of Flowering Shamrock. The little sun-loving flowers have five petals centered by a cone-shaped tube. Mine are *Oxalis cernua* or Bermuda Buttercups and they grow from tiny bulbs that are planted in September and October in a shallow trench in loamy, well-drained soil. I feed them in the growing period with a balanced liquid fertilizer. Sometimes the crown rises above the surface of the soil when the flowers are in bloom, in which case I simply lower them and press soil around them. Oxalis die down and disappear in winter months but are up again in spring. They seem to be particularly pretty after cold winters. Two late summer bloomers are *O. hirta*, a pink and *O. rubra*, a dark-veined rose. *O. crassipes*, pink and *O. Regnallii*, white, are both tuberous-rooted members of this family, almost evergreen, that bloom on and off during the year.

The PINEAPPLE FLOWER or *Eucomis punctata* is probably the most satisfactory summer-blooming bulb that I have ever found. As its name suggests this member of the Lily Family resembles a pineapple, even to the cluster of small leaves at the top. The long strap-like leaves and the flowering scape are all a medium-green, with a faint stippling of purple on the underside of the leaves and the tiny flowers are chartreuse.

I plant it in the fall, usually in October, in my north lily bed with neck showing slightly. Don't be alarmed if it doesn't show immediately in the spring as it is slow to start. The heavy-textured leaves then come up and sprawl out like spokes of a wheel and about May first the scape arises from the center and grows to about sixteen inches. About eight inches from the top, tiny elliptical-shaped nodes begin to cover the scape to the top where a whorl of small leaves appears.

These top leaves have slightly serrated edges and look exactly like the bunch usually found atop the pineapple. On or about May twenty-eighth the nodes begin to open from the bottom showing small chartreuse flowers with deep yellow stamens. These bottom flowers remain open as row on row upwards open. At this point I have to stake the flower stem. The bloom remains intact and lovely until about August thirtieth when signs of fading appear. The time elements mentioned above will vary in locale and with the severity of the winters. I took them from my garden diary and gave them to you as a guide to the length of time the flower lasts.

The Eucomis, which is from the Greek meaning "Topknot", likes semi-shade and grows well and looks beautiful when planted near English Bracken Fern. I give it a single feeding of a liquid fertilizer containing all of the trace elements in March. The foliage dies down in the fall and the bulb remains dormant all winter in the ground. Propagation is by offsets.

Because I have enjoyed this bulb for three years there are two other varieties that I am certainly going to try; *Eucomis pedunculata* with same growth habits but with flowers ranging from green to pure white, marked spasmodically with purple, and *E. Pole-Evansi* a rare new one and a big one with frilled leaves, more upright in habit, reaching three feet. This flower scape is said to reach four or five feet, bearing light green blooms. I have found *E. undulata* to be very much like the *punctata* with the leaves of the topknot somewhat larger.

s c i l l a or Squill is a perennial bulbous plant of the Lily Family that has been widely grown in temperate climates and should be tried here. Known also as Wild Hyacinth and Bluebell, Scilla makes a lovely addition to the group of border plants that bloom in the early spring. It needs an occasional feeding of leaf mold or well-balanced fertilizer. The Siberian Squill, *Scilla sibirica* is hardy if placed in a sheltered spot. It blooms early, showing little clusters of three deep blue flowers on short stems. The variety *nonscripta* is the English Bluebell that reaches twelve to fourteen inches in height and bears a dozen or so fragrant flowers. *Scilla nonscripta caerulea* is a beautiful blue; *S. nonscripta alba* is the white form; *rosea* is a rosy-pink and the lavender is *lilacina*. The variety *hispanica* produces larger blossoms that shade from blue to a rose-lilac. There is one type that blooms in the fall, *Scilla autumnalis*, commonly called Autumn Squill. Planted in the spring, it only reaches six to eight inches in height and bears soft pink flowers, usually in September.

s n o w f l a k e s bloom in early spring and they make you think of Lilies-of-the-Valley. Botanically they are *Leucojum vernum*, hardy bulbs of the Amaryllis Family. The leaves are strap-like, about nine inches high and the scape, about one foot high bears small white bell-shaped flowers that are dotted with green near the outer edges. They nod, resembling little bells. Plant in early fall about two inches deep in well-drained loamy soil. They do best when left undisturbed for years.

SPREKELIA, *Sprekelia formosissima* is known to some as the Jacobean Lily, St. James Lily and the Aztec Lily, the last one suiting it best. I love this exotic-looking flower, a dark crimson perianth and a red spathe touched in brown. The leaves, almost one foot high, appear only with the bloom. The scape is hollow. A small bulb of the Amaryllis Family, it does best when root-bound in a pot which is sunk in the open ground. Plant bulb about one and a half inches deep and keep mulched over the winter. Sprekelia is not particular as to the soil in which it is planted but it does demand sun. Blooms in early summer, usually in June. Don't keep too wet. I bring mine indoors in long rainy spells.

SPRING STAR FLOWER is *Triteleia-milla* or *Triteleia uniflora*, a member of the *Brodiaea* clan of the Lily Family and is one of the few of this group that does well here. Most of them are more suited to the West. The leaves are about one foot long, the scapes shorter, each bearing one small star-shaped fragrant flower of a pretty lavender-blue. The throat is white. These small corms like fairly rich soil, full sun or partial shade and bloom in early spring. Plant two inches deep and do not disturb.

Brodiaea volubilis is commonly called Snake-Lily and this one does well here in any type of soil provided it is not kept too wet. With the exception of giving it plenty of sun you can plant it two inches deep and forget about it. Tiny deep pink flowers appear in umbels in the spring. The leaves are reedy and thin, the flower scape about three feet high. It is climbing in nature so if there is a bush or pole handy it will grab on and begin to twine upwards. It is rather pretty blooming atop fences.

STAR-OF-BETHLEHEM, *Ornithogalum umbellatum*, small bulb of the Lily Family produces strap-like leaves about one foot high with a shorter scape bearing small cup-shaped white flowers that open wide. Like the Daffodil this early spring bloomer has to have good drainage, loamy soil and plenty of sun. Sometimes there is a return of bloom the second year in the lower South if the first winter is cold, otherwise reorder because they are well worth having in the border. Set out two inches deep and do not disturb. *O. arabicum,* smaller and more tender than *umbellatum* does well in a pot and is unusual because the pistil is shiny and black and very striking against the white flowers. *O. caudatum* is a very large bulb with three-foot leaves which are succulent. Flowers are small and greenish-white in racemes on four-foot stems. This variety is some-times erroneously listed in catalogues as the Sea Onion, *Urginea maritima* whose flowers are whitish-brown. The bulbs of the latter are known as Squill and as *Scilla verna,* used for medicinal pur-poses.

STERNBERGIA, *Sternbergia lutea,* is a bulbous herb of the Amaryllis Family, low-growing and bright yellow, blooming in late summer and fall. Some call it the fall Crocus and it does look like a Crocus. This one will multiply rapidly in cooler climates but in the warmer regions it is pretty enough to replant if it does not return. I planted mine three inches deep in full sun in medium-rich soil. Although it can be set out in early spring and still bloom the first year I prefer to plant mine in the fall. I have enjoyed the Sternbergias for two years.

Although TRITOMA has the fairly new botanical name of *Kniphofia, Tritoma Uvaria* will always be known to most of us as the Red-Hot-Poker. It is a perennial rhizomatous member of the Lily Family with small reedy leaves that are outshined by the tall round flower spikes that rise from the center. The top three-quarters of the scape is covered with tiny tubular buds that open gradually from the bottom, yellowish-red to bright red. Although they were originally autumn bloomers, hybridizers have been so busy with this tribe that we now have access to summer and fall-flowering types shading from ivory to red in tall and miniature plants. They are all winter hardy and should be planted in the autumn so that they can be well-established before blooming. Not particular as to type of soil as long as it is loamy and gets full sun. My *Tritoma* Springtime, a tall one to about three feet was beautiful this June, the flowers shading from ivory at the bottom to orange-red at the top. Another pretty one, Coral Sea, a dwarf to about one and a half feet is all coral-red. Both of these are particularly attractive when used in front of blue-flowering shrubs. The clumps can be propagated by division.

T U L I P S mean spring anywhere but when we in the lower South see a whole bed of these lovely blooms as after an exceptional snow and freeze, then we realize why there might have been a reason for the "Tulipomania" of the seventeenth century. These hardy bulbs of the Lily Family have to have cold temperatures in which to grow and bloom so we try to substitute these conditions by placing ours in the refrigerator for at least thirty to sixty days prior to planting. If you order them early enough and delivery is speedy you will have a longer period to refrigerate them. At any rate keep them cold until planting in November or at the latest, December. Place them in full sun in a rich loamy soil that has been turned and cultivated to a depth of nine inches so that the bulb can send down its roots. Set the bulb on a handful of sand at least four inches deep. After blooming allow the foliage to die down normally and then dig, clean and store the bulbs in a cool dry place. If the next winter proves cold the bulbs will return blooms, with stems about one-half the size of those of the first year. If the weather proves to be the usual warm and humid one you may not have any luck at all. In the lower South you cannot count on Tulips as you can farther north.

Most of the Tulips we know are imported from Holland where the Dutch have bred them for years, hence the name "Dutch Tulips". You will find various types of Tulips offered in your bulb catalogues and to help you differentiate, I list the following in the order in which they usually bloom.

1. *Tulipa fosteriana*, a descendant of the wild Turkish Tulip. Red Emperor is a fine example, a great big bright red flower on eighteen-inch stem. Center is yellow and black.

2. The *Kaufmanniana* species have short stems and wide open flowers. These bloom close to the ground and may be had in a variety of colors. They look best when planted in colonies. One of this group, the Peacock Tulip is excellent for border planting.

3. The Single Early Tulips are rather tall stemmed. Couleur Cardinal is a good red, Olympiade a lovely yellow and Van den Neer, pure white.

4. The Double Early Tulips, to twelve inches and very full, resemble Peonies. Orange Nassau is deep burnt-orange, Peach Blossom is a rose-pink flushed with white at the edges and Marechal Niel, a deep gold color tinged slightly with apricot. While the Single Early Tulips can be planted in mixed colors, I do think that these like the later Darwins and Cottage Tulips look better when each variety is massed by itself.

5. The tall-stemmed Triumph and Mendel varieties are hybrids of a cross between the Darwins and the Single Earlies. I like Elizabeth Evers, a fuchsia with silvery-white markings. Bandoeng is almost mahogany color. These do well in the lower South.

6. The Darwin Tulips are long-stemmed and globular in shape and come in colors ranging from white Annie Speelman, to yellow Sunkist, to red Roman Eagle, to mauve Insurpassable, to almost black, La Tulipe Noire.

7. The Breeder type with more oval buds, gets its name because its self-coloring makes it good for hybridizing. Dixie Sunshine is new, a yellowish-buff with faint lavender blush on the outside of the petals. Don Alma is a tawny golden brown, Chinese Bandit a big dark red.

8. Cottage Tulips, last to bloom, have more slender stems, narrower leaves and pointed petals that tend to recurve as the flower opens. Mellow Moon is a wonderful yellow and The Queen of Spain is ivory shading to rose at the edge of the petals. The lily-flowered Tulips belong to this group and bloom at the same time. These closely resemble lilies in their graceful and delicately curved petals. Golden Duchess,

Astor, a salmon and Spitfire are all most attractive, their buds almost urn-shaped.

The Parrot Tulips are exotics. Their veined, ruffled petals look as if they have been fringed. They are sports of the Darwins and bloom at midseason with them. As the name suggests the colors are very vivid. The deep pink Fantasy is well known and Firebird comes a close second. The darkest of all is the Black Parrot, a purplish-black. The Rembrandt Tulips are varieties of Darwins that have stripes of color in the petals. Here again I suggest you stick to one variety. There is a purple streaked in white and a lavender touched in white that make good companions. Midseason.

There is a class of late flowering Double Giant Tulips that are tall and showy and like the Double Early ones, look like Peonies. Symphonia is bright red and Mount Tacoma a beautiful white.

Since Tulip flowers and leaves grow on the same stem be careful to leave enough foliage if you cut the flower for use in the house. If you allow the blossom to remain on the plant until it has passed its peak cut it off short, allowing as much of the stem to remain and die down naturally with the leaves. The bulb needs all the nourishment it can get for next year's bloom.

The only really serious disease to attack the Tulip is Tulip Fire, a fungus that makes the petals of the flower look scorched. It is a type of Botrytis Blight that usually attacks the bulbs wherever they have been injured and the leaves develop rusty spots on which spores form and multiply in wet weather. It is spread by rain, pets or tools to healthy plants so examine your bulbs before planting for breaks or cuts. If this disease becomes evident after planting burn the affected tulip and spray the ground from which you took it with a Bordeaux mixture.

One of the pests that I have noticed on the Tulip bud is the greenish-yellow aphid, and usually a hard spraying of the hose eliminates that character. If it persists use either lindane or malathion. The white bulb mite can be routed with nicotine sulphate or Aramite.

WATSONIAS really should be grown much more than they are. They are corms of the Iris Family and are lovely fresh-cut or dried. They have the same kind of root though smaller, the same sword-like foliage, the same type of flower spike as the Gladiolus and they bloom very much at the same time. There are some botanical differences. The flowers and leaves are not as big and Watsonias like to be set out in the fall so that they can become established by early spring blooming time. The culture and growth habits are much the same as those of the Glad. Plant about two inches deep. There are many named varieties now in different colors but the one I like best is Lucile, a lovely salmon. Mrs. Bullard's White is considered the best white, Clunes is lavender and Adelaide with a deeper pink throat than its petals is a charming large flower.

WINTER GLADIOLUS, a new strain, should be planted in September for December bloom. See Gladiolus.

There are other bulbs that are best planted in late winter, early spring and early summer for bloom later in those seasons, including the following.

ACIDANTHERA is one of the most satisfactory of the small corms of the Iris Family. The corm itself is interesting, covered with fibre that looks like it was matted and flattened. A native of

Acidanthera

the tropics and South Africa, it ranks between the Ixias and the Glads. The culture is the same as that of the Glad with two exceptions. It is planted about one inch deep and the bulbs must be lifted and stored each year. Set them out in the spring, early in March. Place them in a spot where the plants will get full sun.

I have had *Acidanthera bicolor* for a number of years. The leaves closely resembling Glad foliage in shape and color, are about one and a half feet high. The flower scapes bear small fragrant star-shaped blossoms usually with five petals, white with a brownish-maroon throat. Mine bloom steadily from June through September. Lift and store after foliage dies down normally.

Amaryllis Striata, a small bulb of the Amaryllis clan, bears a medium-sized flower that is salmony-pink, with a slight green keel and a green throat. It usually blooms from December to March. The leaves are like those of the hybrid Amaryllis, but shorter and they will either remain on the plant the year around or disappear depending on the severity of the winter. The scapes rarely measure more than a foot in height and the flowers number two to four. Early spring seems to be the best time either to plant or divide.

This attractive plant does not seem to demand any particular soil, but do cover the bulb a little more than you do the big Amaryllis and give it good drainage, semi-shade and moisture. It is exasperating to see a clump of these *Striata* blooming beautifully in a garden with no care at all, when others that are carefully nurtured are not doing half as well. So don't coddle them too much. Let them multiply a few years before you separate. Some of you may still think of this bulb as *Amaryllis rutila*, its old botanical name. Where winters are severe I would recommend it be grown in pots.

The white B U T T E R F L Y - L I L Y that lends such a fragrance to our southern gardens is *Hedychium coronarium*, a rhizomatous member of the Ginger Family. Planted in rich loamy soil this pretty thing needs plenty of water and filtered shade. In height and foliage it reminds you very much of the Canna. The flowers are large, appearing from behind the green scaly bracts that make up the flower head; the wide white petals look like butterfly wings, hence the name. The yellow-orange variety, often called Yellow Ginger, is *Hedychium flavum* which grows to about five feet, producing a slightly different leaf, smooth on the upper side and hairy beneath. The variety *Gardnerianum,* the Kahili Lily offers an exotic flower, much smaller than the other two but growing in long spikes, yellow with red stamens. These lilies will bloom in late summer and autumn. Should they die back in frost they will return the following spring. Do not disturb until the third year, when you may separate if too crowded.

CALADIUMS, grown for their delightful foliage save the day for us in the extreme heat of the summer when we need cool-looking garden subjects. These tubers of the Arum Family may be planted safely in the open ground in April in the lower sections of the South when you feel rather sure that all danger of frost is over. In the upper South they usually have to wait until May to begin growth outdoors. Caladiums can of course, be started earlier in the spring in seed boxes and cold frames where they can be protected while they put down roots. Transfer carefully to garden beds later. The new fibre pots that are now on the market make ideal receptacles in which to start your tubers. Just place the usual small pieces of gravel or broken clay pot into the bottom of the fibre pot and fill with good loamy soil. Set the tuber one and a half times as deep as the height of the tuber. Keep moist and in a fairly warm spot until the weather conditions are favorable for the pots to be moved directly to the open ground. Because of their composition the fibre containers eventually disintegrate. In this way the Caladium receives no shock at all from the transplant.

Caladiums prefer semi-shade and the acid loamy soil in which Azaleas and Camellias are planted. Plant them at the depth specified above in the open ground and keep moist but not wet. If you feed them several times during the growing period with liquid manure or with a liquid food containing all of the trace elements the bulbs will increase in size, thereby producing larger and deeper colored leaves. I think that cutting the flowers as soon as they appear is beneficial to the plant. The blooms are really of no consequence and just take that much more strength from the leaves. In the fall when you notice the leaves beginning to droop dig the Caladiums carefully without removing the leaves and gently lay them in a cool spot to dry for about three weeks. When the foliage is withered gently pull from the bulb. It should come off easily leaving a tiny pointed top, like a pixie cap on the tuber. Brush away the excess dried earth, dust with sulphur and place in old nylon stockings. I hang the partially full stockings in the garage and allow them to remain there over the winter. *But* however you store them whether in stockings or in boxes filled with sand or vermiculite, be sure that the temperature in the garage or room will never go down to freezing. If it does the tubers will either turn to mush or become rock-like.

There are many colors to choose. As each of the following was at its peak, I went out into the garden and entered the description in my garden diary.

Candidum Pure white, heavily veined and bordered in green.

Lord Derby Transparent pink with dark green ribs and border. Fades in too much sun.

Brazilian Butterfly Subtle sheen to medium large leaves. Color ranges from tan to white to pale green with pink veining and some pink mottling.

Sorocabo Small-leaved, a transparent silvery pink suffused with white. Green ribs and veins.

Balinese Dancer Small hazy-green leaves spotted in white with dull pink veins.

Mary Stuart, Queen of Scots Unique! Leaves irregularly mottled in dark moss green, gray-green, gray and deep red. Some nettled and veined in ruby red with occasional spots of bright transparent red.

Pink Cloud   One of the most beautiful I have ever seen. Very large luscious pink leaves slightly mottled in soft green.

Pink Beauty   A close second to Pink Cloud. Large, deeper pink and more heavily marked and bordered with green.

Macahyba   Deep pink-lavender splotches on bronzy-green. Darker pink veins. Exotic.

Mrs. W. B. Haldeman   Medium pink leaf banded in green. Pink is deeper on those that receive more sun.

Edith Meade   White with red veins and narrow green edge.

Annabelle   Unusual. Large pink veining on green leaves that are generously spotted in white.

Hortilania   Big and strong. Green bordered leaf centered with crimson and overlaid with a tinge of blue.

Dr. D. M. Cook   Dark moss-green leaves slightly rippled at edges and shaped a trifle like the lance-leaf variety. Center and ribs are plum red.

John Peed   Bright metallic-red margined in green.

Itacapus   Very beautiful. Leaf all rust color with red marking on border.

Giraud   Two-toned green crumpled leaves spotted in brilliant red. No marked veining.

Crimson Wave   Large dark green leaf with crinkled red center and spotted with red on border.

Fannie Munson   Very deep lipstick red.

Mrs. F. Sander   Unusual round leaf, dark green blotched in deep rose.

Reconcavo   Strong grower with carmine-pink on green and pink dotted leaves.

T. L. Meade   No green here, leaf all metallic-bronze with heavy red ribs.

Triomphe de l'Exposition   Leaves almost round, very large, with bright crimson center, scarlet ribs and light green border. You will have to look twice before you can tell the difference between this one and Red Ensign.

Red Flare   Bright red blotched in gray-green and light green. Nice for pots.

Scarlet Pimpernelle   This one must have been a forebear of Red Flare. Same red but mottled in only dark green.

Texas Wonder   Tall one. Red center mottled with pink and green. Veined with white and yellow. Known by some as Cleo.

Rising Sun   Red center and ribs on metallic gold background. Mottled with faint pink.

Tom Tomlinson   Deep pink center and blotches on green. Very full.

Spangled Banner   Dark red leaf with magenta ribs, spotted in pink.

Arno Nehrling   Metallic white with red veins and very small green edging. Lovely in pots.

The following are the dwarf plants that I have tried.

Red Ensign   Very large leaves, deep red center to green edge. I like this one in pots. It makes a very full many-leaved plant to bring into the house.

Poecile Anglais   Crinkled dark red leaf with metallic green margin. Attractive.

Dr. Groover   Bushy with a pale pink center with narrow green border and few green splotches.

Madam Truall   Shiny red and bronze leaf, ribs darker crimson.

Mrs. Arno H. Nehrling   Bronze red shaded to rusty red with dark crimson ribs and veins.

The Arrow and Lance Leaf Caladiums are semi-rare. Actually not new because they were known some forty years ago, they are now becoming more popular. They are hybrids of dwarf narrow-leaved Caladiums and rather low-growing, ranging from a few inches to one foot in height. The tubers are very small. The Red Arrow is a bright metallic red. Caloosa Hatchee, with its rather wide green leaf and Okeechobee, with deep green pointed leaves and light green veins are perhaps the best known of the Lance Leaf group.

I do think Caladiums make a better display when grouped according to colors. A border of all white or all pink is a cool asset to any summer garden. Caladiums should be ordered well ahead of planting time to insure your getting what you want. Tubers are graded in standard sizes: number 1, from 1½ inches to 2½ inches in diameter; Jumbo, 2½ inches to 3½ inches, and Mammoth, 3½ inches up. They are priced accordingly.

CANNA, of the *Cannaceae,* has been taken for granted for such a long time that it has become almost neglected. But properly trimmed of its spent foliage it lends itself well to mass planting. The leaves, either green or bronze depending on the type, lend a tropical effect. The tall varieties usually reach four and five feet, the dwarf ones from one to three feet and the clusters of flowers now range from soft shades of peach and cream to the deep reds. Plant these thick fleshy roots in early spring in a fairly good moist soil and where there will be plenty of sunshine. Set out one foot apart if you plan to use them as background or farther apart if intended as individual ornamentals. Water well in the growing period and feed occasionally with a well-balanced fertilizer. Although it is not necessary to dig and store the Cannas in the South it is a good idea to take them up after the first frost in upper sections of the area. Allow the roots to dry well before storing in a cool place.

There are many beautiful pastel-colored Cannas. In the Grand Opera Series, a selected group of hybrids, you will find La Boheme, a pearly-rose overlaid with peach; Madame Butterfly, a pink streaked with yellow; Rigoletto, a lovely yellow, all with green foliage. One of the best white Cannas is Eureka, which grows to four feet and bears green leaves. King Humbert produces bronzy-red foliage and deep orange blossoms, the yellow King Humbert bears yellow flowers dotted with crimson. Both of these are tall, to four and one-half feet. Wyoming is very tall, to six feet, with orange flowers and bronze foliage.

Try one of the new hybrids, the Pfitzer Dwarf Cannas, in a tub or large pot for your patio. It rarely exceeds three feet and the colors are lovely, ranging from shell-pink to deep coral. Most of the hybrids are resistant to the bacterial bud rot that made Cannas look badly for so many years. But you do have to watch for the caterpillars that roll themselves up tight in a leaf and chew away. Spray with arsenate of lead.

The DAHLIA is one of our most spectacular plants and does well all over the South. An herbaceous perennial tuber, it was named after Andreas Dahl, a Swedish botanist of the eighteenth century who obtained plants and seeds from Mexico where it had been discovered by a Spaniard in the sixteenth century. It was earlier known as *Acactii*. The first plants were listed as *Dahlia varabilis* but has since been replaced by *Dahlia pinnata* or *D. rosea*. The second form was the Cactus Dahlia, another Mexican-born plant, *D. Juarezii*.

There are four ways to purchase Dahlias from the nursery: as green plants, as rooted cuttings, as tubers or roots and as pot roots. For planting in the South, I recommend buying the tubers. Dahlias are planted in the spring after all danger of frost is over so that time varies in the South from March in the lower sections to May wherever the cold hangs on. They may also be planted in early summer for fall blooms. As a matter of fact there are many gardeners who prefer to hold their prize tubers for autumn flowering because they feel that cooler weather brings forth better plants. In either case the culture is the same.

The bed must be prepared at least a month ahead of time. Choose a well-raised level spot because drainage must be good. Make sure that the soil is rich and loamy. Test your soil. Dahlias do best in a rather neutral medium neither too acid nor too alkaline. Incorporate humus and a fair amount of bone meal into the earth. I use a cupful for every tuber to be planted. Spade the soil and turn it often, especially after rains to keep it from clogging and caking. I also add whatever wood ashes I can get because they aid a little in production of strong stems and tend to keep the earth friable. Next mark the spot wherever you intend to set the Dahlia, about two and a half feet apart for the tall varieties and one and a half feet apart for the miniatures. Drive a tall strong stake at least twelve inches into the ground at the spot where each tuber will go.

When the time for planting arrives dig each hole six inches deep. Dig it wide enough to accommodate the tuber which must be set horizontally, with the eye usually on or near the piece of old stalk on one end of the tuber. Drop a handful of sharp sand in the bottom of the hole and place the tuber on the sand. Fill the hole half way with soil and as the sprout grows fill in further until the level of the bed is reached. When the Dahlia is about ten inches high begin to attach to the stake. Never use string or wire because it will cut the stalk. Instead try using strips of cloth or nylon stockings dyed green. They don't show and they serve the purpose well. Mulch the bottom of the plant with pine needles so that the roots will keep cool and moist through the summer heat.

Begin pinching out the tips of the plant when it reaches one foot in height. This will encourage side branching. Any flower buds that show before September first should also be pinched out. After that allow them to mature. Then if you wish exhibition blooms, pinch further. Allow the center bud to remain and remove the two side ones. The buds next below the top set should also be carefully taken out, thereby lengthening the stem for the terminal flower. This same procedure can be followed for those Dahlias planted earlier in the spring but you need not remove buds before any particular dates. A certain amount of pinching back can be done on the smaller and miniature Dahlias but never disbud because on these little ones you want plenty of blooms.

Dahlias should be fed at intervals during the growing period with a fertilizer low in nitrogen, a little higher in phosphate and quite high in potash, such as 4-6-10. Scatter around the plant not any closer than six or eight inches from the stalk. Cultivate the

pinch back about one inch
of new growth at top of
Chrysanthemum

pinch side buds to strengthen and
enlarge center bud

pinch out about two inches of main
Dahlia stalk when one foot tall and
at intervals thereafter

PINCHING

soil in the Dahlia bed after each feeding and frequently after heavy rains.

Cut only mature blooms when you cut the flowers in early morning or late evening. Burn the cut surface immediately with a match or candle flame and then plunge the stem in cold water up to the flower for several hours before arranging. Or you may cut and plunge into about two inches of boiling water and then after a minute or two plunge into cold water. Either method slows evaporation of moisture.

After you have enjoyed your Dahlias and the first frost has fallen cut the stem back to about eight inches from the ground. Wait about two weeks and then gently raise the tubers from the ground. This operation will take a bit of doing because instead of your original tuber, there should be a clump of five or six. Allow them to dry in the sun, brush off all loose mud, dust with DDT or sulphur and store in perfectly dry sawdust or newspapers in a cold place. In the spring at planting time again use a sharp knife to divide the tubers, making sure to leave a piece of the old stalk attached to the neck of the tuber because that is where the "eye" will eventually develop. And so the cycle is complete.

The Dahlia is certainly not free of pests, especially in very hot summers. Use prepared baits for snails and slugs and spray hard with the hose to get rid of red spider. I have become increasingly aware of the fact that the constant use of DDT has its drawbacks as well as its uses. DDT destroys the parasite that usually kills off red spider. So in using DDT for cutworms, etc., mix with other controls to combat this situation. Red spider is a misnomer. It is actually an eight-legged mite that turns the leaves under from the tip, giving them a scorched appearance. It leaves strings of almost invisible webbing all about the plant. Rotenone or summer strength lime-sulphur or pyrethrum usually gets rid of them and routs aphids as well. Aramite works well too.

Thrips disfigure the bloom by getting into the new bloom when it first forms. They chew away, leaving malformation behind them. Most of the time you are not aware that they are present until the damage is done. Spray as soon as you suspect them with a preparation containing lindane, DDT and malathion.

Dust in the evening with sulphur for powdery mildew but if the temperatures are high be sure to wash that sulphur off early the next morning. The plants may also be attacked by the mosaic disease, discussed under diseases in the beginning of this chapter. This mosaic is spread by aphids so to get rid of aphids is to prevent mosaic. The preparation you use to rout thrips will kill aphids or an application of nicotine sulphate will do the job.

For Termites there is nothing much that you can do. If you apparently have a perfectly healthy Dahlia and all of a sudden you see the leaves wither and droop and begin to turn brown, dig around the surface of the soil close to the stem of your plant. You will probably see the nasty termites busy running from stem to tuber. They have done so much damage in such a short space of time that you will possibly find the tuber nothing but a shell and you have no alternative but to destroy the plant.

The American Dahlia Society has divided the Dahlia into classes according to the formation of the flowers. When you see these blooms listed in catalogues you usually see capital letters after each name. These are the abbreviations of the class to which each belongs. Here are a few of the name varieties and their description.

Oakleigh Champion (IC) Incurved Cactus. Large double blend of orange buff with the twisted petals tinted with pink. Bush to five feet. Midseason.

Clariam Royalty (RC) Recurved Cactus. Large and purple, shading to lavender at tips of the petals that twist backwards. Bush to five feet. Midseason.

Brown Bomber (ST.C.) Straight Cactus. Large, very formally arranged amber-rose petals. Bush to four feet. Early.

Prairie Fire (SC) Semi-cactus. Very large, fully double with orange-red petals that are crinkled half way to the tips. Bush three and a half feet. Early to midseason.

Ceramic Beauty (FD) Formal Decorative. Large dark red, fully double, outer petals pointed, inner ones cupped. Bush to four and a half feet. Early.

Jersey Beauty (FD) Formal Decorative. I just had to mention this old favorite, a beautiful pink of perfect form and long stems. Bush to six and a half feet. Early.

John Butterworth (ID) Informal Decorative. Big rose-red, petals loosely arranged and slightly twisted, shading to buff on tips. Bush to five feet. Early and midseason.

Mary Elizabeth (ID) Another Informal Decorative worth mentioning. Bright cherry red. Bush to four and a half feet. Midseason to late.

Rosy Dawn (Ba)   Ball. Yellow edged with rose-red at rounded tips. About two inches in diameter. Bush to five feet. Early.

Vera Higgins (An)   Anemone. Single row of coral-buff petals with orange "pin cushion" center. Bush to one and a half feet. Early.

Bishop of Llandaff (MP) Miniature Peony. Two or three rows of red petals with yellowish red center. This one has bronzy-green foliage. To four feet. Midseason.

Bronze Beauty (Pom) Pompon. Small ball-shaped flower of rounded bronze-orange petals. Rugged. Bush to three feet. Midseason.

Mitzi (Coll)   Collarette. One outer row of large red petals and one inner row of primrose yellow petaloids edged in white. Bush to four feet. Early.

Davy (S)   Single. Thick single row of orange-red petals. Very good for cutting. Bush to three feet. Early.

Nicki (Dwf)   Dwarf. Cactus formed and one of the best yellows. To two feet. Early.

Lone Star (O)   Orchid-flowering. Creamy yellow petals lined with purple. Good strong stems. Bush to three feet. Early.

Look (M)   Miniature Informal Decorative and a bi-color of carmine and white. To three and a half feet. Midseason.

The TREE DAHLIA is different. It is propagated by stem layers and by division of the tubers. For stem layering, after blooming the stem should be cut up leaving two joints to each section. Pack in sawdust until spring when you plant the sections horizontally with the sprouts at each joint facing up. Known as *Dahlia imperialis,* the Tree Dahlia is a beautiful fall-blooming plant that grows to ten or twelve feet, producing many large single lavender blossoms with yellow centers. I have had one growing in the garden for years. I do not dig the tubers every year but cut the stem instead. Every third or fourth year when I do dig I find the tubers to be enormous. This specimen is quite tolerant of cold.

Dahlias may also be planted from seed.

The GLADIOLUS is a corm member of the Iris Family. The foliage is stiff, ridged and sword-shaped whence comes the name taken from the Latin gladius, meaning sword. The funnel-shaped flowers appear in spring and summer in spikes on tall strong stems. Most of the glads we know come from the South African Cape. Hybridizers have been busy and have produced blooms of nearly every shade, beautifully ruffled, with a long flowering period.

I have found that glads do not thrive in alkaline soils. They must have rich loam fortified with peat moss or leaf mold. The big corms must be planted from three to four inches deep, the smaller size two or three inches deep, and the cormels one to two inches deep. The glads need this depth of planting to be able to hold the tall foliage and stems straight and rigid. Plant them from four to six inches apart in a sunny exposure. Begin planting in very early spring. As a matter of fact in the lower South plantings can start as early as January, and it has been noticed that those planted earliest are almost certain to escape the damage done by thrips. Stagger your planting over a period of several weeks to insure a succession of blooms. I have mine planted at the back of my lily bed in a northern exposure where they get sun for at least four hours a day.

I don't dig the corms every year. Glad corms as you know last only one season but as the old corm dies a new one forms directly above it and at the same time small cormels grow around the corm. Left in the ground over the winter the old corm disintegrates and the following year's bloom comes from the new corm. As for the cormels, left in the ground for two seasons they become flowering corms. The only reason I dare leave the corms in the ground one year and dig them the next is that the bed is well-raised and the drainage is good. On the alternate years in the late summer and early fall, and not later than September, I have to raise them not only because the new corm is nearer the soil surface and does not afford good anchorage to the plant, but because the corm must be cleaned and disinfected against thrip. I soak them in a solution of one and a half to two tablespoonfuls Lysol to about one gallon of water. All of mine have survived snow and freeze with the spring flowers more beautiful than ever. But the freezes down here are not as prolonged as those in the upper South, so in that section the corms must be dug in the fall, cleaned, dried and stored in a cool place over the winter. In the spring prior to planting soak in the disinfectant. Just try to get the glads in the ground as early as you can. The flowers are always more attractive when they bloom before the heat of the summer gets too intense.

Thrips are the main enemy of the glad. These minute insects suck the juices of the leaves and cause burn and wilt. Precautionary measures of early planting and soaking with disinfectant will tend to thwart this pest but if you do find an invasion spray with a mixture of lindane, malathion and DDT or dust with chlordane. These insecticides will usually rout worms and ants as well.

In planning your glad purchases notice how the various bulb growers list the corms. They are usually classed in size, color and time of bloom. There are about thirty-five All-American Gladiolus Trial Gardens all over the country and each year a new winner of the All-America Gladiolus Selections is announced. This year Emperor is tops. A midseason bloomer, tall and vigorous of growth, the white-throated florets of rosy-purple are waved and recurved. Winners of the last four years are Caribbean, a powder-blue shading to blue-violet and very ruffled; Maytime, tall and deep pink with a white throat; the vivid red Royal Stewart and the rose and white Appleblossom. All of these are patented. There are many others equally interesting. Blue Smoke, midseason, is blue and gray with a salmon throat. Chartreuse, an early to midseason, Green Light and Green Ice, midseason, offer varying shades of greenish-cream. Orange Ruff, early to midseason, is a deep red-ruffled orange; Friendship, early, a deeply frilled clear pink; King David, late, is a very dark velvety purple fluted and edged with smokey-gray. Spotlight is a very large yellow with scarlet throat. If you select carefully, you can find glads to fit any color scheme.

Hybridizers have also produced the Miniature or Baby Glads with culture and habits the same as the larger ones. Quite a few of these, like Green Thumb, creamy Flirt and salmon-pink Goblin are very early bloomers.

The new Winter Glads, probably a forerunner of a new strain are the exception to the rule of spring planting. Because they stand colder weather they may be set out in September. They bloom in December. Winter Glow is a dark salmon with yellow throat and Winter Fairy is a pale salmon with a pink throat.

Just don't forget two things. If you have to support your tall glads be careful not to drive the stake too close to the plant for if you do you will ruin the corm. When you cut your flowers leave at least five leaves on the plant because foliage is essential to the maturity of future bulbs.

I would like to call the G L O R I O S A L I L Y the Flame Flower because it so closely resembles a tongue of fire. I have a picture of one of mine, so taken that its dark shadow behind it looks like smoke, completing the illusion. As I write this I can look up and see through the window nine blooming Gloriosa lilies atop my fence. This tuberous member of the Lily Family from South Africa is weak-stemmed so it supports itself as it climbs by means of tendrils that are actually the tip ends of the leaves. And when it attaches itself it really clings! I planted my *Gloriosa Rothschildiana* several Aprils ago at the foot of the chain-link fence in the north bed where my hybrid lilies grow. Each year they reappear having weathered humidity, snow and freeze, and are startlingly beautiful every time. The plant grows to about three feet and the blossoms form on short stems rising from the axil of the leaves at the top, usually in June. The buds hang at an angle to the stem looking very much like little green lanterns. They gradually show color and open face downwards. On the second day, the undulated petals have reversed themselves pointing upward like flames, the ends bright vermilion-red shading to yellow at the base. The six green stamens are long and spread downward and outward, tipped with

THE GLORIOSA LILY

yellow pollen. The flower lasts several days and as it grows older the yellow gradually disappears, leaving almost entirely crimson petals.

The Gloriosa likes full sun and plenty of water in its growing season. Although the tuberous roots can be planted at almost any season of the year in the lower South, springtime is best so if you get hold of the tuber which looks like a short thick white root pack it in clean, dry, sharp sand and keep air-tight until time to set out. Propagation is by separation of roots and by new shoots but don't ever dig up the root until the foliage dies down normally. When you plant place the tuber horizontally about two inches deep on a handful of sand. In the lower South the Gloriosa need not be disturbed even for propagation purposes, for three or four years. *Gloriosa superba's* flowers are orange and red. The variety *citrina* is yellow at the base and tipped with magenta. All of these varieties may be grown all over the South.

The prettiest of the HIDDEN LILIES is *Curcuma petiolata*, a tuberous-rooted member of the Ginger Family and I don't think that any flower has looked as lovely in my flared Dresden vase as has the blossoms of this plant. Set out about one and a half feet deep in the spring in light loamy soil and semi-shade and keep moist. The stemmed leaves are large and sheath-like, pointed at the tips and becoming rounded near the base. They are a medium green and plaited. In May or June, from the bottom of the plant rises the scape covered with tiny yellow flowers surrounded by larger rosy-purple bracts, the top a tuft of lavender and blush-pink.

After the flowers are cut the leaves gradually disappear and from late summer until the next spring you see no trace of the plant. Do not disturb but keep the ground moist the year around or the roots will shrivel and die. Feed in the growing season with well-balanced fertilizer.

I received the tuber of the Indian *Curcuma zedoaria* in the fall and planted it immediately though from growing habits similar to the petiolata, it can also be set out in the spring. The roots of *zedoaria* are very pungent with the scent of ginger. Its leaves are heavily ribbed in purple and the bracts show traces of brown. Both species are perfect for patio use in the lower South. I do not recommend them for the upper sections.

Iris unguicularis or the S T Y L O S A I R I S is hardy and should do well here. It likes hot dry locations and will thrive in poor soil if kept moist immediately after planting. Set out in spring it blooms from November to April and lasts several days if cut in the bud. Variety *stylosa alba* is a large white with a yellow crest. *Stylosa marginata* is violet-blue and very fragrant.

I S M E N E is often called Spider-lily, Basket Flower and Peruvian Daffodil but it is really *Hymenocallis*, another bulbous member of

Ismene

the Amaryllis Family. *H. occidentalis* is often seen in the South, a flat white cup surrounded by slender segmented petals. Foliage is bright green. The fragrant Ismene *calathina grandiflora*, another popular variety has creamy white spidery petals with green stripes down the throat. This one is lovely. It bloomed for me in June and into July. H. Festalis is exotic, a taller white hybrid, larger and more spidery but less fragrant. Plant in very early spring in rich loamy soil in full sun about three inches deep, in the open ground in the lower South and in pots farther north. Water copiously. The bulbs need not be dug in the warmer areas but where the winters are colder lift and store after foliage dies down. Incidentally I feed mine during the growing season with a well-balanced liquid fertilizer.

I planted one dozen L E U C O C O R Y N E bulbs last January because I had been intrigued by pictures of them. These very small bulbs of the Lily Family are also known as *Ixiodes odorata*, and as the name suggests they are very fragrant. I set them out two inches apart just beneath the surface of the soil in full sun in a southeast bed. The earth was light and loamy and the drainage was good. The foliage was thin and reedy resembling grass and the flowers that bloomed in late spring were small, bright blue and six-petaled, with pale yellow throats. Since these blossoms are so small I suggest that you plant more than a dozen in a round area or long border in order to have a good display.

N E R I N E S are striking fall-flowering bulbs of the Amaryllis Family from South Africa. They are noted for the long stamens that give the flowers a feathery look. All bear very lovely umbels of blossoms ranging in color from red to pink to white.

I planted my *Nerine Bowdenii*, neck covered, in a pot filled with loamy acid soil and sank the pot in the ground in full sun. This must be done when the bulbs are dormant during spring and summer. In September the scape appears growing to fifteen inches, and produces a large umbel of about nine flowers of a very lovely pale pink keeled in a darker rose. The leaves appear only after the flowers are through blooming and last through the winter, at the end of which they usually die down. The bulb then goes to sleep. By the way I was intrigued with the shape of *Bowdenii*'s bulb. It looked like a small bottle while bulbs of the other varieties are ovoid.

Bowdenii magnifica is a deeper pink and produces larger flowers on taller stems later in the year. *Nerine flexuosa alba* is a stunning white. Probably the best known is the red-flowered *Nerine sarniensis*, called the Guernsey Lily, named for the island where the bulbs are widely grown.

Feed several times during the winter with liquid manure and then as the leaves die back do not keep too wet. The nice thing about planting the Nerine in a pot is that you can bring it indoors while it is blooming and you can move it to dry quarters if the spring and summer rains are too continuous. Don't disturb too often as the bulb enjoys being pot bound. The next spring check the soil to see if the earth around the bulb is acid enough for the plant to get a good start. You want a moderate acidity.

Some catalogues offer Nerine under the name *Nerine japonica* but this is really a Lycoris. You can differentiate by noting the seeds. True Nerines have green seeds and Lycoris has black seeds. The Nerine is also closely related to the Brunsvigia which has larger bulbs, flowers and leaves.

SCILLA or Autumn Squill, *Scilla autumnalis* is a bulbous member of the Lily Family that produces lovely little soft pink flowers in the fall, usually in September. Never more than eight inches high this plant is perfect for borders and proves to be quite hardy year after year, if protected somewhat from the wind. Give it an occasional dose of well-balanced fertilizer during the growing period.

TIGRIDIAS sound bold and startling and the colors and leaves of these flowers fit that description perfectly. The stem is low; four-inch petals are very vivid shades of fire-red, white, yellow and American Beauty, and the cup-shaped throat is usually gold heavily spotted in red. The leaves are dark green and plaited, giving a ridged appearance. They are referred to as ".the fireworks of the garden" and "Roman Candles" because the buds pop wide open with a burst of color, usually in July. True, they last but one day but a group of these bulbs will really make a conversation piece in your patio. The more sun they get, the deeper the color.

Tigridias are small bulbs of the Iris Family and popularly known

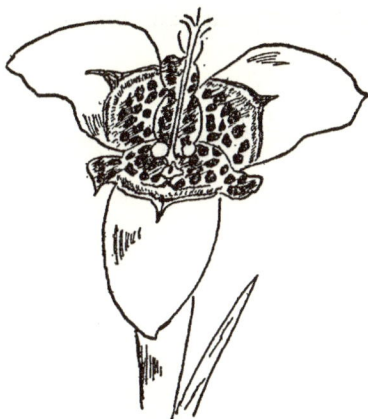

Tigridia

as Mexican Shell Flowers, so-called because they come from Mexico and South America. Their culture is the same as that given to glads except that I dig them every year when the foliage dies back. I clean and store and set them out again the following spring. Plant two inches deep, about six inches apart. The one we know best is *Tigridia Pavonia,* with flowers on stems about one and a half feet tall and sword-shaped leaves. These bulbs are sold in separate colors or in mixed colors called "Fourth of July Mixture".

The T U B E R O S E is really *Polianthes,* a summer-flowering tuberous bulb of the Amaryllis Family. The bright green narrow leaves rise about one foot and then the flowers appear in spikes at the top of the one and a half foot scape. The blossoms are pure white and appear in pairs. Be sure that the spot you have chosen is a sunny one. Cover the bulb with about a half inch of soil, which should be light and loamy. In the warmer sections of the South they need not be disturbed over the winter. Naturally in the upper sections they must be dug and stored when the foliage dies down. Keep in a cool dry place until planted in early spring.

Perhaps the Tuberose has lost some of its popularity because of its heavy fragrance, but don't let that deter you. It does lend itself beautifully to the summer garden and the scent is not objectionable outdoors.

The variety Excelsior or Dwarf Pearl presents long graceful spikes of double white flowers. The Single Mexican Early Ever-blooming type flowers in July and August.

✗ 10 ✗

Roses

I was never more fascinated than when I read the story of roses, and because that flower has become such a favorite in the South, I imagine that you would like a word about the origin.

History tells us that from the time the Empress Josephine planted the famous rose garden in the Palace of Malmaison the rose soared in popularity until by the middle of the nineteenth century there were about five thousand new roses offered to the world. The cross-breeding and hybridization that followed steadily produced new varieties until today the American Rose Society recognizes many more, divided into over sixty classes.

Most rosarians agree that the best way to list these many categories is to divide them into the Summer Roses that bloom once in April, May and June and the Ever-blooming Roses that flower from May until frost. The Summer Roses include the Damask Rose, *Rosa Damascena* which some date back to the Crusades and whence come the Hybrid Perpetuals, such as the dark red Henry Nevard, the pink Paul Neyron and the fragrant crimson Prince Camille de Rohan. Then comes the Provence or Cabbage Rose, *Rosa centifolia* whose Rose des Peintres is a beautiful pink. There follow the Moss Rose, such as the blush-pink Alfred de Dalmas and the Red Moss, and the French or Gallican Rose, whose silvery-red Dumortier is still available. The White Rose of York, *Rosa alba* is the same old-fashioned hybrid, like the Maiden's Blush, that we use in the garden today. Also included are the Sweetbriar Rose, *Rosa eglanteria* which grows to ten feet and makes a deliciously-scented hedge and the Austrian Briar, *Rosa foetida* whose Persian Yellow is noted for its fern-like foliage and double yellow blooms. This one also reaches ten feet. The Scotch Briar, *Rosa Spinossissima* is the thorniest of all roses and Fruehling's Gold is offered by some nurseries. Its bright yellow blossoms contrast nicely with the blue-green foliage and it too lends itself to hedging.

The Banksian Rose, *Rosa banksiae* also belongs to this group. The white variety of this lovely climber, which has a vague aroma of violets arrived in England in 1807 from China and was named after Lady Banks. The yellow variety, with somewhat smaller flowers and leaves and thinner stems, was introduced about ten years later. Both are rampant growers and like to reach great heights. Plant them in rich loamy soil and mulch well with peat. Prune immediately after flowering. I have both growing on a trellis over a doorway, the yellow on one side, the white on the other. They make a beautiful sight usually in April, and after a snow and freeze they really outdo themselves.

Another member of the Summer-flowering group is the Wichuraiana Rose, the trailing rose found in Japan by the noted botanist Dr. Wichura and brought to European gardens in the late nineteenth century. This hardy rose was crossed with the Polyanthas and the Teas and gave us the Dorothy Perkins, the Excelsa and several others.

In the class of the Ever-blooming Roses we find the Hybrid Perpetuals, including the American Beauty and Frau Karl Druschki; the Hybrid Teas, such as Mirandy and Tiffany; the Hybrid Polyanthas, like The Fairy, and the Floribundas, whose new introduction is Frensham.

Also listed are the Grandifloras, the good hedge roses like Queen Elizabeth and Carrousel, the children of Floribundas and Hybrid Teas. Besides these we find the China Rose, Old Blush; the Musk Rose; the Hybrid Bourbons such as Coupe d'Hebe and the Miniature roses. There are also the Noisette, we all know the Marechal Niel, and the Macartney Rose. The latter is the *Rosa bracteata* whence comes my lovely Mermaid Rose Climber which gives so many single yellow blooms for so many months of the year.

The Tea Rose, *Rosa odorata* is also a member of this class. It was introduced from China in the early 1800s and so named because of its delicate perfume that reminds one of the aroma of tea. These are the roses that are budded on to the standards or rose trees.

There is also the Japanese Rose, *Rosa rugosa* a hardy specimen that is the only one to live in sand and salt air. This rose is gaining in popularity used as a hedge. There are several varieties, the pink Max Graf, the red Rose de l'Hay and the white Blanc de Coubert.

Choosing the roses for your garden takes a bit of planning. Begin early in autumn and consider your climate, the spot in the garden and the colors that will be compatible with the surroundings. Just remember that roses do best in full sun and *away* from trees and buildings. Those that get sun from early morning until about four o'clock in the afternoon have all the odds in their favor. They do not seem to mind wind. Having chosen the spot look through rose catalogues and consult the publications of The American Rose Society before ordering. Reputable nurserymen usually label their rose stock by grade. Grade #1 is a dormant two-year-old field grown plant with three or more good branches about fourteen inches high and a strong root system. Grade #1½ carries two or more strong canes and a healthy root stock. Grade #2 offers one big branch and several smaller ones, with a fair root system. Study the specimens and consider their growth habits, resistance to disease, bud and flower form. Most of these details can be secured from the rating lists of The American Rose Society and through your local rose societies, which organizations publish A *Guide for Buying Roses*. It is interesting to note that only since 1931 have patents been issued to rose plants propagated by budding or cuttings, and Patent #1 went to New Dawn, a climber. Since that date many more have been registered.

PREPARATION AND PLANTING

Order your roses early and designate shipping between January fifteenth and January thirtieth which is about the best time in our peculiar southern winters. Roses may also be planted from December through February. It is a generally accepted fact that roses from Texas may be planted as early as December and those from California, from the fifteenth to the thirtieth of January. Two months before planting begin preparations on your rose bed. After removing plants, grass and weeds from the surface take out the first six or eight inches of top soil and set it aside. Then dig a trench about three and a half to four feet wide by two feet deep. Take out all of this earth and use it elsewhere in the garden. Fill the trench with the following mixture:

½ cow manure
¼ peat moss
¼ top soil (that you had set aside) mixed with rich black humus

We in the New Orleans area can use the Kenner rose sod that is available to us. Make sure to order this Kenner soil from a responsible person as you don't want the kind that may have salt in its content. Salt burns the plants and your bed will be ruined before your roses are in.

If you don't have enough top soil for a mixture to fill the trench make up the difference with the black soil to get the required quantity. To the above ingredients add 1 cup of superphosphate and 1 cup of cottonseed meal for each plant that you intend to put into the bed. Mix thoroughly and screen if possible. Sometimes chopping the sod well and continuously mixing it will serve as well as screening. After preparing the bed and watering it frequently, especially if it does not rain, turn the soil in the bed three or four times before date of planting.

As soon as the package arrives open it and examine the plants. If the roots appear moist and springy you know that you can proceed with the planting right away. But if they look dry soak in water overnight and then heel in, covering with soil and soaking well. Keep moist for three or four days before planting.

At last you are ready to place the bushes into the bed! As you

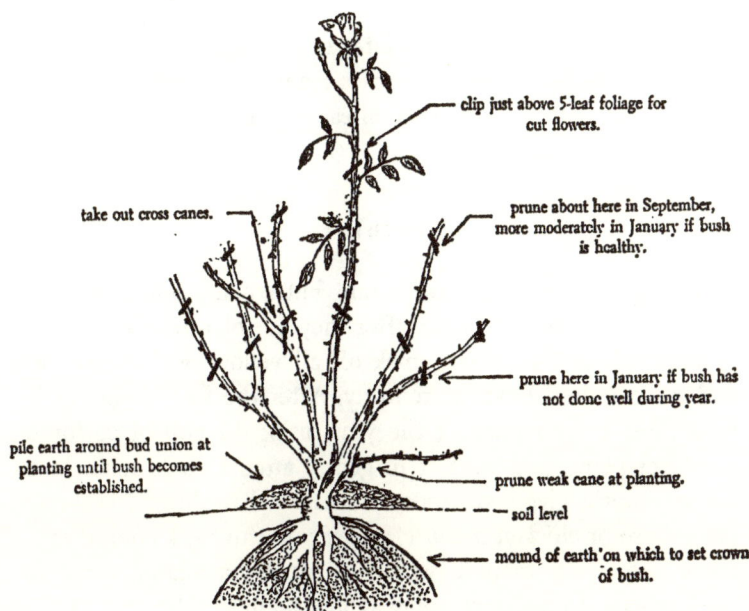

clip just above 5-leaf foliage for cut flowers.

take out cross canes.

prune about here in September, more moderately in January if bush is healthy.

prune here in January if bush has not done well during year.

pile earth around bud union at planting until bush becomes established.

prune weak cane at planting.

soil level

mound of earth on which to set crown of bush.

THE ROSE

lift the plant cut out all bruised or broken roots with a clean sharp shears and loosen the labels so that they do not eventually cut into the plant. Dig holes three feet apart in the center of the bed, making them about twenty-four inches wide and twenty-four inches deep. Fill each hole half full of the soil mixture forming a cone in the center of the hole. Set the crown of the roots on top of this mound, spreading the roots down around it. Add some of the soil around the roots and fill the hole with water, repeating the watering after the first application has settled. When all water has soaked in fill in remaining hole with soil, keeping the bud union about two inches above the ground level. After tamping well mound the earth temporarily about four inches above the bud union to keep the plant from being dehydrated by sudden frost or high winds until the new feeding roots have a chance to become established. As soon as you see new growth on the bush you can remove the mound, always keeping the bud union 2 inches above ground level. Be watchful of this with later mulchings.

If you have purchased your roses from a reputable nurseryman your plants will have arrived already pruned. Keep roses well watered after planting.

FEEDING

Preparing the rose bed is important but equally important is the care that you give your roses after they are planted. Once a week or more often if necessary, pick off all yellow or diseased leaves and remove dead blooms promptly. After the first blooming feed your roses every month of the year, using ½ cup of cottonseed meal per plant, and work it in gently around each bush. In the cooler months give your roses an occasional feeding of well-rotted cow, horse or chicken manure, and if you can't get hold of any of these use sheep manure which is usually available from your nurseryman. In summer apply rabbit manure. Use any of these fertilizers at the rate of 1 cupful per plant.

Sometimes a rose will look anemic or run-down and will have need of a tonic, much as we humans do. If the leaves are yellowed and badly spotted mix 3 parts superphosphate and 1 part iron sulphate and apply about an ounce of this in the spring. Be sure to water well afterwards. Should the stems seem limp and unable to hold the blossom, instead of cottonseed meal feed each bush with about 2 pints of a solution of ¼ ounce magnesium sulphate and 1 gallon of water. Repeat the dose in two weeks.

Mulch with peat moss five or six times a year to keep the soil in good condition and after heavy rains work the surface of the rose bed lightly to keep the earth from packing. Once again let me caution you to be watchful that you do not cover the bud union when mulching. Keep it about 2 inches above ground level.

PRUNING

Cut back your bush and standard roses in January, and again in September. It is always necessary to prune your plants moderately in January because the roses are produced only on each year's new wood and that new wood must be hardy to produce beautiful flowers. The only way to encourage vigorous growth is to remove old, dead, weakened and diseased wood, leaving at least three or four strong canes. If they have not put on much growth during the year cut them back more severely. Make the cuts on an angle just above a dormant "eye" bud or joint (a small protrusion on the stem) and always prune towards an out-pointing bud to encourage the new growth towards the outer edge of the bush. You must always try to keep the center from being crowded.

If your Hybrid Teas are very healthy in September cut them back about one-half the current season's growth. This forces new shoots on which blooms will appear in six to eight weeks' time. The heaviest fall bloom in the New Orleans area is usually between November fifth and November twentieth. If you have several bushes stagger your pruning over a period of ten days in order to prolong flowering.

Standard or Tree Roses are pruned much the same way, depending on how much you cut your roses for use in the house during the year. Floribundas, Polyanthas and Grandifloras are trimmed lightly the first year and then more heavily as they grow older. Cut back two-year-old canes to three eyes from the base of the plant. Dwarf or Miniature Roses demand little more than the pruning of diseased and dead wood.

Weeping Roses have to be treated a little differently. Feel along each drooping shoot until you come to firm, solid wood and cut at this point. Take out all small weak stems that grow out of the top. Then to stimulate good strong growth for the next year pick out one stout cane on each side and cut it back to about ten inches from its starting point. Do this in January.

The Climbing Roses, such as Lady Banksia and Mermaid should be pruned in the spring immediately after blooming and this trimming should be limited to the cutting out of all dead wood and of branches that overlap or tangle. The idea is to let the strongest canes breathe freely with no crowding allowed. If side shoots seem weak and yellowish cut them back to at least two eyes from the base of the plant.

If you happen to have climbing sports of Hybrid Teas, such as Climbing Radiance, Etoile de Hollande and Dainty Bess, remember that to cut them back too severely is to encourage them to revert to bush form. So train the branches horizontally and trim only the laterals and sub-laterals that will bear the next year's blooms. Cut them back lightly, allowing at least five or six eyes from the base to remain.

Since the shoots that have flowered on Rambler Roses will never bloom again, cut these out when you prune this type of rose in the late summer and early fall. Do this so that the new shoots will have plenty of air and light in which to mature.

DISEASES AND PESTS

Roses are problem children when it comes to diseases. We must always be on the alert to combat first one and then another. Our frequent summer rains and heavy dews just pave the way for Black Spot, the chief enemy of roses. Since roses derive most of their food from the sun through their leaves, the plant literally starves to death when Black Spot takes over. This disease is recognizable by black circular spots on the leaves and a yellowing of the area surrounding the spot. It is a fungus that is spread by spores that are blown from plant to plant by wind and rain, so the first step is to remove infected leaves right away and burn them. Pick up all fallen leaves too. The spores multiply when the leaves remain wet for four or five hours, hence the recommendation that roses be watered by soakers at ground level, never from above. Black Spot can make such inroads on a bush that whole canes can die off in a very short time. There are all kinds of effective prepared sprays and dusts on the market but here is a mixture that has proven successful:

 1 Tablespoon manzate
 1 Tablespoon malathion
 1 Tablespoon Aramite
 ⅓ Teaspoon detergent or dried milk
 1 Gallon water

When mixing this solution put the detergent or milk in the sprayer first thing and mix with a little water and then add the poisons. This formula has been popular with the most successful rose growers because it accomplishes its purpose so well that it need only be used twice a month. In summertime spray *early* in the morning before the sun gets too hot.

N-trichloromethylthiophthalimide and N-dodecyllguanidine acetate, known under trade names of Phaltan and Cyprex respectively, are two organic fungicides that are being introduced in other parts of the country as controls for Blackspot and Mildew. The consensus of opinion on Phaltan to date is that it is as good as any other organic fungicide to control Black Spot and Mildew. In this area it is still too early to state that they are better than any other fungicide. Further tests will have to be made. If you wish to try them the prescribed dosages are two pounds of 50% Phaltan to one hundred gallons of water and two pounds of 70% Cyprex to one hundred gallons of water. Both are compatible with Aramite and malathion.

The thing to remember about Black Spot is that no matter what control you use you must be faithful about using it. A regular spraying schedule *must* be followed.

Powdery Mildew occurs after spells of high humidity and is more prevalent on ramblers and climbers than on bush roses. It resembles a white powder on the new leaves and buds and it crinkles the leaves. Dust with sulphur if the weather is cool and the attack mild, otherwise use the spray already recommended for Black Spot or try Karathane, said to be a specific for Mildew. Black Mildew sometimes occurs and is more serious than its powdery cousin. The plant will suddenly wilt, and brownish-black patches will coat the upper leaf, while on the underside you will find gray blotches. The leaves eventually fall. Control this immediately upon detection by cutting off the infected parts and burning them; otherwise this disease will spread to stem and eventually ruin the plant.

If you notice the rose leaves looking rusty, beginning to drop and orange spores on the underside of the leaf you have Rose Rust. The control again is removal and burning of affected parts and spraying with the chemicals recommended for Black Spot.

Galls or swellings sometimes appear on the stem of the bush at ground level. If this occurs cut the gall away very carefully with a clean sharp shears. By the way dipping your cutting tools in 95%

denatured alcohol is a fine precaution against spreading disease from one plant to another.

Someone once said that canker is to roses what cancer is to humans. So far there is no cure. The cane just darkens, turns brown and dry, spreading rapidly unless the cane is cut off well below the infected area. Paint all cut surfaces with Bordeaux paste or a tree-wound paint. Keeping your bushes healthy is the best preventive.

Aphids attack new shoots and new buds, multiplying so rapidly that they injure the new blooms. And Red Spider, so minute that it seems invisible, attacks the underside of the leaf in hot dry weather, sucking the sap and eventually reddening and killing the foliage. The spray recommended for Black Spot is also effective against these two pests.

Sometimes you will see leaves look as though they have been skeletonized with all green color gone. Carefully look on the underside of the leaf and you will see a whole colony of slugworms, lined up in formation as if in ranks. Hand-pick the leaf at once, being cautious not to let any of these worms drop, and burn. If the attack has gone beyond the hand-picking stage spray with DDT or a nicotine insecticide. Spray with arsenate of lead for caterpillars.

STAKING

Every tree rose that you plant in your garden should be staked to prevent wind damage. Supports of pipe or iron are much preferred because they do not rot, as wood does, and never have to be replaced. Enclose the wire that loosely holds the stem to the stake in a piece of rubber tubing so that friction will be at a minimum.

The weeping roses, to be effective, should be trained on umbrella-like frames so that their five-foot canes can arch downward gracefully over the edge of the support.

Pillar roses must be secured to the post or pillar on which they are being grown and climbers must be tied to their supports until they are strong enough to carry the top laterals.

I don't pretend to know all the different name-varieties of roses that are suitable for various spots but I will mention a few that I have worked with in hopes that it might be helpful in your selection.

In the Tree Rose Class, Peace, of the pale yellow petals edged in pink, is very beautiful. Frau Karl Druschki is a pretty white, Picture produces a medium pink bloom and the old reliable Etoile de Hollande offers a dark red flower.

Weeping Roses are really the Multiflora or Wichuraiana rambling species that are budded to a moderately tall briar rose. Lady Godiva is a good pale pink and in the yellows, Emily Gray is most effective.

Pillar Roses are plants of moderate growth habits and, as the name implies must be trained to pillars or other stout upright stakes. I have enjoyed the creamy-yellow High Noon, the pale pink climbing Dainty Bess and the white climbing Kaiserin Auguste Viktoria.

Use regular climbing roses to cover wall and trellis and reserve the rambling types for fence and arches because the latter are attacked more often by pests and fungus diseases and they are better handled where they are more accessible. In the climbers, the old-fashioned salmon Gloire de Dijon (fifteen to twenty feet) and the white Silver Moon do best in a north, northeast exposure. The deep yellow Marechal Niel, another old favorite, the dark red Crimson Glory, the coppery-salmon Mrs. Sam McGredy and the pale yellow Mermaid are good for south, southwest corners. The famous Cherokee Rose, *Rosa laevigata* will grow quickly in any exposure to heights of twenty feet. Give it lots of space wherein to spread, but beware of thorns. The pink-blooming variety is just as beautiful as the white and the glossy foliage is most attractive.

In the Rambler Group, the pink Dorothy Perkins and the deep red Crimson Shower are lovely.

When you use the rose as a shrub, remember to give it plenty of place in which to grow. *Rosa Hugonis* or the Golden Rose of China will reach six or seven feet, bearing pale yellow single blossoms in the spring. The Red China Rose, Gruss an Teplitz, which grows to four feet, is a favorite long used for hedging. For an intriguing terra cotta color try Rosa Moyesii of western China which grows to eight feet. Nevada is a luxuriant grower to seven feet, bearing semi-double roses that shade from palest to deepest pink in hot weather. It is practically pest and disease free, has very few thorns and needs little pruning.

Polyanthas that show small flowers in clusters, and the Floribundas with larger clustered blossoms and with a frame shaped like the Teas, are wonderful for bedding purposes. Their ranunculus-type roses still show after the Hybrid Teas have spent their glory. I have enjoyed the Margo Koster, a salmon-orange Polyantha that grows to fifteen inches. The shell-pink Cameo and the white Charlie McCarthy are two other good ones in this group.

The most beautiful of the Floribundas is the Red Pinocchio which reaches about five feet in height. The bushes that I have seen have been literally covered with the dark velvety-red roses that last well when cut. Pink Pinocchio, also lovely, numbers fifty roses to the cluster. Goldilocks is a good yellow and Vogue has attractive coral-rose blooms. The orange-red Fusilier which bears heavy clusters of frilled blooms and the fragrant yellow Gold Cup are the latest All-American Rose Selections in this class.

My Miniature Roses have been a joy to me since I decided to plant them in a strawberry terrace that I had ceased to use for its original purpose. These tiny bushes are hardy, almost everblooming and like to be cut of their flowers. They are especially a delight to children. They shade from Oakington Ruby's crimson and Red Imp's deep blossoms to Rouletti's rose-pink, Sweet Fairy's blush pink, Tinkerbell's medium pink and the white of Twinkles and Cinderella. Baby Gold Star is a good yellow. There are several others from which to choose and with names such as these, can't you see why the small fry in the family would be fascinated?

Last but certainly not least are the Hybrid Tea Roses. These should be in a bed to themselves in order to show their best perfection of form and tapering buds. Helen Traubel is apricot-pink; Madame Cochet-Cochet, a blend of pinks; Chrysler Imperial, a deep maroon red. Charlotte Armstrong shades from light to dark crimson and of course, there is Peace. Love Song, a hybrid of Peace and Charlotte Armstrong, is interesting. The long pointed buds are deep yellow tinged with pink, a most beautiful bi-color. Mojave, a deep orange, is almost (but not quite) as lovely as a rose that I have seen but have never been able to find, Prince Orange of Nassau. Mission Bells, all-American winner of 1950 has deep shrimp-pink buds opening to salmon-pink flowers. President Eisenhower is a fragrant rose-red with large buds opening to five-inch flowers that sometimes number forty petals. Nocturne is a deep cardinal red and Charles Mallerin seems to be the darkest of the reds. White Knight, as stunning in its greenish-white tapered bud form as it is when its thirty-odd petals are open, is the winner of the 1958 All-American Rose Selection in the Hybrid Tea class. Most of the Hybrid Teas may be had as Tree Roses.

THE OLD ROSES

I have heard it said that if you grow roses long enough you will eventually become curious about the old roses so on the chance that you are interested I list a few of the long-ago favorites that still add beauty to the garden.

The Tea Roses of Grandmother's day withstand the heat and dampness of our deep South and the Duchesse de Brabant is a beauty that grows to five feet. Its delicate shell-pink fragant blossoms are cup-shaped and profuse and show for long periods in spring and fall. La Reine Victoria, to six feet, is a deeper rose color with the same long-lasting qualities. Maman Cochet is another Tea that is splendid for cutting. Its flowers shade from blush to deep pink and its height rarely exceeds four feet. The white Maman Cochet is lovely and there is a climbing variety that reaches fifteen feet in our warm climate.

Souvenir de la Malmaison, an old Bourbon rose, or simply Malmaison as it is so often shortened, is a bush rose, to five feet, or a climber to fifteen feet. Both bloom profusely in spring, showing flesh-pink, many-petalled blossoms. These are really old-fashioned, dating back as far as 1843.

Baroness Henriette Snoy has pointed buds and double flowers of peach-pink. The foliage is strong and abundant. It is one of my favorites. Princesse de Sagan is deep red and a healthy bloomer. William R. Smith, sometimes called "Key West Rock Rose" grows all through the South. It is a beauty, double pale-pink and fragrant.

There are many other roses that are just as beautiful in form and color as those I have mentioned. Because there is so much to be known about the rose, I suggest that you obtain the publications of your local rose groups and those of The American Rose Society. Consult the Encyclopedia of Roses and Rose Culture, edited by Harcourt P. Champneys and Carl Withner. It gives an excellent glossary of rose varieties, their description, care and culture.

✳ 11 ✳

Some Delightful Potted Plants

My love of potted plants began a long time ago when the weather grew too cold and wet to enjoy my garden outdoors and I found that I could still put my fingers in the earth caring for a small potted charmer. I found that I could still enjoy the same wonder of a shining leaf through those potted favorites that I had brought indoors. Then I discovered how much these plants added to the pleasure of the sunporch and the patio when milder weather permitted bringing them outdoors. Some startling effects can be produced with arranging potted plants, and they in turn can thrill you with unusual and exotic blooms.

No one can make a definite rule as to just what plants can be successfully handled in pots. It all depends on how much determination and time you have to devote to the care of such plants, and what facilities you have for facing the problems of humidity, light and temperature. To name all possibilities in the field would take a volume. In this chapter I bring you some that are old favorites and others that are startling enough to add to any collection.

There are certain facts to keep in mind that, once established, may take some of the disappointments out of the care of potted plants. First of all consider the plant's natural habitat and remember that the growth factors of water, light, air, feeding and temperature are very important to success.

A study of the plant's origin will give you a key to the type of soil best suited to it and for all practical purposes, I divide the natural habitats into three sections. First there are the tropical forests or jungles where humidity and temperatures run high, and where the lush growth of tall trees leaves the terrestrial plants beneath in the shade. Here too the epiphytes have taken to growing on shelves of trees and rocks, perfectly satisfied with the food that is washed down to them by the heavy tropical rains. In these conditions plants develop rather sparse root systems that have learned to function out of the soil as well as under the ground level.

For the plants similar to the terrestrials, or those grown on the forest floor, I suggest a potting medium of:

¼ good garden loam or compost
½ peat moss or leaf mold
⅛ builder's sand
⅛ chopped charcoal

For the epiphytes, use:

½ peat moss
¼ perlite or sand
⅛ chopped charcoal
⅛ coarse manure
or
sphagnum moss, provided you feed the plant regularly.

For Bromeliads, also included in this group, you have a choice of:

Osmunda fiber, which is preferred by most Bromeliad enthusiasts
or
sphagnum moss, but with these two mediums you sometimes have

a problem of balance to consider, and you must feed more often than if you use a combination of:

¼ sand or perlite
¼ peat moss
¼ fibrous loam
¼ shredded fir bark, with a little charcoal added.

At the other extreme there are the plants of the desert, those that have learned to live in a medium of low humus and much sand through drought and heat. For these desert plants, such as Cacti I recommend:

½ builder's sand
¼ peat moss
⅛ pebbles
⅛ leaf mold or garden loam, with a little bone meal and pulverized limestone mixed into the medium.
Succulents need more loam than sand and peat.

In between these two climates is the comfortable warm temperate zone, more comparable to ours where plants with a more developed root system thrive in fundamental mediums of sand, soil and clay or sand, soil and peat to which varying amounts of leaf mold and well-rotted organic substances are added. Here too, we become conscious of the alkalinity and acidity requirements of the individual plant. For the subjects in the temperate zone, use:

⅓ peat or leaf mold
⅓ builder's sand
⅓ good garden loam, with a little bone meal and dried cow manure mixed with it. This standard soil formula must variate with more acid peat or leaf mold if the plant needs acid soil, or pulverized limestone must replace the peat if the plant needs an alkaline growing medium.

Having established the potting medium consider the amount of Water needed by the individual plant. I mention this first because of all the growth factors this seems to be the most difficult to handle. Water your plant when the soil around it is dry and no longer able to give the plant the moisture that it needs. Then soak the plant thoroughly so that every bit of the soil in the pot is uniformly wet and all roots are made comfortable. When in doubt that your plant needs water my best advice is don't water, wait another day. The season of the year, the composition of the soil, the relative humidity of the day, the size of the pot and the amount of drainage that the pot offers are all things to take into consideration when you wonder how often a plant needs water. You have to live with your plants to get to know them.

Light is the powerhouse of energy to your plants. They need light for photosynthesis, the chemical process by which they make their food. Again the knowledge of the native habitat of the specimen will guide you as to how much sunlight or filtered shade it can tolerate in which seasons of the year. If you can't place them in a window during the cold months put them where they can get artificial light for several hours each day.

Plants, like humans, must have a certain amount of fresh Air to breathe and again we must take care as we did for our own babies to distinguish between the beneficial air and the disastrous draft. Almost all plants react badly to drafts. The Humidity in the air is another problem to solve. When the pots are outdoors in summer the plants more or less adjust themselves to natural conditions but once they are in the house where the air is constantly being dried out by heating systems we must find ways to humidify, either by containers of water placed strategically about the rooms or by mechanical humidifiers. Placing the pots on trays filled with pebbles or marble grit kept constantly damp and spraying the plants with a fine mist from a hand sprayer will also help adjust the humidity. Grouping similar plants together will tend to raise the humidity around them. Most potted plants will thrive in the

patio or sun porch the greater part of the year. With the exception
of a few tender ones, even the tropical plants can stand cold temperatures until a freeze is predicted. Then bring them indoors.
With the right amount of light and humidity they usually adjust
to ordinary room temperatures.

As to Feeding, nearly all potted plants need several supplemen-
tary doses of nutrients during the spring and summer growing
periods. There are several good plant foods on the market that can
be applied to the plant in solution. Just be sure that the soil
around the plant is moist when you feed it. Frequent fertilizing
is necessary because you water your plant often and each time you
do so you tend to wash away some nutrients, nitrogen in particular. Feeding becomes extremely important to plants growing in
Osmunda, bark or other soilless mediums. How often to feed is
another question answered only by your knowledge of your plant
and its habits. Fertilizers for indoor plants are quite different in
proportion than those we use outdoors and those of inorganic
form that are soluble in water are preferred to the organic fertilizers. As I have mentioned before the organics are slower to act
and they need sufficient bacteria of the soil to put them to work.

A rule of thumb, to be altered to fit the particular plant, is to
feed once or twice a month with a complete plant food. Read the
directions on the label of any fertilizer you buy. Try not to go to
the other extreme and overfeed. You can injure your plant this
way too. When in doubt good gardeners very often moisten a
handful or so of sphagnum moss with a solution of fertilizer and
then apply this moss around the base of the plant for a short time
until the nutrients are absorbed.

Containers must be clean. Either boil the clay pots for ten
minutes (start them off in cold water) or wipe out the plastic and
china pots with a solution of Lysol and water. Since good Drainage
is vital to a plant's very existence, make sure that the container
you choose has sufficient holes in the bottom to guarantee success.
Unglazed pottery allows a certain amount of evaporation through

its walls, thereby making it imperative to water the plant in it more often. Glazed pots allow no such evaporation, so here again you must be sure of the holes in the bottom to prevent the plant from drowning. Over the hole or holes, place several bits of broken pot, concave sides down if possible, and over that either a handful of pebbles or a layer of sphagnum moss. Then fill with your potting medium until high enough to set the plant. Fill in the sides of the pot around the root ball, always keeping the soil about one-half inch to one inch from the lip of the pot. Never pack down the soil around the plant as it prevents the roots from breathing. Instead water thoroughly until the damp earth is heavy enough to settle in the pot.

Another thing to remember is to fit the plant to the proper size pot. I usually like to see an inch of soil between the root ball and the sides of the pot. As the plant's root system enlarges and presents a tightly woven mass, you know it is time to move it to a pot about one inch larger. It is always a good idea to prune the roots as well as the top of the average plant when you repot because it helps prevent wilt and tends to produce bushier growth.

If you wish to sterilize the soil used in potting, use one of the soil fumigants now available on the market.

PESTS AND DISEASES

Of course the best preventive to both pest and disease is to buy a healthy plant in the first place. Good housekeeping should hold any onslaught down to a minimum. The next step towards control is to get in the habit of giving your plants a forceful dose of tap water every two weeks. I put mine in the kitchen sink and use the spray to clean the leaves and wash away any pest or disease that might have just started. If this does not do the trick, there are non-toxic preparations on the market that come in the form of "spray guns" or "spray cans". Use these strictly according to directions on the package. Mealybugs and an occasional sucking insect may be routed with a cotton swab dipped in alcohol, but otherwise for:

1. Aphids and mealybugs, use 1 teaspoon nicotine sulphate to 1 gallon of water.
2. Red spider, use one of the miticides, such as Aramite or an all-purpose spray with malathion in it, according to directions on the label.
3. Cyclamen mite, that stunts and deforms foliage, use 1 teaspoon of 19% Endrin to 1 gallon water or if the infestation is bad, dispose of the plant, washing hands, pot and tools to prevent its spreading.
4. Snails and slugs, use baits sold under trade names.
5. Nematodes, one of the methyl bromides can be used, but they are so toxic that they have to be handled with caution and definitely out of doors. Nematodes are usually so well entrenched in the plant's root system by the time you notice them that my advice is to destroy the plant.
6. Scale, (in various colors, from white and tan to brown and black, and in every shape) try brushing off with soap and water; spray with 1 teaspoon 50% malathion emulsion to 1 gallon water, or spray with 1 teaspoon nicotine sulphate and 2 tablespoons mild liquid soap to 1 gallon luke-warm water.
7. Fungus diseases that cause brown spots and crinkled edges of leaves, use Captan, 1 tablespoon of the 50% wettable powder to 1 gallon water.

Plants listed below, unless otherwise specified will live outdoors, in filtered sun and in the standard potting soil that I speak of for plants of the warm temperate zone. Wherever there is a need for other growing mediums and conditions, I have so noted.

ACANTHUS, *Acanthus mollis* see chapter on Flowering Shrubs.

The AFRICAN VIOLET, *Saintpaulia* is really not a violet at all; it is actually a member of the Gesneria Family. It was discovered in Africa by Baron Walter von Saint Paul and originally all flowers were blue. The African Violet, along with the related Gloxinia is not a plant for the open garden. Both have to have care and attention for ultimate success and both do very well in air-conditioned houses. Grown in a wide variety of soils, the African

Violet needs a potting medium that is slightly acid and one that will drain quickly. Some enthusiasts use ½ compost and ½ peat moss with enough sand or perlite for good drainage.

The African Violet is dependent on the correct amount and intensity of light for successful flowering. It needs 15–30 foot candles (natural or artificial light as measured by a photographer's light meter) for twelve hours each day. The necessary humidity can be obtained by placing the pots on top of gravel in a saucer half-filled with water. A temperature range of 70 degrees in daytime and 60 degrees at night is ideal. The African Violet is very tender and very conscious of sudden temperature changes and drafts. And when it is thirsty you must use water as near room temperature as you can get it. It can be propagated by leaf cuttings started in water or vermiculite. The thing to remember about this plant is that it needs full light but no sun.

Some very lovely varieties are Silver Moon, a beautiful white; Fairy Queen, very large light violet flowers with purple eye and edge; Los Angeles Double with violet flowers; Morning Mists, pale mauve flowers with mauve eye; Temple Belle, violet-blue flowers with white border; Morning Dawn, a pale violet. Dream Girl is white edged in blue; Pink Attraction, large rounded flowers with rose-pink eye; Red Princess, wine-red; Ruffled Queen, blue-burgundy with frilled petals; April Love, a new, delicate, blue and white frilly double with bronze foliage; Sunday Pink is fresh and free-flowering. Pink Puff is a lovely, large, double pink with quilted leaves and Pink Victoria is appealing. White Pride Supreme is a large double white; Masquerade's two upper petals have dark lilac eye and black edges—the foliage is dark; Fire Dance, dark velvety red and Fantasia shows lavender flowers streaked in purple. There are many books written solely on the subject of the African Violet and you should consult them if you have the urge to try growing these beauties.

The FLAME VIOLETS, *Episcias* also of the *Gesneriaceae* resemble the African Violet in appearance and are grown very much like them in that they require plenty of light, no direct sun and a warm temperature. But *Episcias* demand an even more porous soil. Old leaf mold is perfect for them, with no garden soil whatsoever in the pot. You may add small amounts of bone meal or crushed charcoal, or a little well-rotted cow manure that has been sifted but bear in mind that this potting mixture, as porous as it is, will dry out quickly, so check each morning to see if your plant needs water. *Episcias* require constant moisture. Native to the American tropics, their beauty is primarily in the leaves; the flowers bloom singly, not in clusters. They differ from the African Violet in that they will trail downward over the pot, making a perfect plant for hanging baskets or for a small plastic trellis in the pot. The color range is large: *Episcia coccinea* is a brilliant scarlet bloomer with deep bronzy leaves; *E. lilacina*'s cultivar, Fanny Haage, has blue-lavender flowers and bright green leaves; *E. cupreata* Chocolate Soldier has red blooms against reddish-brown leaves; *cupreata*'s other cultivar is Emerald Queen, also red-flowered with silvery-green foliage. *E. cupreata viridifolia*, or the Christmas Flame Violet, is a wonderful combination of bright green leaves and shiny red blossoms.

The GLOXINIA or *Sinningia* Hybrids from Brazil, of the same family as the African Violet and the *Episcia*, requires the same growing conditions as the other two. It likes a potting soil of ½ leaf mold, ¼ fibrous loam and ¼ peat. Never allow the soil to dry out. When you water be careful not to wet the leaves, and feed occasionally with a fertilizer high in nitrogen. The Gloxinia likes a resting period over the winter, so withhold water gradually until the leaves die down. Kiss of Fire is a small red; Velvet Queen, a large ruffled red; Prince Albert is frilled and a dark purple; Mont Blanc, a pure white and Blue Heaven, a lovely blue.

The African Violet, the *Episcia* and the Gloxinia are all definitely house or greenhouse plants, although I have known of occasions when friends have had luck with one or two outdoors.

A C H I M E N E S , *Achimines longiflora* another member of the Gesneria Family, is a tuberous-rooted plant that takes the same culture as the Gloxinia, the *Episcia* and the African Violet. At its best as a potted plant or in hanging baskets, it thrives in a mixture of ½ loamy soil, ¼ peat moss and ¼ leaf mold. Royal Purple and the white Dainty Queen are as lovely as Pink Beauty and Big Boy Blue. There are many other varieties; all do well in warm, light places without direct sun, and require plenty of moisture while growing. Water as you do for Gloxinias. See that the leaves and flowers stay dry and after flowering gradually withhold water until the tuber becomes entirely dormant. Store it in dry sand or peat until spring when you pot it once more.

A L O C A S I A S , of the Arum Family, come from tropical Asia and are noted for their beautifully shaped foliage. They are divided into two groups, the evergreen and the herbaceous species and both demand good drainage. The evergreens grow best in a mixture of ½ peat, ¼ sphagnum, ¼ fibrous loam and some chopped charcoal and granite chips. When they are potted they need to be mulched at least three inches above the edge of the pot with sphagnum moss. A good example is *Alocasia cuprea*, a very compact plant with heavy wavy leaves to ten inches in length, shading from dark green to maroon.

The herbaceous species likes to grow in a medium of ⅔ good garden loam and ⅓ old cow or sheep manure. This group loses its leaves during its dormant winter season, during which time water is withheld gradually. *Alocasia macrorhiza* is one of these, with leaves about three feet long and so blotched with white that some seem entirely white. Both types are tender to cold and must be fed at regular intervals. March is about the best month in which to propagate by cuttings of the rhizomatous roots and by offshoots.

The *Alocasia* Hybrids range from the small, white-veined leaf, A. *amazonica* to A. *Watsoniana* from Sumatra, called the Queen of the Alocasias. The latter has a large corrugated heart-shaped leaf that is silver-veined above and purple beneath; it is not always available from nurserymen. Another rare form is the striking A. *zebrina* from the Philippines, whose plain green leaves and stems are striped in greenish-brown. All three are hardy.

The *Alocasias* are related to the C O L O C A S I A or Elephant's Ear, and to the C A L A D I U M.

A M A R Y L L I S, see chapter on Bulbs.

The A N T H U R I U M Hybrids, also of the Arum Family, are hothouse plants grown for either their unusual velvety foliage or their brilliant blossoms that last for weeks. These tropical aroids can also be grown in the house if carefully tended.

Although all of them flower, some, like *Anthurium crystallinum* from Peru, have very inconspicuous blooms but large, dark green, heart-shaped leaves with glistening, silver-white veining. This foliage type grows best in a medium of ¼ coarse loam, ¼ coarse peat, ¼ sphagnum and ¼ coarsely-chopped charcoal mixed with a little sand. *Anthurium Andraeanum's* foliage is also heart-shaped. Its simple green leaf contrasts strongly with the shiny flowers or spathes that range from six to eight inches long, of a deep orange-red. This species runs into many varieties with blooms ranging in color from white to pink, light rose, salmon, coral and dark reds. The yellow spadix on all is about three to four inches long. This flowering type from Colombia needs a coarse growing medium of ⅓ sphagnum, ⅓ Osmunda fiber and ⅓ mixed sand and well-rotted manure. The trick in making these flower well is to build up the compost or sphagnum around each new root that forms above the level of the growing medium. Both types need good drainage, high temperatures and lots of humidity. Repot and propagate by suckers or division of the rhizome, in January before active spring growth starts.

A P H E L A N D R A, *Aphelandra Chamissoniana* is an evergreen native of Brazil and belongs to the family *Acanthaceae*. It is a tender, erect specimen with silvery-yellowish-white bandings on the slender green leaves. The bracts are yellow with green tips and the flowers are a clear yellow. *A. squarrosa Louisae* is another charming variety. Both are tender and both bloom about twice a year. Prune and start new cuttings when new growth appears.

ARDISIA, *Ardisia crenulata* see chapter on Flowering Shrubs.

ARTILLERY PLANT, *Pilea microphylla* of the Nettle Family, is propagated by seed, cuttings or root division. This lacy fernlike plant is so-called because of its habit of forcibly discharging its pollen from the staminate flowers, and grows best in moist mixtures of loam and leaf mold with a little sand added. One variety of this plant, *Pilea nummulariaefolia* is commonly known by the simple name of "Creeping Charlie" because of the creeping stem that roots at the joints. *P. cadierei* is called the Aluminum Plant because of the silvery markings on its blue-green leaves. Both varieties bear tiny flowers.

ASPIDISTRA, of the Lily Family, has long been known as a border plant. Its variety *elatior* or *lurida variegata*, with leaves half green, half cream, makes an unusual potted plant that is very hardy. Propagation is by division of the rhizome. See chapter on Ground Covers.

To tell you all there is to know about BEGONIAS, *Begoniaceae* would take a whole book in itself. There are bulbous-rooted Begonias; tuberous-rooted ones; rhizomatous members to which the Rex varieties belong, and the fibrous-rooted or *Semperflorens* group. For all practical gardeners who wish to enjoy the Begonia in the patio as well as in the house I suggest leaving the first two divisions for the hothouse and giving attention to the charmers in the third and fourth groups.

The rhizomatous Rex Begonias are hairy and grown chiefly for their colorful foliage. They do best in a coarse mixture of ⅓ loamy soil, ⅓ leaf mold, ⅙ well-rotted manure and ⅙ sharp builder's sand. They like diffused light but no sunlight, and plenty of warm humid air during the warm months; in winter, they will take as much sunshine as you can give them, and they must be protected from the cold. Be careful not to wet the leaves when you water the plant. Propagation of this type is by leaf cuttings, and this is accomplished by choosing a large matured leaf and cutting the big nerves or veins on the underside. Peg the leaf down on the surface of your garden bed and shade it well; in no time roots will form around each cut. As soon as the tiny new leaves appear you can lift the young plant and pot it, at first in a very fine sifted mixture of the soil just mentioned. Bismarck, with a red-bordered green leaf, and Herman Teupel with dark green foliage heavily mottled in plum and raspberry-red, are two outstanding Rex Begonias. Seeds of the Rex Hybrids are available.

The dainty *Semperflorens* or Wax Begonia group is part of the fibrous-rooted division and likes a growing medium of ½ loam, ¼ well-rotted manure or peat and ¼ sharp builder's sand. These are more erect than the Rex, with smooth and smaller leaves of either green or red, and flowers of either pink or red, depending on variety. Gustav Lind, of the green leaves and pink flowers, and Rose Pearl, with reddish foliage and rosy-red blossoms are two very attractive long-blooming varieties. They too prefer good light, fresh air and warmth in the summer; like the Rex, they demand sun and protection from cold in winter. Propagation of this type is by division of the stem, and seeds of the Fibrous F1 Hybrids are available.

BLOOD LILY, *Haemanthus* see chapter on Bulbs.

The BROMELIADS, of the Pineapple Family, *Bromeliaceae* are legion, and all are fascinating. There are about forty-five genera and about sixteen hundred species in this group of ornamentals, including our Spanish Moss and the Pineapple. Natives of South and Central America, where most of them are epiphytes, they usually present rather stiff, leathery, trough-like leaves in rosette formation. Some, like the *Tillandsia* (with the exception of the Spanish Moss) and the *Billbergia*, have a tight rosette in which water cannot collect or stand; and others, such as the *Aechmea* and the *Cryptanthus*, form basal, natural "drinking cups" that hold water like a vase. The foliage ranges from shades of green and gray to striking variations of red and plum. The flowers are for the most part incidental to the colorful bracts which may show but once a year but last for weeks and months when they do. Some, like the *Dyckia*, are "succulents" and need dry conditions, sandy, rocky soil and full sun to bring out the bright red coloring of the leaves at flowering time. Water these only about every two weeks and if outdoors, protect them from the heavy summer rains before too much water rots them. Others, such as the *Guzmannias*, *Vriesias* and *Aechmeas*, prefer filtered sunlight, high temperatures and plenty of moisture. Although they have been known to stand very low temperatures the Bromeliads show some damage from the cold and should be sheltered when a freeze is predicted. All of them have a common demand: good drainage.

Nearly all Bromeliad enthusiasts prefer to grow their exotics in Osmunda fern fiber, and for the small, light-weight plant, this medium is ideal. But the Osmunda, as well as sphagnum and shredded bark does not anchor the heavier plants too well, allowing those Bromeliads with water standing in the cups to topple over, spilling whatever they hold. A layer of marble grit sometimes steadies the plant but in lieu of faulty balance the Bromeliad will also thrive in a porous mixture of ¼ leaf mold or fibrous loam, ¼ sharp builder's sand or perlite, ¼ peat moss and ¼ shredded fir bark to which a little chopped charcoal has been added. Make sure that the bottom of the pot is well filled with broken bits of pot to insure good drainage.

Bromeliads like a monthly feeding of a weak liquid fertilizer either placed in the natural cup or sprayed over the leaves. Use a half-strength solution recommended for foliar feeding. Read the directions on the label of whatever food you purchase and then use one-half as strong as recommended by the manufacturer. Those plants with cups almost make their own organic food when leaf particles and bits of plant matter fall into the cup and slowly disintegrate in the water contained therein. With the exception of the dry ones Bromeliads like a daily spraying of clear water. Those growing outdoors on or under trees may need this syringing even after a heavy rain because overhead branches serve as a shelter.

Bromeliads may be propagated by detaching the off-shoots or removing the tops and rooting them in peat or sand.

The A E C H M E A S of this family are Collectors' Items. They like to be grown in filtered shade in Osmunda fern fiber with bits of broken pot and charcoal and a layer of sphagnum moss in the bottom of the pot. *Aechmea fasciata variegata* has silvery cross-bandings on its gray-green leaves and a stout globular head of blue flowers and striking pink bracts that turn deeper as they mature. *Aechmea Fosteriana* is startlingly lovely with its spined leaves shading from pale green to rosy-green, mottled in a brownish-purple. Golden yellow flowers show between crimson bracts on the flower spike. The rosette of this one is more erect and clustered than the more flaring *fasciata variegata*. *Aechmea marmorata* is often called the Grecian Vase because of its stately leaves that rise tall and straight before they slightly recurve. Their blue-gray color, mottled with wine and green, makes a striking contrast to rosy bract and blue blossoms that hang gracefully from the pendant flower spike. One of the best species is *Aechmea Mariae-Reginae* from Costa Rica whose flower spike rises erect above the foliage to show deep rose-colored, toothed bracts.

The B I L L B E R G I A S are easily-grown Bromeliads. *Billbergia nutans* has pretty, spiky, bronzy-green leaves with pendant blossoms in tricolor effect. The bracts are bright red and the petals green and the edging a vivid blue. *Billbergia* Fantasia's rosy bracts and blue flowers are surrounded by handsome leaves of a coppery-green that are splotched with creamy-white and pale pink. *Billbergia zebrina* has wider spreading leaves of a silvery-gray banded in tan and green. The bracts are a soft salmon color, holding greenish blossoms. These are hardier than the *Aechmeas*. They like more direct sun, drier conditions and a potting medium of peat moss, loamy garden soil, and sand with charcoal and bits of broken pot added. Osmunda fiber may be substituted for the soil mixture if the plant is small and light enough. I have some planted in soil that do beautifully in full sun; others with Osmunda at the roots do equally well in semi-shade.

The low-growing CRYPTANTHUS group known as Earth Stars presents a more flaring, flattened rosette of leaves and thrives in the same soil conditions as the Billbergias. *Cryptanthus bivittatus* (roseus pictus) is quite star-like. Its leaves are slightly toothed, olive-green with two pale longitudinal stripes and an overlay of rose that turns red in a brighter light. *C. zonatus zebrinus* is called the Zebra Plant, an exotic cluster of purple-bronze leaves that are long and rippled, cross-banded in a silvery gray-beige.

TILLANDSIAS, that like to grow in high places, are lovely on tree branches and trunks. They include *Tillandsia usneoides*, our familiar Spanish Moss. These long gray streamers that make up this remarkable plant are epiphytes that grow on other plants without being in contact with the soil and without taking water or nutrition from the plants on which they grow. They hold moisture from the air by means of the scale-hairs that give this Spanish Moss its gray coloring. Please don't confuse it with the Mistletoe or true parasite that feeds and lives on its "host" or bark to which it clings. *T. usneoides* has tiny yellow flowers. *Tillandsia Lindenii* is larger and may be grown in Osmunda fiber. It presents a lovely rosette of thick, recurved, green leaves that are marked with brownish-red lines, with bright red bracts and royal blue flowers on a ten-inch flattened spike. The Pineapple Air-Plant is *Tillandsia utriculata*.

Strictly air plants, the *Tillandsias* really do not have to be planted —and I mean that literally! They will grow on a rock or on an old piece of tree bark, and I have seen some charmingly "sitting" in pieces of driftwood with Osmunda as a cushion. Sometimes the plant is so tiny that it has to be attached to whatever it has to grow on by means of a small staple or nail. Give the *Tillandsias* some sunlight, water the leaves regularly and watch them turn reddish when the flower appears.

NEOREGELIA, *Neoregelia spectabilis* is called Painted Finger Nail because the ends of the recurving olive-green leaves are tipped bright red. The blue flowers are deep in the center and resemble a pin cushion. *Neoregelia Fosteriana* from Rio de Janeiro has a thick rosette of bronzy leaves that are splotched with green. The wine-red at the tip is repeated in the cushion of the rosette. The center flowers are pale blue.

Ananas sativus is our PINEAPPLE grown commercially in Florida and in the tropics. The stiff, spiny-edged leaves that range from gray-green to bronze, rise from a thick rosette and arch downward gracefully. The dense lavender flowers appear with tufty top knot and evolve into the edible fruit. *A. sativus variegatus* looks attractive in a pot, its striped leaves curving over the edges.

Nearly all Bromeliads like to be hung high but as I stated before the size of the plant generally governs where you put it. Feeling a Bromeliad's leaf will help the beginner decide how much moisture it needs. Usually those whose leaves are thick and feel as though they are covered with gray felt tend to hold more moisture and are more accustomed to living on rocks and crevices. Those with thinner leaves that look like they are covered with a gray powder demand daily sprayings and usually like to be hung. But experimenting with your plants will bring the answers to all your questions. As patio plants Bromeliads will take less attention than when they are grown as house plants. They are also wonderful additions to the air-conditioned office if they are given a few days off in the outdoors every now and then. Since Bromeliads are intriguing there may come a day when you will want to know more about them than I could give you in this book. The Bromeliad Society is an international organization and has affiliated local groups that make a study of this plant and publish literature that deals with the culture and hybridization.

To do full justice to the CACTUS Family, *Cactaceae* I would have to write a whole book about it. To glance at it briefly Cacti are roughly divided into two classes: those originating in the desert and those native to the tropics. The desert variety needs sun and a soil that practically falls apart when you lift it, ½ builder's sand, ¼ peat, ⅛ leaf mold or good garden loam and ⅛ pebbles, with a little bone meal and pulverized limestone mixed with it. This group can stand fairly cold temperatures and will bloom beautifully even when bone dry. We all know the appearance of these Cacti—swollen limbs armed with bristling spines and colorful flowers. A little one, like *Mammillaria bocasana* that looks like the Powder Puff that it is commonly called, is just as curiously attractive as the slightly larger *Opuntia*'s Bunny Ears and Prickly Pears. These contrast sharply with the tall gaunt ones in the desert. Although the Cacti can stand drought conditions, be fair to them and give them regular watering and occasional food during the warm months. Propagation is by cuttings, whose basal ends must be allowed to heal over before they are inserted into sand to root.

Those Cacti that are native to the tropics are semi-epiphytic in habits. The E P I P H Y L L U M or Orchid Cactus, sometimes called *Phyllocactus* needs filtered light, adequate moisture and a richer, loamier soil than the desert type. It will not tolerate as much heat as the desert Cactus; as a matter of fact it will stand temperatures down to freezing, especially when planted in a porous mixture of ½ good garden loam or leaf mold, ¼ builder's sand, ⅛ peat and ⅛ well-rotted sheep manure. There should be no limestone in this mixture as there is in the medium for growing the desert Cactus. I have had the lovely pink-blooming Padre for years and I find it does best on a small trellis attached to the pot. Mimi is a smaller flowering red-violet and Cassandra is my favorite, with a golden-buff blossom that opens wide and flat showing a definite terra-cotta center. I also enjoy Young Nun, a cup and saucer variety whose flower is white with yellow and tan back petals. I give them filtered sunlight, keep them moderately moist and feed them once a month in late summer and fall. I give them another dose of fertilizer in the latter part of February and continue the monthly feeding until the buds begin to form. I withhold further food until the flowers appear and then I apply a light dose. I find them remarkably free of disease and pest.

As a note of interest, the name *Epiphyllum* comes from two Greek words meaning "upon" and "leaf". Actually there are no leaves involved on these *Epiphyllums*. The flowers are borne directly on the flat, branched, leaf-like stems.

Although there are many night-bloomers in the *Epiphyllum* group, *Hylocereus undatus* is the most familiar of the Nocturnal Cacti. It is a plant with long tricornered stems that grow tall. The wonderful waxy blooms open at night, usually in July, and it is simply fascinating to watch the petals unfold with incredible activity, the perfume spreading as the blossoms develop. The flowers last but one night.

CHRISTMAS CACTUS, *Zygocactus truncatus* is an epiphyte and a native of Brazil. Its culture is not difficult if you put it in equal parts of loam, leaf mold and sand and give it a wire frame for support. Take it indoors in the cold weather, keep it in an even temperature, avoid drafts and enjoy its blooms in December and January. Let it rest until March without giving it too much water and take it outdoors again in a well-lighted but shaded location. When in bloom these plants require more water than other times because the deep red flowers extract so much moisture from the plant.

The RAT-TAIL CACTUS is *Aporocactus flagelliformis* from Central America. It is an unusual plant that looks best hanging from a tree branch or basket, especially when flowering in the spring. It may be propagated by cuttings and is very easily grown. The RHIPSALIS are also epiphytes and make nice companion plants for the *Epiphyllum*. Their culture is the same, although their flowers are small and their plants have many forms. These may be grown in Osmunda fiber, shredded bark or sphagnum (with the usual additional feedings required) or in a mixture of ½ peat moss, ¼ perlite or builder's sand, ⅛ chopped charcoal and ⅛ coarse manure. *Rhipsalis cassutha* is the popular Mistletoe Cactus that produces white berries. Its leaves are pendant and many-branched. Many of this family are perfect for hanging baskets.

It has been said that "All Cacti are Succulents, but Succulents are not all Cacti". s u c c u l e n t s are to be found in about forty families of plants—some as tough as others are delicate. The skin has few pores, allowing the stem to serve as a storehouse of water and nourishment. These plants can be left outdoors until freezes are predicted or until winter rains go on too long. They do well in a bright light and in a mixture of ⅓ loam, ⅓ coarse sharp sand to which a little gravel has been added, and ⅓ old leaf mold. Do not use leaf mold made of oak leaves as they contain too much tannin for Succulents. But do add a little ground limestone every now and then, and remember that they are not fond of manure in any form.

There are many Succulents, of many beautiful forms and most of them need sun to bring out the variations of color. Here are some of them:

A G A V E , of the Amaryllis Family, not only gives us the huge specimens that serve as ornamentals, but smaller ones that are lovely in pots. *Agave Victoriae-reginae* presents a well-formed rosette of dark green leaves with white margins, keeled to an abrupt point.

A L O Ë , of the Lily Family, is a South African desert plant that needs plenty of sun. *Aloë nobilis* has white teeth at regular intervals on the edges of the green leaves. *A. arborescens* shows sword-like, fleshy leaves, edged in tiny horns, that recurve as they spread. The infrequent flowers are red. *A. latifolia*'s reddish-green leaves are blotched with white and edged with brown teeth. *Aloë* can be grown easily from seed or from offsets that form around the base of the mother plant.

The c u s h i o n a l o ë is *Haworthia margaritifera*, which will grow in the shade. It has dark green, lanceolate foliage spotted in white. The g a s t e r i a s join the h a w o r t h i a s in their preferences for shade. They cannot stand full sun in summer and need filtered sunlight even in cooler weather.

The CRASSULAS from South Africa make wonderful house plants and do very well outdoors until very cold weather. As a matter of fact sun brings out their vivid coloring and cold seems to spruce them up. The SEMPERVIVUMS belong to the *Crassulaceae*, where we find *Sempervivum calcereum* and *S. arachnoideum*, small rosettes of fleshy leaves, native to the mountains of southern Europe; *Crassula arborescens* or *argentea* and *C. portulacia*, our popular Jade Plants; *Crassula falcata*, with its sickle-shaped leaves arranged in shingle fashion; *Echeveria elegans*, bluish foliage set in a small rosette and coral-pink flowers on rosy stems.

The KALANCHOËS come from Madagascar and are winter bloomers. *Kalanchoë tomentosa* or the Panda Plant, is an erect specimen whose fleshy leaves seem to be covered with white felt. The teeth that edge the foliage are brown. *Kalanchoë tubiflora*, often called *Bryophyllum*, grows slender, pencil-like branches that are blotched a pinkish-grayish-brown and bear tiny new plants at the tips. Its flowers are rosy-red. *K. Daigremontiana's* leaves are tricornered and dull green, arching almost back to the stem. The blossoms are a gray-violet. *Kalanchoë Blossfeldiana's* leaves are small, green and clustered below spikes of bright coral-red flowers.

Then come the low, succulent SEDUMS, and I think the one from Mexico called Christmas Cheer, *Sedum guatemalense* is lovely. It is small with thick, fleshy, glossy green leaves that turn red in the sun. *Sedum Sieboldii*, the perennial creeper with its pink autumn flowers is familiar to all of us.

Another beauty in this group is *Sedum Morganianum* or the Burro's Tail, a perfect plant for a hanging basket. Long streamers of small, fleshy leaves that are gray-green with an overlay of silvery-blue, hang gracefully over the edge of the basket. The flowers are a dull pink. For success with this one your best bet is to line the basket with Osmunda and then fill it with a mixture of ½ gravel or chicken grit, and ½ coarse white builder's sand, with a good handful of pulverized sheep manure added. Feed every two weeks with a soluble fertilizer except during the cool season when once a month is adequate. The Burro's Tail likes indirect light. You will find that too much direct sunlight will cause the leaves to lose their lavender-blue-green cast and turn a sickly yellow. Give it some kind of a shelter so that it does not get too much moisture in a rainy season, otherwise its roots will decay.

STAPELIA *gigantea*, of the Milkweed Family has quadrangular-shaped stems and very large yellow flowers that are streaked with red and covered with long filmy hairs. I would not advise bringing this South African plant into the house. Its blossom is exotic to look at but the scent is anything but desirable. It is well-named the Carrion Flower.

SANSEVIERIA, of the succulent branch of the Lily Family is a native of India and Africa and will grow just about anywhere. Given a loamy soil and fed regularly, the plant keeps in robust health. There are many varieties: *S. zeylanica* is gray-green with darker green streaks. This is said to be the true species from Ceylon and differs from *Sansevieria trifasciata* in the way its recurving leaves spread outward from the center. *S. trifasciata Laurentii* is variegated green and yellow with yellow edges on the leaves and flower spikes as tall as the foliage. *S. trifasciata Nelsonii* is a smaller plant and is a solid dark green. *Sansevieria Ehrenbergii* is blue, one of the finest and most attractive; a recent introduction, the leaves are arranged alternately, like a large fan, hiding the stem. Another new one is *S. Liberica,* whose dark green leaves bear milk-white stripes. *Sansevieria trifasciata Hahnii* is the "birdnest" sport of *Laurentii* that was found in New Orleans in 1939, and is altogether different in growth habits. It forms a thick low rosette of leaves that are dark green with a lighter cross-banding. The variety Golden *Hahnii* is outstanding with its yellow stripes along the margins of the leaves and its gray cross-bandings. All of these plants are often called Snake Plants, Leopard Lilies, Bowstring Hemp, Zebra Plants and Mother-in-law's Tongue.

All Cacti and Succulents must have excellent drainage. Too much water around the roots for one day will kill a plant. And just because they are originally desert and mountain dwellers does not mean that they can be mistreated. They need regular waterings and feedings and sufficient air and light.

ICE PLANT, *Mesembryanthemum crystallinum* see chapter on Ground Covers.

CALADIUM, see chapter on Bulbs.

CANNA, Pfitzer Dwarf, see chapter on Bulbs.

CHICKEN GIZZARD PLANT, *Iresine Herbstii* of the *Amaranthaceae* is highly colored. Its deep red leaves are broad, ovate and crinkled, showing prominent veins. *Iresine Wallisii* is a smaller form with rounded leaves that are bronzy-red above and purple beneath. Both look well in pots or in the patio border.

CHINESE EVERGREEN, *Aglaonema modestum* of the *Araceae* has ovate, dark green leaves that droop rather gracefully from a slender stem. The flowers are inconspicuous, followed by red berries that last a long time. Most of the members of this species like semi-shade, are very hardy and have roots well-adapted to growing in water. *A. oblongifolium Curtisii* is a rare form, slow-growing, with silvery veining on the blue-green leaves. The related plant commonly called AFRICAN EVERGREEN is actually *Nephthytis Liberica* or *Nephthytis Afzelii*; the variegated African Evergreen is *Nephthytis variegata*. These plants are very tolerant of gas fumes from heating systems; they may be topped and rooted when they grow too tall.

COLEUS *Blumei*, of the Mint Family grows in soil or water. There are hundreds of different kinds, all strikingly colored, especially if given full sun. Pinch off a piece and root it in water so that you can winter them indoors. All Coleus demand warmth and moisture and all are very susceptible to mealybug. *Plectranthus Oertendahlei* is the prostrate Coleus, also of the Mint Family. It is lovely in hanging baskets, and very easy to root in water. It will grow in any soil and in any light. The small, very dark leaves are veined in silver and edged in purple. The lavender flowers are incidental.

CROTONS, *Codiaeum* bear leathery leaves of many shapes and a variety of colors, although all new growth starts life as just a plain green. Of the *Euphorbiaceae* or Spurge Family, the *variegatum pictum* group comes from Ceylon, Malaya and South India. There are hundreds of varieties, ranging from oak-shaped and elliptical to cockscrew foliage. All Crotons should have direct sunlight to bring out the most vivid colors and they should be kept out of drafts. They will grow in the average loamy mixture, but feed monthly, soak the plant about once a week and keep moist at all times. Try syringing your Crotons two or three times a week with a weak solution of tabasco and water to kill mealybugs and red spider.

I have been asked to say a word about CYCLAMEN because this plant is so often received as a gift during the Christmas season. Cyclamen, of the Primrose Family, usually flower from Christmas to Easter and are distinctly hothouse plants, but if you must keep yours in the house remember that faded blooms must never be *cut* off—they should be *pulled* gently from the bottom of the plant. If you cut the flowers off decay will result. Give your Cyclamen lots of light but never direct sun, and when you water never allow the moisture to settle in the middle of the plant or it will mean decay again. If the leaves look dusty wipe them off with a damp cloth. After the blooms have ceased to show, withhold some of the water that you have been giving your plant and in the early fall, when you notice the pot filling with roots repot into the next size pot, making sure that your growing medium is always a little more soil than equal parts of sand and peat. Keep pinching back the bloom buds until November and feed occasionally with a small cupful of bone meal or sheep manure. Never let your plant become potbound until it requires a six-inch container.

Scindapsus aureus, of the Arum Family from the Solomon Islands is our DEVIL'S IVY, known also as POTHOS, a fleshy climber whose green leaves are often speckled with yellow. The cultivar Marble Queen is richly streaked with white. These plants take about the same culture as the Philodendrons with which they are often confused. They do well outdoors in warm weather and will tolerate heating conditions of the home during the winter.

The DEVIL'S WALKING STICK, *Euphorbia Tirucallii* of the Spurge Family is sometimes called the Milk Bush and the Indian Tree Spurge. It comes from South Asia and makes a tall potted plant, from four to six feet, with cylindrical, pencil-like green branches that grow out at every angle. It bears very small inconspicuous leaves. The milky juice that bleeds from the plant when a limb is broken is poisonous. This specimen is a conversation piece in the patio as well as in an entrance hall. Propagated by cuttings, the basal end of which must be allowed to dry before being planted in a mixture of sand, charcoal and coal ashes.

The most common DRACAENA is *Dracaena fragrans* variety *massangeana*, with long leaves like those of the corn plant. These leaves have a stripe of yellow running down the center. D. *Warnecki* has dark green leaves with white edging and D. *Godseffiana* is different from all other Dracaenas. It is free branching with rich, dark green leaves beautifully marked with creamy-white spots. D. Florida Beauty has very unusual markings: it is almost entirely splotched in white. A rare plant is D. *Goldieana* from the most tropical part of West Africa. This one likes a well-drained, porous soil well fortified with moisture-retaining sphagnum. It needs high humidity. The young, dark green leaves are streaked horizontally with a bright green and when the foliage matures the colors fade to a near white. It reaches two to three feet. Members of the Lily Family, all of the Dracaenas make striking house plants and can stand a good amount of cold. *Dracaena terminalis* also known as *Cordyline terminalis* and as the Hawaiian Ti Plant, has several cultivars, such as the Eugene André and Firebrand, whose satiny leaves turn deep pink to red if they receive enough light. Topped, the Dracaenas will put out new growth.

The D U M B - C A N E P L A N T, *Dieffenbachia* of the Arum Family is so named because a small amount of juice on the tongue will render a person practically speechless for several days. Dieffenbachia has canna-shaped leaves spotted with white; it cannot be grown in direct sunlight, but prefers shade and can stand, and likes air conditioning. *D. amoena* has dark green leaves splashed with white; *D. picta* is pale green with white and cream markings and is the one with which we are most familiar; *D. Rudolph Roehrs* has yellow leaves edged green and marked with ivory; *D. Arvida* has an unusual white leaf pattern. The cane of the Dieffenbachia can be cut in sections and rooted very easily. They are all supremely beautiful with an insouciant grace all their own.

E U C H A R I S L I L Y, *Eucharis grandiflora* see chapter on Bulbs.

The F E R N Family is enormous and for practical purposes I can only name a few. To start with about the largest there are the T R E E F E R N S, *Cyathea arborea* from the mountains of Puerto Rico and Jamaica, and *Cibotium regale* and *schiedei* from the mountains of Mexico and Guatemala. Of the Cyathea Family, all reach great heights in their native habitats but are so slow-growing that they can be enjoyed in their juvenile state in our patios and small gardens. Their arching feathery fronds are particularly attractive in tubs on stands in small pools and conveniently so, because most Fern like moist air and a woodsy porous soil. The *Alsophila australis* is another lovely Tree Fern and this one requires lots of water. *Blechnum gibbum* from New Caledonia is a member of the Polypody Family and has slender arching fronds in a rosette that rises from a central trunk. Do not water this Fern from above or its leaves will blacken. *Dicksonia fibrosa* from New Zealand presents long fairly stiff fronds growing from a stout brown trunk. This one will tolerate more sun than the others, even in the summer heat but the trunk must be watered *every day* when planted in pots. While growing in the open the trunk of the Dicksonias should be watered twice a day during the growing period and then this moisture should be gradually decreased so that the plant can rest in the winter. Nearly all of these Tree Fern are propagated by spores.

The PTERIS group, of the Polypody Family contains the medium-sized ENGLISH BRACKEN, the CHINESE BRAKE or *Pteris serrulata multifida* and the AUSTRALIAN BRACKEN, *Pteris tremula* and *Pteris scaberula*. These grow from two to three feet high on stiff brown stems and arch forward and outward gracefully, carrying leaves that range from three to eighteen inches long, depending on variety. Unfortunately there are not many dealers who offer the *Pteris* group for sale. They more or less belong to those plants that are passed from hand to hand by interested gardeners. A friend gave me a root of the English Bracken years ago and I have thoroughly enjoyed it in the ground and in pots in my patio. The long fuzzy dark brown underground runners send up strong slender stems of the same color. Each stem carries the leaves curled up tightly until it reaches about eighteen inches in height; then the leaf unfurls, showing its lateral and terminal divisions. This Bracken takes plenty of light (no direct sun) and moisture. I bring the potted specimen indoors in winter; those plants that are growing in the ground die down with a freeze but come up again in the spring. Propagation is by division of the underground runners.

We are all familiar with the SWORD or BOSTON FERN, *Nephrolepis exaltata bostoniensis* and its dwarf, *compacta*. See chapter on Ground Covers. The tallest of the feathered Ferns is *N. exaltata Rooseveltii plumosa*. These may be grown in the open ground as well as in pots, in hanging baskets and on tree trunks, protected as much as possible from the cold.

Another member of the Polypody Family is our HOLLY FERN, *Cyrtomium falcatum* that low, glossy, toothed-leaved full-based Fern that is such a boon to the landscape. A native of Japan and India, it does beautifully in semi-shaded corners in the open ground and in large pots or tubs. See chapter on Ground Covers.

The CINNAMON FERN gives us the Osmunda fiber that we

use as a growing medium for so many of our epiphytic plants. Of the *Osmundaceae*, this one grows in clusters from two to five feet tall, showing fronds that change from green when young to cinnamon color when mature. It does best in a northern exposure in partial shade, and in deep moist earth. The black fibrous roots that cover the creeping underground stems of this Fern are dug, cleaned and used as Osmunda fiber.

In the lower group of the Polypody Family, our MAIDEN-HAIR, *Adiantum* has many species. It does better outdoors in shady places because it needs a high degree of humidity in which to flourish. Add more peat and a little charcoal to your standard potting mix. The BIRDS-NEST FERN, *Asplenium nidus-avis* presents a different type with its wider fronds and brown-black midrib. This one will turn dark brown in cold weather if overwatered. It likes light shade. In Florida the RESURRECTION FERN, *Polypodium incanum* can be seen growing on the trunks of the palm trees, on the Cabbage Palm in particular.

The two main requirements of all Fern seem to be the correct amount of moisture and the protection from the direct rays of the sun. When you move a Fern take a very good look at its position as to depth and exposure and try to duplicate these points when you replant. Try not to bury the crowns below ground level.

The STAG-HORN FERN is *Platycerium alcicorne* also a member of *Polypodiaceae*. A true epiphyte it grows best in Osmunda fiber wired to cypress boards or with sphagnum moss around its roots. The formation of this Fern is curious because the fronds that are forked like an elk's horns are the green and fertile fronds. The reproductive spore form in masses on the underside of these fronds, usually on the tips. The sterile fronds, more round in shape grow close against the Osmunda behind the antlers, one over the other, turning from green to brown with age. This cupped section is often referred to as the shield. These sterile fronds help attach the plant to its support, and as they dry and flare at the top they receive bits of leaves and plant matter that fall from the tree above.

In time these decay and form organic food for the roots of the
Fern. The Stag-Horn is adaptable to high and low temperatures.
I hang mine out under the trees in very early spring and leave it
there until very cold weather. I soak it with water whenever the
Osmunda is dry and I give it a monthly feeding of a good liquid
fertilizer.

The FIG, *Ficus Carica* see chapter on Trees with Edible Fruit.

FITTONIAS are low herbaceous perennials that like deep
shade and warm temperatures. By pinching back the leading shoot
they may be kept squatty and full. The beauty of the foliage of this
member of the Acanthus Family lies in the colored veining on the
leaves, carmine-red veins on the dull green leaves of *Fittonia
Verschaffeltii*; bright red veining on the equally bright green
leaves of *F. Verschaffeltii Pearcei,* and white veins on the nile green
leaves of *F. argyroneura,* the Nerve Plant. Root cuttings in early
spring. Occasional feeding of soft-coal soot mixed with water will
bring out the bright markings.

Growing GERANIUMS has become a hobby with many gardeners and who could fail with anyone of the six major groups:
the Zonal, Cactus, Fancy-Leaved, Scented-Leaved, Ivy-Leaved and
Lady Washington Geraniums? In the Pelargonium Family they
like to be grown on the dry side in a mixture of ⅔ garden loam,
⅙ sharp sand and ⅙ leaf mold with 1 teaspoon bone meal to each
five-inch pot of soil. Drainage must be good and remember that
Geraniums like to be kept in as small a pot as possible in order to
bloom. Feed with a liquid fertilizer about once or twice a month.
Geraniums thrive in sun and fresh air (they are not very fond of
gas fumes) and must be placed on rocks or gravel or stands when
outdoors in summer so that they won't develop "wet feet" from
the heavy rains. They are most attractive on plant stands and in
window boxes and they may be left outdoors until very cold
weather. They are easily propagated by cuttings.

Pride of Camden, a dark velvety double red, and Pink Sensation,
a deep salmon-pink, are two lovely Zonals, *Pelargonium hortorum*

so-called because of the reddish-bronze markings on the leaves. I am particularly fond of Comtesse de Grey, a deep pink Ivy-Leaf Geranium, *P. peltatum* that sends its numerous runners down over the edge of the pot. There are many others ranging from the Dwarf Geranium, like Robin Hood, a cherry-red that reaches eight inches in a pot to one foot when planted outdoors; Miniatures, such as Fleurette that grows to ten inches potted, showing double coral flowers and greenish-brown leaves. Lady Washingtons, *Pelargonium domesticum* include Easter Greetings, a deep cerise-rose with brownish-orange markings, and Mrs. Layal, a small pansy-type that blooms early showing deep purple, rose and white markings. The Scented varieties offer the lemony *P. crispum* and the rose Geranium that I knew as a child, *P. graveolens*. The Cactus Geraniums boast of the attractive *P. echinatum* with gray-green leaves on thorny stems and white flowers streaked with rosy-red.

Another particularly satisfying low foliage plant is H O F F - M A N I A *refulgens*, of the Madder Family. Often called the Quilted Taffeta Plant it grows to about six inches in height. The leaves are silky and crinkled and heavily veined, dull green edged in magenta on the upper side, a pale wine color beneath. The small flowers are a pale red. There are other varieties and all need to be brought indoors during the winter.

I V Y is discussed under Ground Covers but I want to mention three *Hedera helix* varieties that are small and make attractive potted plants. *Cristata* or Parsley Ivy has little rounded leaves with frilled edges; *cristata* Curlilocks is even bushier and makes a full, compact pot; Weber's California is very good indoors, compact and bearing notched, wavy, medium-green leaves.

The L E M O N Tree, *Citrus Limonis* see chapter on Trees with Edible Fruit.

The M A N G O, *Mangifera indica* bears outdoors in the open ground in southern Florida and in the warmest parts of central Florida. It is also becoming popular as a tubbed plant in other parts of the deep South. I have seen some in excellent condition, heavy with fruit. Actually a large tree under free-growing conditions, it has long elliptical deep green leaves that are slightly wavy at the margins. The flowers are yellowish-red, followed by the greenish-yellow fruit, two to six inches long, that turns reddish as it matures. This evergreen, native of the Malay Archipelago grows in spurts so to speak, periodically sending up new shoots that are dull rose in infancy and green as they grow older. It likes sun and is not fussy as to the planting medium, but a rich loamy soil containing a good amount of sand has proven best. Late spring seems to be the best time to plant the Mango. Water well until established and thereafter keep moist but not over-wet; it likes to be on the dry side, especially when setting its fruit. Care must be taken when feeding time arrives. A fertilizer low in nitrogen is recommended, such as 3–10–10. Never feed the tree during the fall or winter or when the flowers are beginning to show or you will encourage sucker growth. The Mango needs pruning only when young to promote a well-formed head, which should never be allowed to grow too thick. Protect from frosts. Spraying with nicotine will keep the tree free of red spider and thrip and an oil emulsion will get rid of scale. The varieties *Haden* and *Pairi* are good and *Amini*, which produces a smaller fruit is said to be more resistant to blight. *Cambodiana* seedlings tend to have better fruiting habits. Ripening time is usually June, July and August depending on variety.

M A R A N T A *leuconeura kerchoveana* of the *Marantaceae* a native of Brazil, is known as the Prayer Plant because the leaves close up at night. It is also called Rabbit Tracks because of its coloring. A low compact grower, its oval leaves are light green, blotched on either side of the midrib with chocolate brown markings. Its small lavender and white flowers appear in racemes. There are several other attractive varieties but all thrive best in good light without direct sun. Add a little peat to the standard potting mix and allow the plant to rest in winter, trimming the older leaves and withholding some of the normal water supply. Water freely during the summer, during which season you must also feed regularly. Propagation is by cuttings and by division.

N E R I N E , see chapter on Bulbs.

N O R F O L K   I S L A N D   P I N E , *Araucaria excelsa* is most attractive as a tubbed plant in its juvenile state. Light green in color, the branches have a dignified way of spreading out horizontally and drooping slightly at the tips. It is said that plants grown from cuttings made of the leading shoot prove to have more compact growing habits and tend to mature more slowly. This little tree thrives in a loamy soil in temperatures around sixty degrees, in places where it will not be crowded. It needs plenty of light but no direct sunlight. Planting it in a tub means that it can be conveniently moved to shelter from low outdoor temperatures. *Araucaria Bidwillii*'s foliage is very sharp and pointed, thick and shiny-green. This specimen tends to be narrower than the *excelsa* in growth habits. See chapters on Evergreen, Deciduous and Flowering Trees, and Shrubs for the Landscape.

The O R A N G E   T R E E , *Citrus sinensis* see chapter on Trees with Edible Fruits.

O R C H I D culture is highly specialized and the hobbyist usually depends on publications of national and local Orchid Societies for directions on growing this prized plant.

Briefly, the Orchid is an herbaceous perennial, with the family divided into epiphytic and terrestrial varieties. The epiphytes include the well-known Cattleya, Laelia, Dendrobium, Phalaenopsis and Vanda, and are native to the tropics and sub-tropics where they grow in Osmunda fiber or in shredded bark, in pots and on trees. The Cypripedium, the Phaius from Asia, and the Calanthe from India are among the terrestrial Orchids and are usually grown in coarse mixtures of loam, chopped sphagnum and leaf mold, with the bottom of the pot well equipped with bits of broken pot and sphagnum moss to afford good drainage. Technically Orchids are greenhouse subjects but some of them will thrive outdoors almost nine months of the year. I have found that a sudden drop of temperature will very often shock them into blooming.

Try using a layer of marble or granite chips over the bark to steady the plant when you use shredded bark as a potting medium. And if you attach the Orchid to a tree pick out a host whose bark will not peel off; Live Oaks are perfect because they provide shade throughout the year and their bark is solid. Deciduous trees are not such admirable resting places because when they lose their leaves they allow direct sun to strike the Orchid.

PALMS, of the *Palmaceae* grow to great heights in their native habitats. Fortunately for us we can enjoy them in their miniature or juvenile state as potted plants. Palms are discussed in the chapter on Evergreen, Deciduous and Flowering Trees and the culture is primarily the same for the smaller plant. They should be potted during the warm months in a mixture of leaf mold, peat, builder's sand and well-rotted manure. The medium for the small potted subjects should be a little lighter and a little more porous than that used for the older and larger Palms. Always tamp the soil down well around the trunk. Water well, never allowing the Palm to dry out at the roots. Soak it thoroughly at regular intervals, even setting it down in a bucket of water for saturation.

The larger the Palm the more cold it will tolerate, hence for the young potted specimen some protection must be provided during the winter months. By the same token some, like the *Kentias* or *Howeas,* and the *Rhapis* have to be sheltered from sunburn.

FISH-TAIL PALM is *Caryota plumosa,* with solitary trunk and fronds made up of glossy green fan-shaped segments. *Caryota mitis,* or the CLUSTERED FISH-TAIL PALM is clustered in growth habits, with many suckers forming gray-green trunks. Its foliage is a dull green. These are quick-growing and prefer a warm moist atmosphere.

NEANTHE BELLA, from Guatemala is a slow-growing miniature Palm with very slender stem and graceful fronds of narrow dark green leaflets. The PARLOR PALM is *Chamaedorea elegans* a native of Mexico, a small but fast grower to six or eight feet. The trunk is thin and the pinnate leaves grow more or less in a loose spiral arrangement. The segments are broader than those of the *Neanthe bella.* This one likes shade. *Chamaedorea erumpens* from Honduras is one of the finest new palms and an excellent house plant. The new branches show broad paired segments that balance the narrower pinnate leaves at the top. It is shade-loving and will send up new shoots from the base while still quite small. It needs feeding two or three times a year.

Kentia or *Howea fosteriana,* the PARADISE PALM, and *Kentia* or *Howea Belmoreana,* the SENTRY PALM are the ones much used by florists because they welcome shade and do so well indoors. *Fosteriana's* fronds are shorter and its segments broader than *Belmoreana* whose whole effect is fuller and more graceful.

RHAPIS *humilis* has reed-like stems and semi-circular leaves. It does well in large pots or tubs and needs protection from sun. *Rhapis excelsa* or *Rhapis flabelliformis,* known as the LADY PALM is another attractive tub Palm with leaves that are deeply segmented into five to seven parts.

The PEACOCK PLANT is *Kaempferia roscoeana* of the Ginger Family, a lovely low stemless plant. Growing from a fleshy rhizome, the wide spreading leaves are iridescent, veined and zones from pale green to bronzy-brown. The underside is a grayish-lavender. Small pale lilac flowers with a white eye appear during the summer. It takes a loamy soil fortified with leaf mold, plenty of water and semi-shade.

PEPEROMIAS, of the Pepper Family are tropical and sub-tropical herbs that originate in Brazil. All adapt themselves to central heating in the house and do even better when they can be left outdoors the greater part of the year. Add a little extra peat and sand to the standard potting mix, give them sufficient light, comfortable moisture, a dose of fertilizer in the summertime and they respond beautifully. During the winter they will take full sun and less water. All through the year they appreciate occasional leaf sprayings of tap water. There are a number of varieties, and I know that *Peperomia Sandersii* the Watermelon Peperomia is familiar to all of you. The rosette of leaves is almost stemless, showing dark blue-green leaves on rosy petioles, each leaf striped by silvery bands. There are some technical differences between *P. Sandersii* and *P. arifolia* variety *argyreia;* some claim that they are one and the same.

Peperomia caperata has bushy clusters of quilted, deep green leaves streaked with gray and chocolate brown on petioles that are pink dappled in red. The slender catkins rise above the leaves and show a greenish-white. *P. glabella* is the all-green variety. *P. caperata* Little Fantasy looks well on a coffee table. Its form is similar to the cultivar Emerald Ripple but the leaves are marked a darker brown and gray. *P. prostrata* and *P. nummularifolia* are the creeping varieties with tiny round leaves. Propagation is by leaf and stem cuttings.

PHILODENDRONS, of the Arum Family come from the humid forests of Central and South America where most of them cling to trees by their aerial roots and climb to great heights. These roots also serve as a means of absorbing moisture and nourishment from the air around them. There are also some self-heading varieties that are low and show compact growth. Philodendrons make perfect house plants provided they are kept moderately moist and clean and are given sufficient light. I plant mine in a standard potting soil, give them a thorough soaking once a week and feed them once a month with a liquid fertilizer. Try mulching them with a little sphagnum moss to hold the moisture around them. The trunks of dead Tree Fern are the perfect "totem poles" for the climbing type of Philodendron, but these are not always available, so substitute with a slender roll of hardware cloth or similar wire and fill with sphagnum moss. When you water or apply liquid fertilizer, apply from the top of the pillar or cone so that the roots above the pot will be nourished. Needless to say the Philodendrons make attractive additions to the patio and small garden and will stand considerable cold. They do have to be protected from a freeze.

In the vine-type *P. hastatum* is a favorite one to train on totem poles; its leaves are arrow-shaped and a jade green. *P. oxycardium* or *cordatum* has heart-shaped foliage that is small while young and as long as twelve inches when mature. *P. verrucosum* is really an exotic member of this family with leaves that are dark bronzy-green and satiny above, a maroon color beneath.

Philodendron Evansii is a semi-self-heading variety with glossy, lobed leaves that sometimes grow as long as three feet. *P. Wend-Imbe* is a smaller, more compact semi-self-heading specimen. The true self-heading group is growing in number and the latest of the species to be introduced into this country. Some of the finest are *P. Selloum*, with leaves that are deeply notched and *P. Wendlandii*, with spatula-shaped foliage. Both are quite cold-resistant. *P. Lynette* is more compact and *P. Melinoni* is a lovely rare one.

Although Philodendrons are propagated by topping and division of the stem, they may also be grown from seeds. One plant bears staminate and pistillate flowers and the process of pollination must be carefully timed to be successful.

Monstera deliciosa, CERIMAN, also of the Arum Family is a native of southern Mexico and Guatemala. It is a stout tree climber that puts out long aerial roots along the stem and produces a large calla-like blossom that evolves into an edible fruit. The large leaves are pinnately cut and show a number of perforations, giving rise to the plant's popular name, the SWISS CHEESE PLANT. The Monstera's culture is the same as that of the Philodendron and propagation is from shoots and pieces of the stem with a few aerial roots attached. In its juvenile state when the leaves are smaller and less-perforated, the Monstera is frequently confused with *Philodendron pertusum*, whose leaf pattern is similar. See chapter on Vines.

PICK-A-BACK PLANT is *Tolmiea Menziesii*, a member of the Saxifrage Family. A North-American perennial herb that grows from one to two feet high, it is very easy to cultivate in full or half light. It needs a lot of water in summer and a cool light place in the cold months. If you have children they should be fascinated with the baby plants that form on top of the older leaves, rooting as they fall and touch the ground.

POMEGRANATE, *Punica Granatum nana* see chapters on Shrubs for the Landscape, and Flowering Shrubs.

PONY TAIL, *Nolina Beaucarnea* see Ornamentals in chapter on Shrubs for the Landscape.

A West-Indian member of the Spiderwort Family, *Rhoeo discolor* has leaves that are sometimes one foot long, dark green above and purple beneath. The small white flowers peep out in clusters between two boat-shaped bracts and there may be four to six bracts on the plant at the same time. Often called LOVE-IN-A-BOAT and MOSES-IN-THE-CRADLE, it is also known as SAILORS-IN-A-BOAT. There is a variegated form, *R. discolor vittata* whose leaves are striped with yellow-red. This attractive plant is easy to grow and will tolerate some shade. I have had *discolor* growing in the garden bed for some years but I must admit that it thrives best in a pot.

The ROSARY VINE, *Ceropegia woodii* of the Milkweed Family, is also called HEARTS-ON-A-STRING and the SWEET-HEART VINE. This plant has tiny heart-shaped leaves in a soft shade of green marked with gray. It is most attractive in a hanging pot or basket. The long trailing stems grow from small tubers and the minute flowers are very unusual. Keep it moist and give it plenty of light.

No list of potted plants is complete without the RUBBER PLANT, *Ficus elastica* of the Mulberry Family, *Moraceae*. A native of the Malayan Archipelago, it will do well in the standard potting soil and likes to have its leaves sprayed daily in the summer. It needs to be kept moist and given good light, although it will live in shaded corners. Feed in spring and summer and root cuttings in winter. *Ficus pandurata* or *lyrata*, from tropical Africa is called the FIDDLELEAF FIG because of its large fiddle-shaped leaves of leathery texture. *F. Benjamina exotica*, from Java is the WEEPING FIG, with graceful drooping branches. The new foliage of *F. decora* is dark red in the sun.

ST. BERNARD'S LILY, *Anthericum Liliago* see chapter on Ground Covers.

STRAWBERRY GERANIUM, *Saxifraga sarmentosa* see chapter on Ground Covers.

Schefflera digitata of the Aralia Family is so-called because the palmate leaves look like the five outstretched fingers of the hand. Often referred to as the UMBRELLA TREE, the new foliage is very glossy and a pale green, turning darker as it matures. This plant is one of the most satisfactory potted plants I have ever had. I have even enjoyed it in the open garden bed where it will grow much taller and I have had a small one thriving in water for the past five years. Under these last-mentioned conditions growth is very, very slow but convenient when you want a certain size plant in a particular corner. With water as a growing medium you must feed more often. On the whole *Schefflera* gives a very graceful and unusual effect.

The SCREW PINE, *Pandanus Veitchii* gets its name from the spiral arrangement of the foliage. Its leaves are about two feet long and two to three inches wide, dark green in the center, edged in white and armed with fine sharp teeth. It needs plenty of moisture and good drainage.

The SLIPPER PLANT or REDBIRD PLANT, *Pedilanthus tithymaloides variegatus* a tender member of the Euphorbia Family is so named because of its small crimson bird-like flowers. Its foliage is variegated green and white and the plant does well in full sun or semi-shade. Keep it a little on the dry side. I have often heard people refer erroneously to this plant as the Bird of Paradise. My children are always fascinated by this plant when it is in bloom;

they think the flowers look like a group of birds chattering together, and I am inclined to agree with them!

The SPIDER PLANT, *Chlorophytum elatum* of the Lily Family is ideal for hanging baskets or for pots attached to fences or walls. It grows in a rosette of leaves that are green in the center and white along the margins. Little plants develop at the end of the long scape that droops over the edge of the container, and these may be separated from the parent plant to start new specimen. The Spider Plant resembles the *Anthericum* in growth habits. See chapter on Ground Covers.

STRAWBERRY GERANIUM, *Saxifraga sarmentosa* see Ground Covers.

I have already mentioned the TRADESCANTIA in the chapter on Ground Covers as a subject for hanging baskets. This member of the Spiderwort Family also makes an attractive potted plant. There are many types and varieties, all from South and Central America. They are easy to grow in any soil and in any exposure but sunlight does bring out their deeper colors. I recently saw a charmer called White Gossamer, a sturdy-stemmed plant with crisp green leaves covered with silvery hairs. *T. navicularis* is known as the Chain Plant, its boat-shaped, succulent, paired leaves a bronzy-green above and lavender beneath. A related member of the same family from the East Indies is *Cyanotis kewensis* or the BROWN TEDDY BEAR. It bears fleshy leaves in similar formation to the *Tradescantia,* fuzzy brown above and purple beneath. It is beautiful in a hanging basket.

XANTHOSOMA *Lindenii* is a milky herb from Columbia that belongs to the Arum Family. Grown from a corm for its foliage, the green leaves of the variety *magnifica* are arrow-shaped and almost one foot long, beautifully marked along its midrib and parallel veins with silver. This plant needs warmth and moisture. Propagation is by division of the corm.

❋ 12 ❋

Annuals and Perennials

ANNUALS are plants that live and bloom from the last frost of the spring season to the first cold days of autumn. If you wish to enjoy them the following year you must sow seeds again in the fall and in the spring. Annuals are set out as seeds in open ground or in coldframes or as small plants purchased from the nursery. They mature and bloom and die in one season. Some annuals behave as perennials in sections of the South where the winters are mild, either reseeding themselves or remaining alive if the temperatures are high.

These plants must not be confused with Biennials or those that usually require two years to mature, such as the Hollyhock and Canterbury Bells. In the first season the plant makes top growth and fleshy roots and in the second year it brings forth flowers and seeds. So the next time you buy a packet of seeds and the directions tell you that the plants will not bloom the first year, you can be sure that you have a Biennial. As a class they require no different treatment than given any annual. As a matter of fact, hybridizers have made it possible for most Biennials to bloom the first year.

There are hardy annuals, that can stand frost and therefore can be planted very early and right in the open ground, semi-hardy annuals or those that must be started in flats and then set out in the open early in the spring, and tender annuals or those that must be started in glass-covered coldframes and then transplanted outdoors only after all danger of frost is over.

Many nursery catalogues are offering seeds of an "F-1 Hybrid" and for those of you who wonder what this means I hasten to explain. This is the plant breeding terminology for "first filial" generation. It actually means that a stronger-growing, more productive plant has been achieved as the result of careful pollination. The identical cross between the same parents has to be made each year to produce the seed of an F-1 Hybrid.

Soil in the open bed in which you sow your seeds must be light and friable and prepared ahead of time so that the young roots can grow down easily. When a plant needs acid or alkaline soil as a growing medium, I have so indicated when I list the annuals and perennials in later paragraphs. Depths of planting depends on the size of the seed. The rule of thumb here is to cover the seed with as much soil as its diameter. Minute seeds are just pressed into the soil and not covered. Water lightly with a fine spray of the hose or preferably with a handspray. After germination and after the seedlings have grown the two upper sets of leaves they must be thinned out to a reasonable distance apart to allow the passage of air between them as they grow in height and width.

FLATS AND COLDFRAMES

If the seeds are sown in flats in late fall and early winter and the resulting plants are very tender allow them to remain in place until all danger of frost has passed, then transfer to open ground. If seeds have been started in flats and the tiny plants can stand a fairly good amount of cold get them into the ground as early as you can and then mulch if a freeze is predicted.

My husband devised some coldframes for me some years ago and I don't know what I would do without them! They are frames built on waist-high legs, as big as the window sash that is attached to the back of the box. Mine measure 27 in. x 34 in. x 8 in. deep. The height of the box eliminates stooping and the window sash can be raised or lowered according to the weather, almost making it a miniature greenhouse. I have a set of six to give me plenty of

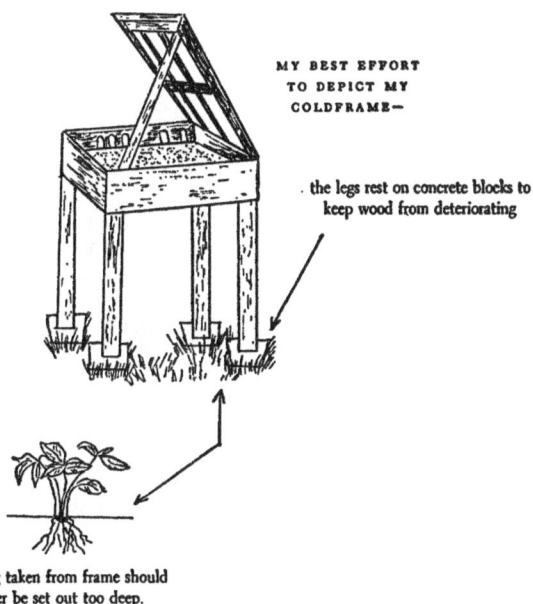

MY BEST EFFORT
TO DEPICT MY
COLDFRAME—

. the legs rest on concrete blocks to keep wood from deteriorating

seedling taken from frame should never be set out too deep.

room to raise cuttings, seedlings and lily bulblets. I have them facing different exposures.

When the coldframe is built I paint it on the inside with aluminum paint and on the outside with a green porch and deck paint. When thoroughly dry, I cover the bottom surface of the box with a good layer (¼ in.) of finely-ground charcoal to aid drainage and to keep the soil sweet. On top of the charcoal I fill the box about two-thirds full with a mixture of ⅓ peat moss, ⅓ sharp, builder's sand and ⅓ good garden loam all of which has been thoroughly turned, run through a soil strainer to make the mix fine and friable and sterilized with one of the soil fumigants.

My tools for the coldframe are also on miniature scale, to make doubly sure that I don't cut into a bulbil or ruin a seedling. After the plants are up in the frame I water them occasionally with a liquid fertilizer.

MULCHES

Those seedlings that are started in open ground or removed from coldframe to ground very early in the spring must always be protected from spring frosts and mulch for this purpose must be easily available. Pine straw, leaves, hay or grass clippings are things that you almost always have on hand. Other mulches, entailing varying degrees of expense, include bagasse, cottonseed hulls, peanut hulls, peat moss and vermiculite. Tests are being made with a black plastic mulch made of polyethylene. So far results show that use of this material tends to eliminate weeding, retains moisture in the soil, and increases soil temperatures as much as fifteen degrees. It comes in rolls long enough and wide enough to cover a garden bed and it has durability. Whatever you use, remove when danger of frost is over.

SHOCK-PROOF METHODS

Some particular plants, like the Godetia and Salpiglossus resent being moved from frame to ground, and in such cases I suggest you try the new planting cubes and fibre pots referred to in the paragraph on Eucalyptus Trees in the chapter on Evergreen, Deciduous and Flowering Trees. The cubes sold in blocks of twelve under a trade name, are fortified with nutrients and are perfect for extra-special seeds. When the seedling is large enough to transfer to pot or open ground, the little cubes can be cut from the block with a sharp knife and lowered into the ground. There is no shock to the plant at all.

One point to remember: when seeds are first planted in flats or open ground it is a good idea to shade them for the first few days, not only from sun but from being washed away by hard rains. Laying several thicknesses of newspaper over the flat or bed will do the trick. The new plastics make excellent covers. Just don't leave the cover on for too long.

In the following lists I have attempted to include the most attractive of the annuals and perennials that do well all through the South. Those that are not particularly at home in certain sections are so noted. The planting times refer only to seeds. I have designated those that are hardy and can be transferred from flat to open ground in very early spring; otherwise, transplant as soon as all danger of frost is over. I indicate which may be planted in the open (o), which should be sown in flats or coldframes (f) and which may be considered possible perennials in the lower South (pp).

ANNUALS TO BE PLANTED FROM SEED

AFRICAN DAISY, *Arctotis stoechadifolia* 1–3 feet. Full sun, summer flowering.
(f) February, March, September, October, November.
(o) April, May, September, October, November.
Variety *grandis* to 2 feet, called Blue-eyed Daisy; Dwarf Glory to six inches, orange with mahogany center; new Hybrids to 1 foot, ivory, cream, yellow, bronze and red.

AGERATUM, *Ageratum Houstonianum* 3–10 inches. Full sun or partial shade, summer and fall blooming. Sometimes called Floss Flower.
(f) September, October, November.

Panicle

Catkin

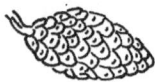
Cone

Spadix and Spathe

Raceme

Flat Head

Corymb
outer buds open first

Spike

Pair

Cone or Round Head

Cyme
center buds open first

Single

Whorl on Whorl

Umbel

TYPES OF INFLORESCENCE

Varieties Blue Ball, Blue Mink, Fairy Pink, Dwarf River and Dwarf White all good. Watch for red spider—use Aramite.

AMARANTHUS, 1–3 feet. Full sun, summer and early fall blooming in loamy soil.

(f) March, April.

(o) April, May.

Varieties *tricolor*, or Joseph's Coat, from 1–2 feet, grown for brilliant foliage in summer; Molten Fire to 3 feet, also bright, shows in early fall. Flowers of both incidental.

ANCHUSA, *Anchusa capensis* called Cape Forget-Me-Not and Blue Bird, to 2 feet. Biennial grown as annual. Full sun, heavy feeder, midsummer to frost.

(f) September, October, November.

(o) September, October, November.

Flowers are red in the bud, turning blue as they open and mature.

ASTER, *Callistephus hortensis* China or Garden Aster. Full sun, rich soil, summer and fall blooming. (pp) Not too successful in lower South.

(f) January, February, September, October, November.

All colors except yellow, 1–3 feet. Varieties offered include single, double, mum, quill, peony and pompon-shaped flowers, giant and dwarf.

BALSAM, *Impatiens Balsamina* called Patience and Sultana. Full sun, summer blooming.

(f) November, December.

(o) February, March, April, May, June, July.

Holstii Hybrids in shades of red, rose, pink, to 2 feet; variety *Sultani nana* to 10 inches. Watch for red spider—use Aramite.

BABY'S BREATH, *Gypsophila elegans grandiflora* 10–18 inches, with pink or white flowers. Full sun, alkaline soil, summer blooming.

(f) September, October, November.

(o) January, February. Thin to 12 inches apart.

Covent Garden Market Hybrids attractive.

BELLS OF IRELAND, *Moluccella laevis* to 2 feet. Full sun, spring and summer flowering. (pp)

(o) February, March, April. Thin to 12 inches apart.

An odd Syrian plant, so-called because the racemes of flowers look exactly like clusters of small bells. The several base-branching stems are filled with bell-calyxes of pale green. Within each calyx is a little white flower. The stems become so heavy with the bells that they droop over and shed seeds easily. Much in demand as a fresh green specimen or dried, in which case the stem and bells turn a lovely golden tan and brown. Leaves must be removed to dry properly. Reseeds itself.

BLANKET-FLOWER, *Gaillardia pulchella* 10–20 inches. Full sun, slightly alkaline soil, summer and fall flowering.

(f) September, October, November, December.

Flowers are now singles, doubles, frilled, quilled; range in color from white to yellow, to orange, bronze and red. Fiesta group is dull red, tipped with yellow, to 18 inches; Lorenziana Hybrids, to 18 inches, offer mixed colors.

CALENDULA, *Calendula officinalis*, Pot Marigold, 12–16 inches. Full sun, slightly alkaline soil, early spring to heat of summer blooming.

(f) September, October, November. Set out as early as possible.

(o) December, January, February. Thin to 12 inches apart.

Mostly orange and yellow, flat, ruffled and quilled petals. Heat Resistant Hybrids in lovely shades of apricot and peach; new Gerbera-like Calendulas are orange with brown centers.

CALLIOPSIS, of the Tickseed Family, often called the Golden Wave. Full sun, summer and fall flowering.

(o) March, April, May, June.

Calliopsis Drummondii from 1–2 feet. Many Coreopsis are listed in plant catalogues as Calliopsis and some say that the Golden Wave is really *Coreopsis Drummondii*. Bailey's Cyclopedia of Horticulture lists Coreopsis as including Calliopsis. Whichever, try it; a very pretty annual.

CANTERBURY BELLS, *Campanula medium*. Filtered shade, summer flowering.
(f) September, October, November.
Double and Single-flowered in blue, rose and white, to 2 feet; dwarf varieties to 18 inches; *Campanula calycanthema* is the Cup-and-Saucer Hybrid to 4 feet, in rose, lilac, blue and white. All these are Biennials treated as annuals.

CANDYTUFT, *Iberis umbellata*. Full sun, spring and summer flowering.
(f) September, October, November. Set out 8 inches apart.
(o) January, February.
Coronaria Giants to 18 inches; Dwarf mixtures include all pastel colors.

CARNATIONS, *Dianthus caryophyllus* 10–20 inches. Full sun, neutral or slightly alkaline soil, summer and fall blooming. (pp)
(f) September, October, November. Set out 12 inches apart.
Best strain is Chabaud, in pink, white, red, yellow. Varieties called Flukes are striped with one color—Orange Sherbet is a pretty one; Picotees have petals edged in another color; Bizarres have petals streaked with many colors. Blooming Carnations should have side buds taken off as they appear and side growth should be removed unless you are saving that growth for cuttings. Flowers will eventually appear on the shoots from the base of the stem. Cuttings can be taken from the lower half of a strong flower stem, using a downward motion to cut off the stem with a heel. After trimming one or two leaves and dipping in a rooting hormone, place in sharp sand and keep wet. Shade the cuttings until ready to transplant into the beds, in about a month.

CHINESE FORGET-ME-NOT, *Cynoglossum amabile* has fragrant sky-blue flowers on 18-inch bush. Full sun or partial shade, spring, summer until frost. Sometimes grown as Biennial.

(f) September, October, November.

(o) January, February, March.

Varieties Pink Firmament, to 18 inches, is mauve pink; White Firmament, a dwarf, is pure white and Amabile Pink, to 2 feet, is deep rose.

CHRYSANTHEMUM, annual

(o) February, March, April.

Doubles and Singles, tall and dwarf in all colors except blue.

CLEOME, *Cleome spinosa* 2–3 feet. Full sun and partial shade, summer blooming. Reseeds itself, so acts as a perennial.

(o) March, April, May.

The attractive ones are Pink Queen, Golden Cleome and Helen Campbell Snow Crown.

COCKSCOMB, *Celosia cristata* to 18 inches. Full sun, summer flowering.

(f) March, April.

(o) May, June.

Toreador, a red; the Gilbert Hybrids, red-gold, green-gold, maple-gold, rose-gold, have crested heads. Pampas Plume Mixture, to 2 feet, has plumy spires in all shades of red, orange and yellow. Golden Fleece most attractive. Do not use commercial fertilizers on Celosia.

COLEUS, *Coleus Blumei* to 18 inches. Full sun, plenty of water, summer blooming. (pp)

(f) February, March.

(o) April, May.

Many varieties. Her Majesty, bronze-red; Glory, creamy with peach and bronze tones; Othello, so dark it looks black; Metallicus, metallic overlay on rust-red; Candidum, old ivory margined in green.

CORNFLOWER, *Centaurea Cyanus* sometimes called Bachelor's

Button, 1–2 feet. Full sun, spring and summer flowering, slightly alkaline soil.

(o) September, October, November, December. Thin to 12 inches apart.

Red Boy, deep red; Blue Boy, bright blue; Pinkie, deep pink; Snowman, white; Dwarf Jubilee Gems to 12 inches.

C O S M O S Hybrids, 4–8 feet. Full sun, sandy acid soil, summer and fall blooming.

(f) February, March.

(o) April, May.

Radiance is rose-red, a bi-color; a new one, Mandarin, to 3 feet, is bushy with double orange flowers.

C U P F L O W E R or W H I T E C U P, *Nierembergia rivularis* sprawly plant, good for rock garden or as ground cover. Sandy soil, full sun, summer and fall blooming. (pp)

(f) February, March, April.

Nierembergia is usually a white flower with yellow throat, but there are new ones: Purple Robe to 6 inches, lavender flowered; *Coerulea* to 4 inches, lilac-blue with yellow throat.

C U P H E A, 1–3 feet. Full sun or partial shade, summer and fall flowering. (pp)

(f) February, March, April.

Sometimes called the Cigar Plant because of the shape of the flowers. Variety *ignea*'s blossoms are completely devoid of petals, the brilliant red being the calyx-tube. It is tipped with black and white. It is still listed incorrectly in catalogues as *Platycentra*. The *ignea* can be grown from cuttings. Variety *lanceolata* to 3 feet, is lavender flowered. There are others, all excellent for bedding.

D A I S Y, Swan River, *Brachycome iberidifolia* 12–18 inches. Full sun, summer blooming.

(f) February, March. Set out 4–6 inches apart.

(o) April, May.

Leaves small; flowers blue, white or pink.

DUSTY MILLER, *Senecio Cineraria* to 30 inches. Full sun, summer blooming. (pp)

(f) February, March.

(o) April.

In demand for its finely-cut white foliage.

EVERLASTINGS, Swan River, *Helipterum Manglesii* 8–16 inches. Full sun, summer blooming.

(f) February, March.

(o) April, May.

Pink or white flowers, foliage grayish. *H. Humboldtianum* has yellow blossoms; *H. roseum* has white or deep pink flowers. All dry well.

GLOBE-AMARANTH, *Gomphrena globosa* 12–18 inches. Full sun, summer flowering.

(f) March. Set out 6–8 inches apart.

(o) April, May, June.

Flower heads resemble clover, one to a stem. Gomphrena *globosa* mixed, to 18 inches. New Dwarf Gomphrena, to 6 inches includes Buddy, a purple; Cissy, pure white.

GLORIOSA DAISY, *Rudbeckia tetraploid* to 3 feet. Full sun, summer blooming. (pp)

(o) February, March.

Large golden flowers with mahogany centers. Var. Goldflame is dwarf to 12 inches with yellow flowers centered in red.

GODETIA, *Godetia grandiflora* 8–24 inches. Full sun or partial shade, summer blooming. Sometimes called Satin Flower.

(f) September, October, November. Set out as early as possible.

(o) February, March.

Flowers are single and double; colors are blue, red, salmon, white, maroon and lavender. Order by color. Var. *amoena*, lilac-rose to 2 feet, sometimes known as Farewell-to-Spring.

HELIOTROPE, *Heliotropium curassavicum*, *H. tenellum* and *H. indicum* 2–4 feet. Full sun or partial shade, summer flowering and more successful in upper South. (pp)

(f) January, February, March.
Blue Bonnet, deep blue; First Snow, pure white, both deliciously scented.

H O L L Y H O C K , *Althaea rosea* 5–10 feet. Full sun, summer and fall flowering. Biennial.
(f) September, October, November. Fussy about being transplanted.
(o) February, March. Needs staking. Thin to 18 inches apart.
Complete mixture of white, pink, rose, red, purple, yellow. Indian Summer and Indian Spring have full double flowers. Triumph Supreme's blossoms have fringed and rippled petals. New Hungarian *Rosea Annua* is dwarf to 4 feet.

I M M O R T E L L E S , *Xeranthemum annuum* 2–3 feet. Full sun, summer blooming.
(o) March, April, May.
Flowers pink, white and purple; foliage is white and fuzzy. Cut flowers before fully open if you wish to dry them for winter bouquets.

L A R K S P U R , *Delphinium* Hybrids 3–6 feet. Full sun or partial shade, spring and summer flowering, slight alkaline soil. (pp)
(o) September, October, November, December. Thin 10–12 inches apart.
Pacific Hybrids, lavender, violet and blue; Imperial Hybrids, all colors except yellow; Hyacinth types have blossoms in pyramids instead of spikes; Regal and Supreme Strains lovely.

L I N A R I A , *Linaria maroccana* sometimes listed in catalogues as Miniature Snapdragons, 10–36 inches. Semi-shade, summer flowering. More successful in upper South.
(o) February, March, April.
All colors, bright and pastel. Northern Lights to 15 inches, brilliant; Macedonia *speciosa* to 3 feet, yellow and orange; *Alpina* to 6 inches, lavender.

LION'S EAR or LION'S TAIL, *Leonotis Leonurus* to 3 feet. Full sun or partial shade, summer flowering. (pp)
(f) February, March.
(o) April.
Bears dense heads of orange tubular flowers. The corolla's upper tip arches over and curves downward. The long calyxes are also curved and stiff. These queer blooms dry beautifully and keep their color.

LOBELIA, *Lobelia Erinus* or the Edging Lobelia, 3–6 inches in sprawly habits. Full sun, summer flowering. Not too successful in lower South.
(f) January, February, March.
Many named varieties, with blue the prevailing color.

LOVE-APPLE, *Solanum aculeatissimum* 1–2 feet. Full sun, summer and fall blooming. (pp)
(f) February, March.
(o) April, May.
Spiny stems bearing berries larger than cherries, of a brilliant orange. The skin on the berries turns papery as it dries, but the bright color remains, making the Love-Apple a choice piece for dried arrangements. The apples are just loaded with seed.

LUPINE, annual, 10–18 inches. Full sun or partial shade, summer blooming. More successful in upper South.
(o) February, March, April.
All colors but not as tall nor as showy as the perennial Lupines.

MARIGOLD, *Tagetes erecta* or African Marigold, 2–4 feet. Full sun, summer and fall blooming, solitary, highly-scented, yellow or orange flower head on tall stems; foliage finely cut.
(o) March, April, May. Thin to 15 inches apart.
New extra-large double flowering variety, Cracker Jack Gigantea has 5–6 inch dahlia-like flowers of yellow or orange; new Climax Marigolds, a Giant F1 Hybrid, in orange and yellow; Golden Trumpet, with bell-shaped petals, are all attractive. Chrysanthemum-flowered or Mammoth Mums have incurved petals; Minia-

ture Africans are scentless, to 6 inches. The French Marigolds, *Tagetes patula*, to 12 inches, do best in acid soil and include reds, yellows and shades of orange. Fine for borders.

M A R T Y N I A , *Martynia louisiana Proboscidea Jussieui* or the Proboscis Flower, 1–2 feet. Full sun, summer flowering.

(f) February, March.

Martynia is the old generic name that is still used in seed catalogues for the Unicorn Plant. This specimen holds the beauty and the beast at the same time—lovely little orchid-like, pale yellowish-pink flowers, with throats dotted with purple, rise above a Devil's Claw of a seed pod! The leaves are heart-shaped, rather damp most of the time and covered, as are the young seed pods with a fuzz even heavier than that found on okra pods. As a matter of fact the seed pods in their infancy look like okra pods, then the point elongates and curls slightly. Finally as it dries the outer fuzzy covering sloughs off, leaving a dried black pod. The elongated point splits lengthwise forming two horns, hence the name Devil's Claw. Flower and pod show on the plant at the same time.

Because I use the dried Devil's Claw pods in plaque-making I decided to try to grow this plant in my garden. The seeds are as black and queer looking as the dried pod. The seed packet recommended Martynia as a border plant but I found that it really grows too high for that. Let me say that it would be better placed just behind the border. I discovered that the flowers are covered with the thickest, stickiest substance that I have yet to encounter on a flower. Evidently the bees are afraid to be trapped on this natural fly-paper because I had to get down on my knees to pollinate the flowers by hand. But it was worth all the trouble. It was fascinating to see the lovely flowers, bright green fuzzy young pods and the weird black claws on the plant at the same time. And besides I reaped a nice harvest of dried material for plaque-making!

Actually this plant belongs to a genus of herbs grown for the curious seed pods that were used while young, in days gone by, as pickles.

MEXICAN TULIP-POPPY or GOLDEN CUP, *Hunnemannia fumariaefolia* 10–20 inches. Full sun, summer and fall flowering. (pp)
(o) March, April, May.
Three-inch yellow flowers and blue-green foliage.

MORNING-GLORY, Bush, *Convolvulus tricolor* 6–12 inches. Full sun, summer blooming.
(o) March, April, May.
Blue flower that remains open all day. Var. *vittatus* is blue and white striped. Royal Ensign, a royal blue, and Rose reach 12 inches. Var. *compactus* is dwarf.

NASTURTIUMS, *Tropaeolum* hybrids have two forms: the climbing variety, to 6 feet, which needs support and the low bush varieties, to 20 inches, that include the Dwarf Gems. Full sun or semi-shade, spring and summer flowering. Will not stand much frost, but bloom best before summer gets too hot.
(o) October, November, December. Protect from frost. Thin to 6 inches apart.
Colors range from ivory to yellow, orange, salmon, rose, red and mahogany. All Gleam varieties good.

NICOTIANA, *Nicotiana alata grandiflora* 3–4 feet. Full sun, summer and fall blooming. (pp)
(f) February, March, April. Set out 2–3 feet apart.
Long green leaves, star-shaped fragrant flowers. Daylight is white; Crimson Bedder is red and dwarf; Grandiflora Hybrids are rose, pink, cream and white.

PAINTED TONGUE, *Salpiglossis sinuata* 1–3 feet. Full sun or semi-shade, summer and fall flowering.
(f) February. Resents being transplanted, so transfer tenderly, or use planting cubes.
(o) March, April.
Gloxinia-flowered Emperor Variety offers these blossoms in colors ranging from white to purple.

PANSY, *Viola tricolor hortensis* 4–8 inches. Full sun, late winter and early spring-flowering, until hot weather.

(f) September, October, November.

Set out plants purchased from nursery in November, December, January; 6 inches apart. Roggli and Canadian Giant good ones.

PETUNIA, *Petunia* hybrids, 12–15 inches. Full sun, spring and summer flowering.

(f) September, October, November.

(o) March, April. Thin to 8–10 inches apart.

Erect single and double types that include ruffled petals, such as Celestine Rose, Commanche Red, Glamour, Snowstorm, Royalty; fringed ones, such as Fire Dance; the Miniatures 6–8 inches, for edging, Allegro and Sonata; Balcony Petunias of many colors; and the Dwarfs. The new F1 Hybrids are Multiflora Sugar Plum, a luscious magenta; Grandifloras Blue Lace and Maytime are delightful.

PERIWINKLE, Madagascar, *Vinca rosea* 10–18 inches. Full sun or semi-shade, summer blooming. (pp)

(f) February, March.

(o) April, May.

Variety Twinkles is blush-pink with red eye; Purity is white; *Kermesina* is red; Little Pinkie or Coquette is 10-inch dwarf.

PHLOX, annual, *Phlox Drummondii* 12–24 inches. Full sun, summer flowering.

(f) September, October, November.

(o) February, March, April.

All colors but yellow, from Gigantea mixtures to dwarf bush varieties. Star Twinkle Phlox grows from six to eight inches in height, making a perfect edging or bedding plant, with compact growing habit. The flowers look like tiny pointed stars of white combined with pink, salmon, rose, red, lavender and purple. I find it more successful to plant this dwarf in open ground in early spring. There is no need to thin out the young plants. They do better when left entirely alone.

P I N K S , *Dianthus* 8–20 inches. Full sun, summer blooming. (pp)
(f) September, October, November.
(o) February, March.
China Pink is *Dianthus chinensis* 12–18 inches. Grass Pink is *Dianthus plumarius* whose new collection of colors is called Winteri, to 9 inches.

P O P P Y , California, *Eschscholtzia californica* 10–24 inches. Full sun, spring and summer flowering. (pp)
(o) January, February, September, October, November. Thin 8–10 inches apart but do not transplant. Bluish-green foliage; deep orange, yellow, white, rose and red flowers.

P O R T U L A C A or Moss Rose, *Portulaca grandiflora* to 6 inches. Full sun, summer blooming.
(f) March, April.
(o) May, June. Whenever possible, use this method of planting; easier and quicker.
This prostrate-growing plant has thick foliage and showy flowers that open only in sunshine. Single-flowered varieties and named varieties include *alba, aurea,* salmon, *coccinea* and *rosea.* Double rose-flowered include Grandiflora mixture of all colors.

Q U E E N A N N E ' S L A C E , *Daucus Carota* 1–2 feet. Full sun or filtered shade, summer flowering. Sometimes treated as Biennial.
(o) March, April, May.
Umbels of white flowers on slender stems.

S A G E , *Salvia* 1–2 feet. Full sun, summer and fall blooming. (pp)
(f) February, March, April.
(o) May, June.
Blue Sage is *Salvia azurea* and its hybrid, *S. grandiflora;* Red Sage is *Salvia splendens;* Gentian-blue Sage is *Salvia patens;* Mealy Cup or Violet-blue Sage is *Salvia farinacea.*

SCABIOSA, *scabiosa atropurpurea* or Mourning Bride. Full sun, slightly alkaline soil, summer blooming.
(f) February, March.
(o) April, May.
Imperial Hybrids to 4 feet; Azure Fairy, blue, to 3 feet; Black Knight, a dark red and Peach Blossom also to 3 feet. Dwarf mixed colors to 18 inches.

SNAPDRAGONS, *Antirhinum* hybrids 12–20 inches. Full sun, summer and fall blooming. (pp)
(f) September, October, November. Transfer early to open ground.
(o) September, October, November. Thin 12–18 inches apart. Pinch and stake.
Doubles include Crimson, Deep Gold, Snowdrift. Giants feature Copper Queen and Paradise Rose. Giant Tetra Snaps offer all colors with ruffled petals.

STRAWFLOWERS, *Helichrysum bracteatum* 12–30 inches. Full sun, summer flowering.
(f) October, November, December.
All colors except blue available in tall and dwarf varieties. Widely used as dried flowers.

STOCK, Night-scented, *Mathiola bicornis* to 10 inches. Full sun, summer blooming.
(f) September, October, November. Set out 6 inches apart.
Bushy plant with scattered bluish-purplish-brown flowers opening at dusk. No varieties. Very fragrant.

STOCK, Ten Weeks, *Mathiola incana annua* 1–2 feet. Full sun, summer blooming. (pp)
(f) September, October, November. Set out 12 inches apart.
All colors—the whites, magentas, purples and pinks are lovely. Trysomic Seven Week Blend most successful—lower than others.

SUMMER CYPRESS, *Kochia scoparia trichophila* called the Burning Bush, 2–3 feet. Full sun, loamy soil, plenty of water, summer and fall flowering.

(f) March, April. Set out 15–20 inches apart.
Grown chiefly for its red or yellow foliage.

S U N F L O W E R , *Helianthus annuus* 8–12 feet. Full sun, summer and fall blooming.
(o) March, April, May.
The familiar Sunflower is nearly all yellow, tolerates heat and turns with the sun. New hybrids offer white, red and yellow. Excelsior Hybrids, to 5 feet, in red, bronze and brown shades. Dwarf Chysanthemum-flowered to 4 feet.

S W E E T   A L Y S S U M , *Alyssum maritimum* 6–8 inches. Full sun, very early spring and summer flowering. Becomes straggly with advent of extreme heat. (pp)
(f) September, October, November. Set out 4–6 inches apart.
(o) September, October, November.
Fine varieties are Violet Queen, Carpet of Snow, Little Gem, Royal Carpet and Tetraploid Violet.

S W E E T   P E A , *Lathyrus odoratus* 4–6 feet. Full sun, winter and spring blooming. Must be supported.
(o) September, October, November.
Turn earth well in advance of planting your seeds, adding about one pound of lime (slaked) to a 25-foot row. Add enough humus or well-rotted manure to make soil retentive. See that your frame or trellis on which your Sweet Peas are to climb is in good shape. Soak your seeds overnight prior to planting and roll them in dust or sand to fascilitate planting. Plant them in a trench about four inches deep and cover lightly, filling the trench gradually to ground level as the small plant grows upward. Feed alternately with liquid fertilizer and wood ashes during the growing period. Protect from extreme cold.

The first Sweet Peas were supposed to have been brought over from Sicily to England in the early eighteenth century. Now, due to hybridization there are the Early-Flowering Spencers; Giants; Cuthbertsons, that will stand heat; *Multifloras* that have 5–7 flowers to each stem. These *Multifloras*, though they begin to flower about a week after the Spencers, are almost replacing the Spencers because of their hardiness, their long stems (some to 16 inches) and the beauty of the florets. The Cuthbertsons are intermediates and bloom longer into warm weather. The little dwarf bush-types, Little Sweetheart and Heidi are perfect to use in front of your regular stand of Sweet Peas. They grow to about a foot in height and fill the usually thin and spindly bottom of the "Grown-Up" Sweet Peas. All are fragrant and come in all colors except yellow.

SWEET WILLIAM, *Dianthus barbatus* 12–18 inches. Full sun, spring, summer and fall flowering. Sometimes grown as a Biennial.
(f) September, October, November.
Singles and Doubles in white, pink, blue, lavender and salmon. Wee Willie is a red and white single dwarf to 4 inches; Indian Carpet, to 5 inches, is white with red and pink eyed zones.

TASSELFLOWER, formerly *Cacalia* and now known as *Emilia flammea* or *Emilia sagittata* is often commonly called Flora's Paintbrush. Full sun or partial shade, blooms from summer until frost. 1–2 feet high.
(f) January, February.
(o) March, April, May.
Long stems bear flowers that look exactly like little paint brushes in dark red, deep orange or pink. I grew the orange colored ones and enjoyed them immensely, the blossoms are so different.

TITHONIA, Mexican Sunflower, to 10 feet. Full sun, summer blooming, sometimes difficult to grow in the lower South, the flower stems tend to be weak.
(o) March, April, May.
Variety *speciosa*, an orange-red, to 10 feet; Tithonia Torch reaches 4 feet.

TORENIA, *Torenia Fournieri* 8–12 inches. Full sun or semi-shade, summer blooming. (pp)
(f) February, March.

(o) April, May, June.
Color usually blue with yellow throat. Variety *alba* is white with gold throat.

ZINNIA, *Zinnia* hybrids, to 4 feet. Full sun, midsummer to frost.
(o) March, April, May and June.
All colors but blue. California Giants, 3–4 feet, with five-inch flowers in soft colors; Polka Zinnias with big striped blooms; Tetraploid Strain, in rose shades and six-inch flowers, to 3 feet; Giant Cactus-flowered group in named colors, to 30 inches; Mammoth Dahlia Type offers Peppermint Stick; Wildfire of the Fantasy Type is a brilliant one. Lilliputs, to 1 foot, is button-flowered; Tom Thumb Gem is a Baby Type and very dwarf, from 4–6 inches. Cupid Type, to 10 inches, is also button-flowered and "Cut and Come Again" variety, 18–24 inches, is fine for cutting.

Below is a short list of ANNUAL VINES. For further information on these and other vines, see chapter on VINES.

BALSAM APPLE, *Momordica Balsamina* 4–8 feet. Full sun, summer blooming.
(o) March, April, May. Thin to 2 feet apart.
Creamy-white flowers followed by queerly-shaped fruit that turns orange and bumpy.

CANARY-BIRD VINE, *Tropaeolum peregrinum* 12–15 feet. Full sun, summer blooming.
(o) March, April, May.
Spur-bearing yellow flowers; quick-growing.

CYPRESS VINE, *Quamoclit pinnata* 10–15 feet. Full sun, summer flowering. (pp)
(f) February, March.
(o) April, May, June.
Feathery foliage, small orange-red trumpet-shaped flowers. Variety *alba* is white.

MOONFLOWER, *Calonyction aculeatum* 10–30 feet. Full sun, summer until frost. (pp)
(o) March, April, May, June. Thin to 4 feet apart.
Night-blooming fragrant white flowers; member of the Morning-Glory Family.

MORNING-GLORY, *Ipomoea purpurea* to 25 feet. Full sun, summer and fall blooming.
(o) March, April, May, June. Soak seeds overnight before planting. Purple flowers open in the morning and close before the hottest part of the day.

WOODROSE, *Ipomoea tuberosa* to 15 feet. Full sun, late summer and autumn blooming. (pp)
(f) March, April, May.
Yellow-flowered. This one will grow here but will rarely hold its few blooms long enough to dry to the lovely wood roses. In Hawaii it behaves as a perennial and climbs rampantly, producing the blooms and later the roses.

PERENNIALS

It has been said that "Perennials are the encouragement of the beginner and the mainstay of the professional". They are herbaceous plants that live more than two years, with stems that die down each year but with roots that live on to send up new growth the next season. They may be grown from seed, or propagated by division of roots and by cuttings. Learn the growth habits of your perennials, so that you can place the tallest to the back of the bed, the mediums behind the lower border plants.

In order to keep perennials in good shape, they must be divided regularly. This is done in spring or fall depending on the plant's blooming habits. Perennials that bloom in the fall, such as Chrysanthemums and Physostegias should be separated in the spring, usually no later than May. Those flowering in early spring and summer are best divided in September and October so that roots may grow and become established before winter sets in. Keep your perennials tidy by cutting down all browned stems and leaves and by weeding around them.

A N C H U S A , *Anchusa azurea* to 3 feet. Full sun, summer and fall blooming.
(f) September, October, November.
(o) September, October, November.
Available in all shades of blue and in dwarf forms.

A R T E M I S I A , *Artemisia albula* the Silver King, to 3 feet. Needs sun to keep white, spring and summer flowering.
(f) September, October, November. Divide in following fall.
Finely cut silvery-white foliage on upright stems; blossoms inconspicuous; neat habit of growth.

A S P A R A G U S F E R N , *Asparagus plumosus*. Filtered shade, summer blooming.
(f) September, October.
(o) February, March.
Graceful drooping fronds; tiny flowers followed by greenish-purple berries in late summer and autumn.

A S P A R A G U S F E R N , *Asparagus Sprengeri*. Filtered shade, summer blooming.
(f) February, March.
(o) October, November.
Whitish-pink flowers followered by coral-red berries in fall. The small tubers that appear at the base of the plant are actually reservoirs of water.

A S T E R , Perennial or Michaelmas Daisies, 1–5 feet. Full sun, rich soil, late summer to frost. More successful in upper South.
(f) January, February, September, October, November.
All colors except yellow. Monarch Strain, to 3 feet, includes many

shades from white to purple; *Novi belgii* Hybrids, 2–3 feet; *Alpinus* Goliath, a good blue, to 1 foot. Many other varieties.

BABY'S BREATH, *Gypsophila paniculata* to 2 feet. Full sun, alkaline soil, summer flowering.

(f) September, October, November.

(o) January, February.

Crimson and Rose Cloud are two pretty pinks to 18 inches; White Queen, to 2 feet; *Gypsophila repens*, a dwarf pink and white, to 6 inches.

BEGONIA, Rex Hybrids, from 6 to 12 or more inches. Partial shade, summer blooming. These are perennial if protected in winter.

(f) December, January, February.

Grown chiefly for decorative foliage. *Picta* has green leaves spotted in white; *rubro-venia*, round leaves, tiny pink flowers.

The large leaf Rex Begonia is rhizomatous, so are the Beefsteak Begonias, *B. Feastii* and the small leaf Rex types. The one called Angel Wing, *Lucerna Begonia* is fibrous-rooted. The little wax plants called Carmen, with reddish-black foliage, and Pink Pearl, with green leaves, are *Begonia semperflorens*. The attractive ground cover that is commonly called Watermelon Begonia is actually *Peperomia Sandersii*.

BELLFLOWER, *Campanula* to 3 feet. Full sun or partial shade, sandy soil, summer blooming.

(f) September, October, November.

Variety *persicifolia* or Peach Bells, mostly blue or white, 2–3 feet; variety *Portenschlagiana*, lavender-blue, 6–10 inches; *carpatica*, blue or white, 8–14 inches.

BLANKET-FLOWER, *Gaillardia aristata* 2–4 feet. Full sun, summer flowering, slightly alkaline soil that needs manure incorporated into it in the spring.

(f) September, October, November, December.

Colors range from yellow and orange to red, maroon and copper.

Tangerine is pretty. Monarch Strain to 30 inches; Goblin, yellow and red, is dwarf.

CANDYTUFT, *Iberis sempervirens* 10–12 inches. Full sun, spring and summer blooming.

(f) September, October, November. Set out 8 inches apart.

(o) January, February.

Color predominantly white, but Queen of Italy is lavender; Jucunda, a dwarf, is pink.

CARDINAL-FLOWER, *Lobelia cardinalis* sometimes called Red Birds and Indian Pink. 2–3 feet tall. Semi-shade, plenty of moisture, summer and autumn flowering. Not too successful in lower South.

(f) February, March, September.

Bright red flowers in spikes; toothed leaves.

CHRYSANTHEMUM, *Chrysanthemum* hybrids, an enormous family of tall, medium and dwarf specimen. A plant I love, but cannot keep it in my garden because I am allergic to it. Full sun and partial shade, fall blooming.

(f) February, March, April. Cut stems after blooming; divide clumps in spring, no later than May. Leaves can be kept green on lower stem by mulching roots well.

There are large hardy Singles and Doubles, Korean Hybrids, Pompons, Spoons, Quills, Cushions, Cascades and many others.

COLUMBINE, *Aquilegia chrysantha* the spurred beauties, 3–4 feet. Partial shade, summer blooming, not recommended for lower South.

(f) April, May, September, October. Plants purchased from nursery may be set out in April and October.

Variety *chrysantha* is yellow streaked with a lovely claret color; *Aquilegia caerulea* is blue, to 18 inches; *longissima*, to 3 feet, is pale yellow.

CONEFLOWER, *Rudbeckia speciosa* 2–4 feet. Full sun, summer flowering.

(o) February, March, April.

Center of flower rises like a cone and petals curve backwards. Variety *hirta* is yellow with black centers, hence called "Black-Eyed Susan". *Triloba*, a Biennial, is yellow with orange centers.

COREOPSIS, *Coreopsis grandiflora* or Tickseed, 1–2 feet. Full sun, summer blooming, not too successful in lower South.

(f) September, October, November, December.

Color usually yellow, but variety *rosea* is a nice pink.

DAHLIA, *Dahlia* Hybrids from 2–6 feet depending on variety. Full sun, summer and autumn flowering.

(f) March, April, May. Growing from seed not nearly as satisfactory as from tubers. Dahlias are tender perennials and so must be dug and stored in winter. See chapter on Bulbs for types of Dahlias.

DAISY, *Chrysanthemum Leucanthemum* sometimes called Ox-Eye Daisy, 1–2 feet. Full sun, summer flowering.

(f) February, March.

(o) April.

Divide established clumps not later than November.

DAISY, English, *Bellis perennis* 6–12 inches. Full sun, spring and summer blooming.

(f) September, October, November. Divide established plants in fall, not later than November.

This is the Daisy of history, predominantly white-petalled with yellow center; leaves basal.

DELPHINIUM, 6–8 feet. Full sun or partial shade, spring and summer blooming.

(f) September, October, November, December.

(o) February, March.

Giant Pacific Hybrids are lovely; Astolot Series includes flowers that range from blush-pink to raspberry-rose to fawn, taupe and brown, all with black "bees" or eyes. Round Table Series includes all colors with white bees; Percival Series is white with black bee.

Delphinium needs more nitrogen than most flowers. Fertilize in late winter and again when stems begin to shoot upwards.

EVERLASTING, PEARLY, *Anaphalis margaritacea* 18–36 inches. Filtered shade, summer blooming. Seeds not easily obtained. These must be lifted in spring as plants from the woods or given from hand to hand.

Flowers are pearly white and resemble buttons, foliage is a grayish-tan. They dry well.

EVERLASTING, WINGED, *Ammobium alatum grandiflorum* 12–18 inches. Full sun, summer flowering.
(f) February, March.
Yellow flower heads surrounded by white bracts. For drying, cut flowers before heads are fully open.

FEVERFEW, *Chrysanthemum Parthenium* 2–3 feet. Full sun, summer and autumn blooming. Some catalogues list this as *Matricaria*.
(f) January, February, March.
(o) April.
Capensis is white, to 2 feet. Ball is a double and the Tom Thumb Group, to 8 inches, includes yellow, cream and white buttons.

FORGET-ME-NOT, *Myosotis scorpioides* of sprawly habits. Partial shade, spring and summer flowering.
(f) September, October, November.
Alpestris alba, white to 1 foot; *Alpestris* Blue Eyes and *Rosea* are good. Cobalt Blue has a yellow eye.

FOUR O'CLOCK, Bush, *Mirabilis Jalapa* 2–3 feet. Full sun or partial shade, summer until frost. Perennial in the South.
(o) February, March, April, May, June, July.
Colors are white, lavender, red and yellow.

FOXGLOVE, *Digitalis purpurea* to 6 feet. Full sun, summer flowering. Sometimes Biennial.
(f) September, October, November.

Usually lavender with darker veining. Horizontal Excelsior Hybrids, all colors, to 5 feet; Giant Rusty Foxglove, rusty-red, to 6 feet.

GERANIUM, *Pelargonium* hybrids 12–18 inches. Full sun, spring until frost.
(f) January, February, March.
Flowers usually white, pink and rose, and various shades of each. The Double Hybrids are interesting; of the *Grandiflorum Hybridum*, the Martha Washington is one of the best. Ivy Leaf Geranium has trailing habits; the Scented Geraniums are very fragrant of rose, apple, nutmeg, etc.

GERBERA, *Gerbera Jamesonii* the Transvaal Daisy and often called African Daisy. 1–2 feet. Full sun, spring, summer and fall blooming.
(f) September, October, November. Divide established clumps after autumn flowering. Lovely hybrids of white, peach, pink, orange, red, yellow.

GLOBE THISTLE, *Echinops Ritro* 2–4 feet. Full sun, summer and fall blooming.
(f) February, March, April.
Segmented fuzzy leaves and spiny blue flower-heads. Variety Taplow Blue is a sultry, smoky shade.

GOLDEN GLOW, *Rudbeckia laciniata hortensis* 6–8 feet. Full sun, summer to fall flowering.
(o) February, March, April. Divide established plants in autumn or early spring.
Tall stems, golden-yellow flowers. Golden Ball a good variety. Control red spider with Aramite.

HELIOTROPE, Garden, *Valeriana officinalis* 2–5 feet. Full sun, summer blooming.
(f) January, February, March, September, October, November, December.
Very fragrant white, pink or lavender flowers. No varieties.

JOE-PYE-WEED, *Eupatorium purpureum* to 8 feet. Full sun or semi-shade, late summer and early fall blooming.

(f) February, March.

(o) April, May.

Deep rose flowers; a rank grower that must be controlled by division. Named after an Indian doctor, Joe-Pye, who used it for medicine in the early days.

LUPINE, perennial, *Lupinus* hybrids, to 3 feet. Full sun or partial shade, summer blooming. Not too successful in lower South.

(o) February, March, April.

Russell Hybrids most attractive; Chandelier, a yellow and Noble-maiden, a white, both grow to 3 feet.

MARGUERITE, GOLDEN, *Anthemis tinctoria* also called Yellow Chamomile, 12–24 inches. Full sun, summer flowering.

(f) March, April, September, October.

Daisy-like yellow blossoms. Variety *nobilis*, to 1 foot, has white flowers.

MARGUERITE, *Chrysanthemum frutescens* or the Paris Daisy, to 3 feet. Full sun, winter and early spring flowering.

(f) February, March.

(o) April, May. Divide established plants no later than June.

This is the Marguerite so popular with florists.

PAINTED DAISY, *Chrysanthemum coccineum* also called Pyrethrum, 1–3 feet. Full sun or partial shade, summer flowering.

(f) February, March.

(o) April, May.

All colors except yellow and blue. Singles and Doubles in white, red, rose and pink.

PHLOX, perennial, *Phlox paniculata* 18–36 inches, sometimes to 4 feet. Full sun or partial shade, summer into fall flowering.

(f) February, March, September, October, November.

Mixed new hybrids in all colors but yellow. Most popular are blossoms of deep pink to purple, borne in terminal clusters on sturdy stems. Divide by lifting clumps, separating, and resetting individual plants. Do this in early spring and space your plants far enough apart to prevent mildew. Those new plants that come up from self-sown seeds rarely come true to the parent plant. Rout red spider with Aramite.

Phlox divaricata or Wild Sweet William, is a lavender phlox from 12–20 inches high.

Phlox subulata or Moss-Pink, also called Ground-Pink is a low perennial that forms a mat about 5 inches high and is evergreen. Flowers shade from white to pink to magenta, and bloom in spring and summer. *Phlox suffruticosa* prostrate to 3 inches, shows early summer blooms of purple, pink and white. It needs full sun.

PHYSOSTEGIA, *Physostegia virginiana* or False Dragonhead, is also known as *Dracocephalum virginianum*. 3–6 feet. Full sun or semi-shade, late summer and fall blooming.

(f) September, October, November. Separate established clumps in spring.

This is a good background plant; needs staking. The variety *virginiana* produces lavender flowers, but there are pink and rose forms, like *Gigantea*, to 6 feet, and *alba*, a white to 4 feet. These are also offered in dwarf sizes. Leaves of all are dark green and slenderly oblong.

POPPY, Oriental, *Papaver orientale* 2–3 feet. Full sun, spring and summer blooming.

(o) September, October, November, December. Divide established plants after flowering, in August when dormant or cut roots into short pieces during the summer, replanting immediately. This type Poppy not too successful in lower South.

Queen Alexandra is rosy-salmon; Toreador is red; Enchantress, lavender; Indian Chief, mahogany.

SAGE, blue, *Salvia pitcheri* to 4 feet. Full sun, late summer flowering.

(f) February, March, April.

(o) May, June.
Bushy plant; gray fuzz on foliage; blue flowers in terminal clusters. No varieties.

SAGE, garden, *Salvia officinalis* 1–2 feet. Full sun, summer blooming.
(f) February, March, April.
(o) May, June.
Foliage silvery-white and very fragrant; blue or white flowers in clusters.

SCABIOSA, hardy, *Scabiosa caucasica* to 30 inches. Full sun, summer and fall blooming.
(f) February, March.
(o) April, May.
Fringed and ruffled doubles, predominantly blue and white.

SEDUM, 2–20 inches. Full sun, poor soil of clay content.
(f) October, November.
(o) March, April.
Sedum acre, called Wall Pepper, is a yellow-flowered ground cover, 2–4 inches high, that blooms in summer. *Sedum spectabile*, or Stonecrop flowers in late summer and fall; Brilliant, a pink and *Carneum*, red, grow from 12–20 inches. *Sedum sieboldi*, from 8–12 inches, has gray-green foliage and pink flowers that show in the autumn.

SHASTA DAISY, *Chrysanthemum maximum* 15–25 inches. Full sun, summer flowering.
(f) September, October, November. Must be replanted every second or third year.
White-petalled with yellow center. Giant Single and Alaska are singles; Marconi is double and fringed; White Swan is fully double.

STATICE or THRIFT, *Armeria maritima* sometimes called Sea Pink, is considered best of the Everlastings. Full sun, sandy soil, summer flowering.
(o) March, April, May. Mulch over winter.

Small clusters of straw-like pink, white and lavender flowers rise on short stem from rosette of evergreen leaves. Variety *Laucheana* rose, to 6 inches; *alpina* is also rose colored, to 3 inches; Glory of Holland, a pink, reaches 15–20 inches.

STOKESIA, *Stokesia laevis* or Stokes Aster 10–24 inches. Full sun, late summer blooming.

(f) September, October, November, December.

Stems are hairy and a dull lavender in color; leaves are lance-shaped and large. Flowers of bluish-lavender are either solitary or clustered, each about 3 inches wide. There are pink and white varieties.

SUNFLOWER, *Helianthus decapetalus* variety *multiflorus*. Sometimes called the Wild or Twin-leaf Sunflower. 3–6 feet. Full sun, moist soil, summer and fall blooming.

(o) March, April, May.

Varieties *flore-pleno* and *grandiflorus* good doubles; Soleil d'Or looks like a dahlia with quilled florets.

SWEET PEA, Perennial, *Lathyrus latifolius*. Can be supported to 6 feet or used as a prostrate, sprawling plant. Sun or shade, summer blooming. Flowers are predominantly red, pink and white. This plant must be kept within bounds to be enjoyed.

(o) February, March, April. May also be propagated by division of roots in the fall.

TEXAS BLUE BONNET, *Lupinus subcarnosus* 6–12 inches. Full sun or partial shade, spring and summer flowering. Thrives best in upper South.

(o) January, February, March, April, October, November, December.

Flowers are blue with yellow or white center.

VERBENA, Garden, *Verbena* hybrids, to 15 inches. Full sun, spring, summer and fall blooming.

(f) September, October, November.

(o) March, April.

Mammoth Hybrid Grandifloras; Apple Blossom, a cameo-pink;

Spectrum Red, a lovely color; Suttons Blue and Lavender Glory all reach 15 inches. Calypso is the candy-striped introduction, to 8 inches. Firelight, Salmon Queen and Crystal are full and grow to 10 inches; Fireball is dwarf and compact.

VIOLETS, *Viola odorata* 5–7 inches. Partial shade, early spring and sometimes fall flowering. Soil needs plenty of leaf mold, wood ashes, soot and a little bone meal.

(f) March, April, May. Separate crowns of established plants in October, November or April, by pulling apart gently with your hands. Plant horizontally about one and a half inches below soil surface and 5–6 inches apart. Keep well watered and feed monthly, alternating with well-balanced fertilizer and well-rotted leaf mold.

Royal Robe is the violet-blue that so many of us have enjoyed for years. I have had thick borders of this one for a long time but I don't remember ever seeing them as beautiful as they were this year after our severe winter. It was wonderful to have a fresh bunch of violets to wear every day! Rosina is a pretty pink and White Czar is entrancing. All are very fragrant.

Violet Scab is present when you notice circular brown spots on the leaves. These brown spots change to resemble scalded areas. These leaves and ones infested with Violet Rust and Gray Mold are best picked off by hand. If this method fails, use Bordeaux mix. Violet Mildew is often caused by improper drainage. Spray with Aramite for red spider, and with nicotine sulphate for aphids. Use commercial baits for slugs and snails.

WALLFLOWER, *Cheiranthus Cheiri* 10–18 inches. Full sun, summer blooming.

(o) March, April, September, October, November.

Low-growing for bedding purposes. Flowers shade from yellow to orange to dark brown and sometimes do not bloom until the second year.

WILD AGERATUM, *Eupatorium coelestinum* or Mist Flower,

to 4 inches. Full sun or partial shade, late summer and fall blooming.
(f) February, March.
(o) April, May.
Bluish-lavender flowers are fluffy and dainty, just like the heads in
the annual Ageratum. The wild variety is particularly well-suited
for borders.

Below is a short list of PERENNIAL VINES. For further information on these and other vines, see chapter on VINES.

BLACK-EYED SUSAN, *Thunbergia alata* sometimes called
the Clock Vine, to 10 feet. Full sun or semi-shade, late summer
and fall blooming.
(f) March, April, May, June.
Yellow-orange flowers with dark lilac centers.

CLEMATIS, *Clematis virginiana* 5–20 feet. Full sun, summer and
fall blooming.
(f) February, March, April.
This one is white-flowered. *Clematis jackmani* has purple blossoms.

CONFUSUS VINE, *Senecio confusus* Mexican Flame Vine, fast
growing. Full sun, summer blooming.
(f) February, March.
(o) April, May.
Bright yellow-orange daisy flowers in loose clusters. Keep in bounds.

DUTCHMAN'S PIPE, *Aristolochia durior* 8 feet or more. Full
sun or partial shade, summer flowering.
(f) February, March.
(o) April, May.
An attraction in any garden.

HYACINTH BEAN, *Dolichos Lablab* to 25 feet. Full sun or
semi-shade, summer blooming.

(o) February, March, April.
Quick-growing with purple or white pea-shaped flowers.

P O T A T O V I N E , *Dioscerea bulbifera* 6–14 feet. Full sun or filtered shade, summer blooming.
Plant by tubers in March, April. Place 2 inches deep in open
ground, 4 feet apart. Inconspicuous pale green flowers and tubers in
leaf axil. Attractive rounded leaves. *D. alata* has most unusual foliage; *D. batatas* has fragrant flowers that smell of cinnamon.

R O S A D E M O N T A N A , *Antigonon leptopus* to 30 feet. Sun or
partial shade, summer and fall blooming.
Pots in February, March.
(o) March, April.
Racemes of small pink flowers. The white variety is very pretty.
This vine forms tuberous roots that remain dormant in ground
through winter; comes up again in the spring.

✳ 13 ✳

The Garden Calendar

This Calendar is intended as a suggestive outline of what to do monthly in your garden. Please think of it as an elastic guide. Because winters in the South are so unpredictable, it is very difficult to state definitely when this and that must be done, so these directions are geared to the average mild year. Should storm, freeze or unusually high temperatures prevail over an exceptionally lengthy period, then use plenty of good old common sense in applying the Calendar. Juggle it back and forth within thirty days to suit the needs.

Please refer to the chapters on specific subjects for further details before planting. For instance, if the Calendar indicates your planting Cape Jasmine, turn back to the chapter on Flowering Shrubs and see just what soil conditions the plant needs and just how it should be set out. If you are directed to prune Tree Wisteria, read up on that particular plant for suggested ways to prune. If the time has come to feed the Violet, look it up in the chapter on Annuals and Perennials and see what violets need in the way of food.

Good luck and happy gardening to you!

JANUARY

SEEDS TO SOW IN OPEN GROUND:

Calendula

Candytuft, annual and perennial

Cynoglossum

Gypsophila, annual and perennial

Poppy, California

Texas Blue Bonnets

SEEDS TO SOW IN FLATS:

Asters, China and perennial

Begonia

Feverfew

Geranium

Heliotrope, annual and perennial

Lobelia

Tassel Flower

BULBS TO SET OUT:

Callas, white

Gladiolus

Leucocoryne

Montbretia

PLANT: Large deciduous trees

Flowering trees and shrubs

Citrus fruit trees; fruit trees

Pecan trees

Bare-rooted rose bushes and rose climbers

Camellias, Azaleas

Ivy

Grape Vines

Pyracanthas may be safely planted this month.

Thryallis

Pansy plants, Gerberas

Last month to set out daisy plants.

TRANSPLANT: Dormant evergreens

Dormant trees and shrubs

Last month to move Magnolia Soulangeana.

Pyracantha.

FEED: Roses

Ixoras

Still time to plug-feed Pecan trees with fertilizer high in potash.
Tree Wisteria
Violets
Give Hydrangeas dose of Copperas and aluminum sulphate to turn
    blossoms blue, lime if you wish to deepen the pink color.

PRUNE: Rose bushes and Rose trees moderately.
Weeping Roses
Prune Duranta bushes of all dead wood.
Pecan trees
Evergreen and deciduous trees and shrubs
Camellias
Golden Rain trees; Finger-leaf tree
Established Fig trees
Grape vines
Summer and fall-flowering shrubs
Clematis vines that flower from old wood.

SPRAY: Azaleas for Petal Blight if necessary.
Roses, twice monthly
Fig trees, while dormant, with Bordeaux mixture to prevent Rust.
Camellias if scale is evident. Use oil emulsion if the weather is mild,
malathion if temperatures are low. Use three teaspoonfuls of 50%
emulsified malathion to one gallon of water.

CLEAN UP: Ground around Camellias of all fallen blossoms to
ward off Camellia Petal Blight.
Rose beds of fallen leaves that might be harboring Black Spot and
bugs.

MAKE CUTTINGS OF: Fig trees
Passion Flower vine
Ivy

ROOT: Fig tree suckers

PREPARE: Beds into which you will be planting spring and summer annuals.

ORDER: Bulbs that you will be planting later in spring.

FEBRUARY

SEEDS TO SOW IN OPEN GROUND:

Asparagus plumosus fern
Asparagus Sprengeri fern
Balsam
Calendula
Candytuft, annual and perennial
Chrysanthemum, annual
Coneflower
Cynoglossum
Delphinium
Dianthus (Pinks)
Four O'Clocks, bush
Gloriosa Daisy
Godetia
Golden Glow
Gypsophila, annual and perennial
Hollyhock
Hyacinth Bean vine
Linaria
Lion's Ear
Lupines, annual and perennial
Phlox, annual
Pinks
Poppy, California
Sweet Peas, perennial
Texas Blue Bonnets

SEEDS TO SOW IN FLATS:

Asters, China and perennial
Begonia
Candelabra tree
Chrysanthemum, perennial
Clematis vines
Coleus
Confusus vine
Cosmos
Cuphea
Cypress vine
Daisy, African
Daisy, Ox-Eye
Daisy, Swan River
Dusty Miller
Dutchman's Pipe vine
Everlastings, annual and perennial
Feverfew
Geranium
Globe Thistle
Heliotrope, annual and perennial
Joe-Pye-Weed
Lobelia, annual and perennial
Love-Apples
Marguerites, Paris Daisy
Martynia
Nicotiana
Nierembergia
Painted Daisy
Phlox, perennial
Rosa de Montana vine, in pots
Sage, annual and perennial
Salpiglossis
Scabiosa, annual and perennial
Tassel Flower
Torenia
Vinca, annual
Wild Ageratum

BULBS TO SET OUT:

Gladiolus	Montbretia
Ismene	Tuberose

PLANT: Rose

Pyracanthas may still be safely planted until February fifteenth.

Broadleaved evergreens

Fig trees

Still time to plant Citrus Fruit trees, until February fifteenth.

Camellias

Grape vines

This is the last month in which it is safe to move deciduous trees, flowering trees and shrubs.

FEED: Established Fig trees

Bulbous plants as new shoots break through the ground.

Climbing Roses, Tree and Bush Roses

Violets

Give Hydrangeas their fertilizer plus another dose of acidifier to turn the flowers blue, a dose of lime if you wish to deepen the pink. I usually put off feeding trees and shrubs until March because there is always danger of a freeze this month, and feeding activates new growth.

PRUNE: Late summer-flowering and fall-flowering shrubs.

Established Fig trees, if you have not already done so.

Poinsettias and Bananas—cut them way back if there has been a freeze.

Hibiscus, only past the blackened area if freeze has occurred.

Clematis vines that bloom from young bottom shoots.

Allamanda and Honeysuckle vines

Don't be in too big a hurry to prune other plants if there has been a series of freezes as the extent of damage is not easily detected immediately.

SPRAY: Glads against thrip.

Give Roses their usual twice-monthly spraying.

Watch Camellias for scale. If necessary use three teaspoonfuls malathion emulsion to one gallon of water. Temperatures are usually still too low to use oil emulsion.

Rout aphids on evergreens and shrubs with nicotine sulphate or lindane.

Kill cutworms in the garden with DDT.

Keep watch for Petal Blight on Azaleas.

Spray Fig trees against mealybug if necessary.

CLEAN UP: Ground around Camellias of dead blooms.

Keep Roses free of all diseased and yellowed leaves.

MULCH: Hydrangeas

DIVIDE: Physostegia, Hardy Phlox, Golden Glow, Wild Ageratum and other fall-flowering perennials.

MAKE CUTTINGS: Fig trees

Hardwood cuttings of Pomegranate.

Softwood and hardwood cuttings of Allamanda vine.

Passion Flower vine

Make cuttings of Bamboo by planting two or three joints of the stalk below ground, leaving same number above the surface.

ROOT: Fig tree suckers

PREPARE: Lawn area for planting new grasses or for resodding old lawns.

Dahlia beds for March planting.

MARCH

SEEDS TO SOW IN OPEN GROUND:

Antigonon (Rosa de Montana)
Asparagus plumosus fern
Asparagus Sprengeri fern
Balsam
Balsam Apple vine
Bells of Ireland
Calliopsis
Canary Bird vine
Chrysanthemum, annual
Cleome
Clitoria
Coneflower

Cynoglossum
Delphinium
Dianthus
Four O'Clocks, bush
Gloriosa Daisy
Godetia
Golden Glow
Gourds
Hollyhock
Hunnemannia
Hyacinth Bean vine
Immortelles

Linaria
Lion's Ear
Lupines, annual and perennial
Marigolds
Moonflower vine
Morning Glory, bush
Morning Glory, vine
Petunias
Phlox, annual
Pinks
Potato vines, by tubers
Queen Anne's Lace
Ricinus (Castor Bean)

Salpiglossis
Sedum
Statice
Sunflower
Sweet Peas, perennial
Tassel Flower
Texas Blue Bonnets
Tithonia
Verbena
Wallflower
Wood Rose vine
Zinnia

SEEDS TO SOW IN FLATS:

Amaranthus
Candelabra tree
Celosia (Cockscomb)
Chrysanthemum, perennial
Clematis vines
Coleus
Confusus vine
Cosmos
Cuphea
Cypress vine
Dahlia
Daisy, African
Daisy, Ox-Eye
Daisy, Swan River
Dusty Miller
Dutchman's Pipe vine
Everlastings, annual and perennial
Feverfew
Geranium
Globe Amaranth
Globe Thistle
Heliotrope, annual and perennial

Joe-Pye-Weed
Lobelia, annual and perennial
Love-Apple
Marguerites, Golden
Marguerites, Paris Daisy
Martynia
Nicotiana
Nierembergia
Painted Daisy
Phlox, perennial
Portulaca
Rosa de Montana vine
(Antignon)
Sage, annual and perennial
Scabiosa, annual and perennial
Summer Cypress
Thunbergia vine
Torenia
Vinca, annual
Violets
Wild Ageratum

BULBS TO SET OUT:

Acidanthera	Ginger, yellow
Amaryllis Striata	Gladiolus
Butterfly Lily	Iris Stylosa
Canna	Scilla autumnalis
Crinum	Sternbergia
Curcuma	Tigridia
Dahlia	Tuberose

WOODY VINES TO PLANT:

All vines in chapter on Vines, except Ivy and Grapes.

PLANT: Bermuda, Carpet, Centipede, St. Augustine and the Zoysia grasses.

Ground Covers, except Ivy. See chapter on Ground Covers.

Bamboo

Cape Jasmine

There is still time to plant Fig trees, broadleaved Evergreens, Azaleas and Camellias.

Caladium in pots.

FEED: Violets

Citrus Fruit trees

Established evergreen, deciduous and flowering trees.

Hedge materials and evergreen shrubs.

Vines that have become established.

Boxwood

Ixoras

Flowering shrubs, including Azaleas and Camellias, immediately after blooming.

Eucomis bulbs that have become established.

Established Fig trees if you have not already done so.

Give Roses their monthly feeding.

If necessary, give Hydrangeas another dose of acidifier to make flowers a deeper blue.

PRUNE: Azaleas and flowering shrubs immediately after blooming.

Established Citrus trees, fruit trees and flowering trees.

Established Fig trees early this month.

Go slow on pruning frozen shrubs and plants, waiting to see how much damage has been done.

SPRAY: Control white fly and scale on evergreens with malathion or oil emulsion. If the temperatures remain low, use malathion.

Lawns and grounds with chlordane for ants.

Fig trees, as they bud, with Bordeaux mixture against Rust.

Hollies with an oil emulsion or malathion in case of scale infestation.

Give Roses their dose of spray every other week.

Watch for aphids on new growth. Use nicotine sulphate, or lindane.

Grape vines with Bordeaux mixture to control Black Rot which spots the leaves. Bordeaux will also help control mildew.

DIVIDE: Dahlias before planting

Amaryllis Striata, if they need it, and replant.

Physostegia, Hardy Phlox, Golden Glow, Wild Ageratum and other fall-flowering perennials if you have not already done so.

CLEAN UP: Ground under Camellia bushes of fallen blossoms to avoid Camellia Petal Blight.

Roses of all yellow and diseased foliage.

CHECK: Camellia and Azalea soil for proper acidity.

Fig trees for mealybug, ants and three-lined Fig Tree Borer.

MAKE CUTTINGS OF: Geranium and Hibiscus

Half-ripened wood of Pentas

Hardwood cuttings of Poinsettias

Four-inch cuttings of Chrysanthemum from new growth on sides of old plant. Keep moist and shade for a few days after planting. Since these cuttings are heavy feeders, keep them happy.

Softwood cuttings of Vitex, Bougainvillea vine.

Passion Flower and Thunbergia vines, from new growth.

PREPARE: Dahlia beds for April planting.

APRIL

SEEDS TO SOW IN OPEN GROUND:

Amaranthus	Calliopsis
Balsam	Canary Bird vine
Balsam Apple vine	Chrysanthemum, annual
Bells of Ireland	Cleome

Clitoria
Coleus
Coneflower
Confusus vine
Cosmos
Daisy, African
Daisy, Ox-Eye
Daisy, Swan River
Dusty Miller
Dutchman's Pipe vine
Everlastings, annual
Feverfew
Four O'Clocks, bush
Globe Amaranth
Golden Glow
Gourds
Hunnemannia
Hyacinth Bean vine
Immortelles
Joe-Pye-Weed
Linaria
Love-Apples
Lupines, annual and perennial
Marguerites, Paris Daisy
Marigolds

Moonflower vine
Morning Glory, bush
Morning Glory, vine
Painted Daisy
Petunia
Phlox, annual
Potato vines, by tubers
Queen Anne's Lace
Ricinus (Castor Bean)
Rosa de Montana vine
Salpiglossis
Scabiosa, annual and perennial
Sedum
Statice
Sunflower
Sweet Pea, perennial
Tassel Flower
Texas Blue Bonnets
Tithonia
Torenia
Verbena
Vinca, annual
Wallflower
Wild Ageratum
Zinnia

SEEDS TO SOW IN FLATS:

Amaranthus
Aquilegia
Canary Bird vine
Celosia (Cockscomb)
Chrysanthemum, perennial
Clematis vines
Cuphea
Cypress vine
Dahlia
Globe Thistle

Lion's Ear
Marguerites, Golden
Nicotiana
Nierembergia
Portulaca
Sage, annual and perennial
Summer Cypress
Thunbergia vine
Violets
Wood Rose vine

BULBS TO SET OUT:

Caladium	Gloriosa Lily
Canna	Nerine
Curcuma	Tigridia
Dahlia	Tuberose

PLANT: Ground covers and vines if you have not already done so.
Still time to plant Bamboo and Cape Jasmine.
Crape Jasmine must be planted in rainy spells of spring.
Not too late to start lawns.
Aquilegia plants

FEED: If you did not get to it in March, feed spring-flowering shrubs that have finished blooming.
Grape vines with a fertilizer high in potash and superphosphate to harden the trunk.
Citrus fruit trees
Avocado trees
Give Roses their monthly feeding.
Feed Camellias and Azaleas if you have not already done so.
Violets

PRUNE: Damaged parts of all plants that might have been affected by earlier freezes. Wait on the Hibiscus as it may not show signs of life until May.
Cut all Iris and Lily foliage as it turns brown and dies.
Spring-flowering shrubs immediately after blooming period. Be sure to prune your Azaleas as soon as they have finished flowering because they set buds for next year's blooms within a month or so.
Grape vines
Climbing Roses as they finish blooming.
Keep your hedges sheared and clipped during the growing season.

SPRAY: Give Camellias, Azaleas and hedge materials their yearly power-spraying. Weather should be mild enough (between fifty and seventy degrees) this month to use oil emulsion.
Use 50% wettable chlordane to fifty gallons of water for ants on grounds.
Give your Roses their twice-monthly spraying early in the morning in warm months.
Spray Glads against thrip.

DIVIDE AND RESET: Crowns of established Violets.
Chrysanthemum, if you plan to use old root stock.

MAKE CUTTINGS OF: Half-ripened wood of Pentas.
Chrysanthemum
Abutilon
Softwood cuttings of Vitex.

MAKE AIR-LAYERINGS OF: Viburnum, Magnolia Soulangeana, Honeysuckles, Jasmines.

CLEAN UP: Camellia beds of all fallen blossoms if you happen to
have a late bloomer.
Rose beds of yellowed and diseased leaves.
All beds of spent foliage.

PREPARE: Dahlia beds for May planting.

MAY

SEEDS TO SOW IN OPEN GROUND:

Amaranthus	Hunnemannia
Balsam	Immortelles
Balsam Apple vine	Joe-Pye-Weed
Calliopsis	Love-Apples
Canary Bird vine	Marguerites, Paris Daisy
Celosia (Cockscomb)	Marigolds
Cleome	Moonflower vine
Clitoria	Morning Glory, bush
Coleus	Morning Glory, vine
Confusus vine	Painted Daisy
Cosmos	Portulaca
Cypress vine	Queen Anne's Lace
Daisy, African	Ricinus (Castor Bean)
Daisy, Swan River	Sage, annual and perennial
Dutchman's Pipe vine	Scabiosa, annual and perennial
Everlastings, annual	Statice
Four O'Clocks, bush	Sunflower
Globe Amaranth	Tassel Flower
Gourds	Tithonia

Torenia   Wild Ageratum
Vinca, annual   Zinnia
Violets

SEEDS TO SOW IN FLATS:
Aquilegia   Thunbergia vine
Dahlia   Wood Rose vine

BULBS TO SET OUT:
Caladium   Nerine
Canna   Tuberose
Dahlia

PLANT: Still time to set out ground covers and vines.
You may continue to plant Bamboo and Crape Jasmine.
Set out Chrysanthemum cuttings made last month.

FEED: Violets
Established lawns, evergreen hedges, flowering shrubs after they have bloomed.
Ixoras, Hibiscus
Clematis vines
Give Roses their monthly feeding.
All bulbous plants as new shoots show.
Established Palms.

PRUNE: Bauhinia as blooming ends.
Rose climbers as they stop flowering.
Gardenias while in bloom.
Relieve bulbous plants of their brown and spent foliage.
Now you can see if your apparently frozen Hibiscus has any living parts; it usually shows some signs of green by May.
Pinch back Chrysanthemums, about an inch of new growth at top of stem.
When Dahlia is about one foot tall pinch out about two inches of the main stalk.

SPRAY: Since summer heat is approaching rapidly this will probably be the last month in which you can safely spray with oil emulsion, if you have not already done so in April. Look over your shrubs and hedges for evidence of white fly and scale and for lace bugs.

Use chlordane to get rid of ants.

Watch for Thread Blight on Fig trees—see chapter on Trees with Edible Fruits for recommendations.

Red spider becomes prevalent in warm weather so get out your miticides.

Tent-caterpillars usually begin to show on Pecan trees this month. Spray with arsenate of lead or burn those that you can reach.

Give Roses their twice-monthly spraying in the morning during the warm months.

DIVIDE: Clumps of Chrysanthemums
Lycoris bulbs if too crowded.

DIG AND STORE: Tulip and Hyacinth bulbs

CLEAN UP: Rose beds of all fallen foliage. Keep Roses picked of yellowed and diseased leaves.
Relieve Iris of their spent foliage.

MULCH: Hybrid Lilies, Amaryllis, Louisiana Iris and Roses against summer heat.

MAKE CUTTINGS: Half-ripened wood of Pentas.
Azaleas, Camellias, Hibiscus, Ixora, Ardisia, Abelia, Clerodendron, Buddleia.
Hardwood cuttings of Vitex.

PREPARE: Dahlia beds for June planting.

WATERING: Keep up steady watering program during dry spells. Ground soaking is preferable to overhead watering. To wet leaves is to encourage mildew and sun scald. If you must use a hard spray of the hose to rout red spider, do so very early in the morning when the leaves can drip and dry before the extreme heat of the day.

JUNE

SEEDS TO SOW IN OPEN GROUND:

Balsam	Moonflower vine
Calliopsis	Morning Glory vine
Celosia (Cockscomb)	Portulaca
Cypress vine	Sage, annual and perennial
Four O'Clocks, bush	Torenia
Globe Amaranth	Zinnia

SEEDS TO SOW IN FLATS:

Thunbergia vine

BULBS TO SET OUT:

Dahlias   Nerine

PLANT: Palms

Gardenia Veitchii

FEED: Camellias and Azaleas, Ixoras, Tibouchina semicadendra.
Watch Azaleas and other shrubs for the anemic look. They may need iron.
Give Roses their monthly feeding.
Citrus fruit trees
Bamboo, Chrysanthemum, Violets.

PRUNE: Keep flowering shrubs and plants free of dead blooms.
When you cut your flowers to bring into the house, you actually keep the bushes lightly pruned and at the same time you prolong the blooming season.
Bauhinia trees after blooming if you did not get to it in May.
Oleander after flowering. Use gloves here because nearly everything about this plant is poisonous.
Remove tops of Glad foliage that has browned normally.
Pinch back Chrysanthemum and Dahlias.

SPRAY: Be on the lookout for Chinch Bug, Brown Patch, other fungus diseases and pests on lawns, and spray accordingly. See chapter on Lawns.
Watch Fig trees for Thread Blight, red spider and thrips in dry weather and fungus in wet spells.
Keep chlordane ready for ants.
Don't forget to spray your Roses twice this month, early in the morning in warm months.
Rout caterpillars from vines, especially the Passion Flower vine, with arsenate of lead or DDT.

DIG AND REPLANT: Rhizomes of Bearded Iris and flags, scrub with disinfectant and replant immediately.

MULCH: Azaleas, Camellias, Gardenias, Hollies, Roses, Dahlias, Chrysanthemums, Hydrangeas against summer heat.

CLEAN UP: Ground in Rose beds, Lily beds and flower beds of fallen leaves, weeds, etc. Keep Roses picked of yellowed and diseased foliage.

MAKE CUTTINGS OF: Half-ripened wood of Pentas. Softwood cuttings of Pomegranate.

JULY

SEEDS TO SOW IN OPEN GROUND:
Balsam   Four O'Clocks, bush

PLANT: Palms
Gather bulbils of the Enchantment Lily and plant in coldframes. This is a good month to start Japanese Yew from seed. Remember that you must have both head and body of the seed for germination.

FEED: Ixoras, Clivias, Hibiscus.
Give Roses their monthly feeding.
Chrysanthemums with a fertilizer rather high in nitrogen.
Violets

PRUNE: This is the last month in which you may cut back your Poinsettias, to one-half the current season's growth.
Hydrangeas as soon as they are through blooming.
Tree Wisteria, after July fifteenth.
Pinch Chrysanthemum until mid-July.
Continue to pinch Dahlias.

SPRAY: Dahlias for thrip.
Shrubs for red spider.
Watch for signs of Die-Back on Camellias and Azaleas.
Give Roses a spraying twice this month, in early morning during hot months.
Chrysanthemum for aphids.

DIG AND STORE: If this is the year to dig your Glads, or if you prefer to dig them annually, when the foliage has dried sufficiently carefully lift, dry, clean and store in a cool dry place until spring.

RAISE: Amaryllis bulbs if they have sunk too low.

CLEAN UP: Ground around Roses of yellowed leaves.
Keep Roses and other plants picked of spent and diseased foliage.

MAKE CUTTINGS: Softwood cuttings of Pomegranite, Poin-
settias.
Japanese Yew
Camellias, about five or six inches long, under glass.
WATERING: Keep up steady program if rains are not adequate.
Camellias are approaching their blooming season and need plenty of
moisture.

AUGUST

BULBS TO SET OUT:

Daylilies   Louisiana Iris

PLANT: Palms
Continue planting bulbils of the Enchantment Lily in cold frames.
Camellia seed pods should split about this time. Plant seeds immed-
iately and cover with glass frame or glass jar for moisture retention.
FEED: Ixoras
Give Roses their monthly feeding.
Check soil around your Gardenia or Cape Jasmine bushes to see if
conditions are sufficiently acid.
Chrysanthemums until buds show color.
Violets
PRUNE: Hydrangeas, if you have not already done so.
Tree Wisteria, until August fifteenth.
Rambler Roses
Pinch Dahlias
Disbud Camellias to increase size of the remaining bud.
SPRAY: Give Roses their twice-monthly spraying early in the morn-
ing.
Fig trees with Bordeaux mixture for Rust.
Watch Chrysanthemums and Dahlias for red spider, aphids.
DIG AND DIVIDE: Louisiana Iris and replant immediately.
If your Glad foliage is spent and you wish to dig the corms, do so
now. Clean and store.
CLEAN UP: Rose and flower beds of fallen foliage.
Keep Roses and other plants picked of all yellowed leaves.

MAKE CUTTINGS: Softwood cuttings of Poinsettias.
Hydrangeas, Oleander, Croton, Pentas.

WATERING: This is another usually dry month, so keep the hose
going on the ground around the plants. Camellias and Azaleas especially need this moisture because they are maturing their buds. If you
see manifestations of red spider, use a hard spray of the hose under
and on the leaves of the troubled plants, in early morning or in the
cool of the evening.

PREPARE: Beds for Lilies and other bulbous plants that you plan
to set out in October.

ORDER: Hybrid Lilies and other bulbs to be planted in fall, from
reputable bulb house. Specify October as delivery time because Lily
bulbs must be planted as soon as they arrive.

SEPTEMBER

SEEDS TO SOW IN OPEN GROUND:

Cornflower
Daisy, African
Larkspur
Poppy, California
Poppy, Oriental
Snapdragons
Sweet Alyssum
Sweet Peas, annual
Wallflower

SEEDS TO SOW IN FLATS:

Ageratum
Anchusa, annual and perennial
Aquilegia
Artemisia
Asparagus plumosus fern
Asters, China and perennial
Bellflower
Calendula
Candytuft, annual and perennial
Canterbury Bells
Carnation
Coreopsis
Cynoglossum
Daisy, African
Daisy, English
Daisy, Shasta
Delphinium
Forget-Me-Not
Foxglove
Gaillardia, annual and perennial
Gerberas
Godetia
Gypsophila, annual and perennial
Heliotrope, perennial

Hollyhock

Lobelia, perennial

Marguerites, Golden

Pansy

Petunia

Phlox, annual and perennial

Physostegia

Pinks

Snapdragons

Stock, Night-scented

Stock, Ten and Seven Weeks

Stokesia

Sweet Alyssum

Sweet William

Tritoma

Verbena

BULBS TO SET OUT:

Callas, white

Daylilies

Easter Lilies

Habranthus

Hyacinths, in pots

Kaempferia

Louisiana Iris

Mertensia

Oxalis

Snowflakes

Winter Gladiolus

Zephyranthes

PLANT: Clematis vines

FEED: Chrysanthemums until they show color.

Give Roses their monthly feeding.

Ixoras and Hibiscus

Established Amaryllis and other bulbs with a solution of one teaspoon of muriate of potash to one-half gallon of water to harden bulbs against winter cold.

Violets

PRUNE: Rambler Roses

Bush and tree Roses, cutting back one-half of the current season's growth. This forces new shoots on which blooms will appear in six to eight weeks' time. Heaviest fall bloom in the New Orleans area is usually between November fifth and November twentieth. If you have several bushes, stagger your pruning over a period of ten days in order to prolong flowering.

Cut off old Duranta berries.

SPRAY: Give your Roses their twice-monthly spray early in the morning.

Keep watch for red spider on shrubs and plants.

DIVIDE: Still not too late to divide and replant Louisiana Iris.

Daylilies, Amaryllis.

Established Violets and replant crowns immediately.

Spring and early summer perennials that have finished blooming.

DIG AND STORE: Tigridias

Glad corms if foliage is dried sufficiently.

CLEAN UP: Rose beds of all spent foliage.

Flower beds of fallen leaves and weeds.

Keep Roses and plants free of yellowed and diseased leaves.

Relieve bulbs of all browned foliage.

Remove old annuals from flower beds.

Some Camellias will start to bloom this month. Begin a rigid program of picking up all fallen blooms from the ground around the plant. This is a sure way to prevent Camellia Petal Blight.

MAKE CUTTINGS: Hydrangeas.

PREPARE: Beds for Pansies—rich, loamy soil, well-turned to at least nine inches.

Begin to plan your Rose bed.

ORDER: Bulbs for planting in October.

OCTOBER

SEEDS TO SOW IN OPEN GROUND:

Anchusa, annual and perennial

Cornflower

Daisy, African

Larkspur

Lathyrus (Sweet Pea, perennial)

Nasturtium

Poppy, California

Poppy, Oriental

Snapdragons

Sweet Alyssum

Sweet Peas, annual

Texas Blue Bonnets

Wallflower

SEEDS TO SOW IN FLATS:

Ageratum

Anchusa, annual and perennial

Aquilegia

Artemisia

Asparagus plumosus fern

Asparagus Sprengeri fern

Asters, China and perennial

Bellflower

Calendula

Candytuft, annual and perennial

Canterbury Bells

Carnations

Coreopsis
Cynoglossum
Daisy, African
Daisy, English
Daisy, Shasta
Delphinium
Forget-Me-Not
Foxglove
Gaillardia, annual and perennial
Gerbera
Godetia
Gypsophila, annual and perennial
Heliotrope, perennial
Hollyhock
Marguerites, Paris Daisy

Pansy
Petunia
Phlox, annual and perennial
Physostegia
Pinks
Sedum
Snapdragons
Stock, Night-scented
Stock, Ten and Seven Weeks
Stokesia
Strawflowers
Sweet Alyssum
Sweet William
Tritoma
Verbena

BULBS TO SET OUT:

Agapanthus
Allium
Alpinia
Alstreomeria
Amarcrinum
Amaryllis
Amaryllis Belladonna
Anemone
Banana
Bird of Paradise
Brunsvigia rosea
Calla, white
Calla, yellow
Clivia
Crinum
Daffodils
Daylilies
Easter Lilies
Eucharis Lily
Eucomis

Freesia
Ginger
Glory-of-the-Snow
Grape Hyacinths
Habranthus
Haemanthus
Hybrid Lilies
Iris, Dutch, English, Spanish, *Juno*, *Reticulata*, flags, *germanica*, Siberian, Bearded, *Spuria*, *Evansia*, *Kaempferi*, *Pseudacorus*, *Marica gracilis*, *Oncocyclus*, Vesper, *foetidissima*. See chapter on Bulbs.
Ixias
Jonquils
Kaempferia
Narcissus
Oxalis
Ranunculus

Scilla
Snake-Lily
Sparaxis
Sprekelia
Spring Star Flower

Star-of-Bethlehem
Sternbergia
Tritoma
Watsonia
Zephyranthes

PLANT: Winter Rye grass
  Hollies may be set out this month.
  Bamboo, Cocculus and Oleander may be moved safely this month.
  Aquilegia plants
FEED: Boxwood
  Established lawns with cottonseed meal.
  Clivia
  Give Roses their monthly feeding.
  Established Palms
  Give *Gardenia Veitchii* a light mulch of well-rotted manure to aid in flower development.
  Violets
PRUNE: Hedge materials and shrubs now because any later pruning will produce new growth which may be easily damaged by cold.
  Geraniums
SPRAY: Roses twice monthly.
  Use malathion for white fly and scale if temperatures are still too high for oil emulsion.
  Keep on the lookout for red spider.
DIVIDE AND REPLANT: Perennials, including Shasta Daisies and Stokesia, that need to be separated.
  Crowns of established Violets, Gerberas, Daylilies.
  Amaryllis
DIG AND STORE: Caladiums
MULCH: Roses with peat.
CLEAN UP: Pull up all worn annuals.
  Keep Rose beds clean of old foliage.
  Freshen up garden beds by adding humus or leaf mold, and by turning the earth well.
  Pick off all yellowed and diseased leaves of Roses and other plants.
  Keep Camellia beds free of fallen blossoms.
  Keep lawn raked clean of leaves.

S T A R T : Compost of raked leaves and clippings.

M A K E C U T T I N G S O F : Hydrangeas

R E F R I G E R A T E : Tulips and Hyacinths.* Place them in the bottom of the refrigerator, *not* in the deep freeze.

P R E P A R E : Hyacinth and Tulip beds.
  Rose beds for planting next month.
  Camellia beds for future planting.

O R D E R : Roses, designating shipping dates.

B R I N G I N : Golden-Rain blossoms to dry.

What you accomplish in the garden in October is very important. Your spring garden depends on what you do this month.

NOVEMBER

SEEDS TO SOW IN OPEN GROUND:

Anchusa, annual and perennial
Cornflower
Daisy, African
Larkspur (Sweet Pea, perennial)
Lathyrus
Nasturtium
Poppy, California

Poppy, Oriental
Snapdragons
Sweet Alyssum
Sweet Peas, annual
Texas Blue Bonnets
Wallflower

SEEDS TO SOW IN FLATS:

Ageratum
Anchusa, annual and perennial
Artemisia
Asparagus Sprengeri fern
Asters, China and perennial
Balsam
Bellflower
Calendula
Candytuft, annual and perennial
Canterbury Bells

Carnations
Coreopsis
Cynoglossum
Daisy, African
Daisy, English
Daisy, Shasta
Delphinium
Forget-Me-Not
Foxglove
Gaillardia, annual and perennial

* Trials have proved that refrigeration is as beneficial to Hyacinths as it is to Tulips.

Gerbera
Godetia
Gypsophila, annual and perennial
Heliotrope, perennial
Hollyhock
Pansy
Petunia
Phlox, annual and perennial
Pinks
Physostegia

Sedum
Snapdragons
Stock, Night-scented
Stock, Ten and Seven Weeks
Stokesia
Strawflowers
Sweet Alyssum
Sweet William
Tritoma
Verbena

BULBS TO SET OUT:

Anemone
Calla, white
Calla, yellow
Daffodils
Freesia
Hyacinths
Iris, same as October

Jonquils
Lycoris
Montbretia
Narcissus
Ranunculus
Tulips
Zephyranthes

PLANT: Pecan trees
Camellias
Hollies and deciduous shrubs and trees may be safely moved this month.
Not too late to plant winter grass.
Begin setting out Calendula and Pansy plants from your coldframe.
Start Narcissi in water.

FEED: Ixoras
Give established Roses their monthly feeding.
Clematis vines
Violets

PRUNE: Shrubs and flowering trees that have bloomed in late summer and fall.
Woody vines

SPRAY: Pansies with DDT if there is any evidence of cutworms.
Calendulas for aphids.
Give Roses their twice-monthly spraying.

DIVIDE AND REPLANT: Still time to separate crowns of established Violets.

DIG AND STORE: Tubers of Dahlias and Acidanthera corms that have been cut back by frost.

MULCH: Shrubs, such as Hibiscus, Datura, Plumbago, Duranta; and bulbs, such as Amaryllis, against cold. At least have mulches easily available in case of a sudden freeze.
Lily bed
Gerberas
Woody vines

CLEAN UP: Ground around Camellias of all fallen blooms to prevent Petal Blight.
Keep Roses clean of yellowed and diseased foliage.
Rake lawn of fallen leaves.

ADD: Continue to add leaves and clippings to compost heap.

MAKE CUTTINGS OF: Boxwood
Coleus for rooting in water in the house, so that freezes will not kill all that you have outdoors.

PREPARE: Rose beds if you have not already done so.

ORDER: Roses for planting in December and January.
Gladiolus corms for January planting.

DECEMBER

SEEDS TO SOW IN OPEN GROUND:

Calendula	Nasturtium
Cornflower	Poppy, Oriental
Larkspur	Texas Blue Bonnets
Lathyrus (Sweet Pea, perennial)	

SEEDS TO SOW IN FLATS:

Balsam	Heliotrope, perennial
Begonia	Papaya tree, in pots
Coreopsis	Stokesia
Delphinium	Strawflowers
Gaillardia, annual and perennial	

BULBS TO SET OUT:

Calla, white
Calla, yellow
Hyacinths
Iris, see chapter on Bulbs

Lily-of-the-Valley, in open and in
pots
Lycoris
Montbretia
Tulips

PLANT: Roses, ordered from Texas
    Deciduous and flowering trees and shrubs.
    Begin planting Citrus fruit trees from December fifteenth.
    Fig trees
    Pecan trees
    Magnolia Soulangeana
    Camellias
    Pansy plants
    Gerberas

FEED: Give established Roses their monthly feeding.
    Plug-feed Pecan trees with a fertilizer high in potash.
    Violets

PRUNE: Top and shape Golden-Rain tree.
    Evergreen and deciduous trees, shrubs that have bloomed in summer
    and fall. *Do not* prune spring-flowering shrubs.
    Cut down Chrysanthemums that have bloomed.

SPRAY: Give Roses their twice-monthly spraying.

DIG AND STORE: Dahlia tubers if you have not already done so.

MULCH: See that all shrubs and bulbs are mulched against cold.
    Keep extra mulch available.

CLEAN UP: Ground around Camellias of all fallen blooms.
    Keep Roses free of yellowed and diseased foliage.
    Rake lawns of leaves and clippings.

ADD: To compost heap.

MAKE CUTTINGS OF: Fig trees

ROOT: Fig tree suckers

PREPARE: Rose beds for those arriving in January.

Bibliography

The Amaryllis Manual, Hamilton P. Traub (1958).
Better Lawns, J. C. Harper II and M. A. Hein; Home and Garden Bulletin No. 51, U.S. Department of Agriculture (1957).
Camellias for the Yard, W. D. Kimbrough, R. H. Hanchey, J. S. Roussel; Bulletin No. 391, Louisiana Agricultural Experiment Station (1956).
Encyclopedia of Roses and Rose Culture, Harcourt P. Champneys and Carl Withner (1957).
Exotica, Alfred Byrd Graf (1957).
Field Book of Insects, Frank E. Lutz (1948).
The Fig: Its History, Culture and Curing, Gustav Eisen; Bulletin No. 9, U.S. Department of Agriculture, Division of Pomology.
Fig Culture, A. C. Van Velzer (1909).
Fig Insects, C. E. Smith, E. H. Floyd, K. L. Cockerham; Department of Entomology, Louisiana Agricultural Experiment Station (1954).
Flowers of the South, Wilhelmina F. Greene and Hugo L. Blomquist (1953).
Flowering Plants from Cuban Gardens, The Women's Club of Havana (1958).
The Gardener's A B C of Pest and Disease, A. W. Dimock (1953).
The Gardener's Bug Book, Cynthia Westcott (1946).
Growing Camellias in Florida, E. W. McElwee; Bulletin No. 161, Agricultural Extension Service (1955).
The Guide to Garden Flowers, Norman Taylor (1958).
Handbook on Lawns, Brooklyn Botanic Gardens (1956).
Hawaiian Flowers and Flowering Trees, Loraine E. Kuck and Richard C. Tongg (1958).

Hibiscus for the Yard, R. H. Hanchey and W. D. Kimbrough; Bulletin No. 489, Louisiana Agricultural Experiment Station (1954).
Hibiscus in Florida, R. D. Dickey; Bulletin No. 168, Florida Agricultural Experiment Station (1958).
The Home Book of Trees and Shrubs, J. J. Levison (1949).
House Plants—A Handbook, Brooklyn Botanic Gardens (1954).
House Plants, Farmers' Bulletin No. 1872, Furman Lloyd Mulford; U.S. Department of Agriculture (1941).
Indoor Plants, Eigil Kiaer.
Knowing Your Trees, G. H. Collingwood and Warren D. Brush; The American Forestry Association (1948).
Landscape Plants for Florida Homes, John V. Watkins; Department of Agriculture, State of Florida.
Louisiana Trees, A. S. McKean (1955).
Louisiana Trees and Shrubs, Clair A. Brown (1945).
Native and Exotic Palms of Florida, Harold Mowry; Bulletin No. 152, Agricultural Extension Service, Gainesville, Florida (1957).
Plants and Gardens, (*Lilies*), Brooklyn Botanic Garden Record, Summer 1949.
Soils and Fertilizers, George D. Thornton, W. W. McCall, R. E. Caldwell and F. B. Smith; Department of Agriculture, Tallahassee, Florida (1953).
Some Woody Ornamental Plants Grown in Louisiana, Dr. D. L. Gill and Donald H. Spurlock.
The Standard Cyclopedia of Horticulture, Liberty Hyde Bailey.
Taylor's Garden Guide, Norman Taylor (1957).
Trees and Shrubs for the Southern Coastal Plain, Brooks E. Wiggington; University of Georgia (1957).
Tropical Plants and Their Cultivation, L. Bruggeman (1957).
What Flowering Tree Is That?, Edwin A. Menninger (1956).
Wise Garden Encyclopedia, edited by E. L. D. Seymour (1959).

Index

www.ingramcontent.com/pod-product-compliance
Lightning Source LLC
Chambersburg PA
CBHW031229090426
42742CB00007B/125